The Italian Resistance

THE ITALIAN RESISTANCE

Fascists, Guerrillas and the Allies

Tom Behan

 PLUTO PRESS

First published 2009 by Pluto Press
345 Archway Road, London N6 5AA and
175 Fifth Avenue, New York, NY 10010

www.plutobooks.com

British Library Cataloguing in Publication Data
A catalogue record for this book is available from the British Library

ISBN   978 0 7453 2695 5   Hardback
ISBN   978 0 7453 2694 8   Paperback
ISBN   978 1 8496 4371 9   PDF eBook
ISBN   978 1 7837 1551 0   EPUB eBook
ISBN   978 1 7837 1552 7   Kindle eBook

Library of Congress Cataloging in Publication Data applied for

10   9   8   7   6   5   4   3   2   1

Designed and produced for Pluto Press by
Chase Publishing Services Ltd, Sidmouth, England
Typeset from disk by Stanford DTP Services, Northampton

Contents

PART II

List of Illustrations

Front COVER (paperback edition) – The partisan column that liberated Milan enters the city's main square, *piazza del Duomo*, on 28 April 1945. Key as follows:

Cino Moscatelli (centre of the car saluting), born 1908, lathe worker, joins Communist youth wing and Communist Party in the early 1920s, spends three years in Moscow 1927–30. He then moves to France, from where the party sends him into fascist Italy in 1930, where he is arrested after a few months. He spends most of the next 13 years in jail, and like many other activists is released in the late summer of 1943. He is commanding the column entering the city, which has just come down from the mountains after two years of guerrilla warfare.

Teresa Mondini, 'Maruska' (to Moscatelli's right), a female radio operator, member of Moscatelli's division up in the mountains. She has a Russian nickname because she was born in the Soviet Union, the daughter of two anti-fascists living in exile. When the Resistance began she first asked to be parachuted into Yugoslavia, and then crossed the border into Italy.

Don Sisto Bighiani (behind Teresa Mondini), born 1920, a young priest who immediately joined the Resistance, taking part in many military actions. A political commissar of Moscatelli's 82nd 'Osella' brigade, famous for the phrase 'On your knees to pray, on your feet to fight!'

Pietro Secchia (the silhouette of the top of his head is just visible, slightly behind both Bighiani and Moscatelli), born 1903, joins the Socialist Party youth federation in 1919 and is a founder member of the Italian Communist Party in 1921. Receives his first jail sentence at the end of 1922. He spends most of the 1920s in France and Russia, and is arrested in Italy in January 1931, and held in prison until July 1943. He is the overall political commissar of all the communist-inspired Garibaldi brigades in occupied Italy, and is the party's main military organiser.

Luigi Longo (the right profile of his face is visible, behind Moscatelli's left shoulder) born 1900, he joins the Socialist Party in Turin as a teenager, and is a founder member of the Communist Party in 1921. In 1926 he is forced to emigrate to France, and then to Russia. In 1936 he joins the Spanish Civil War, quickly becoming Inspector General of the International Brigades. Returning to France, in 1940 the authorities deport him to Italy when the Second World War began and he is imprisoned until the summer of 1943, when he quickly becomes the Communist Party leader in occupied Italy. He becomes the commander of the PCI-inspired Garibaldi brigades, and deputy commander of the CVL, the overall military structure of the Resistance. Later, from 1964 to 1972, he was the leader of the Communist Party.

Alessandro Vaia (in front of Longo and to Moscatelli's lower left) born 1907, organiser of the Communist Youth wing in the early 1920s, arrested and given a four-and-a-half year sentence in 1927. Released in 1932, he first moves to France, then the USSR, then to Spain in 1937 and became Garibaldi

Brigade commander. In the Italian Resistance he was initially commander in the Marche region, and then commissar for the whole of Milan.

Giovanni Pesce (dressed in a raincoat, in front row, with a machine gun cradled over his left arm) born 1918. From an anti-fascist family, which was forced to migrate to France when he was five. At 11 he was herding cows, at 14 he starts work in a coal mine in southern France. He joins the International Brigades in the Spanish Civil War aged just 18, where he was wounded three times. As with Luigi Longo, he was deported back to Italy from France in 1940 and imprisoned for three years. Released in August 1943, he began organising urban 'terrorist' groups in Turin, where he was again wounded. Because his face was known, he moved to Milan where he rebuilt clandestine resistance groups, personally assassinating dozens of fascists and Nazis.

Abbreviations

AMGOT – Allied Military Government
ANPI – National Partisans' Association
CLN – National Liberation Committee (based in Rome)
CLNAI – National Liberation Committee for Upper (occupied) Italy (based in Milan)
CVL – Liberty Volunteers Corps
DC – Christian Democrat Party
GAP – Patriotic Action Groups
GDD – Women's Defence Groups
MSI – Italian Social Movement
PCI – Italian Communist Party
PNF – National Fascist Party
PSI – Italian Socialist Party
RSI – The Italian Social Republic (or Republic of Salò)
SAP – Patriotic Action Squads

Acknowledgements

This is a history book that still just borders a period of 'living history', so thanks to those who over the years agreed to be interviewed about their experiences: Luigi Fiori, Luigi Moretti, Gianni Ottolini, Giovanni Pesce, Silvano Sarti, Laura Seghettini and Mario Vezzoni.

Several organisations have been generous with their time and resources, among them the Archivi della Resistenza Circolo Edoardo Bassignani, the Centro di Documentazione Ebraica Contemporanea, the Istituto Storico della Resistenza in Cuneo e Provincia, the Istituto Storico della Resistenza di Parma and Yo Yo Mundi.

Thanks to those individuals who provided important logistical help and advice, including Cesare Bermani, Filippo Colombara, Simona Rampoldi, Reda Sironi and Charles Young. Thanks are also due to those who read the book in draft: Chris Bambery, Jon Flaig and Barbara Rampoldi – whose help as ever was invaluable. I am grateful to all of them even though I did not follow every piece of advice.

Chronology

28 Oct. 1922   Mussolini becomes prime minister and begins to transform his government into a fascist dictatorship.

March 1943   After an absence of 20 years, mass strikes involving at least 100,000 workers take place in northern cities.

9 July 1943   Allied invasion of Sicily.

25 July 1943   Mussolini deposed and arrested in a palace coup. Marshal Badoglio leads a new government over the next '45 days'.

8 Sep. 1943   The Italian government announces an armistice with the Allies. The Germans invade Italy from the North.

9 Sep. 1943   Formation of the National Liberation Committee (CLN) by the six anti-fascist parties.

19 Sep. 1943   Freed by the Germans, Mussolini proclaims his puppet government, the 'Republic of Salò'.

28 Sep. 1943   First of the 'Four Days', a spontaneous and successful insurrection in Naples.

4 June 1944   The Allies liberate Rome.

2 Sep. 1944   After three weeks of street fighting, partisans liberate Florence.

April 1945   Successful insurrections in northern cities. Mussolini is executed and taken to *piazzale Loreto*.

18 April 1948   Overwhelming Christian Democrat victory in Italy's first postwar election.

14 July 1948   Spontaneous insurrectionary general strike in protest at the attempted murder of PCI leader Palmiro Togliatti.

30 June 1960   Semi-insurrectionary general strike stops conference of the neo-fascist MSI in Genoa.

April 1994   The MSI joins the coalition government led by Silvio Berlusconi.

Introduction

It is very difficult to spend any time in Italy without being reminded of the Resistance movement of 1943–45. In many towns and cities throughout the country the name '25 aprile' is invariably given to a main square or street – the day in 1945 when many Italians liberated themselves from Italian fascism and Nazi occupiers. Alternatively, a street is simply called *via Resistenza*, or *piazza Partigiani* – partisans' square – after the name given to the anti-fascist fighters.

It is a period that has become almost a modern legend. Based on real events, tales both truthful and exaggerated have been handed down through the generations. While the Italians obviously recall their own history intensely, the historical memory handed down through British and American films and general culture often depicts Italians as having been mesmerised by Mussolini, even though nothing could be further from the truth. Mussolini became prime minister in 1922 with just 35 MPs out of over 500. It was during the next few years that he developed his dictatorship, banning opposition parties and a free media. Over the Alps in Munich, one man was writing in his prison cell: 'In this period – I openly admit – I conceived the profoundest admiration for the great man south of the Alps ... his determination not to share Italy with the Marxists, but to destroy internationalism and save the fatherland from it.'[1] The man was Adolf Hitler, who when he first met Mussolini asked him for his autograph.

Outside Italy most people today are simply unaware of the scale of Resistance to fascism during the Second World War. Yet writing in May 1944, Allied commander-in-chief General Alexander calculated that partisan activities in the North were pinning down six out of 25 enemy divisions.[2] Allied supreme command admitted in December 1944 that 'the resistance forces have been so powerful that the Germans have had to employ mechanized troops against them'. In other words, the Allies needed the Resistance as part of their war effort, as the same report stated: 'if they are obliged to cease this activity, through lack of food and equipment, four enemy divisions may become available to the enemy for employment on the front of the Allied Armies in Italy'.[3] In March 1945 the US secret services (OSS) estimated there were 182,000 partisans, with a further 500,000 potential recruits.[4] After the war the British Hewitt Report also came to the conclusion that 'without these partisan victories there would have been no Allied victory in Italy so swift, so overwhelming or so inexpensive'.[5]

On the opposing side, German commander Field-Marshal Kesselring was honest enough to admit to the partisans' existence in his memoirs.

1

Above all though he was at pains to discredit them as human beings, saying that partisans:

> violated the laws of humanity ... the criminal element being strongly represented among them. Riff-raff who robbed, murdered and pillaged wherever and whatever they could – a national scourge. ...
>   Altogether the Partisan groups presented the picture of a motley collection of Allied, Italian and Balkan soldiers, German deserters and native civilians of both sexes of widely different callings and ages with very varying ideas of morality, with the result that patriotism was often merely a cloak for the release of baser instincts.[6]

From Kesselring's perspective of belonging to the master race it was correct to define partisans as 'riff-raff'. Recent research from the central region of Emilia-Romagna has shown that the three largest social categories of the partisan movement were industrial workers (32 per cent), agricultural workers (31 per cent) and artisans (11 per cent).[7] The social breakdown of individual partisan brigades tends to bear this out, although they varied according to their catchment area. The Sinigaglia brigade, which operated to the south-east of Florence, was made up of 33 per cent engineering workers, 33 per cent artisans, 20 per cent students, 7 per cent peasants and 7 per cent white collar workers and technicians.[8] Furthermore, thousands of priests volunteered to join the movement and lived as either priests or fighters, some even as both, with 191 being killed by Italian fascists and 125 by the Germans.[9] Italian soldiers stationed abroad also joined foreign partisan forces, particularly in Yugoslavia. For example, 500 men from the Garibaldi battalion fought for several days to liberate Belgrade from the Germans in October 1944.

While it is impossible today to judge whether Kesselring was consciously telling lies or whether he genuinely believed in the partisans' apparent lack of humanity, one should remember that this was written by a core member of the Nazi machine, a man who fought for Hitler until the bitter end – indeed he went on fighting as senior military commander for a week after Hitler committed suicide.

Whatever the accuracy and veracity of his opinions, elsewhere he does admit that the partisans caused him significant problems. In August 1944 he ordered that his troops 'must tactically put the struggle against the armed bands on the same level as that of front line warfare'.[10] On 1 October he wrote to all his commanders: 'Supply traffic is being seriously constrained. Acts of sabotage are growing. We must fight these difficulties with all the means at our disposal ... [Partisan] bands have an excellent intelligence network: in the majority of cases they are supported by the Italian people and informed about all German troop movements and preparations.'[11]

But for reasons he explains, the Nazis never came close to eliminating the Resistance:

> In small groups or singly they ran amok without restraint, doing their nefarious work everywhere, in the mountains, in the Po valley, in woods

and on roads, under cover of darkness or of fog – but never openly. To the work of these bands must be ascribed most of the many acts of sabotage to military installations, dumps, railways, roads, bridges, and telegraph lines and the equally frequent crimes against humanity.[12]

And even when German soldiers were taken out of the front line for a rest period they could not relax. As Kesselring points out, in whole areas of the country German domination was far from total: 'the German soldier in the infested areas could not help seeing in every civilian of either sex a fanatical assassin or expecting to be fired at from every house. The whole population had in any case helped in or connived at elaborating a warning system which placed every German soldier's life in danger.'[13]

All the time partisans were in contact with the Allies: both forces had a common enemy in the Nazis and fascists. One of the factors that particularly worried Kesselring was when these two forces coordinated their actions: 'While acts of sabotage on railways, depots and dumps were more or less localised and routine, the rest of Partisan activity was governed by the situation at the front, the areas and the frequency of surprise attacks changing constantly.'[14] The scale of sabotage of the railway network in three of the most active regions was remarkable. In Emilia, Liguria and Lombardy railway lines were brought to a halt on 800 separate occasions, while 220 locomotives, 760 carriages and 275 bridges were destroyed.[15]

Obviously the Resistance developed in the wider context of the war. As was the case in many other European countries, the Allies were willing to form an alliance with a movement that also wanted to defeat Italian fascism and German Nazism. Although, as we shall see, the long-term goals of Allied leaders were often very different to those of the Resistance, the two managed to forge a meaningful coalition during 1943–45 – which quickly fell apart once politics could be practised freely again after liberation in April 1945.

It has been estimated that by the spring of 1945 there were 300,000 people fighting in the Resistance,[16] but even this probably underestimates the reality of popular military activity. A person only officially became defined as a partisan if they had carried arms for at least three months in an officially recognised unit, and taken part in three armed actions or acts of sabotage. Those arrested and held in jail as anti-fascists were only classed as partisans if they were held for longer than three months; and those providing logistic support for partisan units needed to have done so for six months.[17] In addition, to keep one partisan in the field, it has been estimated that another ten to 15 people were needed to obtain finance and weaponry, provide food, clothes, medicine, messages, and so on.

In 1945 a new democratic Italy emerged from a war-torn country. It was the left that laid the major claim as the inheritors of the Resistance, given that three left-wing organisations (to be closely examined in this book – the Action, Communist and Socialist Parties) had provided 80–85 per cent of partisans.

THE MEANING OF THE RESISTANCE

In essence the Resistance is about democracy, direct democracy. And perhaps the most subversive idea of the entire movement was that you can defeat a far more powerful enemy – in this case by successfully conducting a campaign of guerrilla warfare. When the Italian government signed an armistice and collapsed in September 1943, the Nazis brought large numbers over the Alps in a great rush to occupy the country, and to block the Allies, who were already in the South. The idea that the most ruthless and efficient fighting machine in the world could be brought to a standstill seemed like a joke back then – yet less than two years later German Field Marshals were forced to surrender to ordinary communist industrial workers.

The story of the Italian Resistance movement is the story of how ordinary people (a people who are often racially stereotyped as being cowardly), who had lived under a dictatorship for 20 years, played a key role in ending a system which seemed set in stone, totally unbeatable. It is the story of how a society which seemed extremely stable and controlled, destined to continue in the same way forever, suddenly exploded from below with mass activity, such that for a brief period *everything seemed possible*.

How could such an organisation grow so quickly? First of all, the situation was so dire that many people felt they had nothing else left to lose. A historian hostile to the ideals of the French Revolution of 1789 once captured the common causes of so many huge social upheavals, which were also applicable to Italy during the Second World War: 'Hunger and nakedness, and nightmare oppression lying heavy on twenty-five million hearts; this, not the wounded vanities or contradicted philosophies of philosophical advocates, rich shopkeepers, rural noblesse, was the prime mover in the French Revolution; as the like will be in all such revolutions, in all countries.'[18]

By 1942 many Italian cities were being bombed nightly by the Allies, jobs were becoming scarce, as was food. A young worker in Milan recalled: 'Parents' body weight fell to 40–50 kilos, so they could give what little they had to their children. You reached the point that out of dying of hunger or dying from a bullet – it was better to die from a bullet.'[19] Similarly, many families had loved ones fighting in Mussolini's armies who had either been killed, wounded or captured. For many conscript soldiers and their families, the idea of fighting alongside the invading Nazis, or dying for Mussolini's puppet regime created in September 1943 by the Germans, was simply never taken seriously.

People behaved in unusual ways: who would expect a Vice Chancellor in a speech to first-year university students to invite them to take up arms against the government? Well, it happened at Padua university in 1943.[20]

The Resistance is important not just because it was a military movement which involved much of society, but because it was also a political movement, a movement for democracy against fascist dictatorship. Very few of the participants ever visualised their future in terms of the kind of stale parliamentary systems we know today; most were fighting for much more radical and participatory forms of democracy. Be that as it may, one simply cannot understand modern Italian society and politics without understanding the Resistance. Modern Italian democracy comes directly from the Resistance, it comes from below.

This is why it is has been so popular for many Italians – it was a war fought by volunteers. All Resistance fighters made their own personal decision that it was right to risk their own lives for a cause – a very different decision from that of someone joining an army because they receive their call-up papers through the letter box.

HOW THIS BOOK IS STRUCTURED

Most of the book – Part I – tells a broadly chronological story, while Part II contains four thematic chapters which could be approached on their own assuming the reader already has some background knowledge. Chapter 1 deals with the fascist period of 1922–43. Because of what follows later in the book, it begins with a description of how the regime repressed all dissent, although most of the chapter is taken up with Italian colonialism and racism. This is important not only due to revisionist attempts to whitewash this period of Italian foreign and social policy, but because Mussolini's foreign adventures – crucially his participation in the Second World War – created the conditions for the regime becoming severely weakened at home. This chapter then ends with a description on how Italy's disastrous experience in the war favoured the beginnings of opposition on a far larger scale than had been seen in the police state of the previous 20 years.

The following chapter deals with the two key dates of 1943: 25 July and 8 September. On the former, Mussolini was arrested in a palace coup led by other fascist leaders, and on the latter the Badoglio government announced an armistice and literally disappeared into the night. The Germans responded by pouring troops in from the North and occupying the country, immediately engaging the Allied armies already in the far South. The chapter concludes with the 'Four Days of Naples', a spontaneous insurrection that drove the Germans out of Italy's second largest city.

Chapter 3 is devoted to the social and political response to this crisis. The three main left-wing parties – the Action, Socialist and Communist Parties – are analysed separately. However, the creation of a coalition National Liberation Committee (CLN) involving all parties was an equally important event, as were the mass strikes of March 1943, which demonstrated the existence of a widespread clandestine network, mostly dominated by the Italian Communist Party (PCI).

The next two chapters describe the two main arenas of the Resistance struggle. All kinds of people – disbanded soldiers, those facing the call-up, local peasants, activists forced out of the city, even escaped Allied POWs – went up into the hills and mountains and formed guerrilla units. Chapter 5 outlines the conditions which led people to take part in acts of resistance in the cities, concentrating on strike action in large workplaces. The chapter ends with a description of an organised insurrection which liberated a major city, Florence.

Chapter 6 is devoted to the high-point of the Resistance: the liberation of the three main industrial cities of the North (Genoa, Milan and Turin) on 25 April 1945, which took place several days before the arrival of Allied forces. The following chapter looks at how partisans were treated after April 1945, and stresses the reasons for their frustrations, both as regards their own treatment and with respect to the policies of the PCI in particular.

Chapter 8 examines the fate of the defeated side in the Resistance, the fascists. Disturbingly, fascism was never fully eradicated from the Italian state, and for many decades neo-fascism enjoyed some degree of protection and sympathy within government machinery, which explains two attempted coups and many acts of neo-fascist terrorism which went unpunished. In recent decades fascism has sought rehabilitation by political rather than military means, and the chapter concludes with an examination of revisionism and the undermining of the Resistance.

The first chapter in Part II outlines the significant contribution of women to the Resistance, both as combatants and as support staff – actions that were largely 'hidden from history' until rediscovered in the 1970s. Chapter 10 examines the creation of, and democratic life within, three of the 15 to 20 liberated areas the Resistance was able to create and maintain for several weeks or months in mountain areas. Chapter 11 is devoted entirely to the organisation and impact of urban 'terrorism', contrasting activities in Rome and Milan.

The final chapter broadens the discussion to examine the wider context within which the Resistance was acting, taking into account the military and political needs of the Allied powers, including the Russians.

PART I

1
Midnight in the Century

When Mussolini became prime minister in October 1922 the powerful politicians who supported his election thought they could control him. In a parliament of 535 seats, his party had just 35 MPs, yet 479 parliamentarians voted for the formation of his government.

Another group in society was also backing Mussolini – his party was highly reliant on financing from the rich and powerful. For the period 1921–24 the breakdown of contributions to the Fascist Party has been calculated at 25 per cent from individuals, 10 per cent from banking and insurance, and 64 per cent from industrialists and the business world at large.[1] These finances were forthcoming because the fascists had quickly shown themselves willing and able to make physical attacks on the left. Early examples were the attack on the Italian Socialist Party (PSI) daily *Avanti!* in Milan on 15 April 1919, and the beating up of Socialist MPs on the opening day of the new parliament on 1 December.[2]

The reason such a violent new movement received rapid funding from some of the most powerful financial forces in the country lay in what happened during the *biennio rosso*, the 'two red years' that followed the First World War. The left had grown massively for a combination of reasons: hardships during the war had increased radicalisation, and the idea of solving problems through revolution was growing in popularity, particularly following the Russian Revolution of 1917. The PSI had grown from a membership of 50,000 in 1914 to 216,000 by 1921, and from 50 MPs before the war to 156 in 1919, when it became the largest party in parliament. *Avanti!* sold 300,000 copies a day – 50,000 alone in Turin. Similarly, the largest union federation, the CGL, rose from just below 250,000 members at the end of 1918 to 1 million in 1919 and 2.2 million in 1920, with the semi-anarchist, semi-revolutionary syndicalist USI federation claiming 500,000 members in 1919.[3]

Not surprisingly, strike statistics shot up, but so too did the level of wage increases won as a result. In 1918 real wages had fallen to 65 per cent of their 1913 level, but they rose to 114 per cent in 1920 and 127 per cent in 1921.[4] This whole period culminated in the 'occupation of the factories' in September 1920, when hundreds of thousands of engineering workers occupied their workplaces, sometimes with weapons, for nearly a month. While the PSI and the trade unions publicly debated whether to use this movement as a springboard for revolution, factory owners were faced with the difficulties of stopping armed strikes with the use of force, and the intractable problem of democracy having made the PSI the largest party in parliament.

Hence the financing of fascist squads, committed to destroying a resurgent working class. For example, in August 1922 ship owners in Genoa spent millions financing a fascist 'punitive expedition', which in three days of fighting saw five dockers killed and 50 wounded.[5]

It was this 'great fear' which also explained the political as well as the financial support for Mussolini. For his part, Mussolini had a considerable talent for making promises people wanted to hear. Once he had assured business leaders that his movement would not enact any radical or populist economic measures, in early October 1922 the industrialists' organisation the *Confindustria* came out in support of Mussolini joining government. Similarly, since the fascists had made it clear they would not close down private Catholic schools, the church was on side too. And the country's two most important military leaders, Marshals Pietro Badoglio and Armando Diaz, also made it clear on 7 October that the military would not oppose a government led by Mussolini.[6]

The government sworn in on 30 October was a coalition made up of five parties, with the Liberals taking one cabinet post and the Popular Party three,[7] given that leaders such as Ivanoe Bonomi and Alcide De Gasperi had voted to make Mussolini prime minister. Bonomi was not only leader of the Liberal Party, he had also been prime minister during 1921–22 and was elected on a joint ticket with the fascists (on more than one occasion he had allowed his ministerial car to be used in 'punitive expeditions').[8]

The Popular Party was much larger, and in effect Mussolini could not pass laws without their agreement or abstention. Although his methods were not immediately as dictatorial as they later became, Mussolini quickly began to engage in highly reactionary policies. Nevertheless, six months after the formation of Mussolini's government the Popular Party held its conference in Turin, and in a speech their young MP, De Gasperi, called for his party to adopt the following policy towards government: 'I ask that conference approves the attitude adopted by the party so far, an attitude of frank and loyal collaboration.'[9]

Even though the party conference voted 70 to one to stay within government, Mussolini, rapidly growing in power and self-confidence, ejected them. Nevertheless, a meeting of the Popular Party parliamentary group chaired by De Gasperi again expressed the view that 'an attitude of sincere collaboration with the government should be maintained'.[10] The historical peculiarity here is that both these men – Bonomi and De Gasperi – were to take on an important institutional role in Mussolini's downfall during the Second World War, although their practical contribution was perhaps small.

Mussolini, meanwhile, ruled more or less constitutionally in the first two or three years of his government, although press freedoms were quickly curtailed. But over time internal pressure built up within the fascist movement, which demanded that the party's 'revolutionary' agenda be put into action. Part of this involved continuing to annihilate the left, a strategy that culminated with the kidnapping of Socialist MP Giacomo Matteotti in 1924.

When his body was found several weeks later, a profound political crisis developed: Mussolini's personal bodyguards were involved in the murder, and Mussolini too was implicated in the plotting before the attack and the cover up afterwards. In the meantime many anti-fascist MPs left parliament and created their own alternative structure in opposition to Mussolini's mockery of democracy. The Liberal and conservative politicians who remained in parliament disagreed with the fascists' violent methods, but did not have the numbers to unseat Mussolini with a vote, and neither did the king want to sack him. Crucially, the Popular Party remained in parliament rather than joining the alternative democratic assembly.[11] The only way to end Mussolini's rule therefore would have been unconstitutional – it would have meant calling for a popular uprising or revolution, and while many spontaneous protests had already broken out, these concepts were not part of conservative and Catholic political traditions. Left-wing parties, meanwhile, were suffering terrible harassment and were also politically divided after the Communist Party (the PCI) had been created from a split within the Socialist Party in January 1921.

In the face of all this instability fascist hardliners were demanding that Mussolini face down all his critics. Mussolini had to either resign or accept responsibility for Matteotti's murder, which he did on 3 January 1925, banning *all* opposition and effectively creating a dictatorship. His hand had been forced by fascists who had been rattled by the possibility of prosecution over the Matteotti affair, and who were considering removing Mussolini himself.

This was the beginning of a full-blooded dictatorship.

The fascist Special Tribunal, which sat from 1927 to 1943, gave out prison sentences to 4,000 communists, 323 'generic anti-fascists', 24 anarchists and 12 socialists. In all the Tribunal inflicted a total of 28,196 years imprisonment against 4,596 anti-fascists: not for theft, rape, or murder, but for being anti-fascists. Their social composition is interesting to note because it revealed what kind of people were actively opposing fascism: 85 per cent were workers or artisans.[12] Another 12,000 anti-fascists, for whom strong evidence could not be presented to the Tribunal, were sent not to jail but into 'internal exile' in remote areas of the South or small islands. Others were forced to sign on at a police station twice a day. Many more were followed and spied upon.

However this working-class opposition to fascism did not come from some kind of moral superiority they possessed over other classes. Whilst workers and peasants might be ideologically more opposed to fascism than other classes, it was the anti-working-class policies of fascism that drove many to oppose Mussolini's government. Once a fully fledged dictatorship had developed, huge wage cuts were imposed on workers: 10–20 per cent in October 1927, 8 per cent in December 1930 and 7 per cent in May 1934.[13]

Given the risks, opposition to fascism was therefore unlikely to involve the rich or the middle class, by and large – a fact borne out by the social status of those convicted for anti-fascism. Overall Mussolini was careful about protecting the wage levels and savings of the middle class; while overall real wages only regained their 1922 level in 1938 – in a society where the eight-hour day had been won and then abolished. By 1940 Italy had the lowest per capita consumption of sugar in Europe, and by the end of the 1930s there were near starvation conditions in many areas of the South, as outlined in *Christ Stopped at Eboli* by Carlo Levi, an anti-fascist sent into 'internal exile' by the Special Tribunal.

Individual Italians might complain about the government in private but would be foolish to do so in public. But even in their own home parents often would not criticise fascism in front of their children, for fear that the children would innocently betray them as a result of devious questioning at school, or simply through a careless word in the street or the playground.[14] Society was highly regimented, and people were fearful of speaking their mind. The risks were enormous: if neighbours saw someone going in and out at odd times, or thought people coming to visit looked suspicious, they might tell the police. The police were also very good at turning captured anti-fascists into spies, so ultimately any anti-fascist activity was likely to end in long-term imprisonment.

Many people died from beatings, or were simply murdered, never appearing in court. And some prisoners such as Antonio Gramsci, the main theoretician of the 1920 'occupation of the factories' and leader of the PCI from 1924, died in prison. This did not go on for just one or two years, but for two decades. If anything, the Tribunal became more vicious as time went on, and as fascism felt under more pressure. For example in 1941 it handed down a three-year sentence against Corporal Francesco Castiglione for complaining about the war during a train journey between Naples and Caserta. In Salerno Eduardo Adinolfi Borea was sentenced to sixteen years for distributing anti-fascist leaflets.[15] Although he was writing about the horrors of Stalinist Russia and Nazism, Victor Serge's definition of the inter-war years as being 'midnight in the century' seems very appropriate.

Many anti-fascists were driven into exile abroad, with many settling in France. In essence it was a small band of communists who kept the flame of anti-fascism burning for 20 years. Yet in many towns and cities all links with the party leadership now living abroad, and all publications, were cut for years on end – 'the darker the night the brighter the star' was a phrase they used to keep themselves going.

To take one city and one year out of 20, 1927 was a devastating one for Milan communists – a total of 1,960 people were arrested and accused of party membership. Repression was harsh: on one occasion 150 workers were beaten up en masse on suspicion of communism, with five dying of their wounds. In January the printing press of the party newspaper *l'Unità* was discovered, and in July, through the infiltration of spies, the police discovered the PCI's offices for the whole of northern Italy, duly arresting the PCI treasurer for Milan and the person responsible for distributing party literature throughout Italy.[16] By mid 1928 the PCI in Milan had not surprisingly almost collapsed: their youth organisation had just over 30 members.[17]

Opposition to fascism continued by and large to be a working-class affair, and those who had doubts about fascism were compromised if they remained in influential positions. As one speaker recalled at a recent congress of the ex-partisan's association, ANPI: 'there is a difference between Antonio Gramsci who dies in a fascist jail and senator Benedetto Croce, who in the very same period donated his Senate gold medal to the fascists in support of the war against Abyssinia, fought with poison gas'.[18] Although more famous as a philosopher, Croce had also been a senator and Minister of Education in 1920–21 and voted for Mussolini to become prime minister in 1922. Furthermore, in a key vote of confidence during the Matteotti crisis he again voted for Mussolini in the Senate in June 1924. The following month he explained why: 'Fascism has met some important needs and has done a lot of good, as every fair-minded person knows.'[19] Although he later distanced himself from fascism, the significance of Croce's track record lies in the fact that he was to play a key mediating role between the fascist establishment and the radical forces of the Resistance during 1943–45, becoming a Minister without Portfolio in both the Badoglio and Bonomi governments.

ITALIAN COLONIALISM, RACISM AND THE SECOND WORLD WAR

The history of Italian racial apartheid in Africa even predates fascism. The town of Asmera in Eritrea was first occupied by Italian forces in 1889, and as the city developed entire urban areas were racially segregated by 1914, as well as cinemas and local transport.[20] But the country which suffered the longest history of Italian colonialism – 32 years – was Libya. Still today, many Italians are surprised by Libyan hostility towards their country, yet the blood-chilling statistic of one in eight of the Libyan population dying to achieve independence explains the essence of the bitterness. As the First World War raged in northern Europe, Italian forces continued the land grab which had begun with their first invasion in 1911. During 1914–15 Colonel Antonio Miani, with just 1,200 men and ten cannons, managed to conquer the Fezzan region of Libya, an area as large as Italy itself.[21]

In line with his strongly nationalist ideology, Mussolini's foreign policy was openly imperialist, and therefore broadly similar to previous governments. This emerged first in 1923, the year after he became prime minister, when Italy invaded Corfu only to retreat after threats from Britain.

The first war crime of the fascist period occurred at Merca in Somalia in October 1926, when Italian colonisers massacred a hundred people in the mosque. From 1925 to 1927 large numbers of Italian occupation troops under Governor Cesare Maria De Vecchi engaged in a scorched earth policy in the north of the country, an area essentially outside of Italian control due to support for local rebels.

Meanwhile in Libya, mustard gas was first used by Italian troops in 1928, and again in 1930. Entire populations were displaced in Italy's African colonies following orders given by the governor general of Libya, Pietro Badoglio, which were carried out by Marshal Rodolfo Graziani. Of the 100,000 people assigned to displacement camps in 1930, only 60,000 had survived when the camps were closed three years later. This is not surprising, given that for the 33,000 held in the camps of Soluch and Sidi Ahmed el-Magrun there was just one doctor.[22] In 1930, in a portent of future attitudes, Badoglio stated that the dominant attitude among Libyan Jews was 'selfishness, lack of interest in others, moral and material laziness'.[23]

These kinds of attitudes and policies formed the background to the better-known invasion of Abyssinia/Ethiopia, which began in October 1935 and lasted until 1939, during which Italy mobilised nearly a million men. Furthermore, weapons of mass destruction were used on a large scale – at that time the 500 tonnes of bombs dropped was a significant amount. This was made up mainly of mustard gas bombs, but arsenic shells were also used.

Resistance was repressed mercilessly. When the Viceroy, Rodolfo Graziani, suffered an attempt on his life in February 1937, he laid waste to large areas of Addis Abeba – burning down huts and for three days shooting on the spot anybody captured in a fascist round-up. Indeed Mussolini urged Graziani that 'all suspects must be executed immediately', and that in any village where resistance was suspected 'all adult males must be shot'.[24] Mussolini's eldest son Vittorio later wrote a book about his exploits in the war, writing of groups of tribesmen 'bursting out like a rose after I had landed a bomb in the middle of them'.[25]

Mussolini's proclamation of an Empire gave a huge impulse to fascist racial policy. A major fascist anthropologist wrote in 1935: 'In negro races the mental inferiority of women often approaches stupidity; furthermore, at least in Africa some aspects of female behaviour have very little of the human, bordering those of animals.'[26] The danger therefore was of mixed-race children polluting the purity of the Italian race. This is why a Ministry of African Italy publication could write in 1939: 'it is essential that every Italian in the colonies is intimately and totally convinced of being the carrier of a seed that must not be polluted, because its purity has been the condition and guarantee of the strongest contribution to civilisation in the world'.[27] Therefore there were jail sentences of between one and five years for the Italians who married Ethiopians; Italians were also banned from living in Ethiopian areas given that there was a catch-all crime of 'damaging racial prestige'. Public transport and buildings were racially segregated, as were sporting activities.[28]

Italian fascists also took part in the Spanish Civil War in 1936–39, with Mussolini sending around 100,000 men. Indeed, the Italian military used the skills they had developed in Abyssinia; the dress rehearsal for the far more notorious bombing of Guernica occurred in the nearby town of Durango three weeks earlier, and was carried out by Italian bombers and fighters. At dawn on 31 March 1937 four bombers began dropping 500lb bombs on this Basque town of 9,000 people, followed up by nine fighter planes. In four days of attacks 366 civilians were killed and hundreds more injured.[29]

However Mussolini's forces sometimes found themselves fighting Italian anti-fascists in the International Brigades, battles which were in turn a dress rehearsal for the Resistance period of 1943–45. Many activists living in exile, or their family members, rallied to the anti-fascist cause represented by resistance to the coup launched by General Franco. A typical example was Giovanni Pesce:

We emigrated to France in 1922, when Mussolini took power. Dad had to leave because of his politics. He was an anti-fascist, but he wasn't in a party or even an activist. We moved to a pit village: there was nothing inside our house, just one big room where my parents and their three kids slept. There was no bathroom – absolutely nothing.

Growing up I could see the living and working conditions of miners. What struck me even more were the wooden shacks in which five or six migrant workers lived, mainly Algerians, Moroccans and people from the Balkans. When you passed by them at night you could see one of them snoring, the other tossing and turning, a third getting drunk while the fourth was dying of silicosis. This was a huge political education for me. ...

I can remember these huge demonstrations throughout France demanding help for the Spanish people, including the buying of guns. What really struck me was that so many intellectuals and scientists, including a French Nobel prize-winner for Physics, and so many others from the world of cinema and the arts – from America, Britain and all over the world – called for solidarity with the Spanish people. Then the issue of sending volunteers to Spain came up. A group of Italians such as Nicoletti and Carlo Rosselli had left immediately: Communists, Socialists, anarchists and republicans, and from this grew the idea of organising an Italian contingent.[30]

A leader of the libertarian left organisation *Justice and Liberty*, Carlo Rosselli in particular had been among the first of Italian anti-fascists exiled in France to understand the importance of the Spanish Civil War, writing on 31 July 1936: 'The Spanish revolution is our revolution; the civil war of the Spanish proletariat is a war for all anti-fascists.'[31] He quickly went on to coin the phrase that encapsulated the motivations of Italian anti-fascists: 'Today in Spain, tomorrow in Italy'.

The left came together instinctively over this cause, often from below. Enthused by these developments, although aged just 18, Giovanni Pesce wanted to go and fight in Spain but his fellow communists thought he was too young. But he ignored their advice and finally managed to cross the border into Spain. He was one of 3,354 Italian volunteers, most of whom joined the 'Garibaldi brigade', one of the numerous International Brigades; 600 of them were killed, and 2,000 wounded. The Italians made up about a tenth of the volunteers who came to fight in Spain from over 50 countries.

At Albacete, a town halfway between Madrid and Valencia, Pesce met Guido Picelli, a man from whom he and others received first military training and then leadership in the field.[32] In many respects, the generation of activists who had been defeated during Mussolini's rise to power in 1920–22 was handing over the baton to a younger generation. Picelli was now 47; he had first joined the Italian Socialist Party during the first World War, and personally led the largest successful act of resistance against Mussolini's blackshirts in Parma in 1922.[33]

Pesce continues his account:

I was wounded three times, for example I took part in all the battles for the defence of Madrid. The battle I'm proudest of took place at Guadalajara, where we defeated the Italian army.

The order came through to go and fight these Italian fascists. Lots of us were confused and worried, because many of those people were unemployed or very poor, and had been forced to come to Spain.

So two of our leaders, Longo and Nenni, came and explained that we all knew those people had been conned. Therefore we had to behave differently, like real soldiers, there were to be no acts of revenge. We should try and talk to them across the trenches, so we used a megaphone to try and persuade them that they should surrender. Many of them had gone to colonize land in Abyssinia, but it had been a disaster, and we explained they had just been used. I think all this helped to lower their level of confidence and create demoralisation.[34]

This was confirmed by the Italian Foreign Minister, Galeazzo Ciano, who wrote to Mussolini explaining that years of fascist political indoctrination could quickly dissolve under difficult conditions or upon hearing a counter-argument.[35] Indeed, this is exactly what happened in the closing stages of the Second World War less than a decade later.

One of the fascist soldiers captured by Pesce told him this emblematic story:

I've always been anti-fascist. In 1931 I had two children and in 1935 I became unemployed; and I started going from one employment exchange to another. But when they found out I didn't have a Fascist Party card they slammed the door in my face. ... In a fascist meeting they talked about the need to recruit lots of workers and send them to Abyssinia: the government would guarantee lots of subsidies to the families of those who accepted. I thought about it for a long time, but in the face of so much misery and with no prospects for the future I joined up.[36]

While these were the trends at a rank-and-file level, a new political leadership emerged during the Spanish Civil War, honing skills that would be used on a far greater scale during the Resistance. Luigi Longo, a PCI central committee member aged 36, quickly came to the fore, initially organising the involvement of Italian communists.[37] He then took on a major political role, indeed he became the senior political commissar for the International Brigades. In a communiqué released as the Brigades were about to leave Spain in late 1938 he wrote: 'Although we are leaving Spanish trenches, this does not mean our struggle for freedom is over. New and larger battles await us.'[38] Giovanni Pesce viewed his Spanish experience in a similar fashion many years later: 'Spain was a huge moral, political and military training ground. It gave experience to hundreds and thousands of people who then led the European Resistance.'[39] Neither man could have known of the bigger battles that awaited them. Longo was to become the senior communist leader in occupied Italy during 1943–45, and Pesce became a feared urban 'terrorist' leader in Turin and Milan. Both men would meet again, but this time during a successful insurrection, in Milan in April 1945.

Returning to fascist diplomatic developments, as with Nazi Germany, Mussolini wanted to have a friendly relationship with Russia to create greater room for manoeuvre with other competing imperialist nations, so in 1933 the two countries signed a non-aggression pact. One of the outcomes was that the USSR supplied Italy with oil during the sanctions imposed by the League of Nations for its attack on Abyssinia. So once again, the much better-known August 1939 non-aggression pact between Russia and Nazi Germany had been a later application of a precedent already created by Mussolini.[40]

Italy entered the Second World War a year later than many other countries, in 1940, and its conduct in the Balkans, where it stationed 650,000 troops, was no different to that of the Nazis. Indeed it was built on a 20-year policy of virtual ethnic cleansing of Italian territory which was inhabited by both Italian and Slav populations, in which tens of thousands of people deemed to be resisting the Italians were sent to detention camps in southern Italy.

The official policy towards local people, who as Slavs were considered inferior to Italians, was their 'fascistisation'. Schools were Italianised, Slovene or Croat teachers sacked or forced to emigrate, hundreds of sporting, youth and cultural associations were closed down. And just as in Italy, political parties and a free press were banned.[41] And for those who disagreed, there was prison: from 1927–43 the fascist Special Tribunal convicted 615 Slavs to a total of 5,418 years of imprisonment, and condemned 34 to death.[42]

This was the background to whole areas of Slovenia, Dalmatia, Bosnia and Montenegro being simply annexed to Italy when they were invaded in April 1941. Resistance would not be tolerated, so mass executions began in Montenegro in July 1941, and in March 1942 General Roatta issued a circular about how to respond to partisan attacks: 'armed rebels, or those who work with them or help them must be executed. Built-up areas in which arms or munitions are found, or which have shown themselves to favour the rebels will be burnt.'[43] A subsequent war crimes commission estimated that in the 29 months of occupation a thousand Slovenes were killed as hostages, 2,500 civilians were killed during round-ups (200 due to torture), 900 partisans executed, and 35,000 men, women and children deported.[44] Many of those deported, often to Italy proper, were families who had a member 'absent without clear motive'.[45] Overall, it has been calculated that 1,600,000 Yugoslavs died or went missing in the Balkans during 1941–45, a figure proportionally similar to the deaths suffered by Germany and the Soviet Union.[46]

Events followed the same pattern in Greece. In November 1940, after early reversals on the Greek-Albanian front, Mussolini ordered his command to: 'destroy and raze to the ground ... all urban centres of more than 10,000 inhabitants', the purpose being 'disorganisation of civilian life in Greece, sowing panic everywhere'.[47] Incendiary bombs were dropped on several cities, while economically Italian businesses were favoured and a special occupation currency was introduced, causing devastation of the Greek economy. In the islands under Italian control it was forbidden to speak Greek, and Italian teachers were appointed to replace Greek ones who had been sacked.[48]

Mussolini was constantly informed of events in the Balkans, and wrote in August 1942: 'I am convinced it is necessary to respond to partisan "terror" with blood and fire. The stereotype that depicts Italians as sentimental, incapable of being tough when necessary, must come to an end.'[49] Although nobody knew it at the time, these events were a dress rehearsal for how fascist forces were to treat presumed partisans and their supporters in Italy the following year; indeed for many senior military officers the 'Italian campaign' would be their third, after Africa and the Balkans.

Back in Italy, a media campaign against Italy's 40,000 Jews developed during 1938. On 4 September, for example, the main newspaper in Naples ran a large banner headline which read: 'In Naples Jews have infiltrated all the professions', whereas news on a major eruption of nearby Vesuvius was well down the page.[50]

Later that autumn a series of 'racial laws' was announced. A 'Manifesto of the race' which accompanied the laws argued: 'The majority of Italy's current population is Aryan, as is its culture. ... It is time for Italians to openly declare themselves racists.'[51] Jews could no longer study or teach in public schools or universities, or work in banks, insurance companies and local or national government. Furthermore, they could not publish books or go on holiday to popular resorts. They could not own land over a certain value, own or manage companies involved in military production or which employed over a hundred people; neither could they marry non-Jews. Worst of all perhaps, Jews who had been naturalised after January 1919 lost their citizenship and became aliens.[52] Such was the bureaucratic obsession that in November 1938 the Italian embassy in the UK wrote to its consulates in London, Glasgow, Liverpool and Cardiff: 'Please urgently communicate the names of the consular employees who appear to be of Jewish religion or of Jewish descent by listing also the uncertain cases. Enquiries must be extended also to these employees' wives.'[53] All this was taking place several years before the holocaust started to be organised in central Europe.

Such was the government's zeal that in February 1942, in the midst of a disastrous campaign in North Africa, a minister ordered that all Jews in Libya be sent to concentration camps, whether Italian citizens or otherwise, and later organised their deportation to Italy at the rate of 200 per day.[54] On

6 May the Ministry of the Interior ordered all Jews in Italy aged 18–55 to report for forced labour.

Another group targeted, which has recently become subject to government discrimination again, was gypsies. In September 1940 the chief of police ordered that all Italian and foreign Roma be arrested and sent to the dozens of internment camps scattered around the country.[55]

When the Second World War broke out Mussolini believed that Germany was on the verge of dominating Europe, and wanted to be on the winning side. But the Italian armed forces in 1939 were in a terrible state of preparation, badly equipped and trained. Mussolini heeded his advisers and did not join the fray during the first year of 'phoney war', that is, before Germany launched

Figure 1.1   Trieste 1942: 'Closed forever – Jewish shop'.

a major invasion of France; but when in 1940 German forces sliced through France like a knife through butter, Mussolini declared war against France believing that the fighting would last just six weeks. He cynically admitted his reasons: 'we need a few thousand Italian dead to make some weight to our claims at the conference table'.

Mussolini had made the biggest blunder of his life: three years later he would be deposed in a palace coup, and two years after that his dead body was strung up in a Milan square by partisans.

THE ICE MELTS

As the Second World War approached the only anti-fascist party to have kept a presence in Italy throughout these two decades, the Communist Party, was in serious disarray. The international organisation to which it belonged, the Comintern, had originally called for a united struggle for peace involving working people, but also capitalist states such as Britain and France, and condemned the Nazis as the chief instigators of war. But following the non-aggression pact signed between Germany and the Soviet Union in August 1939, for Moscow and national Communist Parties throughout Europe it was now Britain and France who suddenly became the main cause of the second great imperialist war. The pact was a 'pact for peace', and a blow against the old imperialist powers. The Comintern even went so far as to say that German workers preferred Hitler's rule to a British victory.

The PCI was obliged to swing into line with this tortuous logic, alienating many other left-wing forces and its own membership and periphery in the process. Yet the switch would be reversed again in 1941, when Germany attacked the Soviet Union – once again the British and French governments became anti-Nazi allies.

Meanwhile, on the ground in Italy, a war economy enabled employers to turn the screw further in workplaces. When Italy declared war in July 1940 companies were arbitrarily allowed to raise their working week to 48 hours, and by February 1941 60 hours was the average working week in engineering. With these long hours, and many workers forced to commute, it was not uncommon for some to sleep in the factory or in nearby barns. Some firms even asked for permission to build huts to house workers temporarily. In the big cities in the evening, people would frequently walk out and sleep in the surrounding countryside. There were very few air-raid shelters, and little in the way of public transport.

Any war almost inevitably leads to food shortages and price rises. In the industrial region of Lombardy official statistics show that real price levels (both official and black market) rose by over 30 per cent from July 1942 to July 1943, while pay for industrial workers was generally static throughout 1942.[56] People began to keep their hunger at bay by using unusual methods, so much so that in March 1943 the prefect of Bologna issued an order banning the killing of cats, since 'a reduction of the animals in question creates an increase in rats'.

Given these kinds of pressures and the length of the working week, it is not surprising that dissent slowly began to surface after years of repression. By the second half of 1942 there was an average of two strikes a month in Italy, rising in the first two months of 1943 to five strikes a month.[57] This industrial dissent grew at the same time as more widespread concerns developed throughout society – by 1942 it was clear the war was going very badly, and millions of Italians had loved ones under arms. An experienced communist activist in northern Italy, Pippo Coppo, describes how his job of developing anti-fascist activity started to become easier:

because mothers and parents, all those who had sons under arms, knew they were at war they started to rebel, and therefore discontent began growing. This happened here. Therefore making contact [with people] became easier; even though we were always as cautious as we could be – nobody could know more than two other people, and people worked on their own.[58]

People were also rebelling because they were being bombed. A young Jewish intellectual in Turin described coming out of an air-raid shelter after one of the first big raids in November 1942:

I go up with dad and see an incredible sight – for miles and miles the sky is red. The front shutters of shops are blown away or bent, there are large white stains on the ground – the phosphorous dropped by the British. It seems that a cloud of fire, made more luminous by the darkness, is hanging over Turin. I imagine this is what the last hours of Sodom and Gomorrah were like – tonight I have witnessed something that most people have never seen – it looked like the funeral pyre of a city of 600,000 inhabitants.[59]

By early 1943 the anti-fascists had grown in confidence, as they could see more and more people agreeing with them. The small conspiratorial groups were no longer tiny and inward-looking, but experience had shown that fascism would have to be defeated physically – there was no 'rule of law' or 'democratic process' to appeal to as there was in conventional democracies. But for many working-class people, influenced by far-left ideas, anti-fascist activity was also seen as an opportunity to overturn the relationship between the classes.

As we shall see in Chapter 3, events started to move quickly when the original financiers of fascism saw their world literally crumbling around them in 1941–42. They began to withdraw their support and quietly suggest within the establishment that Italy sue for peace.

2
The Mafia and Street Kids: How Fascism Fell in the South

In November 1942 two events indicated that the tide had turned in the Mediterranean: the Italians suffered a decisive defeat at El Alamein, and US forces landed in North Africa. On 9 July 1943, the Allied invasion of continental Europe began in Sicily under the command of Generals Montgomery and Patton, who led 150,000 men onto the southern shores of the island. A brief look at what happened in Sicily shows what the rest of Italy, and Europe, had to look forward to when the Allies 'liberated' them.

The Allies were invading a devastated country. Shortly before the fall of fascism, the biggest reason for discontent and protests among agricultural workers was the price and availability of shoes. Due to the dislocation of the war, production had fallen from 12 million to 3 million pairs. Prices had therefore rocketed, from 150 lire before the war to 1,000 in 1943.[1] Another source of great discontent was that peasants were forced to send a significant amount of the food they produced to state warehouses, which led to local shortages in foodstuffs. As men were called up into the armed forces, the women and old men left behind were called upon to produce even more, but Italy's economy could not withstand a major war. By the end of 1942 the police chief in Agrigento risked his job by writing to his superiors to explain that poor people

> have seen their primordial diet of bread and pasta decrease; the effects of this are visible in people's complexion, especially in the countryside. It is therefore understandable that there is discontent and suffering, and an expectation that these privations would not last long. The ruling classes have never done anything for this country, and have only shown cold selfishness.[2]

In more general terms a poor island economy which had already been seriously harmed by general war shortages was further disrupted by becoming a war zone. A black market quickly sprang up, and many peasants virtually starved to death.

In strategic terms it may well have been easier to start the invasion of Italy by attacking Sardinia, which was not as strongly defended as Sicily and only slightly further from the Allies' North African bases. One explanation is that the Americans had close links with Italo-American 'advisers' with Sicilian connections, who provided them with two vital services: military information about Sicily itself, and the ability to guarantee social order once fascism had collapsed – neither of these conditions applied in Sardinia.

A few months before the actual invasion, a man named Colonel Charles Poletti – an American businessman of Italian background who was to become the senior allied administrator in occupied Italy – travelled secretly to Sicily. Poletti had been deputy governor of New York state before the war and was also a freemason. One writer subsequently commented: 'After the war it was anything but a secret that Charles Poletti, Governor of Sicily after the occupation, had arrived clandestinely in Palermo at least a year before the end of the war, and had lived for a long period in the villa of a mafia lawyer.'[3]

The Allied invasion overthrew a dictatorship that had lasted 20 years. But the attitude of the Allies was motivated by self-interest, and contained internal tensions. Neither America nor Britain had any specific plans for postwar Italy when Churchill and Roosevelt met at Casablanca in January 1943 and decided to invade the country. Strategically, the US was concentrated on the defeat of Germany and Japan, whereas Britain had a specific interest in gaining control of the Mediterranean so as to better protect its colonies. Both countries, however, gained tactical advantages from having the Mediterranean open to shipping; furthermore, airports in southern Italy were within easy range of targets in eastern and southern Germany.[4]

The political attraction of invading Italy lay in the weakness of Mussolini's government, and the possibility of creating a political crisis which would take Italy's armed forces out of the war – a calculation that was broadly proved correct. However, this created the problem of what was to come next, politically speaking. The Allies' problem was that opposition to Mussolini and fascism was dominated by socialists and communists, whose demands hardly coincided with American plans for postwar Italy. The political legacy of fascism in Sicilian society was that very little middle ground existed. The Christian Democrat (DC) party had only just been formed, so the Allies had to enlist the help of anyone who was not on the left. Rather than working with these mass democratic organisations they turned to a different kind of power structure, and simply put known Mafiosi in positions of power.

Naturally Poletti appointed specialised staff to help him, such as his interpreter Vito Genovese. Apart from being fluent in two languages Genovese had a long criminal record, given the fact he was one of the main bosses of the US Mafia – indeed he had fled New York in 1936 to escape several charges of murder. Poletti went on to use his position as head of Allied administration first in Palermo, then in Naples and all the way up to Milan, to trade in foodstuffs with Vito Genovese and Damiano Lumia (a nephew of Calogero Vizzini – see below) in Sicily, and with Jimmy Hoffa of the Teamsters Union in New York. The company run by Poletti in Italy collapsed into bankruptcy soon after the Allies' withdrawal, suggesting that his business lifeline involved the creaming off of Allied goods for sale on the highly profitable black market.

The Allies acquired partners who were able to police society very effectively.

There is no doubt they were aware of what the Mafia was, but for both the Americans and the British, the thought of encouraging real anti-fascists, that is, socialists and communists, was completely abhorrent. So when three American tanks drove into the central Sicilian town of Villalba on 20 July 1943, the soldiers immediately asked local people to call Don Calogero Vizzini for them. Eight days later US Lieutenant Beehr, from the Allies' civil affairs office, presided over a ceremony at the local police station in which Vizzini became mayor of his home town.[5] Superficially Vizzini seemed a very respectable middle-aged man: two of his brothers were priests and one of his uncles a bishop. The Allies, however, knew he was the head of the Mafia, and they also knew about his criminal record: he had been tried for four murders under fascism but acquitted each time, although he was convicted of Mafia membership and spent five years in jail.[6] He had also been charged with, but not tried for, many other crimes: 39 murders, six attempted ones, 36 robberies, 37 thefts and 63 extortions.[7]

A similar event occurred in the town of Mussomeli, just a few miles away. A newly appointed councillor, Giuseppe Genco Russo, had been acquitted of five murders in 1928, four in 1929, and three in 1930, together with three attempted murders; in 1931 he escaped conviction for being a member of a criminal organisation, and in 1932 was once again acquitted of three murders. He was however convicted of conspiracy to commit a crime in 1932, and served three years of a six-year sentence.

Given the weakness of the Christian Democrats, the Allies were happy to encourage a movement for Sicilian autonomy, a demand that verged on calling for complete independence at times. One of its leaders was a large landowner named Lucio Tasca, who was appointed mayor of Palermo by the Allies in October 1943. Six weeks later, on 6 December, he arranged a meeting of 40 people in his villa just outside Palermo; one of the guests was Don Calogero Vizzini who, as he put his gun on the table, said: 'it digs into my stomach when I'm sitting down'.[8] In many ways the problem facing the Allies was both political and military: democracy had caused an explosion of trade union and left-wing activism all over the island. The static defence mechanism that landowners had used – the Mafia – was no longer enough. Appealing to traditional Catholic values and national unity through the Christian Democrats was not enough either, so a popular political alternative had to be created to combat the influence of the left.

Perhaps this is what Aneurin Bevan had in mind during a House of Commons debate on 3 August, in which he described AMGOT (Allied Military Government) as 'un ugly word to cover an uglier deed'.[9]

The defeat of fascism had seen huge radicalisation across the island. In October 1944 council workers went on strike in Palermo against abuses in the rationing system, troops began firing and throwing hand grenades into the crowd, killing 30 and wounding 150.[10] In January 1945 protests broke out in the town of Ragusa when call-up papers arrived. Young people did not want to join the army – some had already fought in Mussolini's army. Workers and students shouted: 'We're not cannon fodder.' Their parents supported them, chanting: 'If they're going to die, it's better they die here.' The Communist Party said they should obey the call-up. When the soldiers came to round up people who had not joined up, women lay down in front of the trucks. The soldiers then opened fire on them.

Things really exploded the next day. A priest said to an officer: 'What do you want from these young men? Everybody's fed up with the war.' In response the officer threw a grenade at him, tearing his head from his body. At that point the town rose up in armed rebellion, using their own weapons and those the Germans had abandoned. They took hundreds of prisoners. In the fighting, which went on for several days, there were at least 37 killed and 86 wounded.[11] As with the Palermo demonstration three months earlier, the violent response of the newly 'democratised' Italian army, in a 'liberated' area of Italy, showed up starkly the reality of the kind of 'new Italy' the Allies were prepared to condone.

25 JULY 1943: THE FALL OF MUSSOLINI AND 'THE END OF THE BEGINNING'

The effect of the Allied conquest of Sicily on the political establishment in Rome was electric – a mood of paralysis and fear dominated. Fascist leaders refused to hold public rallies demanding greater support from the Italian population, because they were frightened crowds might turn against them. The more dissident leaders demanded the convening of the Fascist Grand Council, which had last met in 1939. If these dissidents gained majority support at the Council it would have given the king, who had slowly come to the conclusion that Mussolini was a liability, an institutional justification to order his arrest.[12] However as we shall see, throughout this period the king was very cautious, and above all was consistently against creating greater democratic openings.

Signs of popular unrest were producing responses that were unheard of. On 19 July the Allies launched their first major bombing raid on Rome, killing thousands throughout the capital. When the king went to visit one of the worst hit areas, the working-class suburb of San Lorenzo, people started throwing stones at his car and shouting 'Send us the other guy' – meaning Mussolini.[13] Meanwhile, on 22 July, the American army entered Palermo.

The Fascist Grand Council, after nearly nine hours of argument, passed their motion for a 'return to legality' at 2 a.m. on 25 July by 19 votes to 7, with one abstention. Mussolini was arrested after a meeting with the king at 5 p.m. that afternoon.

For the fascist leaders who had ruled the country for 20 years, the arrest of *il duce* was terrifying. Roberto Farinacci, one of the most hard-line fascists, turned up at the German embassy in Rome soon after the vote. According to an attaché at the embassy, Colonel Eugen Dolmann, he was 'pale-faced and shaking with fear; all he wanted was the first plane leaving for Germany'.[14]

The impact on anti-fascists was the opposite. Amerigo Clocchiatti, who had spent several years in fascist jails, and was forced into exile in France and

Russia, had been interrogated in Parma jail on 25 July, and feared he would be shot the next day:

On the morning of 26 July I was woken up by a loud chorus of the *Internationale*, the best version I had heard in my life. It was announced that Mussolini had been deposed – a noisy version of *Bandiera Rossa* (Red Flag) followed – sung by 300 Yugoslav political prisoners, and you know how Yugoslavs love to sing.[15]

The hope of fascist leaders, once they had decided to get rid of Mussolini, was simply to carry on without him. This is why the new prime minister, Field Marshal Pietro Badoglio, a fascist general who had played the leading role in Italy's bloody colonial wars in Africa, made it clear in his first proclamation that 'Italy, seriously damaged in the areas which have been invaded, in its destroyed cities, will keep its word ... whoever imagines they can undermine the normal running of things, or tries to subvert public order, will be punished inexorably.' The key message was this: 'the war continues'.

On the same day Badoglio's government announced a curfew, and a ban on more than three people meeting together in public. The armed forces received a circular in which they were ordered, in the case of 'public order' being broken by demonstrations, to 'move forward in battle formation and open fire without warning from a distance, including mortars and artillery, as if advancing against enemy troops. ... If the ringleaders of disorder are caught in the act they can be executed.'[16]

In Reggio Emilia troops opened fire against striking workers at the *Officine Reggiane* factory, killing nine. In Bari crowds celebrating Mussolini's fall were massacred: 23 dead and 70 wounded.[17] One author has estimated that in the first few days of demonstrations and strikes after 25 July, 83 people were shot by the army.[18]

Only existing newspapers were allowed to be published, and the king intervened to stop the legalisation of anti-fascist parties.

Nevertheless, as soon as news of Mussolini's arrest came over the radio there was mass euphoria. People poured out into the streets to celebrate, destroying symbols of the regime, hunting for known fascists, fraternising with soldiers. As we shall see in the next chapter, the mass strikes in northern cities in March had been specific factory-based actions; the 25 July celebrations, by contrast, were very public and city-wide affairs. In Turin a young Jewish anti-fascist wrote in his diary on 28 July:

The situation is confused and unclear, but it is legitimate to hope. ... The only real progress is this: in the streets, on the trains, in shops people speak more freely, they criticise Badoglio even more openly than they did Mussolini, the attacks of Radio London and secret broadcasts against the new government and the "poison gas" general [Badoglio] are repeated without fear.[19]

Despite the intimidation, not everybody was prepared to watch passively the changing of the fascist guard and remain immobilised by fear. On the evening of 25 July some anti-fascists in Rome occupied the city's main newspaper, *Il Messaggero*, and by 2 a.m. had already produced a new democratic edition headlining with the title 'Long Live Free Italy'. The police chief immediately impounded this version, and an official edition – strikingly similar to the first one – came out at dawn.[20] Overnight 36 Fascist Party branches in Rome alone were attacked, burned and vandalised.[21]

Events were highly volatile, and people had no clear political agenda to follow. A communist leader in Turin, Luigi Capriolo, noted in his diary on 25 July: 'the national flag is the only one I saw in the streets of Turin during the whole morning'.[22] Nevertheless this was not a sign of passivity: fascist headquarters were burning here too, as were fascist newspapers. The following day Capriolo made an impromptu speech in the city centre, in front of the jail. The crowd then stopped the next passing lorry, commandeered it, and crashed it through the gates of the jail. Many experienced communist and socialist leaders were immediately set free.[23]

From there Capriolo went to the offices of the fascist trade unions. Twenty years earlier, in a democracy, it had been the trades council building. To show their dominance, the fascists had taken it over in the early 1920s, and so for 20 years Capriolo had never been inside it. He made a speech from the balcony: 'for 20 years this building has been a symbol of oppression. We're going back into it with our ideas unchanged. Many struggles await us – above all the struggle for an immediate end to the war.'[24]

In Milan anti-fascists were very worried about how the police and troops would react when crowds tried to congregate in the city's main square on the afternoon of 26 July. A socialist activist recalls:

it was a miracle. At the same time as our demonstrators came into contact with the barriers that had been set up, you could hear a loud noise coming from the other side of the square. In fact a column of lorries from Sesto San Giovanni was coming in from *Corso Vittorio Emanuele*, and in a second everything was overwhelmed. Columns of demonstrators poured in from the side streets and mingled with the fascist militia, soldiers and the odd policeman who had been roped in. Lorries full of workers lined up in front of the *Galleria*. By now the square was a sea of faces.[25]

The fascist regime was in disarray. It was trying to carry on in its own typically brutal fashion, but it had lost consensus. More than that, despite the level of violence suffered in demonstrations and strikes, ordinary people were no longer frightened. Perhaps their biggest problem was coordinating their actions in a practical way, and mentally grappling with what kind of society they wanted to see once fascism had been destroyed.

The 45 Days

The whole country was in turmoil, and politically at a crossroads. What followed were 'the 45 Days' – which were to end with the announcement by the Allies on 8 September that Italy had agreed to an armistice, in other words that it was no longer at war.

The first worrying signs came at dawn on 26 July – eight German divisions were streaming through the Brenner pass into northern Italy.[26] At the same time the 305th German infantry division moved into north-west Italy from France.

After Mussolini's arrest Italy began to inch towards democracy. The king, the fascists and the generals all hated the idea on principle. But as with all ruling classes, they were aware of how angry people were, and became frightened, oscillating between violence and uncertainty. As one author has commented, the king and Badoglio 'were conditioned by fear of losing control of things internally, terror as regards the Germans' reaction, lack of confidence in the Italian armed forces and the need to keep things secret'.[27] In any event, they slowly started to think about compromises, since making no concessions at all opened up a scenario of uncontrollable change, even revolution. Everyone knew that the current situation – with massive Allied bombardments and a country split in two politically and militarily – could not continue for long. Therefore throughout these 45 Days both Badoglio and the king were engaged in secret negotiations with the Allies for an armistice.

Despite the continuation of Badoglio's military dictatorship, democracy began to seep through the cracks. There was a slight liberalisation, and most anti-fascist leaders were released from jail, but on the other hand a free press was still not allowed. In terms of anti-fascist activity, the genie could no longer be put back in the bottle, though the regime certainly tried: when *Mirafiori* workers went on strike in Turin on 18 August, machine guns opened fire killing two and wounding three.[28]

The Badoglio government clearly represented the continuation of a profound division between what people wanted (peace, freedom and food) and the political ideas held by government leaders. However the logjam and its uncertainties were resolved neither by working-class revolution nor by violent reaction – the Allies having finally lost patience with Italian delays, at 18.30 on 8 September General Eisenhower announced the armistice on Allied radio. They certainly could not wait any longer, given that they had a massive amphibious fleet at sea and due to land at Salerno at dawn the following morning – Italian soldiers needed to know that their government had agreed to end the war. Incredibly, despite the lengthy secret negotiations that had taken place, the king, Badoglio and several senior generals immediately called an emergency meeting to discuss whether to repudiate the armistice. Notwithstanding their misgivings they decided to honour the agreement, so Badoglio announced the news at 19.45 on Italian radio.[29]

8 SEPTEMBER 1943: THE FALL OF FASCISM

Badoglio's brief radio message, reproduced on the front pages of all newspapers the following morning, encapsulated the contradictions of his government. While stating that all hostilities with the Allies must cease, he also added that

Italian armed forces would 'react to any attacks from any quarter'. The only possible interpretation was that this meant resisting German invasion.

But in the meantime Badoglio's priorities were very different. As early as mid-August, General Giuseppe Castellano had raised the issue of organising the flight of the king and other important individuals to Allied occupied southern Italy. So just before dawn on 9 September seven cars carrying Badoglio, the king and other members of the royal family left the Ministry of War and headed out of Rome. A few hours later other senior military commanders left the capital too. Badoglio and the king boarded a corvette at about 10 p.m. in Pescara, and later, further down the coast at Ortona, other generals were picked up, bringing the total to 57 passengers. Overnight, the boat travelled down to the South, now under Allied control.

No clear instructions were left for military leaders, who had three million servicemen under their command. Italian institutions had dissolved themselves. All senior commanders, politicians, and the head of state knew that an armistice was imminent but had refused to deal with the problems that would inevitably ensue, such as what kind of government there would be and what to do with the armed forces. Senior members of the government and key institutions simply ran away – which was one of the main reasons Italians voted for a republic and not a monarchy in a national referendum in 1946.

One notorious scandal was that throughout late August and early September the military high command had discussed plans to defend the Italian passes over the Alps against the inevitable German invasion, but no decision had been taken to put them into action.[30] On the other hand, why should career generals, trained under 20 years of fascist rule, ever have agreed to democratic resistance to Nazism? Meanwhile, the Nazis themselves had started planning for an Italian military collapse as early as April, and the number of troops stationed in the country increased significantly after 25 July.[31]

The Resistance of the Military

The supreme military commander of the Badoglio government, General Mario Roatta, also abandoned Rome along with the king, giving orders for Italian military units to leave the capital; thus leaving it defenceless and wide open to German occupation.[32]

The tragedy for anti-fascists was that if the Italian military had coordinated its actions with the Allies then German occupation could have been thwarted. On 8 September the Germans had only two divisions around Rome, which were vastly outnumbered by Italian forces, and the plan was for the US 82nd airborne division to be parachuted into the capital immediately after the announcement of the armistice. However US General Maxwell Taylor, on a secret mission to Rome, realised on the evening of 7 September that the Italian high command were not to be trusted. Luckily, his order to stop the operation came through just as planes full of parachutists were about to take off for the drop zones.[33]

Away from these machinations, on 8 September ordinary people celebrated the armistice by thronging the streets (there were also celebrations inside military barracks), believing briefly that the war was over. Many people were keen to resist the Germans, as a young anti-fascist illustrated in his diary on 9 September, recounting a conversation he had had in front of the German consulate in Turin, when a group of workers wanted to rush the guards and steal their machine guns. An argument developed in the street, with class differences emerging immediately: 'A well-dressed man of about 40, with a brightly-coloured bicycle, intervened by saying it was impossible to oppose the Germans. Then everybody insulted him and said: "We're tired of taking orders from the middle class; we've had enough of 20 years of fascism".'[34]

But what were ordinary soldiers meant to do? Were they now neutral or were they fighting the Germans? They got no answer from their senior officers, who had no orders from their superiors to give to the lower ranks. Faced with the lack of any command structure, military units often reacted on the basis of the political ideas which prevailed on the ground. Consequently most soldiers, seeing there was no army to speak of, decided to try to return home. Given the numbers involved, a virtual mass migration began. A British Intelligence officer who had just landed on the Salerno beachhead remembers: 'Italian soldiers who had walked away from the war were plodding along the railway line in their hundreds on their way to their homes in the South. ... they were in tremendous spirits, and we listened to the trail of their laughter and song all through the day.'[35] In military terms, as soldiers fled their barracks leaving them empty, with many of them handing over their weapons in exchange for civilian clothes during their travels, the Resistance outside the cities began to seriously arm itself.

Overall many soldiers chose either to resist the Germans, or at least not to surrender to them and give up their weapons. Many thousands did this on the eastern border, often joining the local Yugoslav resistance movement. In central Italy troops fought for five days to stop the Germans gaining control of the port of La Spezia, allowing the Italian fleet to set sail and avoid capture. But most of the high command were thorough fascists – such as General De Vecchi who had been one of the four military leaders of Mussolini's March on Rome back in 1922.[36]

One of the difficulties for the left was that it pursued a policy of national unity – a weakness we shall examine in future chapters, and a forlorn hope that many scholars have chosen to downplay. The notion was to stress that Italy was facing a war of national liberation alone, ignoring what were equally if not more important motivations such as a political war against fascism and class war against bosses and landowners.

On 9 September the left was openly agitating among military officers or sometimes senior policemen to form a kind of National Guard, or popular army. Yet time after time this policy failed. In Milan General Ruggero refused to release any weapons and allowed the Germans to enter the city unopposed. But the possibilities of widespread popular resistance had been immense, as one author points out: 'Lorries full of workers from some big factories, which had moved towards the mountains around Lecco to organise defensive positions, had to then travel back to the city within 24 hours.'[37] On the morning of 9 September the leaders of the Resistance in Parma went to see the military commander of the city: 'Their requests for a serious struggle against the Germans they were met with laughter.'[38] At the same time communist activists in Sarzana persuaded the local mayor to go with them to the police barracks to demand the distribution of arms. Although the commander initially seemed very sympathetic, he eventually declined, and in the evening attempted to arrest the very same anti-fascists who had come to see him.[39] In Turin, a socialist member of the nascent National Liberation Committee recalls going to see the military commander, General Adami Rossi, to ask for weapons to defend the city: 'there was not only a negative reply but a threatening one against the individuals who made up the delegation, who had to leave immediately to avoid arrest'.[40] After the last in a series of fruitless meetings with the prefect, another socialist activist took the communist leader Osvaldo Negarville by the arm saying: 'Come on, let's go and look for weapons. If we can't defend ourselves in the city, we'll go up into the mountains like the Russians, French or Yugoslavs.'[41]

Despite the PCI's repeated appeals to the dangers 'the nation' faced, senior commanders would not change the political habits of a lifetime and trust 'the nation' to defend itself. As occurred at times during the Resistance, the PCI leadership's moderate line led to paralysis or confusion, meaning that the whole movement lost any impetus in moving towards radical change.

There was however one key positive response in and around Rome, where General Giacomo Carboni played an important role. For weeks he had been negotiating with Resistance leaders Luigi Longo, Giuseppe Di Vittorio and Antonello Trombadori. They had agreed on an insurrectionary plan, but the announcement of the armistice was made four days earlier than expected. Nevertheless, on the night of 8–9 September two large lorries moved through Rome, and six men unloaded weapons at various points – one of them was Luigi Longo, another the son of General Carboni, along with three other communists and an anti-fascist monarchist.[42] On 9 September, the Germans outside Rome encountered significant resistance from the Italian military. In just one battle to the north-west of Rome, at Monterosi, they lost 40 tanks and at least 700 men. At Monterotondo, to the north-east, they lost 300 men and two airplanes.[43]

Luigi Fiori was a young lieutenant in an infantry battalion stationed at a military airport to the south of Rome, and remembers on the evening of 8 September:

a German colonel arrived in a sidecar and spoke to our commanding officer, and told him if the regiment didn't surrender by tomorrow morning his men would attack. Our colonel then made some phone calls and found out that grenadiers were forming up at Porta San Paolo in Rome, so he gave the order for all our equipment to be put on mules – because we didn't have motorised transport – and for us to move to the city.[44]

At dawn on the morning of 10 September there was serious fighting at Porta San Paolo between the Italian army – with light tanks, and joined by volunteers from the PCI and the Action Party – against the Germans. When Fiori arrived the Italians had already lost the battle: 'I saw absolute chaos – gun carriages being pulled by horses without a driver. Shops were being looted – I saw people running home with olive oil poured into their hats – that was the level of hunger. Parents were using their prams and filling them up with coal.'

On the Istrian peninsula between Trieste and Rijeka (at the time Italian territory), a major insurrection broke out on 9 September. Italians, Slovenes and Croats all fought together to keep the Nazis at bay. After three weeks of fighting the partisans were defeated and the Germans extracted a terrible revenge on the civilian population.[45] However the scene had been set for a high level of cross border cooperation between Italian and Yugoslav resistance movements.

FOUR DAYS IN NAPLES

Italy's second city has always been poor, but such was the poverty in August 1942 that the city's prefect warned people not to get themselves arrested 'just to be able to get something to eat in jail'.[46] Death rates had risen sharply even before the war had made its effects felt, from 20.9 people per thousand in 1940, to 26.1 in 1942.[47]

What decided much of Naples' fate was its strategic importance – it was the country's major port. The war in north Africa, on the southern shores of the Mediterranean, made it a key city for both sides, and Naples began to suffer years before the popular uprising which exploded at the end of September 1943. The first air raid took place on 13 June 1940, just three days after Mussolini had declared war, with the first major attack occurring on 15 December, causing 36 deaths.[48] The bombing continued over the next two years, with the worst raid probably being that of 4 December 1942, which caused at least 900 deaths.[49]

The war moved closer with the Allied landing in Sicily on 9 July. A week later Naples suffered its worst raid so far: in seven hours bombs fell mainly on industrial areas. The news of Mussolini's arrest came out late on the radio on the evening of 25 July, and it was only the following morning that people started to congregate in the streets. As in the rest of the country, many fascist symbols and statues were attacked, as were Fascist Party offices. Organised anti-fascists quickly came to the conclusion that the fascist regime, despite announcing Marshal Pietro Badoglio as its new prime minister, had been badly wounded. So the next step was to come out into the open and demand change.

On 28 July the Naples police chief wrote to his counterpart in Rome about how the news of Mussolini's arrest had

> created the blossoming of passions which had been repressed for a long time ... This surprising event has seriously disoriented fascists ... I must add that

after the enthusiasms of the first day ... a certain unease has grown due to the fact that people are beginning to understand that the war will continue, perhaps with increased harshness ... On several occasions, particularly in the provinces, fascist offices have been attacked and vandalised ... The strongest effect has been on the press, which overnight has taken up a completely different position to the day before; and that anybody believes themselves to now be free to communicate their own ideas and to push their own principles, whether they be socialist, Catholic, liberal, communist or anarchist.[50]

On 30 July Italo de Feo, an anti-fascist soldier, noted in his diary that at his anti-aircraft battery 'Fascist badges have disappeared – even party members have taken them off. We've got one here, a foreman, who is now walking around with his tail between his legs – like a dog that's been beaten.'[51] On 16 August 500 steel workers at a factory in Torre Annunziata demanded the sacking of fascist workers; the response they got was for the police to fire at them. In nearby Portici on 29 August at least a thousand people demonstrated against the war in the presence of German troops.[52] Four days later an almost identically sized demonstration of shipyard workers took place just down the coast at Castellammare di Stabia; police threw hand grenades to disperse the crowd, wounding five, and arrested 60. However in the afternoon large numbers of women organised protests in working-class areas of the town, and in the surrounding countryside houses draped white flags on washing lines as a sign in support of peace.[53]

By way of applying greater pressure for the Italian government to sign an armistice, on 4 August the Allies launched another violent air raid destroying more than a hundred buildings in Naples' city centre; 3,000 people were killed or wounded – many churches were damaged, with the Royal Palace taking 23 hits. Overall, during the Second World War somewhere between 8,000 and 22,000 Neapolitans were killed during Allied bombing raids.[54] The city emptied out even more. Nearly all the middle class had left. By the middle of the month de Feo noted: 'Food is getting scarce and the city gets fed almost exclusively by the black market. But in these conditions I wouldn't say the black market is getting difficult, rather it's impossible.'[55] There were still at least half a million people in the city, and food was running out. Indeed the Nazis' order in early September to close shops provoked a lot of resentment, but in reality made little difference.

Yet resentment had already begun to take an organised form. After 20 years of silence due to fascist repression, in May and June there had been strikes at engineering factories because bosses refused to pay for the time workers spent in air-raid shelters. Local anti-fascism had always existed in the city – for example when Hitler visited in May 1938 some factory walls were painted with anti-Nazi slogans, and leaflets were distributed clandestinely.[56] As conditions worsened during the war, local activists managed to regroup, albeit in a limited fashion. The local PCI had resurfaced in summer 1942, when *Il Proletario* (The Proletarian) was produced in Capua, to the north of the city. In December anti-fascist leaflets start appearing to the south of the city too.[57]

But much of the local communist leadership was still 'workerist', believing that the only battle worth fighting was one in which industrial workers played a major role. They were also used to slow conspiratorial work and not attracted by reckless open activity. Not having seen any example of it, they did not believe guerrilla warfare could be successful. So, not surprisingly, during the Four Days communist and socialist leaders were not really prominent in a leadership sense, though their rank and file were active.

However, what was taking place among many sections of the population, perhaps in an unconscious and unstated way, was a deep-seated politicisation. After 20 years of fascism, the sheer hardships people were experiencing were pushing them to look for political alternatives.

Neapolitans were overjoyed by the announcement of the armistice on 8 September: no more war meant no more bombing raids. Logically, it should also have meant the withdrawal of German troops from a now neutral country. But Germany was still at war, and the Nazis were enraged by what they saw as Italian 'betrayal'. Suddenly Neapolitans saw German armoured cars speeding up and down the main streets, pointing their loaded guns at them; for the Germans Italy and Naples were now enemy territory.

As for the Italian military, given the officer class's overwhelming fascist indoctrination, military officers did not call for any organised resistance to the Nazi takeover. The senior military commander in Naples gave the following advice to junior officers demanding action against the invading army from the North: 'don't irritate the Germans and treat the British well'.[58] At a lower level the ordinary ranks often had anti-fascist sympathies, sometimes gave out arms to civilian anti-fascists, and on occasion even joined them. This happened in *piazza del Plebiscito* on 9–10 September, when there was a lengthy battle between German soldiers and a mixture of sailors and civilians. The fighting extended down onto the sea front, and both sides suffered losses. At roughly the same time, a newly created 'anti-fascist parties' committee' began to demand that local people be armed.[59] All civilian authorities also sat on the fence in those crucial early days after the armistice, further facilitating the consolidation of a strong German presence in Naples.

Meanwhile, on 9 September, the Allies launched an amphibious landing in the Gulf of Salerno, just to the south of Naples. The Germans had spotted the invasion fleet at sea the day before, so their troops were ready and greeted the Allied landing with a massive artillery barrage. Rather than retreat, the Germans decided to try to repel the attack, and two days after the landing had managed to push the Allied front line back nearer to the sea. The implications of the Allies establishing a bridgehead in Salerno, just an hour away from Naples by train, were clear, so the Germans decided to destroy the city and take all resources – both human and material – away with them.

This meant turning on the entire population; one of the first moves was to disarm Italian soldiers and policemen, then they began to requisition any vehicle that took their fancy. By now thousands of deserters and men were being hidden by families all over the city. It was an extremely widespread act of solidarity, which had mushroomed due to a clear understanding of what was happening, despite the very negative consequences of what would happen to these men and their helpers if discovered by the Germans. A 14-year-old boy later looked back on how the deserters contributed to a growing popular awareness about what had happened throughout Italy since 8 September:

> the fascists have run away, maybe Mussolini is dead, the soldiers are coming home. This was happening throughout the area. People spread the news, and the soldiers who returned and who had escaped from prison camps and had come here – everybody had their own story to tell – because there were no telephones, no radios, there was nothing.[60]

On 20 September the Germans destroyed parts of the port, railway lines, power stations, water and electricity lines, as well as banks, public buildings and large hotels. The anti-fascist army officer Italo de Feo noted in his diary for 22 September: 'Throughout the city not only have the Germans taken heart, but so too have the ex-fascists.'[61] On 23 September the local population – about 35,000 families – were given 20 hours to abandon houses within 300 metres of the coast, due to German fears of an Allied landing. This caused huge human upheaval and displacement, as it covered a very densely populated area of up to 100,000 people.

On the same day a poster was put up: 'All men resident in the city of Naples born between 1910 and 1925 are called up for obligatory national labour service. Those who do not attend will be made to do so with force, and sanctions applicable under war regulations will be applied to those who do not comply.'[62] This meant going to work in Nazi Germany as forced labourers. Men started hiding in sewers, attics, cellars, caves, church catacombs and in the countryside. Some even dressed up as women. Virtually nobody went to the transportation points – the Germans expected 30,000 but just 150 people turned up. The following day the Germans published another proclamation, in which they said that those not reporting for labour service 'will be executed by patrols without hesitation'. It also added that civil servants, council workers and those in public utilities were also now under the same obligation.[63]

These continuous turns of the screw pushed people's backs to the wall, and the only potential outlet was popular resistance. Such were the terrible circumstances that these people, thrust together, started to think differently. As an eyewitness account recalls, some of them

> decided to resist using violence, and they brought improvised weapons and ammunition into their hideouts – weapons not handed in during the first days of German control and other guns which had been obtained in a hurry ... they met in groups; ... improvised formations were created, each one numbering a few dozen or few hundred men, some were armed, others

were not. They were all committed; because their destiny was either death in a foreign country, remaining free, or dying through resistance.[64]

The Germans now began their scorched earth policy: factories, transport, gasometers, telephone exchanges, the university, archives were all destroyed or damaged. Naples was like a ghost town. At night many families would – until the electricity was cut – gather round silently and listen to Radio London for news of what was happening in Salerno. The German counter-attack had failed, the American bridgehead was safe, and the British 8th army was moving up the mainland from Calabria to join them. And in the Gulf of Naples, the Allies had taken control of the three islands of Capri, Ischia and Procida. Despite all the difficulties, liberation could not be far away.

The Germans knew they were about to lose Naples to the Allies. On 26 September they took a massive quantity of food out of the starving city. The following day another large round-up began. Ignoring the Geneva convention, men were dragged from their hospital beds. About 8,000 were rounded up, and the Nazis threatened to kill them for not obeying their orders and reporting for deportation. When the Germans started taking people out of the city the local population began to react with violence, and the Neapolitan resistance finally came out into the open – the German lorries carrying menfolk were stopped and attacked. Food shops were looted, and military barracks broken into and weapons stolen.[65]

All of this was spontaneous, there was no coordinated plan or an organisation directing activity. That evening on the hill of Capodimonte six Nazis and six fascists were captured. They revealed that the entire water supply to the city had been mined.[66] Overnight activists took control of three major arms dumps and began to distribute weapons.[67]

The First Day

The following day, 28 September, was the first of the 'Four Days'. At dawn many lorries were parked in the city centre, in *piazza Dante*, carrying men ready to be deported.[68] At the same time young men in the hilly area of the Vomero saw Allied ships on the horizon in the Bay of Naples. They came out of their attics and cellars with guns, and started shooting at the Germans and fascists who were continuing their round-ups and destruction.[69] Rumours were rife that the Allies had landed to the west of the city.

Near Capodimonte anti-fascists were able to get a whole anti-aircraft battery ready, and were quickly involved in an action which influenced all the battles that followed. A column of Tiger tanks and armoured cars wanted to move down the hill into the city but were stopped by the artillery fire. Another five tanks tried to make it down a nearby road but mines drove them back. This resistance had stopped the Germans moving heavy weaponry into the city centre. Elsewhere, trams were turned over to make barricades.

By about midday there was sporadic communication between the different groups, and by early afternoon most areas were experiencing street fighting. Groups tended to come together spontaneously: both civilians and soldiers participated in the fighting, while others would carry baskets of munitions. Young boys carried news or requests to other groups – a vitally important task because the Germans had cut the public telephone system weeks before.[70]

That evening an extra German battalion, with tanks and artillery, was ordered to Naples. The command of the Germans' XIV Army Corps reported that in Naples 'a revolt has broken out, and the commander is surrounded'.[71]

The Second Day

More people were involved in fighting on the second day: the Resistance had held its ground and that gave people more confidence. Barricades were still up in the Vomero and in the old town, and overnight many people had worked hard at defusing German mines aimed at destroying the city's infrastructure. In the old city, in *via dei Tribunali*, a 'Partisans' revolutionary action' committee had been created, which resisted German incursion into the narrow streets, repelling them with salvos of hand grenades. One of the key problems the Germans had was that most of their forces were motorised, moving in tanks and armoured cars. In the narrow streets this meant they were sitting targets for people armed with hand grenades. The Germans had managed to get three Tiger tanks into the city, but they were stopped by more barricades.

In the Vomero a communist ex-military officer, Antonino Tarsia, had begun to set up a command centre. In the morning a proclamation from a 'Revolutionary United Front' was distributed throughout the area,[72] and a major siege of a football stadium in the Vomero continued for the whole day. Eventually the 50 Germans inside were allowed to leave, but on condition they released the 47 hostages they were threatening to kill.

Ordinary Neapolitans had effectively turned the tables: the Germans were now besieged in their strongholds. Down in the old town, the Resistance was now in full control, and there were no more German soldiers to be seen.

The Third Day

One clear sign of German defeat was the secret overnight departure of the German commanding officer, Colonel Walter Scholl. By the dawn of this third day, in the old town, Italian fascists were largely on their own, facing an uncertain future if captured. Small groups were left to make isolated and ineffective attacks, which quickly fizzled out.[73] It is worth remembering that throughout the major battles in Naples, those fighting the Germans had often suffered sniper attacks from the rear from fascist snipers. Furthermore, the fascists gave the Germans vital information, back-up and help with interpreting.

By now the Germans were on the defensive and in retreat, although on the edge of the Vomero the largest battle of the whole insurrection now took place, after which, at dusk, the Germans withdrew to Marano, a suburb outside the city. By the evening partisans were in radio contact with British forces stationed on the island of Capri, but were told that no men – or, crucially, ammunition – could be sent.

The Final Day

The fourth day began with the Germans repeatedly shelling the city from the hill of Capodimonte, where they had set up all their heavy weapons. There seemed to be no end to the city's torment: it had been without gas, water and electricity for the last three days, and apples were the only item of food still on sale. Rubbish was piled up everywhere.[74] But at about 11 a.m. the news spread through the city like wildfire – the first dusty Allied jeep had just driven into the city from the Pompeii motorway, followed soon afterwards by a column of the King's Dragoon Guards.

After the war Naples was awarded a military gold medal for its resistance. Four who were given individual posthumous gold medals were incredibly young: 12, 13, 17 and 19. Many of the combatants were no more than children. Official figures mentioned 307 dead and 192 wounded, but the reality was much starker – recent research estimates a total of 663 dead,[75] a figure probably far higher than the number of deaths which occurred in the northern cities in April 1945.

From the safety of his house on Capri, the influential philosopher Benedetto Croce defined what had happened as a *jacquerie* – a kind of primitive spontaneous apolitical revolt. It was nothing of the kind. This was the first major defeat for the Germans on the Italian mainland carried out by Italians, and it was a sign of the scale of popular resistance they were to encounter for the rest of the war throughout the country. The account of the revolt transmitted by Radio London was listened to by many people in the rest of occupied Italy, and would have done nothing but encourage them to engage in similar acts.[76] The social make-up of those who died in the fighting reveals the nature of the revolt: 30 per cent were industrial or manual workers, 30 per cent were artisans, 14 per cent deserters and 19 per cent women.[77]

A criticism that has been made of the Neapolitan insurrection was that the level of formal influence exercised by political parties was low, but this was the norm throughout the country in September 1943. From the end of July to early September a rudimentary 'National Patriotic Front' did exist in the city, and from 24 September a Neapolitan National Liberation Committee, representing all major democratic parties, had come into existence.[78] Nevertheless, it remains clear that the insurrection was not a planned and coordinated action.

But the 'Four Days of Naples' were not an exception, rather they began to become the rule. Twenty long months later, cities in northern Italy would launch their own insurrections, having had time to create stable structures, organise militarily and make detailed plans. Indeed as one of the main military commanders of the Resistance, Luigi Longo, wrote a few years later: 'After Naples the call for a final insurrection took on a sense and a value, and became the guiding example for the most audacious elements of the Italian resistance.'[79]

The influence of the Neapolitan insurrection was noticeable in many of the broadcasts by 'Radio Free Naples'. For example, in early October Ciro

Picardi, a communist who had been exiled under fascism, made the following appeal to workers under Nazi occupation:

Act as a bloc, hit the right target. Workers' solidarity must become people's solidarity. Comrades – don't be frightened by German words and threats – they are despicable. They run away in the face of danger and organised resistance. ... This magnificent victory, which has saved thousands of Neapolitan lives, and which cost the Germans men and material, was due solely to the practical application of the principle of solidarity.[80]

Mussolini, meanwhile, had been freed from his mountain jail in Italy by German paratroopers on 12 September, and quickly taken to Berlin. After meeting Hitler a week later he made a radio announcement from the German capital that he was now leader of the 'Italian Social Republic', also known as the 'Republic of Salò' after the town on Lake Garda where the majority of ministries were located.

But very few people, including diehard fascists, were unaware that Mussolini was now a puppet leader, beholden to the Germans. In reality, several new fundamental truths were now clear in Italy. First, fascism was totally discredited – on one hand millions of people hated it, on the other the ruling class had decided to ditch it. Second, the nature of postwar Italy would now be decided to a large extent *before* the Allies' final victory (if Italy was liberated without having put up any resistance it would be treated as a thoroughly fascist country; but if people played a part in their own liberation, not only would the Allies find it hard not to concede independence and democracy, the Italians themselves would be confident and aware enough to create an entirely new system). Third, many people felt they had to resist Nazi invasion and fascist repression – part of the reason for this shift was the common understanding that fascists were much weaker and anti-fascists much stronger than before. A 'critical anti-fascist mass' had been created.

3
People, Parties and Partisans

The strike wave that began on 5 March in Turin, and which rumbled on for a month in northern Italy, indicates what was perhaps unique about the Italian Resistance compared to other European countries under fascist or Nazi occupation – it was the first in a series of coordinated national strike waves.

In Italy it had multiple effects. For the fascists it meant thinking the unthinkable: their totalitarian regime was no longer functioning as such. The entire Italian state was caught by surprise, because to shift hundreds of thousands of workers – secretly – from a mood of resigned fear and frustration to an open challenge against a fascist regime needs a huge amount of preparatory work. And a lot of work had gone into convincing and preparing the workforce, but uniquely in the history of the dictatorship, virtually nobody in authority had got to hear about it. Only on the morning of 5 March 1943 did fascist leaders realise, metaphorically speaking, that there was an iceberg beneath them; and as is the case with icebergs, they had no idea of its full size or shape.

For the factory owners it meant they no longer had control over their workforce. A document written two weeks later by the senior management of FIAT, the largest car manufacturer and employer in Italy at the time, admitted that 'subversive propaganda is widespread – including the use of leaflets – distributed by a vast, well trained, and expert organisation'.[1]

So how had it been possible to organise so many workers without being found out? Context is everything here. Bombardments had started the year before; the Italian military was losing on all fronts, and more importantly, people were losing their loved ones on all fronts. Then there was the extreme rationing, which led to extreme hunger: it was common for people to lose 10 kilos in one year. By September 1943 the daily ration for workers was just below 1,000 calories – about 500 less than what is burnt up doing nothing, just sitting in bed all day.[2] This was the background to the two main economic demands of the strike: higher wages and greater rations and availability of foodstuffs. The main political demand was an end to the war.

In this rapidly changing situation, people's ideas changed rapidly too, so those who had rejected anti-fascism now began to look upon it with interest, because its criticisms and demands constituted both an outlet for their frustrations and material demands they could agree with. The first strike during the war was recorded in July 1941, and from then on there were a series of 'manifestations of discontent', as the police called them. These included both disturbances within factories and demonstrations in the streets, particularly women demanding more bread.

The role of the Communist Party was crucial. Its membership had grown over the previous couple of years, and they now had enough members and resources to begin launching campaigns on a bigger scale. The use of clandestine publications had a major impact due to fascist censorship, given that the regime kept certain facts hidden for long periods. For example, people first read about the D-Day landings in the Communist Party paper *l'Unità* – likewise for many of the victories on the Eastern Front. Not only did this generate huge credibility for those publishing this information, it also showed those in or on the verge of joining the anti-fascist struggle that they were not isolated.

In more direct agitational terms, the PCI was now able to print thousands of leaflets calling for a strike, and had enough people to distribute them, with a reduced risk of being reported to the police. The long and dangerous work by anti-fascists was finally about to pay off. They had partially opened up from their rigid conspiratorial structure – of one communist factory worker being allowed to identify himself only to two others – to a more agitational stance. The number of party members was still not particularly high in major workplaces: 80 members out of the 21,000 working at the FIAT *Mirafiori* factory, 30 at Lancia, and so on.[3] What paid off was the changing political situation.

The Turin strikes began on 5 March, and in one respect were easier to organise than those in Milan. Once the major FIAT factories were on strike, virtually the whole city quickly took notice, and the very high concentration of industrial workers also meant that activists were able to focus their resources at a single point. The demands raised were partly economic, such as the payment of the 192 hour bonus promised in January, as well as for an end to the war. One of the more general propaganda points was an insistent demand for anti-fascists to create some kind of national unity.

Although the regime reacted by repeatedly sending armoured cars to scour working-class areas to prevent the formation of marches, and police were placed outside factory gates, members of the Fascist Party and its militia generally joined the strike. As the days wore on – and in a common tradition in the Italian labour movement strikes would last a few hours rather than a whole day – factory owners and fascist officials tried to stop the factory hooter from sounding at 10 a.m., the agreed signal every morning to walk out.[4]

The sense of confidence created then inspired another action unthinkable as far as fascists were concerned – women organising against the regime. Over the next couple of days, 7,000 leaflets were distributed in Turin calling for a demonstration in *piazza Castello* on 8 March, International Women's Day,[5] although in the end the demonstration did not take place.

From Turin the strike wave spread to the rest of Piedmont, such as the national centre of the woollen industry around the town of Biella, 40 miles to the north. As with every town and city, the move to strike action meant an abrupt political gear change for the small groups of communists and anti-fascists who had managed to avoid arrest. When the first PCI publications calling for joint action with socialists and perhaps even Catholics arrived from abroad in 1941, most experienced communists initially thought they were forgeries.[6]

Given that striking was such a rare phenomenon, there was a high level of unevenness. Some strikes were organised by experienced activists, others broke out spontaneously when news of a nearby factory strike arrived during a tea break. One method used was to daub slogans on factory walls – 'send the fascists to El Alamein' for example. Some factory owners refused all demands, whereas others – perhaps looking to the long-term – told their workers they were not members of the Fascist Party, and agreed to pay overtime. At the Luigi Botto woollen mill, a good example of 'civil war' and 'class war' occurred. Striking workers were called out to hear a local fascist leader give a speech, in an attempt to persuade them to go back to work. As the fascist called for common sacrifices since the nation was at war, an activist called out from the back, noting that the speaker was wearing an expensive gold watch.[7]

The same demands and activities surfaced throughout northern Italy. The main demands – 'bread and peace' – were both political and economic, and for those with long memories carried echoes of the 1917 Russian Revolution. Where economic demands were conceded, such as the payment of 600 lire personally promised by FIAT boss Giovanni Agnelli at the RIV plant at Villar Perosa, workers responded: 'Now that we've solved the economic question we've got to solve the political one', stating in mass meetings that their strike 'has the aim of weakening and shortening the war'.[8]

When strikes broke out in Milan and elsewhere, fascists were no longer caught by surprise, and although their response was more repressive, the stoppages were still successful. On 2 April the government was forced to announce a general increase in wages, trying to hide its embarrassment by specifying that the increase would be paid from 21 April, the anniversary of the foundation of Rome, a day of fascist celebration.[9]

Fascist leaders could read the writing on the wall. Giuseppe Bottai, a senior leader who had run many different Ministries, described in his diary for 26 March a rally he had given three days earlier. He complained of 'not even a jump, a shout or a song. All I heard was the sad and uninspiring noise of feet passing over cobblestones. As if these feet themselves had come to a rally to hear me speak.'[10]

Another senior fascist leader, Roberto Farinacci, vividly expressed the widespread sense of shock in a letter to Mussolini written on 1 April:

> I have experienced the demonstrations of workers in Milan, naturally from the shadows. I felt deeply embittered both as a fascist and as an Italian. We were incapable either of predicting or repressing them, and we have broken the principle of our regime's authority. ...
>
> The party is absent and impotent ... Unbelievable things are taking place. Everywhere – on trams and trains, in bars, cinemas and air-raid shelters – there are criticisms and attacks against the regime. No longer are just

individual leaders being criticised, but the *Duce* himself. And the terrible thing is that nobody reacts any more. Even the police headquarters are absent, as if their work was now useless.[11]

The fascist regime was faced with a catastrophic lack of consensus and control.

Mussolini had said in a speech exactly 20 years earlier, in March 1923: 'I want to govern, if possible, with the greatest citizen consensus. But, until this consensus can be formed, nourished, and fortified, I stock up the greatest amount of force available. Because it may be that force will lead to consensus and, in any event, should consensus be lacking, force is there.'[12] Both consensus and force were now lacking, and the regime understood it could no longer create consensus – and neither did it feel confident about applying force. Furthermore, workers had demonstrated their own force, and had gained an infinite sense of their own power.

Mussolini clearly understood the importance of what had happened – over 200,000 workers striking against his government. At a meeting of the National Fascist Party (PNF) leadership held on 17 April he defined the strikes as possessing historic importance: 'This decidedly nasty and extremely deplorable episode has suddenly thrown us back 20 years.'[13] The Allies too, understood that something profound had changed in Italy. A few weeks later Radio London repeatedly broadcast news of the strikes not only to Italy, but to the whole of occupied Europe.[14]

Another important collective player aware that the situation had changed were the industrialists. The Allies' bombing of the three cities of the industrial triangle began to focus their minds: Genoa was heavily bombed during the nights of 22–27 October 1942, many schools were damaged, as well as a hospital, while a famous church was completely destroyed. In Turin during 18–20 November the Allies' 4,000 pound bombs had partially destroyed FIAT's *Mirafiori* factory, including details on how to programme production lines. At the company's SPA factory, production of Italy's first heavy tank was delayed for six months because of widespread damage. At the end of the year FIAT boss Giovanni Agnelli estimated that 50 FIAT and supply factories had been totally or seriously damaged.[15] This is why in the very same period industrialists began secret talks with the Allies. In early 1943 Alberto Pirelli, Vice President of the Milan rubber and tyre company of the same name, and Guido Donegani, boss of the chemical giant Montecatini, began talks with the Allies in Switzerland.[16]

Given the growing disengagement of industrialists from the regime, in the long term the only way out for Mussolini was to take steps to bring Italy out of the war. Italy's ally, Germany, would need to be informed about moves towards neutrality – but this was a path Mussolini was not prepared to go down. When Hitler was informed of the first strikes he told his generals: 'For me it is unthinkable that people go on strike in eight factories and nobody intervenes. ... I've always said that in these cases those who show any weakness are lost.'[17] So things just drifted, and the regime's credibility continued to be undermined.

THE BIRTH OF A NATIONAL UNIFIED MOVEMENT

Ever since the war had started to go badly for the Axis powers, the dislocation and discontent this caused in Italy had led anti-fascist parties, most of which had their headquarters in France, to believe they could launch a wave of mass struggles which could eventually lead to the end of fascism. After 20 years of arrests, isolation and impotence, anti-fascist forces could now look forward to rapid growth and widespread influence in Italian society. Indeed just two days before the March 1943 strikes broke out the Communist and Socialist Parties held a conference with the Action Party in Lyons, in which they

affirmed their willingness to move forward in the work of the Italian state's democratic reconstruction; and the destruction of fascism and the economic, political and social causes which made it possible (finance capital, the monarchy, etc.), and to carry out this reconstruction in the context of a democracy in which the primacy of labour will be created.

This is a hybrid formulation in some ways: just a single section of capital – finance – is identified as having supported fascism, whereas other component parts of capitalism are not singled out. Democracy is called for, but intriguingly one in which 'labour' will be the prime element. The motion went on to specify how these changes would come about: it will be necessary 'to save Italy from fascism's ruinous policy of war through a national insurrection'.[18] There was no other way to defeat fascism but through insurrection; a brutal dictatorship rarely hands power to its opponents.

The ambiguous formulations contained in this 'pact of unity of action' are the result of the heterogeneous nature of the three organisations that had agreed to them, which will be examined below. One of the signatories for the PCI, Giorgio Amendola, has pointed out that the agreement contained 'all aspects of a future unitary policy, that in Italy will be created through the CLNs' (these National Liberation Committees will also be examined below). Since all those signing were aware that Italy was entering a state of flux, they were all, as Amendola points out, quite pragmatic: 'unity had to be created in the course of struggles – from the most basic to more advanced – including strikes, sabotage and armed action by partisans.'[19] But while the spirit was willing, the flesh was very weak. The average period an anti-fascist activist sent into Italy lasted before arrest was just one month, so senior leaders had to think of ways of working round the problem.

Indeed it was Giorgio Amendola and Celeste Negarville, who had spent twelve years in fascist jails, who had been working on sympathisers living in Vichy France over the previous couple of years. One Italian exile they visited regularly lived in Saint Tropez in 1941–42, and they either wanted him or other people to take publications into Italy and find out what was happening on the ground. The man, Gillo Pontecorvo, came from a comfortable background in Pisa and was married to the daughter of a rich industrialist. Given his lack of a criminal record, in the summer of 1942 Pontecorvo was given the job of taking propaganda into Italy in a false-bottomed suitcase. He immediately took his commitment seriously, and after further discussions agreed to join the Communist Party, being persuaded to go back to Italy permanently in the closing months of 1942.[20]

On paper the agreement made in Lyons reads in a perfectly logical and linear fashion – however it would be quite another issue how communists and socialists in Italy, long separated from their leadership, would interpret these condemnations of fascism and capitalism and assertions of the need for a national insurrection. In the chaos and tension of war and clandestine activity, there would be ample scope for widely differing interpretations of what the agreement ought to mean in practice.

The three organisations who met at Lyons formed the political left-wing of the Resistance, and were very much at its organisational and military heart, with the communists being far the largest. But in many ways it is the nature of the two smaller organisations that is intriguing; together they constituted a 'critical mass' in terms of a potential left-wing bulwark against the more moderate elements which would join a national alliance in Autumn 1943. All three will now be examined in turn.

THE SOCIALIST PARTY

At the beginning of the Resistance the Socialist Party was a shadow of its former self. Founded in 1893, it had been the largest party in the country during the last fully free elections, held in 1919. Both socialists and communists were still scarred by their split of 1921, but once again the socialists came out of it with far the largest membership. But for various reasons socialists had been unable to resist the fascist onslaught, and in the years before the Second World War the party had no active organisation within Italy whatsoever. Furthermore, it had always been a party that was internally divided, and the inevitable frustrations of the politics of exile simply exacerbated the phenomenon.

As a result, it was very weak going into the March 1943 strikes, and indeed it was organisationally split. The most militant grouping under Lelio Basso, the Movement for Proletarian Unity (MUP), had been created in autumn 1942 and was to last until summer 1943, when it merged with the old Socialist Party, the PSI, to create the PSIUP. (It also continued to be known under its old name, the PSI, which it later reverted to after 1945).

Despite the fact that the MUP lasted just under a year, the ability of Basso and others made it a force to be reckoned with. Basso was 39, and had been active in left-wing politics since 1926. The precise origins of the MUP derived from the shock produced by the Hitler–Stalin pact of August 1939. The PSI leader Pietro Nenni had been strongly in favour of the 'pact of unity in action' he had signed with the communists in 1934, but the Soviet Union's alliance with Hitler created massive anger among socialists and other left-wingers. So Nenni was jettisoned as leader by Angelo Tasca and Giuseppe Faravelli, who had always opposed working closely with the communists. They quickly convinced another socialist leader, Giuseppe Saragat, to join them, and co-opted a leading socialist trade unionist, Bruno Buozzi, into their leadership group.[21]

The MUP had nothing but ambition: it wanted to create an entirely new united organisation of the working class, as the two major organisations had been shown to be wanting. However, it also insisted on a total separation between the working classes and the middle classes. Compared to the PCI's rapid shifts following Moscow's latest diktat, and what would soon be revealed to be a more pragmatic stance in terms of building an active Resistance, what the MUP brought to the Socialist Party was a clear commitment to classical Marxist principles.

Yet in its brief life the MUP suffered from being intellectually top-heavy, and apart from in Milan and Bologna it did not have much of a working-class following. From the March strikes until negotiations with traditional socialists over the summer, the MUP realised that its small size meant it risked being isolated by a growing movement increasingly under communist domination. This was to be a fundamental dilemma for all forces involved in the Resistance: make compromises by joining an umbrella organisation, or maintain principles by staying outside it. As time wore on, it became clear that the growing sense of unity in action had a centripetal influence on all major organisations, and those who chose to stay outside were overall condemned to irrelevance.

Avoiding any risk of isolation was very much the instinct of Pietro Nenni, the old Socialist Party secretary. His leadership of the party before the Second World War could be summed up in his notion of a 'policy of alliances'. It was an understandable principle, considering the fact that divisions on the left had been a major contributory factor in fascism's rise to power in 1921–22. What had changed in Nenni's world was that his style of socialism had finally started to resurface in Italy. Four months before the creation of the MUP in Milan, in September 1942 a group of 70 met in Rome to refound the PSI.[22] Yet their weakness was even greater than that of MUP in the North, in terms of their inability to build a mass working-class following. Oreste Lizzadri, a supporter of Nenni, was acutely aware of what was happening to the competition, and wrote at the end of May: 'We need to look at the reality of things. In Italy a Communist Party exists and exercises – on the basis of what we have seen in recent months – widespread influence over the working masses.'[23]

This was the long-term background to the fusion of August 1943: divided, both socialist currents were unlikely to count for much; better to settle differences or try to put them to one side. Both currents were worried about the need for broader left unity – the imminent collapse of fascism and the Allied invasion meant that the working class needed to move even further and faster than they had initially thought, if it was to seize the revolutionary moment.

Despite unification, the tensions were unresolved and erupted almost immediately when Nenni decided to lead the PSIUP into the CLN. This was bitterly opposed by the left of the party, as they believed that the party's room for manoeuvre would be severely limited, and above all that the interests of the working class would be poorly represented. The signing of a new 'pact of unity in action' with the PCI on 28 September produced even more disagreements,[24] as it opened up old socialist wounds. What counter-balanced these tensions was the growing involvement in active resistance. One man more than any other represented this emphasis – Sandro Pertini. He led the socialist contribution to the battle with invading German forces at Porta San Paolo in Rome on 9 September, although his activities were cut short by his arrest the following month. However when Pertini escaped from a Rome jail in January 1944 he began to organise very efficient socialist brigades throughout Lazio, commanding a total of 2,500 men.[25]

The strike wave of March 1944 witnessed significant socialist involvement, a sure sign that the party had finally managed to create a significant mass following. In the mountains, by the spring of 1944, socialist 'Matteotti brigades' (named after the Socialist MP murdered by fascists in 1924) began to develop as a serious force. But tensions never left the party. When PCI leader Palmiro Togliatti declared in March 1944 that his party would no longer refuse to work in an anti-fascist government under Pietro Badoglio with the king as its titular head, the socialists initially agreed. But later, in December of the same year, after repeated compromises, the Socialist Party, unlike the PCI, refused to join a government under Ivanoe Bonomi. Specifically, they argued that the necessary purging of fascists from the state apparatus had been lacking, and that the monarchy continued to wield too much influence.[26]

THE ACTION PARTY

In terms of the relative strength of the three left-wing anti-fascist parties, two major historians of the Resistance (Secchia and Frassati) have argued that, although the Action Party was only formed in the summer of 1942, by the following year it was stronger than the Socialists.

What is beyond doubt is that ideologically it was a substantially new force. Much of its thinking came from Italians exiled in France during the 1930s. Until his murder by fascist agents in 1937, Carlo Rosselli had been developing the view in his *Justice and Freedom* organisation that Marxism had become too deterministic, and had run its course. He argued that socialism could find new life through accepting conventional democracy and a liberal state: in his view, socialism had to be separated from Marxism. At the end of his book *Liberal Socialism*, he came out strongly in favour of the British Labour Party.

While Rosselli argued explicitly for liberal socialism, others stressed the need for a radical and revolutionary rupture with politics as it had been known up to that point. The philosopher Norberto Bobbio, himself a member of the Action Party during the Resistance, sums up the party's thinking: 'Since total renewal implied revolutionary transformation, the new ideology opposed all forms of restoration of the prefascist past that the Liberals held dear, but it also rejected any attempt at revolution that slavishly imitated the Soviet revolution, which had already exhausted its capacities for the creation of a new society.'[27]

The Action Party was created in the summer of 1942, and although its origins and influences were distinct from the Socialist Party, it had similarities in the sense that it was the fusion of several distinct elements. Some leaders such as Leo Valiani had left the Communist Party in 1941, disgusted at the Nazi–Soviet pact. Others such as Vittorio Foa, perhaps the dominant grouping, were influenced by the ideas of 'liberal socialism' developed by Carlo Rosselli. Others still were demoralised ex-fascists, confused and curious about new ideas given the regime's bankruptcy. Yet another grouping led by Aldo Capitini was developing ideas about European federal government.

Groups began to coalesce in towns and cities in late 1942, and the need for a centralised party structure began to be felt more strongly. A newspaper, *L'Italia libera*, started publication in January 1943 with a print run of 3,000.[28] While the presentation of its position referred back to liberal socialist thinkers of the 1920s and 1930s, the editors were at pains to stress that this was a new party with new ideas.

The organisation agreed a seven-point programme at a conference in Florence in the first week of September 1943: development of local autonomy, nationalisation of monopolies, land reform, trade union rights, religious, political and civil freedoms, a European federation and for Italy to be a republic.[29]

Overall, the Action Party tended to be more unwilling than the Communist Party to compromise on what it viewed as questions of principle, and this intransigence over principles was often why radical elements were attracted to its banner. Harking back to its pre-war origins of *Justice and Freedom*, a leading Action Party theorist outlined his thinking in a lecture given in November 1944 entitled 'Democracy at the crossroads and the third way', that is: a new route between conservatism and communism:

The road to democracy is a high road that stretches toward the horizon. But at a certain point it comes to a crossroads that conceals the direction in which the true road continues. To the right there is the detour of liberalism, agnostic or conservative: the road of liberty without justice. To the left there is the detour of authoritarian collectivism: the road of justice without liberty. The Action Party takes neither the one nor the other because it knows the true road, the third road, the way of union, of congruity, of the indissoluable joint presence of justice and liberty.[30]

This passage is useful because it illustrates both the strengths and the weaknesses of the Action Party: its ideas were appealing, but the organisation spent too much time debating them and never managed to develop a stable working-class following.

However it did create significant partisan forces up in the mountains. Their youth, republicanism and lack of sectarian dogmatism – which sometimes characterised some of the left – made their mountain brigades particularly appealing. The political commissar of a Justice and Freedom brigade once said in a speech to his men: 'I'd like it if soldiers from Badoglio's groups came here and see how we live – they who stand to attention in front of officers and live like the old army – where a soldier worked and got a penny a day, and the officers gave orders and got fifty.'[31] In his diary a few months earlier he had summed up his ideological thoughts thus: 'Communism and the Action Party are parallel; the former tends towards freedom through justice, the latter justice through freedom, but their actions are the same.'[32]

Although accurate figures are now impossible to verify, an impartial source has estimated that the Action Party's Justice and Freedom brigades amounted to 20 per cent of the national total of partisan forces, while the Communist-linked 'Garibaldi' brigades totalled around 50 per cent. There may have been up to 20,000 volunteers under Action Party leadership in the mountains, and a further 11,000 involved in military actions in towns and cities.[33]

THE COMMUNIST PARTY

Whatever the appeal and relative strength of these other two parties, the determining weight throughout the Resistance was clearly the PCI – a weight that became clearer to all during the 45 Days. With the slow but steady disintegration of government authority in this period, approximately 3,000 communist prisoners were released from jails in the second half of August – a figure that gives an indication of the party's potential.[34]

Most had been held in prison on the island of Ventotene, just south of Rome. One day in late July a small boat docked in the island's harbour, but when the prison governor was told who his new prisoner was, he immediately ordered it to set sail for another island. The governor said the new prisoner 'would be cut to pieces' by the inmates and he was probably right – it was Benito Mussolini, the man ultimately responsible for the ten years or more of prison that many Ventotene inmates had endured.[35] While Mussolini's arrest on 25 July was a sign of fascism's growing weakness, the liberation of political prisoners testified to the growing strength of anti-fascism. Badoglio had promised to free them but their release was continuously postponed; it was only when Resistance leaders began telling him that they would call a general strike that the jail doors finally started to open.[36]

The vast majority of these activists had long experience of anti-fascist struggle, often including participation in the Spanish Civil War, and all would play a leading role in the PCI's activity in the Resistance – the same was true of Socialist and Action Party leaders. One of the many 'Ventotenisti' was Pietro Secchia, who had been in jail since 1931. The day after his release he was in Rome and making contact with other PCI leaders. He soon moved to Milan, where for the rest of the Resistance he was the commissar general of the communist-inspired Garibaldi brigades.

The new members who began to flood into the party were a cross-section of working-class Italy. One writer has assessed their nature very critically: 'politically inexperienced, ignorant and immature ... There was the discovery of a rather simplistic communism which, with the stroke of a magic wand

– and back then this wand often came in the form of a magazine containing forty rounds – would create a new world.'[37] Despite these rather disparaging remarks, tens of thousands of young activists did join the PCI and the Resistance, enthused by both the feeling of power that having weapons can give, and by the communist ideas they were now starting to absorb.

What is clear is that the PCI membership was highly uneven and varied, and far from the stereotype of the monolithic machines which ran the Eastern bloc countries in the second half of the last century. At the top were experienced politicians and activists, operating in a difficult situation and trying to reach a variety of strategic objectives. Yet despite their experience, in late 1943 the party had 'a remarkably heterogeneous leadership'.[38] At a meeting of the leadership in Rome on 4 November, the influential leader Giorgio Amendola said that the radio broadcasts from Moscow by long-time leader Palmiro Togliatti 'cannot constitute for us directives that we are obliged to follow'.[39] Towards the end of the month another leader, Mauro Scoccimarro, made the same point concerning these Moscow broadcasts: 'made so as to appear like directives given to the party, [they] were absolutely inopportune, and it is to be hoped they are not repeated.'[40] Contrary to what many historians have argued, Togliatti, still in Moscow, did not rule the communist roost in Italy. This was hardly surprising, since he had been out of Italy for more than 15 years, and had been living in Moscow in recent years due to his senior role in the Communist International, the Comintern.

In any event, given that the primary strategy of the leadership was to defeat fascism and Nazism, rather than any immediate attempt to create communism – the arguments they put forward in their press frequently had a nationalist tone, not what one would expect from the highly international ideology that is communism. For example, in mid-March *l'Unità* argued on its front page: 'The objectives facing the Italian people today are determined by the duty we all have to save the country from total catastrophe before it is too late.'[41] In other words, this was a national struggle of the whole people. Like much of the PCI's policy this emanated from Moscow, where the Russian leadership had motivated its population against German invasion along strongly nationalist lines. This contradiction between the PCI's official propaganda of national unity and its supposed tradition of working-class power is a theme that will resurface repeatedly in future chapters.

As regards leadership activities, negotiations with the more moderate parties had begun even before the 45 Days. By May 1943 Ludovico Geymonat and afterwards Concetto Marchesi had started talks on behalf of the PCI initially with Liberals such as Count Alessandro Casati. (Casati had been Education Minister in Mussolini's government during 1924–25, although he later distanced himself from fascism. He was close to the royal family, and a friend of senator and philosopher Benedetto Croce. Casati later became Minister of War in Bonomi's second and third governments in 1944–45.) If the immediate strategy was to liberate 'the nation', then the PCI was obliged to work with far more moderate forces. While arguments between left-wing parties often involved abstract discussions about socialism and communism, when dealing with more conservative forces the name of the game was making concrete compromises.

These PCI representatives first agreed that the party would work with the army for the overthrowing of the regime, as long as in any future anti-fascist government communists would not be discriminated against. They also made it clear they would work with the king to oust Mussolini, and would participate in a new democratic government led by a titular monarch.[42] Since allying with the Badoglio government – a force that was both shooting down workers striking against fascism and fighting against the PCI's beloved Soviet Union – was something that was at the very least highly debatable, this meant that on the ground very few activists were prepared to embrace these compromises immediately and uncritically. Those with long memories knew that the king had supported Mussolini's rise to power and had never acted in a hostile fashion towards his regime; similarly Badoglio had been one of fascism's senior military commanders in its colonial wars. The fact that the PCI leadership was negotiating with these people did not mean that their ordinary members approved, far from it – once again allegiance towards the PCI was far from being monolithic; given the chaotic and fraught situation of wartime Italy it was easy for highly conflicting views to co-exist within the party.

Following Geymonat's initial meetings, several weeks later Marchesi restated the PCI's willingness to serve under the king in two meetings held in Milan. Such was the moderation of the PCI's position that the Christian Democrat representative was moved to remark: 'In that case we Christian Democrats are further to the left than the Communists.'[43] This tension was finally resolved in early 1944, when Palmiro Togliatti returned to Italy after his long exile. Before leaving Moscow, on the night of 3–4 March, he was summoned to a meeting in the Kremlin with Stalin, who had decided that the division into two camps (Badoglio and the king versus anti-fascist parties) kept Italy weak, and this was a bonus to the British. So Stalin wanted the left to unite with the Badoglio camp; Togliatti duly obliged and changed a document he had written from expressing opposition to the king to an agreement to join his government.[44]

This is the policy he announced in the town of Salerno. Although some leaders had been negotiating such a policy privately, the public announcement came as a real bombshell. When he heard the news – a complete reversal of the policy that had been followed until then – Mauro Scoccimarro disowned the decision, stating: 'You are going to enact this policy [not me].'[45] The rest of the left was in turmoil, with the PSI opposing the PCI decision.

In an immediate sense this new policy meant all argument over state institutions would be decided once the war was over. With the benefit of hindsight, it is clear this represented a profound change: primarily, it created a continuity of the Italian state, opening up the possibility of a smooth transition from fascism to democracy. As one historian has argued: 'Togliatti had acted as a statesman, but had compromised the progressive development of democracy in a way that was to prove decisive.'[46] In an immediate sense it weakened the National Liberation Committee (CLN): 'it was clear, in Naples as in Rome, in Milan as in Turin, that the CLN – as an embryo of power, as the central pillar of a new democratic state, had suffered a very serious blow'.[47]

THE CLN

The tense negotiations between political parties became far more urgent following 8 September 1943 and the German invasion. At 8 a.m. the following morning Ivanoe Bonomi chaired a meeting with Giorgio Amendola and Mauro Scoccimarro of the PCI, Pietro Nenni and Giuseppe Romita of the PSI, Ugo La Malfa and Sergio Fenoaltea of the Action Party, Alcide De Gasperi of the Christian Democrats, Count Casati from the Liberals and Meuccio Ruini who represented Badoglio. The meeting had been convened as an 'anti-fascist committee', and by the afternoon had passed a brief motion: 'At a time when Nazism tries to restore in Rome and Italy its fascist ally, anti-fascist parties are creating a National Liberation Committee (CLN) to call Italians to struggle and resistance, to restore the place that Italy deserves among free nations.' They also issued an appeal which concluded: 'The Italian people will make a judgement on the responsibilities for the current tragedy once the enemy has retreated over the Brenner pass. Today, for the sons of Italy, there is only one position: that of defending peace against the Germans and fascist fifth columnists. To arms!'[48]

This unitary CLN structure was slowly reproduced throughout occupied Italy. Most cities, towns, villages and factories had their own CLN, and within each one there were generally two separate bodies – one party political, the other military. To the extent that the five main political parties were united against a common enemy there was unity – but disputes immediately arose over what could seemingly be instinctively unitary matters, such as how to defend oneself. At its more extreme, the most conservative wing of the CLN wanted to simply wait for the Allies and ensure that a mass movement did not develop, while the most radical wing (which was fairly widespread amongst the rank and file, but was not shared by left-wing representatives on the Rome national committee) wanted the military struggle of the Resistance to culminate in a political revolution which would usher in socialism or communism.

Two days after the meeting in Rome representatives of these parties met under Nazi occupation in Milan and decided to form the 'National Liberation Committee for Upper Italy' (CLNAI), which effectively meant occupied Italy. While the Roman committee often spent a lot of time discussing the nature of a future democratic Italy, Milan concentrated more on the practical needs of the struggle. For example, one of its first urgent tasks was to ensure that ex-soldiers, who had walked up into the hills of Lombardy preparing to fight, were not captured by the Germans and were given some help to organise into a Resistance force.[49]

Radical hopes were created in the minds of many people, something perhaps surprising considering that the CLNAI, like its Roman counterpart, also included the Christian Democrats and the Liberal Party – which in Italy is a conservative party. But certainly in early 1944 there was genuine unity given the strength of the fascist threat. The following motion passed by the CLNAI in January 1944 outlines how it conceived of the future. One of the reasons it emerged was that all parties understood that the fascists, with their constant propaganda about communist violence and treachery, were trying to divide the movement:

> Tomorrow there will be no space for a lighter form of reaction or a weak democracy. Our political, economic and social system can only be one of definite and effective democracy, and today the CLN is a harbinger.
>
> In tomorrow's government the weight of workers, peasants and artisans – all popular classes – will be decisive. And the parties that represent them will make up an appropriate part of this weight. This includes the Communist Party, which is part of the CLN on the basis of perfect parity with the other parties, with equal authority today and power tomorrow, when the pact of national liberation will be realised.[50]

This coming together of different political forces also led to some prestigious figures breaking ranks and using their position to influence events. One such individual was Concetto Marchesi, Vice Chancellor of Padua University, who in the inauguration of the 1943 academic year, a traditional event at all Italian universities, praised the centrality of the working class in his speech: 'Today labour has straightened its back, thrown off its chains, lifted its head and looked around and upwards. This former slave has also been able to throw off the chains that for centuries have held back his soul and intelligence.' The effect of his speech was electrifying, as soon as he stopped speaking students threw out the armed fascist students who had also been in the main hall. Marchesi resigned his position and had to go into hiding, but as he did so he released a manifesto that was distributed around Padua, and then throughout occupied Italy: 'together with young workers and peasants, you have to rewrite the history of Italy and rebuild the Italian people. ... Students – I'm leaving you in the hope of returning among you as a teacher and a comrade, after the brotherhood of a struggle fought together.'[51] Marchesi's words certainly produced action: a hundred students from Padua University were killed during their participation in the Resistance.

ANTI-FASCISM ON THE GROUND

Besides serving soldiers, the other main grouping of young men catapulted into the Resistance were those about to be called up. But there were also significant numbers of people simply swept up in the events. One such man was a married 30-year-old, Roberto Battaglia, father of one child with another on the way, who later wrote one of the most authoritative histories of the Resistance: 'On 8 September 1943 I was a placid art historian, enclosed within a small circle of friends and interests. By 8 August the following year I was commanding a partisan division that created more than a few problems for the Germans.'[52]

This was the scale of the transformation for tens of thousands of young people. Many had a strong commitment to creating a country radically different to the one they had known, and to varying degrees they rapidly developed a sense of confidence and collective power. Writing just two years later, Battaglia remembers that in the first half of 1943: 'the goal I had set myself in those first years of war seemed to have been reached – my book on Bernini was now at the printers'. But during the 45 Days: 'I remember ... I started to avidly read all newspapers, trying to resolve a critical problem – what could really be understood by the word "freedom".' On 8 September he saw government literally disappear from Rome: 'everything that had made life liveable or comprehensible suddenly disappeared: government, newspapers, public services, the police. And with this tangible collapse what disappeared forever inside of me was the placid nature of a scholar, which had already been seriously eroded.'[53]

The old order, and the old certainties, no longer existed. In November a young intellectual with progressive but not communist ideas, who had recently gone up into the mountains, revealed in his diary his worries about the unpredictability and simplicity of some partisans' thinking: 'Many young people understand communism to be a system of anarchy, disobedience and plunder. The day before yesterday one of them stated there were no longer officers and other ranks, while another promised himself he would end up with one of Agnelli's villas.'[54] (Agnelli was the owner of FIAT, and the country's most powerful capitalist.)

In any event, once individuals made the choice to join the Resistance it was difficult to turn back – in February 1944 the fascist authorities announced the death penalty for those who avoided the call-up. But things were already too late – in late 1943, 50 per cent of those called up avoided the draft, by early 1944 it was as high as 66 per cent,[55] and by June that year practically nobody obeyed the call-up. (It must be said that some of this refusal had nothing to do with anti-fascism; what was really feared was deportation to Germany.) These facts show the lack of credibility of the puppet Republic of Salò declared by Mussolini on 18 September 1943, as well as the general disintegration of any common system of government accepted throughout the country. Another incredible statistic concerns the Italian soldiers the Germans transported over the Alps after September 1943. These 650,000 men were asked to recognise the legitimacy of, and to therefore fight for, Mussolini's puppet regime. Only 1.3 per cent agreed, while a further 5 per cent agreed to work in German labour camps. The rest went into concentration camps, where they were not classified as normal POWs – 16,176 of them died as a result.[56]

There were other categories of people, those who unconsciously joined the Resistance through individual acts of resistance, but who were then forced to take to the hills. It could be anybody: people who complained too much, or who argued with the policemen, but more commonly those who helped partisans and were then betrayed by their neighbours. Whatever the reason for joining the Resistance, it involved the coming together of large numbers of inexperienced young people, and smaller numbers of experienced activists.

In the far north of Italy an 'old timer' named Pippo Coppo recalls how he organised the first groups:

> We found ourselves with lots of young men who had no real political education, but who had changed their views during the early stages of the war – veterans of the Greek or Russian campaigns. They took the road to the mountains with a different kind of enthusiasm to that of old communist activists, or at least some of them. These men felt betrayed by the education they had been given, I had many people like this with me. ... A big contribution came from the technical and military training they had received in other areas of anti-partisan warfare.[57]

This perhaps naive enthusiasm of the new recruits was not shared by experienced communists. Coppo remembers that when old anti-fascists came back from prisons such as Ventotene after 25 July they started saying: 'We've got to get ready for a fight, because the ruling class doesn't die on its knees but on its feet.'[58] In other words, many new recruits looked no further than to the ending of fascism and German occupation, whereas many middle-ranking communists in leadership positions wanted to create a communist society. Indeed such was the attachment to communism, regardless of the varying perceptions of individuals, that it was not uncommon for partisan units to organise attacks on German or fascist barracks to celebrate the anniversary of the 1917 Russian revolution.[59]

For all strands of these new resistance organisations, what 25 July clearly represented was great hope for the future, and a huge leap in self-confidence. A worker from the Bemberg factory in Gozzano, near Novara, recalls how things suddenly changed:

> I remember that on 25 July 1943 I was working at Bemberg, and in every section there was a picture of the *duce* – but on the following day there were none. I can recall one detail: there was a welder from San Maurizio called Riz, who went to have his lunch of bread and cheese in front of this picture: 'Jesus Christ', he said, 'you've really made me eat a load of bread and cheese' and 'wham' – he smeared the cheese over the photo, which stayed there until it fell off of its own accord.[60]

But the 45 Days between the fall of Mussolini and the German occupation of 8 September did not allow for much stable work to be done. As Pippo Coppo has stated, during this period: 'our main task was to try and forge links with people from other organisations. ... But on 8 September our first job was to order everybody to not obey the call-up, head for the mountains and prepare for the battle that was going to take shape.'[61]

Organisations came into being through improvisation. Dante Gorreri remembers a meeting in a barn near Bardi, in the far south-west of Emilia-Romagna, on 23 September:

You entered via a stepladder. The furniture was bales of hay, which were used as tables and chairs.

There were no windows but it wasn't cold – it was comfortable.

There were Serbian, Croat, Montenegrin, British officers sitting around, plus a US air force lieutenant from Chicago.

The Italians who had been in hiding on Sette Sorelle mountain were the last to arrive. But the very last was a Slovenian major, who had walked for five hours to get to the meeting.[62]

The strategy that most groups quickly arrived at, almost instinctively, was that of relatively small groups changing their base as often as possible. Guerrilla warfare meant organising many things: finding safe places to stay, food to eat, a communication network, supplies of weapons and ammunition – issues that will be looked at in greater detail in the next chapter.

THE THREE WARS

The Resistance was a semi-spontaneous mass movement made up mainly of working-class people, among whom there were varying motivations and desires as regards the nature of the new Italy they were fighting for. While everyone might agree on who the enemy was, the reasons for which they were fighting were often significantly different. An ex-member of a Patriotic Action Group (GAP) in Verona once explained things in the following fashion:

on one side there was the national war and on the other the people's war. The PCI had organised the people's war, and military personnel had organised the national war. If we fought together it was because at that moment we had no alternative. In that period the national struggle got mixed up with the class struggle because of reasons beyond our control: the German invasion of Italy. And also for us, the first thing to do was to get rid of the Germans. The class struggle should have continued afterwards, but it didn't, perhaps because we were too weak.[63]

Historian Claudio Pavone, himself a partisan in a Justice and Freedom brigade, has provided a highly influential formulation of these complexities. Taking the Resistance as a whole, he argues there were three wars being fought simultaneously: a patriotic war, a civil war and a class war. Each category will be analysed below, but the particular usefulness of this formulation is its recognition that many partisans were fighting two or three different types of war simultaneously.

Patriotic War

For those fighting a 'patriotic war', the king was the authority looked to by the more conservative elements of the Resistance. For these people the main enemy was the German invader, and national honour had to be restored through the liberation of Italian territory. Albeit not a monarchist, one young man wrote in his diary on 8 September 1943: 'half of Italy is German, half is British – there is no Italian Italy any more'.[64]

Tactically these patriotic anti-fascist forces had a deep ideological problem: the system under which everybody had been living – fascism – had been intensely nationalistic. So promoting an anti-fascist war by simply stressing the need to free 'the nation' was always going to be difficult. And similarly, given the nature of the discredited monarchy, it was problematic to call for a war under the banner of the king.

One of the unifying factors this section of the Resistance emphasised – though the left were not immune to this either – was to hark back to the *Risorgimento*, the movement to unite Italy that had culminated successfully in 1860. As Pavone has written: 'the *Risorgimento*, with the strength of its heroic and unifying stereotypes, was useful as ideological cover for a politics of unity – whether in its left-wing version or its moderate version'.[65] Furthermore, on a practical level, people with a traditional and socially subservient outlook found it difficult to join a guerrilla war that had no legalistic justification, such that sometimes they were hesitant about acting 'illegally'.

The most influential in this group were career army officers and conservative politicians. Part of their propaganda could be racist towards the German people, making references to 'barbarians', 'teutons' and Attila the Hun. Concrete examples are the 'autonomous' formations or the *Badogliani*, such as the 'Fazzoletti azzurri' (Blue Neckscarves) of Major Mauri in the Monferrato and Langhe areas of Piedmont, the Osoppo Brigades in Friuli, and the 'Fiamme verdi' (Green Flames) in the Brescia area. Officers in these formations wanted to see a new Italy dominated by tradition and royalty, whereas nearly all partisans thought the monarchy had had its day. Having said that, these groups were all loyal in their anti-fascism.

Civil War

In an idealistic sense, this was a war against 'a fact that weighed heavily upon society, culture and the Italian people'.[66] Fascism was born in blood: it had come to power in a violent low-level civil war during 1919–22 when thousands were murdered, and had maintained power for 20 years through systematic and widespread repression. Fascism was ending in violence too; so some of those who fought a 'civil war' had personal scores to settle, and frequently took up the fight on that basis. Pavone has even put forward the notion that it was the end of a civil war which had begun just after the First World War: 'In fact the civil war between fascists and anti-fascists can be viewed as the summing up and final act, under the pall of German occupation, of a conflict which began in 1919–22.'[67] Perhaps in the countryside it was this kind of war that was fought by the majority; if people involved in the Resistance did not consider that they were fighting a 'civil war', it was certainly a 'people's war'.

As civil war involved fighting against fascism, and its objective was liberation from fascism, the primary enemy had to be Italian fascism rather than German Nazism. Of course there were close links with the patriotic war, in the sense of recovering lost national pride, or re-establishing the true values of the nation, but in this case there was also a progressive ideological motivation, namely to eradicate fascism and all its causes and traces. In a very visceral sense it was a war against an ideology – fascism – which had been created in Italy.

Perhaps, of the three wars, this has been the one that Italian anti-fascist historians have avoided the most: first because fascists themselves have since tried to stress there was indeed a civil war, in an attempt to put their side on an equal footing (and anti-fascist historians did not want to grant fascists legitimacy by accepting this argument); second, because it broke the taboo of denying the 'national unity' that was apparently involved in the creation of a new democratic Italy; and third, the right-wing of anti-fascism, and conservative parties and elements in the decades since 1945, have since stressed the existence of a civil war because they wanted to attack the Communist Party.

Yet to deny the validity of people having had such a motivation is to deny the reality of events. At the time it was widely acknowledged that this was what was happening. On 16 October, in one of its first major motions, which was widely published, the national CLN criticised the strategy of new Republic of Salò: 'the latest Mussolinian endeavour – behind the mask of a so-called Republican state, to encourage the horrors of civil war'.[68] In the same month, the PCI began to publish a new theoretical journal, in which it was argued: 'It is time to shoot, it is time for partisans, a time of civil war, a time of war actively fought against Germans and fascists.'[69]

While for some people the Nazis may have been the main enemy, their occupation of Italy and their brutality over 18 months could never have been sustained without the help of Italian fascists. And besides, many of the attacks against partisans in the mountains were carried out by Italian fascists, who also had responsibility for maintaining law and order in many cities. So inevitably, Italian partisans spent much of their time fighting Italian fascists.

Class War

As Pavone has put it, in this war: 'the main enemy was the traditional one of workers' struggles, that is the boss – whether factory owners or the big landowners who had financed fascist gangs and made use of them. ... The boss and the fascist ended up coinciding.'[70] Inevitably, therefore, this conflict had at its heart those anti-fascists who worked in factories or other large workplaces. Indeed a good summation of workplace involvement in the Resistance was the last headline of *l'Unità* before the northern cities began their insurrections: 'With strikes and guerrilla warfare towards the decisive battle!'[71]

Although the traditional method of the workers' struggle, the strike, was common throughout the Resistance, it needs to be appreciated in a different way. Hundreds if not thousands of people were shot for striking, and thousands of striking workers who were deported to Germany died in labour or concentration camps. None of this happened just because Nazis or fascists simply lost control of themselves, it was part of a very public policy – for example, in June 1944 a fascist decree was passed instituting the death penalty for organising strikes. The fact that any strikes took place at all is testament to a deep sense of commitment and grievance. Most of those arrested and deported – about 8,000 – were taken to Mauthausen, from which many never returned. For example, 67 per cent of the 250 workers deported from La Spezia after strikes in March 1944 died in the camp, as well as 73 per cent of the 215 workers deported from Sesto San Giovanni in Milan.[72]

Historically the motivation for fighting the class war coincided strongly with the political origins of fascism; at the time of its emergence the fascists were the armed wing of the ruling class, rising to power because the working class had become too threatening. But this is also a war that needs to be analysed further, because broadly speaking it probably motivated a clear majority on the left-wing of the Resistance. Essentially, the model people looked to was the Soviet Union, but it was the *propaganda* of the Soviet Union rather than the reality which became increasingly public only from the 1960s onwards. The model was then a new Italy without bosses, a country of both political and economic democracy. But even within this sphere there were many middle-ranking leaders who spoke only of nationalisation rather than full-blooded socialism, and national leaders who were in alliance with the monarchy.

There were nevertheless elements of a classic revolutionary situation in Italy during the Resistance – that is, the coming together of the two classic factors once developed by Lenin. The first was that the ruling class was no longer prepared to carry on in the old way – it wanted rid of fascism and an end to the war – but was divided about how to go about it. Equally important for all powerful capitalists was the rate of profit; most large companies earned high profits in the early years of war,[73] but these were severely under threat by late 1942. The second factor was that the working class was no longer prepared to live in the old way and, potentially, was prepared to annihilate its historic enemy. As early as January 1943 an uncompromising leaflet was found by the authorities in Turin: 'The openly murderous bourgeoisie of yesterday is today secretly afraid, and is trying with any means to save what it can. We will overthrow this puppet government but we are intelligent enough to recognise our shadowy oppressors and will strike without pity.'[74]

But perhaps it was the fraught nature of any industrial struggle during the Resistance that sometimes made 'class war' a far more uneven and ambiguous phenomenon. On one hand, a report from a Milan factory in December 1943 stated: 'There are persistent rumours that if the strike is not fully successful on the 16th then most of the responsibility will be laid at their door (the bosses), and that four or five of them will be put up against a wall.' Yet six weeks earlier a communist report from Turin had noted the following attitude from the country's most powerful capitalist: 'Agnelli seems willing to give a lot of money to the CLN.'[75] Large sections from both sides of the class divide were prepared to cooperate warily in prosecuting the other two kinds of wars outlined above; while absolutely rigorous and uncompromising acts of class war from the working class were rare on an extended basis.

To sum up, as Pavone has written: 'There were very few who just fought a patriotic, civil or class war.'[76] The nature of these individual wars was clear, yet in reality they overlapped in many people's minds; nevertheless the categorisation is useful because it highlights the tensions within the movement. These were exacerbated by the fact that all participants were reacting to a fast-changing situation, and were used neither to political debate nor even to being free to discuss different ideas.

4
Resistance in the Mountains

All three of the left-wing parties within the Resistance had suffered under fascism for 20 long years, and therefore had a keen sense of history. As two historians of the Resistance – who were victims of fascism themselves – have suggested, when a coordinated movement started to emerge after 8 September 1943 it had, as the Italians say, 'come from afar':

> September 8 was not the date on which the Resistance was born, it was the date it turned into armed struggle. The Resistance had its origins way back in 1919, with the first fierce battles against fascism, and had continued in overseas emigration and in secrecy internally, forging itself in fascist jails. The Spanish Civil War was its university; it had been led by Communists, Socialists and the Justice and Freedom movement, and now that long experience was priceless and placed those parties at the head of the war of liberation.[1]

Yet none of those experiences were appropriate to the situation in 1943. Battles between fascists and anti-fascists before 1922 occurred in a democracy and in familiar surroundings, while the Spanish Civil War saw large formations engaged in conventional mass warfare. The Resistance, by contrast, involved guerrilla warfare against the world's most formidable fighting machine, and was developing spontaneously, week by week.

Luigi Longo, a senior commander in both the Spanish Civil War and the Italian Resistance, outlined his thinking: 'creating large military units would have no sense in the current situation. The organisational recommendation for operative units remains that of small, highly mobile but well-structured squads of not more than 40–50 people.'[2]

These kinds of numbers were not only recommended in order to avoid being discovered by the enemy, but also because of the difficulties of finding food in remote valleys. For large units of outsiders stationed in hill country or on mountainsides to be able to survive, good relations with the local peasantry were absolutely vital. Because it was impossible to hide the presence of hundreds of men, even in the remotest areas, if partisans antagonised local people their safety would be immediately compromised.

Furthermore, the partisans relied on peasants as one of their main sources of food, and from whom they would buy or ask for clothes and medicine. Virtually every kind of help partisans wanted from the peasants had to be requested, and often negotiated. One political commissar Paolino 'Andrea' Ranieri remembers having to discuss with local peasants the terms on which the partisans could use donkeys to carry their equipment. The eventual agreement was that half of the local donkeys – 15 – could be used on rotation. One half would be used by partisans at night, the other half by peasants during the day to work the fields; that way the animals could get some rest and everybody could use them.[3]

The partisans also used peasants' barns or abandoned farmhouses to sleep in. Not surprisingly, their appearance and lifestyle was often similar to classical tramps, as one outlines:

The first time I noticed I had fleas was a bit tough, I remember I cried ... You could tell they were happy to be with me ... they kept me company. ...

I remember once I lived on bread and water for 10–11 days, or rather bread and snow because we were up in the mountains. Then we came across a herd of sheep so we bought a goat from the shepherd and cooked it over a fire without salt or anything ...

We chose where to sleep at the last minute because that kept us safe. We decided when we were on the move ... there were [normally] four walls without any windows and a concrete floor. We couldn't use hay or leaves because otherwise it would have left a sign that we had been there, we always had to keep the concrete clean.[4]

These newly formed brigades were a melting-pot of Italian society, and they needed to be turned into a cohesive fighting force very quickly. Although Luigi Fiori had been a lieutenant in the regular army, and so had a high level of military training, his problems were different to most other partisans:

I was from a wealthy bourgeois family – peasants and workers had nothing in common with me. Finding yourself there, with these kinds of people: burping when you eat, or the fact that we had about seven bowls to share among 50 ... I was used to everyone having their own cutlery ... or going to the toilet – I used to wander off somewhere so they wouldn't see me.

It wasn't easy to adjust to all of this. For them I was a dandy, I had good clothes, or otherwise I used to wash them regularly in streams.[5]

Another young partisan wrote to his girlfriend in October 1944: 'In a week more or less three meals made up of cabbage collected from the fields, and some bread given to us by peasants. The sky deals with our cleanliness (our bed is the woods), I haven't changed my clothes in three months – they can stand up by themselves. Best not to mention the fleas.'[6] In the same month, Laura Seghettini moved her small organisation to a new base in the Apennines: 'To our delight we discovered that there were some sulphuric springs used as public baths, and therefore, after so many months, we now had the chance to wash ourselves.'[7]

All this meant that partisans acted very correctly towards local peasants, who, though they may not have understood some of the politics, generally saw that the partisans were poor working-class people like themselves, and so

Figure 4.1   Members of the 53rd Garibaldi brigade near Bergamo, Lombardy.

felt an instinctive solidarity towards them. In essence, however, partisans were often walking on eggshells: 'All that was needed was some kind of resentment, personal rancour, or having been rude to certain individuals to be spied upon and condemned by an anonymous [letter], with all the consequences that can be imagined.'[8]

The Germans and the fascists tried to undermine these links by implementing a policy in which, for every German or fascist killed, ten Italians would be killed. They would sometimes be selected from partisans held in jail, but would more often be people from the town where fascist or Nazi barracks had been attacked, or from a village near to where their patrols had been ambushed. After the entire population of the town had been rounded up, victims were selected at random and herded into the main square. It was a sign of the depth of the link between partisans and local communities that cases of betrayal were relatively rare. Essentially most people believed the partisans were in the right, and the Germans and fascists in the wrong. This positive view of the partisans came from their own belief that working-class people were the key to creating a new Italy, through an alliance of workers and peasants. For the fascists, working-class people were an irritation, and they treated them with contempt as they had always done.

This was one of the reasons why discipline was so harsh within partisan groups. Executions for indiscipline were not infrequent and would take place in the field after a trial involving large numbers of the formation. To take just one example from northern Italy: a partisan had originally been expelled from a brigade for lack of discipline but was re-admitted. He had then been caught drunk, harassing some local nuns. After a trial held by a four-man court, a death sentence was passed. Two partisans who observed the trial remembered years later that this was a perfectly normal and correct decision to make: 'We often said to ourselves – if we didn't respond like that, if we didn't behave properly – we would never have been able to tell the people of Ossola and all the others who helped us how grateful we were. Without the help of the local population we wouldn't have lasted a fortnight up in the mountains.'[9] A group near Bologna maintained equally severe but necessary discipline: 'a thief would have been executed. We weren't bandits! A partisan on guard duty who feel asleep would have been shot.'[10]

Another example also suggests the idea that in some ways partisan groups were in effect a new if rudimentary kind of civil society: 'we executed another one up at Cortevecchio for rape – we were hardly in a situation to send him to jail for a year'.[11] Although partisan groups were by definition mobile units subject to unexpected attacks, there were some that managed to survive intact for over a year.

Apart from discipline as regards relations with the outside world, there were also severe difficulties in terms of internal cohesion, or measures taken to ensure the safety of the whole group. Most people were questioned when they asked to join up, but strangers from widely differing backgrounds were often allowed to join partisan groups. Laura Seghettini estimates that the 40 men she commanded came from the following backgrounds:

> There were people from the local area and others – such as southern soldiers who had stayed in the North after 8 September. There were three South African officers from the British army who stayed with us for about a month waiting to cross the front line, a group of *Bersaglieri* from Emilia-Romagna, one of whom was a doctor in Reggio Emilia. Some young people, such as Giorgio Giuffredi, had been sent into the mountains because they had already been activists in the Communist Party. Others, however, after obeying the call-up had then deserted from the army.[12]

The harsh reality was that some people joined up not because they believed in the cause but because it was the most convenient thing for them to do – or, in very rare cases, because they wanted to use the new situation they were in to their own advantage. Punishments for lesser crimes were obviously less severe than execution, such as this example from December 1943: 'One young man has stolen some grain from the group and sold it. Zama, his officer, made him undress completely apart from his shoes and underwear, and had him tied to a post in the snow at 5,000 feet for several hours. He untied him when he turned blue.'[13]

The nature of how the partisans operated meant that anybody could simply melt away without warning. Not surprisingly, suspicions of all kinds were widespread, and were based on the relatively high number of betrayals from within the groups. If someone arrived with brand new weapons, for example, people would wonder how he had got them. Similarly, why would someone put on a headscarf every time he went into battle – was this a signal to the other side not to shoot at him? On the other hand, if someone who had been viewed with suspicion suddenly left the camp overnight, this was almost inevitably taken as a sign that an enemy attack was imminent.

With a view to keeping morale and order, as well as maintaining physical security, the number of executions for spying could be very high. For example, in Tuscany, Roberto Battaglia's Lunense division executed 90 people for collaboration with the enemy.[14] Luigi Fiori is quite matter of fact about events in his brigade: 'We executed two. They used to go off at night and come back in the morning – they were stealing from peasants – they forced them to hand over gold rings and necklaces. It was the same thing with spies – once you'd established the facts you didn't have any choice. Besides, we were hardly set up for running prison camps.'[15]

In terms of the local community, there was no Chinese Wall stopping local peasants from joining the Resistance. To the limited extent that they were able, brigades would paste up bulletins on the walls of towns and villages outlining the Allies' progress and local partisan actions on a weekly and occasionally daily basis.[16] A truthful account of events, as opposed to fascist propaganda, clearly helped to move local people towards the partisan cause. But in reality the Resistance was pushing at an open door, since far more peasants than urban industrial workers had been enrolled into the armed forces and suffered in fascism's disastrous campaigns of the war. After 8 September many returned embittered to their towns and villages, while those due for the call-up were strongly inclined to go on the run – the most obvious choice being to join a partisan group. Just as with any other Italian, they were suffering the effects of a failed war which had ended up with Nazi occupation. One anti-fascist peasant family became famous for tragic reasons: On 28 December 1943, seven brothers of the Cervi family were shot without trial in Reggio Emilia in revenge for the assassination of a local fascist leader.

Elsewhere, in the hamlet of Giucano, above Sarzana:

> The population became very close to the partisans very quickly, and several young people joined the group. It was relatively easy to create a supply network by using supporters enrolled earlier; this was a varied and lengthy chain. Many families donated things spontaneously, although always within the limits of their own circumstances. The others did not create any problems, and accepted the vouchers they were given. Besides, when the group managed to buy cattle for slaughter local people ate for free.[17]

The vouchers mentioned were promissory notes produced by large partisan units, committing Italy's new democratic government to reimburse the owner of the note for the goods that partisans had used; repayment invariably did occur.

Figure 4.2   Promissory note given by partisans to people in exchange for goods or services, which were then repaid after the war. The lower part of the note reads: 'Accepting this note means having faith in an Italy independent from the Germans and free of fascism.'

Two miles to the west of Giucano, in the hamlet of Ponzano Superiore, half of the town's population were refugees, and here partisans generated support among local people by setting up a local bakery, which they were able to do thanks to an agreement with local railway workers, who stole flour from the large convoys that passed through the station.[18] A resourceful and alert group of partisans often had occasion to get local people onto their side – such as in the town of Barge in Piedmont, when a German truck full of milk destined for troops was seized and the milk then distributed to the local population for free.[19]

When a young commander was parachuted into a rural area to the north of Carrara he noticed that 'almost every family had a young man who was a partisan. And what was more important was that the formation's activities didn't exclude those who operated from home – it was a new "job" that was added to or was alternated with that of a peasant or shepherd.' Writing immediately after the war, this commander remembers that the first hard argument he had with partisan groups in the Garfagnana area concerned whether they should enrol new members who wanted to work their land as well, 'through shift work'.[20] They were allowed to do so, and the group was then largely made up of 'partisan-peasants who by day laboured agriculturally and by night, by rotation, went down onto the roads to try out those new weapons which had come from the sky, and also – if possible – to get hold of a brand new pair of boots'.[21]

The importance of good relations with local people increased as the Resistance grew geographically, spreading its theatre of operations down into more densely populated areas. In late 1944 a partisan newspaper discussed how to relate to the civilians partisans were meeting for the first time:

They're now starting to really get to know us down in the lowlands, because before they only knew us vaguely, or more commonly through second-hand accounts. So every step we take has to be a careful one, because we all know that first impressions last in terms of how you judge someone. When people see partisans they have to see, ... if they have personal dealings with them, friendly and courteous people.

So no more threatening faces, multi-coloured ribbons or other adornments, useless bravado, telling tall tales so that kids in villages look at you open-mouthed. Whether you're in uniform or not, you need to be spotless and serious. And a military demeanour even if your clothes are ragged and you're barefoot. So no angry attitude, even when you're going to get water![22]

A NEW KIND OF ARMY

The largest number of partisans belonged to the Garibaldi brigades, which were dominated by the Communist Party – although many partisans within these brigades would not have considered themselves communists. Influenced by the structure of the Red Army in the Russian Revolution and civil war of 1917–22, and the International Brigades in the Spanish Civil War of 1936–39, after 8 September the PCI decided to set up the Garibaldi brigades, which were open to everyone. Luigi Longo was overall commander while Pietro Secchia was political commissar. Years later Secchia remembered:

As Communists we gave the order, and back then it meant an order, that each one of our organisations had to send at least 10 per cent of its leading members and 15 per cent of its ordinary members into partisan groups: a total of 25 per cent. Today this might not seem very high, but in many areas it was a difficult number to reach.

The first serious battles these new brigades were involved in took place near Lecco and Varese in Lombardy during the second half of October.[23]

Figure 4.3   Partisans and local people build a road-block together in a Piedmont town.

This key move on the part of the PCI broke with the passivity of career military officers, who found it very difficult to accept the unconventional command structure and strategy of the new groups. These officers may have been genuinely interested in resisting the Germans, but their reluctance to join and in some cases outright plotting against the Resistance delayed many initiatives. Particularly in the second half of 1943, the PCI had to conduct a political battle against such people, who just argued for more waiting: to wait for the Allies, for better weapons, for better organisation, for better weather, to wait until the Nazis and fascists were on the verge of collapse. This attitude became known as *attendismo*, literally 'waitingness', but translated correctly as something like 'adopting a wait and see attitude' or 'fence-sitting'.

An article in the Communist Party's theoretical journal in November spelt out the kind of actions that were needed: 'the struggle needs to be waged with all means, from sabotage of production, machinery and transport, to the cutting and destruction of telegraph, telephone and electrical lines, the burning of warehouses, supplies and arms dumps, to direct attacks on German positions and command posts, etc.'. The article, written by Pietro Secchia, went on to argue that by engaging in such actions the war would be shortened and thousands of lives saved, but in addition, the party would be tested and would come out of the war far more cohesive and united. Perhaps most important of all were the political reasons why it was necessary to fight:

We cannot and must not await our freedom from the Allies. The Italian people will be able to have the government they have wanted for so long – a government that will really act in their interests – and not one linked to reactionary imperialist cliques – only if they will have fought to conquer their own independence and freedom, only if they will have shown that they have the strength to impose their own government.[24]

For 18 months this would be a continual political battle within the partisan movement, which would be particularly fraught on the eve of the imminent liberation of a big city. It was never an easy argument to win, not least because of the fascist and Nazi policy of revenge killing, often on the ratio of one to ten, and often through a random selection of civilians. Those who argued that the Resistance should not fight with the possibility of execution hanging over innocent heads, and in a situation where enemy forces were clearly superior, naturally got a hearing. But the fact that, apart from the failed or half-hearted liberation of some cities during 1944, the Resistance won the argument overall illustrates the level of support it had.

The issue of German and fascist reprisals was posed most starkly for the local populations living near partisan camps. Luigi Fiori, by now commander of a moderate non-communist brigade, recalled:

German reprisals were a huge problem. You found yourself in a situation in which if you didn't attack the Germans they [local peasants] would say – 'Eh, you sit around here drinking tea, but when the Germans turn up ... you disappear.'

But if you attacked them there were reprisals, and then you got – 'you've caused all this'. I'd have people on their knees in front of me, crying ...

One day I got really fed up with hearing 'when the Germans turn up you run away', and that when I wanted to attack, I shouldn't. I remember there was an old peasant, aged 60–70, and I said to him – 'come here you, let's put our cards on the table. Do you know why I'm here? Living like a dog? Hungry? A death sentence on my head? It's because you, 20 years ago, did nothing to stop fascism and now Mussolini has taken us into this war.

'I'm not here to make trouble for you – it's people like you who have put me in this situation. I'm here for you – I could have stayed home and done nothing.'

There's a saying where I come from – 'the pains of childbirth stay in the mattress.' In other words, 48 hours after the Germans had passed through they were rational again, they realised it wasn't our fault, we were all in the middle of a war.[25]

Perhaps it was the increasing solidification of fighting forces that also made a difference: the left-wing of the Resistance could see very quickly that their fighters were deeply committed and bonding as a group. For all individual partisans this was to be a life-changing experience. To an extent, the social hierarchies of normal life simply did not exist in partisan brigades. For example, the commander of a brigade operating in southern Tuscany wrote of the single aristocrat in his formation: 'What with his long beard and holes in his clothes, and the pistol in his belt, up here in the woods he too is just a partisan.'[26]

Once people had decided to join the Resistance very few ever looked back: in a short while it became known to the authorities that they were absent from where they were supposed to be, or from the army, and so they could never really go back home. This meant spending months and months in the hills and mountains with the same group. Individuals virtually took on a new identity, because for security reasons they would be known only by a nickname – which, for those who survived, would often be used for the rest of their lives after the war, particularly if they remained politically active. Indeed many funeral announcements of ex-partisans in the postwar decades gave more prominence to their partisan nickname than their official name.[27] ('Nickname' is a very poor translation of the Italian 'nome di battaglia' – literally 'name for battle'.)

Command Structure: Commissars and Commanders

One of the great mistakes people make when imagining warfare is to think that soldiers spend most of their time fighting. In reality, much of a soldier's life is spent waiting around. Partisan groups were no different, except that arranging shelter and the provision of food were two very time-consuming activities. Since guerrilla warfare has very different rhythms and practices to conventional warfare, in partisan units a 'strong egalitarian spirit is widespread, in nearly all formations food is shared out equally, commanders and troops eat the same things'.[28] The major organisation within the Resistance, the Garibaldi brigades, attempted to strike a balance between conventional hierarchical structures and a democratic army. As the Piedmont military committee once wrote to a local brigade: 'We certainly don't want the discipline of a bourgeois barracks, but neither [do we want] anarchy.'[29] This was not a regular army under conventional authority, but an unconventional army fighting for a new world, a world whose rules had not yet been written.

But since some kind of structure had to exist, the brigades had two leading members: the military commander and a political commissar, positions which were subject to both election and recall. It was the element of democracy and accountability that not only created cohesiveness and motivation, but, crucially, brought the most talented individuals to prominence. Often, commanders, 'apart from their attributes of physical courage, intuitive responses and imagination, possessed an awareness of the central rules of partisan warfare, that is the wise management of scarce military resources, clothing, and essential goods'.[30] The division of roles between the commander and the commissar was very clear, as Dino Borrini, a military commander of a brigade in Lunigiana in north Tuscany remembers: 'when we were on a mission the commander controlled everything, but back at base camp he didn't count for anything – the word from headquarters was law. All responsibilities at base were held by the commissar.'[31] Aldo Aniasi, military commander of the Redi division near the Swiss border, writes in similar terms of his relation with his political commissar, Pippo Coppo: 'Pippo never interfered in military decisions, that is, in the conduct of a guerrilla campaign. I used to consult him and we discussed the targets together, but I was the one who made the decisions and took responsibility.'[32]

The image of a political commissar can easily create notions of boring men with beards using long words that few people could understand, but the truth of the matter was very much the opposite. People had a thirst to discuss ideas that had been repressed for two decades, and which would guide the building of a new Italy after the war. Partisans had chosen to join the Resistance, it was a volunteer army, and a large part of making that choice involved the desire to create a better society. In general, the commissar in Garibaldi brigades was often an experienced communist activist. But it was not uncommon for the commissar to be a university student, hardly an authoritative figure, but obviously a more educated person in a society where a university education was still very much a minority experience. Their job was 'to organise "the political hour", a mixture of explaining the reasons behind the struggle, party propaganda and starting to develop political and social horizons'.[33] The commander of a brigade largely concurs on the importance of the 'political hour':

due to the way life was organised in a Garibaldi brigade, despite so many difficulties and unmet needs – especially food – it was a coming together ... a moment of collective debate among equals, information about developments in the war, explanation of the political objectives and social goals to be reached in the transformation of our country. People looked forward to it because it was an amalgamation due to the fact we were heterogeneous, there were demobbed soldiers from the South, maybe someone who had got out of jail, students, there were all sorts.[34]

Sometimes precise educational instructions were sent out to the groups in the mountains. A week before Christmas 1943 the Parma federation of the PCI wrote to its commissars:

Every squad should have a small library, a few good choices of various kinds of books. The librarian freedom fighter must look after the books they are responsible for.
Form study groups so as to encourage reading and discussion of all the party's literature. A good vanguard fighter is not created – and only improves – through action, but also through the development of a good political and ideological understanding.[35]

Since many partisans were probably only semi-literate, it is clear that there were never study groups in the modern sense of the word, nonetheless, a deputy commander of a Brigade remembers what used to happen in the evening, after leaders or couriers had arrived back at base: 'When we gathered to eat, those who had other duties carried them out. The rest of us drew together as a group to listen to party documents being read'.[36] Partisans would reflect on events, great and small, as they unfolded. As a young man fighting in north-east Tuscany in September 1944 wrote to a friend: 'I'll tell you quite frankly, I'm worried that our freedom will be wasted in compromises and political battles which will not be particularly clean. The news I'm hearing on this score from the South saddens me; it seems that the fate of our freedom is being put back into the hands of those who only offered minor resistance to fascism!'[37] Many of the concerns that developed out of this new political education were about the future as much as the present. As the same partisan argues: 'we're going to free this Bologna of ours, and we'll hold a party that will never end – but we'll chuck out cowards and those who just waited. The people who have never taken a stand are the permanent and real enemies of freedom: it will take nothing for them to become fascists again.'[38]

Each brigade tended to have a dominant political ideology, although it was not uncommon for a small number of partisans to move between a few brigades until they felt fully comfortable with the environment they were in. Every commissar had to be careful not to overstep the mark: many partisans were very young men who had known only fascism, so to try to ram Marxism or any other new set of ideas down their throat would probably have been counter-productive. As ever, it was better for people to learn on the basis of what they saw and heard, as well as being encouraged to learn about new ideas. The following long quotation concerns a partisan group that by mid-March 1944 had not even given itself a name. Based on the recollections of seven participants, it recounts the speeches given over several evenings by Paolino 'Andrea' Ranieri, the PCI political commissar, to partisans resting in a barn in the Apennines:

> He outlined the Italian political situation, the purpose of the CLN, the need for unity among the anti-fascist forces in the struggle against resurgent fascism and the German invaders ... the need to reinforce within the group they were building not a fake unity ... Audacity and prudence were needed, as were courage and humility, seriousness and correctness, discipline and freedom at the same time ... they had to view themselves as being the nucleus of a popular army in which no ranks or differences exist. People are chosen for political and command responsibilities on the basis of knowing how to wield these powers efficiently and democratically, regardless of their social background or qualifications.
>
> 'Andrea' stressed the need for everyone to cooperate without reservations in making the group's life and activity a model of free and democratic cooperation. It was also necessary to create and maintain links with the local population if you wanted them to be friendly and helpful, and furthermore, to develop them democratically and socially ...
>
> Many of those young people were hearing these concepts for the first time, and they were fixed indelibly in their minds.
>
> It was true that nearly all of them had heard people talk about socialism and communism, Soviet Russia and the PCI, but all this had been instinctive, vague, perhaps even mere fascination ... it had not entered their brains as a living and operative concept ...
>
> They listened to an outline of Marxist economic theories albeit at an elementary level, concepts such as class struggle, the overthrowing of

capitalism, the dictatorship of the proletariat, the creation of a classless society which would have guaranteed social justice and peace among peoples.

At a certain point, both during the first and second evenings, several people showed not so much irritation as a sense of tiredness, as if it had very little to do with them. Others did not understand a great deal of what 'Andrea' was saying ...

During the following evenings the majority paid more attention and there was more interest ... Horizons expanded, the education that many had received emerged in all its emptiness; the cultural values learnt by the few who had attended secondary school were shown to be lacking. ...

After so many adventures and dangers, and their hard, precarious and uncertain existence, a flame of hope had been lit. These young people needed to believe in something noble and worthwhile, and to create real values which would substitute the empty frippery of the past. It was that classless society of human brotherhood which emerged shimmering and distant, yet it was not a dream – it was the final goal in a process which had already begun.[39]

In 1972 the PCI political commissar Pippo Coppo looked back on his experiences:

As commissars our task was to explain to young people why they had to fight, why we had to fight fascism, and what we wanted after its end. It's not as if we wanted the society we got, we wanted another society, the kind of society that workers and students today are fighting for. No longer a society dominated by the power of capital, but one in which the Italian people could have had a louder voice and have mattered far more. ... at the end of the day the Italian people are made up of workers as well, so wasn't it more natural and logical to create a government with working-class forces? ... This is why I agree with young people today, when they say the enemy to be defeated is a party which comes across as democratic [the Christian Democrats], that gives lectures about democracy, that uses all these lovely words but in action behaves differently. When have we ever seen a Minister of Labour worry about a factory closure ... or acting so that the working class no longer lives with a sword of Damocles above its head, because from one moment to the next people could find themselves on the street without a job?[40]

What Coppo expresses here is the frustration of many partisans at the missed opportunities of the Resistance, and perhaps also an underlying bitterness that PCI commissars were under pressure at the time to reduce the enthusiasm for communism shown by their members. Paradoxically, it was widespread ignorance that helped make the appeal of communism so strong. Although the PCI leadership had by now no allegiance to the kind of revolutionary communism represented by Lenin, there was virtually no awareness among partisans of the demise of revolutionary Soviet society and its degeneration into oppressive Stalinism. These conscious or unconscious tensions emerged in many different ways. For example, the political commissar for the Ossola region wrote to Pietro Secchia, Commissar-General of the Garibaldi brigades, in November 1944: 'We have insisted on the appropriateness of military saluting but with very few results – the vast majority salutes with a clenched fist. Almost all the local population salutes with a clenched fist: men, women, children and old people. When vehicles from our headquarters pass through these towns people stop and salute using the same method.'[41] This resistance to saluting was not confined to communists; there was a fairly universal aversion because it was used in hierarchical army units, and in the fascist army in particular, which many partisans had fled from. Cino Moscatelli, the popular political commissar in the Sesia valley, wrote to his local PCI federation in August 1944 mentioning the same problem:

If you ask partisans what their political ideas are or what party they belong to, nearly all of them answer that they are Communists. They would let their buttocks be stencilled with a hammer and sickle; Stalin is a god. You can't criticise Russia, and above all the Red Army. They all salute with a clenched fist. ... Personally I've never saluted anyone with a clenched fist, whereas policemen, local people, even priests, all salute me with a clenched fist.[42]

An interesting character, Moscatelli was born in 1908 and had joined the communist youth wing in 1925. His talent was quickly discovered by communist leaders, and he was sent to party schools in Switzerland and Berlin. From 1927 to 1930 he lived in Moscow, and the following year moved back to Italy where he was quickly arrested and sentenced to 16 years for being an anti-fascist, although he only served five. Upon his release he went into business, and became an object of suspicion for local communists. Once the Resistance began, however, he threw himself into it, and perhaps it was his recent distance from the party that gave him a more original vision. In the same letter he continued:

Many times have I had to intervene to remove red trimmings from uniforms, red flags from lorries; I have had to ban little red flags from machine guns and rifles. ... And the more I intervene the worse it gets. Many of our officers have asked to join the party. I've banned them from singing *Bandiera Rossa* when they march: they sing and sing yet they always end up with that song.[43]

The bigger picture behind these concerns is that of a lifelong communist trying to keep his organisation open to others, especially Catholics. For centuries, particularly in poor rural areas, the worldview of the church and its values had been handed down to peasant families. But not only were socialists and communists traditionally anti-clerical, fascist propaganda had strongly emphasised the attacks on churches and priests during the Spanish Civil War.

Moscatelli went so far as to design a portable altar which could be carried as a rucksack, and wrote the *Garibaldino's prayer*, which he printed in thousands of copies, with an image of St Michael slaying the devil on the back.[44]

Many Catholics, however, had their faith severely tested, for a variety of reasons. As one partisan recalls: 'Let's say I started to work things out during Easter '44, when I went to communion in Prato. The priest refused [to give me communion] because I was a partisan, so I started to understand things.'[45] Indeed large numbers of Catholics joined the Communist Party during the Resistance, with many of them continuing to practise their faith.

The paradoxical problem for the PCI was that it was a popular party. Communist ideas were popular. While on one hand the PCI feared that the prominence of their ideology might antagonise some and drive them away, on the other hand the militancy of much of their rank and file, many of whom were anti-clerical, also needed to be accommodated.

WHY THE PARTISANS WERE SUCCESSFUL

According to conventional military wisdom, the partisans never stood a chance. For a start, they had very little equipment: 'On average, partisan groups' ammunition did not allow more than an hour's firing in any engagement.'[46] Most had no military experience, and they were badly clothed, fed and housed. They were continually subject to betrayals, and faced the most formidable fighting machine in the world. Yet if we take just one partisan division as an example – the Lunense division in north-west Tuscany, led by the 30-year-old art scholar Roberto Battaglia – the scale of success is undeniable. Over a four month period, from August to December 1944, it carried out 50 acts of sabotage against railway lines, destroyed about 90 enemy vehicles, killed about 1,000 of the enemy and lost about 150 of its own.[47]

The advantages guerrilla fighters enjoy against a stronger enemy are numerous. The fact that the partisan brigades had no permanent base meant that it was unlikely the enemy would be able to engage and destroy the entire organisation. Although brigades were often almost surrounded in battle, thanks to their intimate knowledge of the local territory the enemy build-up had already been noticed, so most partisan forces managed to escape either as a group over the mountains, or by splitting into small groups and conducting rearguard actions before melting away. In other words, fighting was largely conducted on the partisans' terms. Likewise, partisan offensive actions would often consist of large numbers of heavily armed men launching an attack against fascist soldiers in barracks, blowing up bridges or railway lines, or attacking arms dumps. They normally outnumbered whoever they were attacking, and had the element of surprise.

But the reasons for the partisans' military success were also political. Quite simply, the partisan army was a volunteer army, people were fighting because they wanted to fight, and they freely risked their lives in the hope of creating a better world. Many armies, by contrast, are conscript organisations, made up of soldiers who are by and large forced to be there, and who often resent

Figure 4.4 Members of the 36th Garibaldi brigade help with the harvest south-east of Bologna. Credit: Luigi Arbizzani.

the highly dictatorial methods most armies use. The partisans' personal and political commitments were mirrored by political support from the local population, without which most groups would not have been able to survive. Although this support was widespread and genuine, it was not overtly ideological. The PCI in particular repeatedly pointed out in articles that peasants were an integral part of the movement:

> After the battle it is the peasants who, crawling through the woods and clambering from rock to rock either on mountain peaks or on river beds, go and look for wounded patriots. They hide them and nurse them, snatching them away from the search parties of the Nazi-fascists. Every day hundreds of young peasants go up into the mountains to join partisan formations, and fight shoulder to shoulder with workers and students.[48]

The same article goes on to point out that 'Older peasants undoubtedly remember the magnificent struggles conducted in the past against large landowners, struggles that sometimes lasted for several months culminating in real armed and insurrectionary movements.' Essentially rural areas were part of class society too. For example, large landowners would frequently hoard essential goods bought at official prices, such as petrol, seeds and fertiliser, only selling them on at black market prices. The PCI repeatedly argued for organised partisan groups to encourage peasants to set up their own trade-union type organisations, which were very thin on the ground.

Perhaps the greatest political encouragement the partisans received at the time was the creation of a series of democratic republics in high remote valleys, which held out for several weeks or even months, offering a very tangible sign of their success. These republics will be analysed in greater depth in Chapter 10.

5
Resistance in the Cities

While the conflict in the hills and mountains was one of guerrilla warfare, the clash in large towns and cities took a different, though equally extreme, form. Compared to the mountains, the cities were perhaps a more decisive battleground. Italy was already a significantly urbanised country, as modern as any in Europe. In the countryside the Germans and their fascist allies could devote resources to the military struggle against a clearly definable enemy, but what they faced in cities was a more invisible resistance, harder to fight and tactically more destabilising. The military problem was that, as a rule they could not identify their enemy. The partisans might suddenly attack and then, hiding their guns, melt back into the crowds. Not only did the Nazis and fascists have to use up significant military resources to keep things under control, they were also demoralised trying to catch these guerrillas.

The importance of the cities lay in the fact that they were places where both strategic decisions were made, and where the central economic components of Italian society were located. Exercising control over a city's main economic activities and communication centres was tantamount to exercising control over the country as a whole. This is why the Germans were often so intransigent in response to military actions against urban communication channels. Following attacks on telephone and telegraph lines in September 1943, the commander in the city of Livorno had a poster put up announcing that he had taken 50 male hostages, and that if German soldiers were fired on again – or if their lines of communication were disturbed – five hostages would be killed. If attacks continued after that, then a greater number of hostages would be executed.[1]

As in the mountains, the development of the Resistance movement in the cities was the result of exasperation at the increasingly desperate living conditions. Faced with growing complaints about lack of food, in July 1942 a group of fascist propagandists in Turin decided to weigh a group of factory workers. They discovered that large numbers of workers had decreased in weight over the previous year by 10 to 15 kilos, and that men over 1.70 metres tall weighed only 53 to 55 kilos.[2] Resistance occurred in many different ways, starting with the lowest level of passive resistance, or turning a blind eye. Then there was the low-level propaganda activity carried out mainly by Patriotic Action Squads (SAPs) – producing posters, throwing leaflets from the back of trams or from bridges, distributing newspapers, making 'flying speeches' in cinemas and factories, writing slogans on walls. (These activities will be discussed further in Chapter 11). Fund-raising was another vital activity. It cost money to buy weapons, ammunition, clothing, food, and to pay rents. Since people will usually only volunteer money for a cause they believe in, drumming up the necessary finance was primarily a matter of winning political arguments with potential supporters. The urban resistance could not be sustained without constantly renewing and increasing its popular support, and new recruits were always needed given the deaths and arrests the movement suffered. As such, an ongoing political discussion had to be maintained, in order to defend the legitimacy of the Resistance.

Although there were a significant number of 'terrorist' attacks in cities, the greater scale of resistance in the mountains – and the harsher physical conditions experienced there – meant that solidarity for the partisans in the mountains also became an organisational focus. On 10 December 1943, the PCI leadership in Pistoia sent a message to all its members in which it insisted that during the run-up to Christmas: 'Communists must organise collections so that anything that can be of help to partisans (food, clothes, shoes, money, etc.) floods into sorting centres. ... the collection of a Christmas parcel for partisans should be a true plebiscite of popularity towards those who are giving the most in the struggle.'[3]

The most demanding kinds of military action in cities were carried out by the full-time 'terrorists' of the Patriotic Action Groups (GAPs). (Again, these will be looked at in greater detail in Chapter 11.) For their surprise military attacks to be successful, a network of support was needed. Since they needed somewhere to hide their weapons or wounded fighters, a number of safe houses had to be established. The people involved had to be sympathetic to the cause before agreeing to any concrete involvement, since intimidating them into cooperating would only have increased the likelihood of betrayal.

The underlying political support for the urban Resistance grew out of a series of social and economic factors. The cities far more than the countryside were targets for Allied bombings, and the fascists had no solution to the problem. Following the first heavy air raids in the North, in early December 1942 Mussolini gave a major radio speech in an attempt to improve morale. Given that most cities were without air-raid shelters, he suggested that people 'organise an evening exodus'. Incredibly, this advice was followed to a significant extent, though police reports warned of the anger and discontent such experiences, in the depths of winter, were creating. In Siena the police chief wrote to Rome at the end of the year: 'it is beyond doubt that in the mass of the population there is a daily growing sense of unease about victory in the war which, in a best case scenario, is viewed as being uncertain'.[4] In Turin, by October 1943 gas had been unavailable for three months, 50 per cent of houses were damaged in some way, and the vast majority had had their windows blown out.[5]

While peasants had far easier access to food in the countryside, in cities people increasingly found that food shops and markets had empty shelves, and that black market prices were out of their reach. And while salaries remained largely unchanged, official statistics from Turin council reported that, taking the cost of living as 100 in 1941, it had risen to 135 by January 1943, to 168 in September, and to 221 in December.[6] Throughout the Resistance period, hunger was to be a highly unifying factor. By 1943 a kilo of bread was five times more expensive than in 1938, the price of pasta had tripled, and the price of cooking oil had risen by 800 per cent. A bottle of olive oil bought on the black market cost the equivalent of a month's wages for an average textile worker.[7] Or, as one scholar has put it: 'What one could have bought for 100 lire in 1938 would have required 858 lire in 1944, 2,060 in 1945.'[8]

As time went on the gnawing hunger became a focus for anti-fascists, reaching a crescendo in the winter of 1944–45. On 25 November 1944, *l'Unità* argued in a special edition: 'Workers have asked for food and coal and the enemy has answered with hunger and arrests. There is only one response: to storm food and fuel dumps, compel the industrialists and Nazi-fascists through force to recognise our people's right to exist.' However the key action, involving the highest number of people, was strike action. Many cities were dominated by large workplaces, and the collective nature of big factories turned them into places where the Germans and the fascists could be challenged more openly. A successful strike demonstrated the level of confidence and degree of organisation the Resistance now had, not only to the enemy but to ordinary Italians as well.

STRIKE ACTION IN THE CITIES

Going on strike under a fascist regime is difficult enough, since clandestine preparation is not the most reliable way of organising industrial action. Although the PCI was the dominant force, it is important to remember that the vast majority of workers did not take its positions and proposals as being written on tablets of stone, and the confidence that PCI activists managed to create sometimes led to situations outside of their control.

The first major strike wave in northern cities took place in Turin in March 1943, as described above in Chapter 3. The next broke out in November, again in Turin. Following a particularly heavy bombardment of the FIAT factory in Villar Perosa, a wildcat strike developed beyond the control of local communists. The spark was management's refusal to suspend work when air-raid sirens sounded, which led on this occasion to many workers being killed. A more long-term demand was higher wages, as well as a reduction of the delays in paying the increases that had been agreed. Indeed the mixture of anger, desperation and confidence was such that FIAT *Mirafiori* workers demanded either a 100 per cent increase in wages, or else 50 per cent and the equivalent given in larger rations.[9]

Management, beginning to fear the day when the fascists would no longer be in control, immediately announced they would pay higher wages – although they were unable to increase rations since that was beyond their control. FIAT boss Giovanni Agnelli had written a long report to Rome on New Year's Eve 1942, commenting that 'the chaos which ensued during the latest enemy air raids is largely the result of the easing of discipline between superiors and inferiors which has taken place recently'. Agnelli was thinking about the long term, and worried that management were losing control of the shop floor: 'the future could hold more painful surprises'.[10]

Figure 5.1   Sabotage of a tram during a strike.

After the March 1943 strikes the main players began to reposition themselves. One very bold move was made by Agostino Rocca, managing director of the Ansaldo steel and engineering group. This was the key company for the war industry, producing all Italian tanks in 1943, 65 per cent of artillery and 50 per cent of warships.[11] A few days after Mussolini's arrest on 25 July, Rocca called a meeting with communist shop stewards in Genoa, who, for reasons either of inexperience or opportunism, agreed to work closely with him. After the meeting, Rocca wrote:

> While many within the ruling class believe that the fall of fascism means the end of 21 years of the regime and a return to where we started from – and with such an illusion they busy themselves reacting with a 1921 mentality – from day one the leaders of the labour movement have shown a very intelligent approach.[12]

In other words, the business world had to accept that fascism was finished, and that in the interim it was necessary to work with left-wing leaders in the factories.

Meanwhile, fascist trade unions now tried to put themselves at the head of strikes in order to recover some credibility. When a strike wave broke out in November it was supported by fascist trade union leaders, who negotiated with fascist authorities, announcing victory when their meeting ended. Rejecting this manoeuvre, workers struck again, only to encounter the third big change since March – there were now Nazi authorities on the ground. Colonel Klaus went to *Mirafiori* and confirmed the increases in wages and rations, but threatened that if there were any more strikes, the 'shop stewards will be held responsible'.[13] Indirectly, workers' representatives had become German hostages.

The only way to respond to this kind of threat was to go fully underground again, which was what happened, leading to a third wave of strikes on 1 December. The German response was to place heavy weapons in front of factories, and let the threat and sense of insecurity run its course – this third strike was suspended without a clear victory. But a victory of sorts had been achieved: a total of nine days of strike action in a vital war industry had been successfully conducted.[14]

As in March, Milan quickly followed Turin, but this time the PCI organised the events beforehand. Mass leafleting of factories on 1 December led to walk-outs starting at 10 a.m. This wave of strikes functioned more successfully: the PCI press made it clear what the demands were, and the fascist unions were unable to influence events. The difference here was that factory owners immediately let the Germans intervene, and they duly arrested a small number of striking workers from every factory. But the solidarity of the movement was such that they were quickly released. The bravery of these workers is hard to imagine. After three days on strike, with workers refusing to go back to work after the first German promises, SS General Zimmermann arrived at the *Unione* factory. According to a contemporary account he threatened: '"Whoever doesn't go back to work must leave the factory. Those who leave will be treated as enemies of Germany." *All* workers leave the factory.'[15] Some improvements were obtained, but once again the clear political result was that workers in the major industrial factories had managed to strike for over a week.

The third city in the Italian industrial triangle to enter the fray was Genoa. A major strike wave was preceded by a tram drivers' strike at the end of November, an action that was obviously noticed in all areas of the city, but the more generalised movement was soon nicknamed 'the olive oil strike', since one of the main demands was an increase in the ration. Perhaps due to the relative success obtained in Turin and Milan, workers in Genoa went a stage further and marched out of their factories, to be immediately joined by a significant number of local people. The authorities responded by shooting three workers on the third day. The Resistance answered by declaring public mourning across the city. In the areas where the workers lived everything was closed down, and there were pickets outside the major theatres and cinemas. When work was due to resume on the Monday morning, a political strike was called against the executions. The movement had now extended beyond factory workers and involved bakers, street cleaners and hospital workers.

Another significant factor during the strike days was the response from GAP groups: a column of Germany artillery was attacked in the city's main street, killing two mounted officers. The Germans suffered more dead and wounded in attacks just outside the docks, and two fascists were killed elsewhere.[16] Despite the manoeuvres of management over the summer, the Ansaldo artillery factory also went on strike.

For the PCI, however, the outbreak of these strikes had been a worrying event since they began spontaneously, without any premeditated coordinated preparation. Activists who had led previous strikes had generally been arrested, so the numeric weakness of the left meant that angry workers took matters into their own hands. As a leading PCI activist in the city wrote: 'given the speed with which action broke out, party branches could do nothing but … try to lead the movement'.[17]

By the end of 1943 it was clear that in the major cities of Italy the Resistance had mass support among the working class; it was also clear it could launch significant surprise attacks on its enemy, both economic and military. But this increased strength and sense of confidence gave rise to a different kind of problem – how should the people be mobilised in the future, and for what objectives? The Resistance had clearly developed a network within major cities that their opponents could weaken but not destroy. Likewise, the Resistance could periodically attack the enemy, but could not finally destroy them alone. Tactically, however, the Germans and the fascists were on the defensive. As events unfolded, it became increasingly clear that it was only a question of time before they would be defeated. Among the Resistance, perhaps too much triumphalism sometimes crept in. Final victory might have been fairly certain, but the whole point of the movement was to arrive at the day of liberation with the largest and most self-confident movement possible, so as to be able to build the most progressive Italy imaginable.

The difficulties regarding popular mobilisation may have led to easy solutions being proposed. In any event, at the end of January 1944 the PCI decided to organise a national wave of strikes. Despite miscalculations and exaggerations, these were nevertheless among the biggest strikes ever organised in occupied

Europe, in the face of one of the most violent and repressive state machineries in history. After the series of strikes in 1943, new problems and demands had arisen. As punishment for strike action the Germans had frequently resorted to mass deportations of workers, so opposition to deportations had to be a key demand in order to maintain morale. Other, more 'clandestine' concerns, which could even be communicated to management privately, included worries over machinery being dismantled and transported to Germany – something that had already begun to happen on a small scale. Another issue was that of reducing or sabotaging production – a tactic that was bound to incur the wrath of the authorities once it came to light.

The anti-fascists' plan was to organise a simultaneous general strike throughout northern Italy. Given the scale of organisation required, this meant that the element of surprise would be lost, and the fascists and Germans would be able to plan their response. But the Resistance was prepared to take the gamble: success would mean a further demonstration of the movement's growing strength. German and capitalist preparations were thorough: the Germans pinned up lists of suspected 'subversives' who would be deported or sacked if strikes broke out – and obviously it was the employers who provided the names. Alternatively, the Germans threatened that a certain number of strikers would be deported, with names selected at random. *L'Unità* in return would regularly attack the major employers, referring for example to 'Mr Valletta and his Nazi-fascist bosses' and identifying Valletta, the managing director of FIAT, as one of a number of 'sinister individuals'[18] – an accusation that seems wholly justified given that he had joined the Fascist Party back in September 1930.

The fascist authorities ordered many factories to close down for holidays once the planned strikes were due to start on 1 March. The numbers involved on this first day in Turin have been estimated at 60,000, rising to 70,000 the following day. The precise demands were for higher rations and an end to deportations, arrests and violence. The strike lasted a week, with many lock-outs in the factories, and 150 workers deported. Just outside the city, partisan formations in the mountains blew up several suburban railway lines, and in the high valleys electricity lines were cut.[19]

In Milan the strike was perhaps more generalised: tram drivers joined in, and GAP groups blew up a major railway line. At the university, students ran fascist lecturers off the premises. Many clerks at companies such as Edison and Montecatini went on strike. Printers at the country's major newspaper, *Corriere della Sera*, prevented it being published for three days – this was perhaps the most telling event, since the newspaper as a means of communication was so crucial in the days before television. The Germans began threatening mass deportations, and ordered the closing of many factories. The workers' response was to declare they would stay on strike until their side decided to go back to work – and the date decided was the same as for Turin.[20] The 60,000 leaflets distributed in Milan at the end of the strike were triumphalistic: 'The end of the strike must mean the beginning of partisan guerrilla warfare with the intervention of all working masses inside and outside the factories ...

The Italian people only have one solution for survival: answer violence with violence.'[21]

Fortunately very few people took these instructions literally. The time would come for open warfare, but the movement was not yet strong enough to stand up to the enemy in open battle.

One of the most interesting aspects of this wave of action was exemplified in the town of Castel Maggiore in Emilia, where a contemporary account records that 'women and peasants demonstrated in front of the town hall ... [and] demonstrators made the following demands: Freedom to buy products directly from peasants, and peasants demand the right to freely sell their products.'[22] Similarly in the Tuscan town of Empoli, peasants 'demonstrated against having to deliver another 15 kilogrammes of wheat to state warehouses, and demanded the right to mill freely'.[23] Although not widespread throughout the North, this shows that there was peasant support for an initiative that had come from the cities. And in the cities themselves, securing higher rations – i.e. extra food – was becoming more important than wage rises as a demand of the strikes.

One estimate has spoken of 1,200,000 workers taking strike action in this period, and the news was even broadcast on Radio London.[24] The *New York Times* commented on 8 March: 'in terms of mass demonstrations, in occupied Europe nothing can come close to the revolt of Italian workers'. However, in a long article published in the PCI's theoretical journal after the strikes, a fairly frank assessment was made of a series of weaknesses. One problem stemmed from the workers leaving their factories: in a situation of military occupation where public meetings are banned and repression is on the cards, big workplaces constituted a rare space in which to meet and distribute newspapers. Genoa had also presented a particular problem, where poor preparation meant that very few strikes had taken place. Equally the Germans had successfully intimidated significant numbers of workers with their posters threatening strikers with deportation.[25] An even greater weakness was the lack of action generally by public sector workers such as railwaymen, tram drivers, post office workers, and gas and electricity workers. And in Turin the strike 'ended in workers' demoralisation due to the lack of concrete results; ... in Genoa there were no strikes at all, due to workers' lack of confidence in an insurrection and fear of leaving yourself open to a head-on clash for which people did not feel ready.'[26]

It took several months for urban anti-fascism to regain its confidence. In Turin this occurred on a more sustained level when, in September, train drivers completely stopped railway traffic for several days, and while two-thirds went back to work, the remainder stayed on strike until liberation. Even more crucial were sabotage, strikes and go-slows in war production. The average production of tanks at the Turin SPA factory was 1,095 between January and July 1944, falling to just 73 between September and November. Although the slow down was partly due to bombing and lack of raw materials, a further significant cause was resistance in what was a highly militarised factory.[27] The problem as ever for factory owners was that they needed their workforce,

RESISTANCE IN THE CITIES 85

but if they opted for strike negotiations they had both the fascists and the Germans breathing down their necks. When Sunday working was demanded at the *Mirafiori* and *Lingotto* factories towards the end of 1944, the workers refused, and bosses responded with a lock-out, suspension of wages, and the arrest of 200 workers. A strike wave then developed throughout the city, forcing management to back off from its belligerent stance, provide back pay for the lock-out and release all arrested workers.

Industrial relations and the partisan struggle were by now inextricably linked, presenting a new and very difficult problem for management since 'economic' issues and political issues had always tended to be kept separate. When nine partisans were executed in a central Turin street, there were continuous strikes throughout the second half of October as well as street demonstrations. On 2 November, the traditional 'day of the dead' in the Catholic calendar, anti-fascists commemorated their fallen in large numbers at the city's main cemetery, in front of stunned fascist militia.[28]

As strikes and 'terrorist' attacks continued in the cities of the North, the Allies – having liberated Rome on 4 June – were slowly advancing up the peninsula. Resistance forces were now faced with the test of launching a significant insurrection in a major city. As will be explained in Chapter 11, since there was no insurrection in Rome, by the summer of 1944 the only important city to have liberated itself was Naples, which had done so in a semi-spontaneous fashion back in October 1943.

THE LIBERATION OF FLORENCE

The next major city in the Allies' path was Florence. Along with the rest of Italy, anti-fascists in the Tuscan capital had been outraged by the Italian military's refusal to hand over any weapons on 8 September 1943. Deportations to Germany began quickly, particularly following a raid on the city's synagogue in early November.[29] Despite this, the PCI developed its military network, and agitation committees sprang up within the factories. The Action Party meanwhile often concentrated on political propaganda, preparing false documents, and helping Allied prisoners escape.

There were, however, many reactionary forces attempting to stop an insurrection developing. When a GAP group eliminated Colonel Gino Gobbi, military commander of Florence and a key local fascist, on 1 December 1943, the city's Cardinal Elia Della Costa attacked them for doing so.[30] A few days later the Cardinal called for 'humanity and respect towards German officers and soldiers'.[31] In his Christmas message he criticised the 'struggle between children of the same earth', and went on: 'every act of violence, every beating, every illegal use of weapons is criminal because nobody can exercise justice on their own'.[32] One factor playing in the conservatives' favour was the high number of irreplaceable works of art housed in Florence: there was some pressure not to turn the city centre into a battleground and so risk ruining them. On the other hand, resistance meant resistance, and there were important monuments and resources in any medium-sized Italian town. Development of the movement in Florence therefore tended to follow the national trend, with significant participation in the March 1944 strikes.

The fascists made the first move in attempting to blunt the local Resistance by proposing the freeing of political prisoners in exchange for their own immunity. In mid-July 1944 both the Germans and the fascists proposed creating a 'civic guard' to ensure a smooth transition of powers and no need for a battle. As with Rome, there was talk about Florence becoming an 'open city' in which military forces would neither be stationed nor fight – an idea supported strongly by the Cardinal who intervened with a proposal to ensure 'a peaceful handover of power' which included giving the Germans the right to leave the city undisturbed. An integral part of these discussions saw the senior clergy in Florence intervening to try to pull the Christian Democrats away from the local CLN.[33] In other words, the classic bourgeoisie was thrown a lifeline in the attempt to stamp out radicalism, and the Tuscan CLN was forced publicly to denounce the *attendismo* of those who just wanted to wait for the Allies. Other 'notables' pulling in this direction were the Vice Chancellor of the university and many other art and archeological experts and lecturers.

This was all the more ridiculous given developments on the ground. On 25 June PCI leader Antonio Roasio wrote in a party journal:

> The army of the so-called republican regime is melting like snow in the sun. Some groups are heading home, some are in hiding and waiting for the Allies, and a significant number has gone over to the partisans. Fascists and their militias are escaping to the North even before the Germans' withdrawal. Fascist leaders are the first to run away. ...
>
> Some senior fascist leaders and bigwigs would like to negotiate with us in order to save their skins.[34]

Although the enemy was clearly weak, in a report sent to PCI leaders in Milan two days later Roasio outlined that the anti-fascist side had its weaknesses too: 'The activity of the Tuscan CLN is still too vague, too bureaucratic – they're too worried about the future and do not worry enough about the daily struggle. It's still a talking shop and of very little use in the struggle.'[35]

It was clear by now that the fascist system was breaking down quickly, even before the arrival of the Allies. This was partly due to GAP attacks: several leading fascist leaders had been assassinated in the spring, creating such panic that other leaders moved around with 20 bodyguards. On 18 June the fascist leader Alessandro Pavolini wrote to Mussolini: 'The *carabinieri* are disappearing almost everywhere, often with their weapons. Even more serious is the widespread disappearance of the police, contaminated by the *carabinieri* and the general situation. Even more serious is what has happened to army units.'[36] As regards the military struggle itself, Roasio says in his 25 June report that 'Two-thirds of active combatants are Communists', but that politically '*Attendismo* is strong among the population and also among our members. Workers hate and despise the Germans and the fascists but don't want to fight – they're waiting impatiently for the Allies and don't want to take any risks when it's just a question of days.'[37]

Another key problem over the summer was that despite the growing general collapse, the Germans and fascists were very efficient at hunting down GAP members. On 13 July fascists killed Elio Chianesi, a major GAP organiser, and another four members. Four days later another four were captured, and were executed on 23 July along with another eight anti-fascists. All of this created a lot of demoralisation. At a CLN meeting on 10 July the minutes record: 'After having outlined the situation created after the arrest of various Florentines, Christian Democracy asks the CLN to call for the suspension of any action which could give the German authorities a pretext to carry out the executions threatened in their latest communiqué.' The PCI took a completely different position, arguing that 'the Tuscan CLN cannot agree to such a request without relinquishing the very basis of its functioning as the coordinating body of the Italian people's armed struggle against Nazi-fascist tyranny'.[38] The outcome of the argument, crucially based on a request from relatives of the anti-fascist prisoners, was to launch actions to try to free those prisoners, and to take some German hostages.

Whenever the insurrection was going to come, large industrial workplaces would not be its organisational centres, partly because of partisan actions in the mountains such as the blowing up of electricity pylons.[39] Roasio, however, outlined on 25 June most of the major reasons for the lack of activity in industry:

60 per cent of workers have left their factories. They have been taking action for several weeks, demanding living conditions appropriate to current circumstances. Almost all factories have handed out one or two months' wages, or 1,000–2,000 lire credit.

Food has been distributed in many factories.

Despite these successes, in the last few days workers have left their factories in large numbers because the Germans have tried rounding them up to deport them back to Germany. In a few days there will be nobody left in the factories.[40]

For example, the *Officine Galileo*, which normally employed 5,000 workers, was empty. Because the Nazis had made no secret of their intention to dismantle factory machines and take them away, workers dismantled the machinery first and hid them for the duration.[41] Workers' fears were far from exaggerated; following successful strikes in March, the Germans deported a thousand workers from the *Officine Galileo*, *Pignone* and other factories to the death camp of Mauthausen.[42]

What with the German occupation, extreme hunger and rationing, the streets themselves became an organising centre:

In queues for food and coal, in factories and artisan workshops – the hatred towards the Germans and resentment against the fascists, hostility to the war and mistrust of the authorities, exasperation due to hunger and the black market – day after day they become elements in a new class solidarity due to the action of both young and old anti-fascists who were linked to the struggle. From the outskirts to the centre there were collection points: hand carts, bicycles and prams carrying weapons all pass under the noses of the fascists and the Germans.[43]

The most unthinkable events could occur. A major institute for the blind in Florence not only hid away the machinery in its workshops, it also hid Jews and partisans in its cellars.[44] On 3 July the Allies liberated Siena, 35 miles to the south, and at virtually the same time several senior fascists left the city, including Pavolini, who stole five million lire out of a government safe before he left. Fascist newspapers also ceased publication. On 21 July the CLN agreed it would refuse any negotiations with the enemy and would launch an insurrection. Ten days later it issued a proclamation which openly attacked the notion of an 'open city': 'there is only one thing that can reduce or stop people suffering from German violence and the destruction of their city: armed insurrection ... The CLN invites everyone to remember this, and for everybody to get ready to fight to save everything which is dearest to us: our families and our civilisation ... Long live liberty, out with the barbarians.'[45]

The last few days of German occupation resembled events in Naples before its liberation. The Germans ordered the south of Florence, that is, south of the Arno river, to be evacuated. By 3 August the city was without water, electricity and bread, and the streets were deserted. Scabies began to break out in many areas, a few cases of typhoid had been recorded, rubbish was rarely collected and dead bodies remained unburied.[46] There were now about 500,000 people in the city, double the normal number – many having left surrounding towns and villages after German massacres and looting. The authorities declared a state of siege, ordering people off the streets and warning that anyone seen looking out of their window would be shot. People had no water at home, so were forced to risk being shot in the streets when they went to find standpipes. Since all this meant there were no crowds in the streets, the build-up to the insurrection was to be unique in Florence, as the city started to resemble a ghost town.

The Germans had mined all the major bridges, so some of the first partisan actions were attempts to take control of the bridges and defuse the bombs, but they were beaten back at every attempt.[47] Fearful of a sudden Allied advance, on the night of 3–4 August the Germans blew up five bridges across the city, including that medieval masterpiece, the Holy Trinity bridge. The only bridge left standing was the *Ponte Vecchio*. The city was effectively split in two, and serious fighting began in the south on the 4th. There were 780 partisans in the south of the city, and 2,000 in the north. The first Allied patrol entered the far south at dawn on 4 August, but it was to be many long days before significant Allied forces came to aid of partisans across the Arno.

The Allies' arrival undoubtedly produced jubilation, and on the afternoon of 4 August Antonio Roasio spoke at the first democratic rally in the Porta

Romana area, held outside of the *Casa del popolo*, the building that had been the organising centre for socialists and trade unionists before fascism. But problems immediately arose; the following night Aligi 'Potente' Barducci, commander of the Arno Garibaldi division, called all his brigade commanders to a meeting in the *Casa del popolo*, together with a British 8th Army colonel, who, following orders from General Alexander, demanded the immediate disbanding of the entire division: 'there was a moment of confusion, then everybody wanted to give voice to their protest and indignation – three-quarters of Florence was still in enemy hands, the people of Florence were preparing an insurrection'.[48] All brigade commanders were against the proposal, and said they would raise the issue with their men in the morning. If anything, their men were even angrier, a stance that was then communicated to the Allies, who repeated their order and moved tanks up to positions outside partisan camps. The partisans replied by setting up road blocks, 'and let it be known that anybody who came to impose the surrender of weapons gained from the enemy through so much blood would themselves be treated as an enemy'. The following day the Allies relented, announcing that the partisans would be allowed to liberate their own city.[49]

Meanwhile on the north side of the river the Christian Democrat representative on the CLN, Mario Augusto Martini, described what life was like in the city in his diary for 4 August: 'People look out from half-open windows. It creates a very strange impression to see an entire city imprisoned. Apart from when mines or cannons explode, or the machine guns fire, the lack of noise allows you to even hear the inmates' muted conversations.'[50] A state of emergency followed for several days, during which there was neither peace nor an insurrection.

Tension with the Allies continued. On 6 August some partisan leaders managed to cross the river – using the lofts of the buildings of the *Ponte Vecchio* they literally passed over the Germans' heads. (The irony was that this passage, the *Corridorio Vasariano* originally built in 1565, had been especially improved for a visit by Adolf Hitler in 1939.) At a meeting with other partisan leaders and the British high command, they outlined the desperate situation the main part of the city was in, and the British assured them they would soon launch a pincer movement on both sides of the city to apply more pressure on the Germans.[51]

The PCI federation published a newspaper on 7 August which was also stuck up as a poster on walls. It detailed Allied advances on the Eastern Front, and the fact that the Allies were just 200 kilometres from Paris, as well as now on the southern outskirts of Florence. The main article was entitled: 'Popular Insurrection is our salvation'. The need for carrying this out was spelt out politically, criticising moderates who had argued for simply waiting for the Allies:

Those kinds of people who held on to the disastrous vain hope of seeing Florence respected, should now understand the correctness of our predictions. After having devastated all industrial units, destroying as much as they could of what will be of use to us tomorrow, the Germans have blown up the bridges over the Arno and other famous works of art loved not just by us, but by all civilised people. Then they launched themselves into the theft of precious objects, money, clothing, looting shops and homes as well as launching manhunts.[52]

The following day the same PCI wall newspaper used even stronger tones:

Let's attack our killers! With no bread, gas, electricity, water or medicines; between the explosion of mines, the rumble of mortars, the hissing of bullets – what more could frighten us? Hunted down in the street, attacked in our houses, machine gunned on our doorstep, what more is there to be afraid of? ... Let's move, and with weapons in our hands earn the right to live.[53]

Martini wondered in his diary on 10 August: 'How many friends will never see each other again? And you, old clock, when will you strike the hour of liberation?'[54] At dawn the following morning, 11 August, the agreed signal rang out. The bells at *Palazzo Vecchio*, the city's town hall, began to toll. Soon after, another enormous bell situated just behind, the *Bargello*, began ringing for the first time since the start of the Second World War. The same morning the CLN issued a proclamation in which it took on the role of provisional government. It went on to say that the people of Tuscany had conquered 'the right to be a free people fighting and dying for freedom'.[55] The battle had finally begun: ordinary people spontaneously joined organised partisan groups in the streets. Fighting would only stop in the suburbs on 2 September, three weeks later: this was the first organised insurrection in a major city, and it was to be the longest.

Compared to both the Neapolitan insurrection, and the insurrections in the big northern cities in April 1945, Florence was very much a half-way house. Although it was not spontaneous like the Four Days of Naples, their opponents were still fighting a world war which at that point was far from over. The partisans' plan had been to first save the bridges, then relentlessly attack the Germans in the city centre, followed by attacks on the north bank of the Arno, thus pushing the enemy further to the north. None of this worked. One of the problems was the sheer imbalance in men and weaponry. However, on the first day of the insurrection partisans on the north bank were helped by the arrival of fresh forces from outside the main part of the city. On the morning of 11 August the Arno division managed to wade across the river from the south under enemy fire. At roughly the same time, three socialist 'Rosselli' brigades also arrived – a total of 1,200 men.[56]

Over three long hot weeks street fighting raged in the city. The first major battle was at Pino bridge on 12 August, with the PCI youth organisation having its baptism of fire: five dead, eight wounded, out of 30 young fighters. The main battlegrounds were the *Manifattura tabacchi* (a factory turned into a fortress by the Germans), the train station, and a major medieval fortress, the *Fortezza da Basso*. The partisans had only light weapons to counter the

Germans' tanks and heavy weapons.[57] At night the Germans would bombard partisan positions with artillery, while fascist snipers would hole up in a variety of buildings.

Figure 5.2 Partisans liberating Florence.

The Allies' interventions continued to create problems. When the insurrection started the CLN had announced that an old socialist, Gaetano Pieraccini, was to be mayor. The Allied military government then countered by saying members of the local aristocracy would take on full powers. The CLN replied on 20 August, warning that 'The Allies need to understand that the removal of the mandate from Pieraccini could reduce the Allies' popularity.' The Allies then backed off, announcing that a Colonel R.S. Rolph would be commissioner for Florence, and would work alongside the CLN: 'negotiating local affairs with it rather than with the local aristocracy, which has done nothing in the city's current crisis'.[58] In the meantime, the first Allied forces crossed the Arno on 13

August, and only seriously began attacking the Germans two days later. These battles raged for several days, with Allied soldiers and partisans fighting side by side.[59] Only on 31 August did the Germans stop shelling the city – people were still sleeping in cellars – and all fighting stopped on 2 September.

Even while certain areas of the city were a battleground, democratic newspapers began to be sold openly. Socialist leader Sandro Pertini remembers selling his party's newspaper during liberation: 'A man stopped me in *piazza San Marco*, he must have been 70–75. Without saying a word he held out his hand to take the paper, and held it just as a Christian might hold a sacred object. And he kissed it – he kissed *Avanti!* and started crying.'[60]

But not everybody thought the ending had been a totally happy one. Angiolo Gracci, commander of the Sinigaglia brigade and author of the first book to be published on partisan activities, was demoralised by his organisation's passing out parade in the *Fortezza da Basso*. In front of British generals, a few days after the end of the fighting hundreds if not thousands of partisans marched out: 'in the poorest streets, where the walls are worn by age and bullet holes, where people have broken shoes and are wearing just a few rags, there is applause. They shout and sing along with us.' But as the march passed through the more affluent city centre and today's tourist attractions: 'they look at us silently, questioning and dubious. Most of them don't understand.'[61] It was an indirect sign of the class divisions implicit in the very existence of the Resistance.

6
'Aldo says 26 for one'

From the beginning of 1945, all sides knew that within a few months the war would be over in Italy. Germany was now being invaded from both East and West. For the Allies, this meant a greater focus on how the new postwar Italy should come into being. For the fascists, it meant either a fight to the death or some kind of effort to ensure their own personal safety and wealth once the war had been lost. The situation was similar for German Nazis, although the final destiny for most of them would be played out in their homeland. For the Resistance, it meant preparing for the final push against the enemy, as well as jockeying for positions of influence in a postwar Italy.

The very decision to launch insurrections says a lot about the Resistance movement: they could have simply waited a few days or weeks for the Allies to arrive. The reason for this act of self-sacrifice was political: those who chose to rise up against fascism were collectively inoculating themselves against the risk of history repeating itself; similarly, the insurrections would remind the Allies that most Italians had always been democratic and anti-fascist. While there were deep tensions between the competing ideologies that co-existed uneasily within the Resistance, perhaps the rifts were even deeper within the major ideology of the movement, that of the communists. Disquiet had been building, particularly since Togliatti's return to Italy in March 1944 when it had become increasingly clear that the PCI was arguing for a 'self-limiting revolution' and was prepared to compromise with reactionary forces. In the heat of battle these disagreements were put to one side, and were avoided in party publications, but there is a weight of evidence pointing to widespread unease and wariness among ordinary and middle-ranking members.[1]

Nevertheless, the Communist Party still needed an insurrection for political reasons, although mobilising millions of working-class people to launch one was worrying for them. Any insurrection is a calculated risk since the outcome is not guaranteed beforehand. It was necessary to motivate and mobilise as many people as possible, and in large towns and cities that meant general strikes. In Reggio Emilia the local CLN produced a poster entitled 'Insurrectionary General Strike', which called on workers to 'defend factories from Germans and fascists. Workers battalions must move out from these centres of struggle.' Peasants were called upon 'to sweep the countryside clear of fascist bandits and occupy towns and villages'. Women had 'to fight by the side of your men for your family's safety, and so that in the future your children will never know fascist barbarity'. The manifesto concluded with the words: 'Death to the Germans – Death to the fascists'.

In the event of a successful insurrection, not only would participants feel immensely powerful, many of them would feel tempted to fight a 'class war' alongside a struggle for national liberation. After all, communists could only be expected to further the cause of communism, to want a society run initially by the working class, which would move towards the creation of a classless society. But the PCI's strategy clearly contradicted communist theory: it was now quite happy for its partisans to enter into alliance with the traditional 'class enemy'. And indeed industrialists had not been slow to take advantage of the PCI's position. From March 1943 onwards many factory managers began to face two ways at the same time: on the one hand they paid bribes to fascists to persuade them not to interfere with management policies, thus enabling them to distort the reality in their factories – both in their negotiations with the Germans, and in terms of their clandestine links with the Resistance. (As regards the Germans, many managers gave out names of known activists, while others feigned ignorance or invented excuses.) On the other hand, managers began to turn a blind eye to anti-fascist propaganda and military organisation within factories – often giving money to CLNs, and going so far as to warn activists of the imminent arrival of a fascist or Nazi round-up. In some cases, such as in the OM factory in Milan, the leaders of the factory CLN were also members of management.

The chemical company *Snia Viscosa*, located near the Yugoslav border, was another example. Franco Marinotti was both president of the company and mayor of the local town, and from this position of local dominance decided to finance all partisan brigades – both the communist brigades and the more moderate ones. Yet earlier in the war Marinotti's company had made extensive war profits, and worked very closely with the Nazis. In late October 1944 Marinotti, now playing the role of intermediary for the Allies, met General Harster, head of the Gestapo in Italy, to suggest a 'separate peace' that would benefit the two warring parties.[2] In general, industrialists had accepted that they had to work with the fascists and the Nazis, but as defeat became increasingly inevitable not only did they have to start thinking about their own track record, they also risked having their machinery stolen by the Germans – a further reason to cooperate with anti-fascists. Such close contacts could have a corrupting or compromising influence on younger and less experienced anti-fascist workers, as they were sometimes drawn into a close and non-antagonistic working relationship with management. The surprising thing was not that industrialists wanted to extricate themselves from recent alliances and bet on partisan horses, but that the partisans generally accepted their donations, rather than simply taking the money by force – something which happened sporadically, particularly in Piedmont. Despite the fact that partisans were fighting a bloody war to completely change society, none of the left organisations encouraged the creation of such a rupture between partisans and industrialists.

One of the clearest examples of a major firm's ducking and weaving comes from the country's most powerful company, FIAT. It first developed links with the forerunner of the CIA, the OSS, as early as October 1943, even as, in various FIAT factories, six different types of military vehicles were being produced or planned, including a tank, a bomber and a fighter plane. The company was literally being pulled in different directions, with managing director Vittorio Valletta called in by General Zimmermann on 1 December 1943 and accused of 'fomenting' his workers, at the same time as the firm agreed to build tanks according to German specifications and develop engine parts for V2 rockets. Meanwhile, the company was also giving money to moderate elements within the CLN in Rome, and deepening its links with the Vatican.[3] A substantial shift in the company's direction came about following owner Giovanni Agnelli's response to the March 1944 strikes. According to his biographer, Agnelli could now see 'the significant level of political consciousness and organisation of the labour movement. Alongside the more immediate objectives of opposition to the fascists and Germans, the principle of class struggle as the propulsive element in popular participation in the Resistance had clearly emerged during the strikes.'[4] Eventually, as the war continued and the partisan movement grew, Agnelli and other FIAT bosses such as Valletta were forced to assess their future. This was the background to approximately 55 million lire being handed over by FIAT to the Resistance during the winter of 1944–45.[5] Even here there was controversy: a local leader of the Action Party, Vittorio Foa, with support from the communists, proposed to refuse the regular payments of 50,000 lire being sent to the Piedmont CLN, but the motion failed to gain majority support.[6] Alongside the financial support was the fact that 700 workers were deported to Nazi Germany from the *Mirafiori* factory alone, with very few of them ever coming back.

The financing increased in the final months, particularly to those partisan groups operating near the outlying FIAT factories in Piedmont. Indeed once the amount of cash, petrol, transport, medical aid and other material help is added together, it is possible that FIAT financed the partisan movement to the tune of 500 million lire.[7] The leader of the *Mirafiori* CLN, however, was under no illusions about the purpose that lay behind such 'generosity':

> Agnelli and Valletta had understood in '44 that the war was lost. Both, but Valletta in particular, had no scruples about facing in several different directions at the same time to safeguard their primary interest: profit. I've never believed they had any real anti-fascist spirit, they were committed to safeguarding production whatever way the wind was blowing.[8]

The final link in the chain for FIAT was its connections with the Allies. Company bosses had held meetings in Switzerland with the head of US secret services, Allen Dulles, from late 1944. As will become clear in the following section, the arrival in Turin of Colonel John Stevens as leader of a permanent Allied mission to the Piedmont CLN was a further help to Agnelli. And indeed, one can only presume that the secret radio link between FIAT and the Allies installed in company offices helped to reduce the number of air raids against FIAT factories.[9]

SPRING COMES IN MANY COLOURS

Despite all the worries, compromises and divisions within the Resistance, the vast majority of forces all agreed that the decisive factor would be the liberation of the big northern cities. The first to be liberated was Bologna, where, as in many other cases, the ground had been thoroughly prepared. By the spring of 1945 the city was in the hands of the Resistance at night, with the fascists holed up in their barracks. On 16 April a group of women decided to organise a demonstration with placards demanding an end to the war, the surrender of fascists and the departure of the Germans. This was a risky enterprise, so partisans were ready on the pavement in case the women encountered any problems. As they marched down one of Bologna's main streets people opened their windows and applauded, and the numbers grew, reaching just over a thousand by the end, when a primary school teacher gave a speech. On the evening of 20 April partisans heard that the Germans were about to leave the city and immediately took over the main public buildings. Although fighting was brief, the Germans suffered 300 dead and 1,000 soldiers were taken prisoner. The Allies arrived the following day to find a democratic Bologna already functioning normally.[10]

Turin

Massimo Mila was a commissar of a Justice and Freedom division based in the mountains to the north of Turin. He wrote in his diary on 25 April:

> Things have kicked off in the valley floor: Castellamonte, Cuorgnè, Pont are burning like matchsticks in a row. Our divisions have divided them up and freed them with audacious and tough actions ... but now a new and far more important task awaits our men: the secret code has been transmitted – *Aldo says 26 for one*. That is: on the 26th at 1 a.m., carry out the first phase of the insurrectionary plan ... the paradise dreamt about for twenty long months is about to become real: Turin! ...
> Rapid rush to the valley bottom. Cuorgnè free and full of flags is an inebriating spectacle ... A quick look-in at home, no more than half an hour – get changed, fill your bag, greet your wife if you've got one. A quick hello so as not to let the emotion get to you, a kiss on the lovely face that smiles at you bravely: *ciao dear, keep your chin up, it'll be easy, a real doddle*.[11]

This was not romantic literary licence written decades later, it is highly representative of the partisan experience. Many fighters were based close to where they had grown up and had families, and cities like Turin and Genoa were very near to the mountains. What partisans had been dreaming about had been crystallised by sitting round campfires at night for months on end, looking down at the lights of their home towns and cities.

As Mila and his men moved slowly towards Turin they took the surrender of two German officers in the town of Rivarolo, who showed 'their amazement at the efficiency and seriousness which the partisan movement had suddenly demonstrated ... the penny dropped: all of this, therefore, had been created under their noses, and they knew nothing about it?'[12] In Turin itself a full dress rehearsal had been held the previous week. A general strike 'against hunger and terror' literally exploded on the night of 18–19 April with partisans coming down from the mountains and attacking road blocks and fascist barracks. City-based activists covered walls with huge slogans – 'Milk for children!' 'Fascists: Surrender or Die'. In the morning factories and shops were shut. There were no trains or trams, and telephones did not work. Senior PCI leader Giorgio Amendola had had a sleepless night; hearing gunshots coming from the outskirts, he decided to risk arrest and go out into the streets:

> at 10 a.m. we saw happy children racing out of a primary school shouting a new word they had learnt – 'Strike, Strike!'. Workers, often a majority of women, marched through the city carrying placards calling on fascists not to shoot but to surrender. Sometimes marchers were singing *Bandiera Rossa* [*Red Flag*, probably the most famous working-class song of the period], under the noses of the Germans. Democratic rallies were held in working-class areas. At one point an armoured car appeared near the front of a march and fired shots in the air; partisans immediately responded in kind and there was no further confrontation.[13]

Amendola then recounts the reports he received from middle-aged activists: 'They say they haven't seen such huge strikes since 1920, and state that back then you never had such widespread solidarity, of workers and office staff, technicians, schoolteachers, professionals, shopowners and even judges.' But the politics of the demonstration had to be nationalist and not communist, although as Amendola says of the singing of *Bandiera Rossa*: 'I wasn't at all upset given that it was a working-class area. But then I saw a comrade move to the front of the march and shortly afterwards they stopped singing *Bandiera Rossa* and struck up the national anthem.'[14]

The regime's response was verging on the surreal. Late on the 18th the Prefect had a poster put up around the city announcing the strike's failure: 'A tiny minority of Communists, paid by the enemy – and equally as guilty as their "criminal" bosses for the barbaric bombardments which several areas have suffered (having requested such bombardments), tried to create chaos in the city this morning.'[15] All the government had left was bombast.

A week later, word had come through to launch a definitive insurrection. One of the 2,000 women employed at *Mirafiori* recalls: 'we grouped all the workers together in the courtyard, the gates were shut and wouldn't open again until the insurrection was over, the factory was occupied ... and we said "We'll not hold anyone against their will, whoever wants to go home can go. For those who want to stay and fight, whatever will happen will happen."'[16] By mid-morning, Amendola recalls: 'Not only the working-class areas, but also the wide boulevards were patrolled by patriotic forces. But the partisans hadn't arrived.' Several messengers were sent out but no large columns arrived, and the situation started to become dangerous.[17]

What was happening? The previous evening hundreds of partisans had arrived on the city outskirts by 9 p.m. when their commanders received an order from the Turin high command: 'do not proceed to your objectives in the city without a specific order from the high command'.[18] This order was a forgery; it had come from the local British liaison officer, Colonel John Stevens, who had parachuted in the previous December to join the Resistance, but who had moved to a safe villa owned by the Agnelli family as the insurrection was about to start. His hostility to a large-scale insurrection, inevitably dominated by communists, had clearly emerged in meetings even before the final order was given – although it was often couched in more general military terms. Francesco Scotti, commander of the Garibaldi brigades throughout Piedmont remembers that:

> I tried to explain that we were not so militarily stupid as to not fill the streets of Turin with partisans and people. We had some very relevant experience: among other things I told him we had lived through the defence of Madrid, in which I had taken part, so he didn't need to worry about us not knowing how to launch an urban insurrection.[19]

In a gesture of compromise, Italian political parties had agreed that the number of partisans due to be moved into the city at H-Hour would be reduced from 8,000 to 3,000.[20] Given this compromise, and the negative intervention by Stevens, on the morning of the 26th Resistance forces were forced to confront the Germans on their own. Factories were an obvious target for the Nazis, partly out of the temptation to destroy or transport material away, and partly due to widespread awareness that they contained the greatest numbers of Resistance activists. Trenches had been dug in many courtyards, and steel girders served as barricades, while machine guns were placed on roofs. The fascists and the Germans, sensing an opportunity, attacked *Mirafiori* at 6 p.m., using three tanks and ten armoured cars. Although they penetrated the first defensive line, they were driven back with grenades, petrol bombs and machine guns, losing a tank and several armoured cars. A second German attack followed, which managed to get just a few feet from the doors to the factory shop floor: 'What are we going to do if they come in? The SAP commander orders that all armed workers, even if they've got a single pistol, must stay on the shop floor among the machinery. Eventually they'll have to get out of their tanks and when they do we'll kill the lot of them'.[21]

The attacks failed at the last minute. The Germans had also attacked at FIAT's SPA factory, but here workers had managed to build three rudimentary tanks with 75mm guns, and their emergence from the factory caused the enemy's immediate withdrawal. At around 9 p.m. three Tiger tanks attacked the *Lancia* factory, but were again repulsed with hand grenades and petrol bombs.[22] Meanwhile, there was fighting around all the strategic buildings in the city centre, particularly the railway station. However, it was not as if factories were separate from the rest of the city: groups of workers often left their factory to come to the aid of other partisans under heavy fire. Despite these reinforcements, during this first day of fighting the fascists regained control of a major newspaper, the police headquarters and the town hall.[23]

By the evening of the 26th the first partisan units started entering the city – their numbers and heavy weapons were desperately needed given that the Resistance inside was facing attacks from tanks and armoured cars. Larger numbers moved into the city on the morning of the 27th – the spoiling manoeuvre by Colonel Stevens had been recognised for what it was and commanders were now ignoring it. The city's main jail was seized and all political prisoners released. One new inmate was the fascist governor, who had held sway until just a couple of hours before liberation.[24]

The fact that the telephones were not working has provided a huge bonus for historians: the only way to coordinate the insurrection in such a large city was to send couriers with written messages – many of which have survived. So for example at 5 p.m. on 27 April the high command received a message from a factory where five workers died during the insurrection: 'FIAT *Ferriere*: the SAP garrison, fighting since 3 p.m. yesterday, was reinforced this morning by two lorry-loads of partisans. Two enemy tanks are circling and firing on the factory. We are resisting well but lack anti-tank weapons and are apparently now low on ammunition.'[25]

Workers at *Mirafiori* were overjoyed to see fresh forces – they had been under constant attack for nearly 48 hours. Vittorio Valletta had rashly decided to stay inside the factory, almost the last decision he ever took, as the head of the *Mirafiori* CLN recounts: 'Valletta expressed his desire to go and pay his respects to two of our fallen. We gave him permission but in the corridor that led to the mortuary some partisans raised their machine guns to shoot him. We stopped them and probably saved his life.'[26]

Figure 6.1   The fight to defend and liberate FIAT's *Ferriere* factory in Turin, where five workers died.

Fighting still continued elsewhere, with Germans and fascists controlling large areas of the city centre. But by the early morning of 28 April it was clear that the battle had been won. Overnight some fascists had disappeared from the city centre using a secret tunnel, while a major German armoured force had broken out from partisan encirclement and headed off northwards. The next two to three days were full of tension: there were many fascist snipers throughout the city, and to the west German forces continued to demand free passage through Turin, threatening that otherwise they would bombard the city. All told, the Resistance suffered around 320 deaths in five to six days of fighting. Nevertheless, when the Allies finally arrived on 2 May they found a major city with electricity, transport, and a democratic council in full control.

Meanwhile, other events were taking place which were even more sobering for the future. On 24 April leading partisans of the Justice and Freedom Third Division arrived from the Langhe area at a very spacious villa in *via Giacosa*, in one of the city's most exclusive areas. The group's commander, Alberto Bianco, had led a sizeable force up in the mountains for nearly two years, and his men now installed their division headquarters on the first floor of the villa and stayed there for several days as fighting raged in the city. The villa was the home of FIAT boss Giovanni Agnelli, who remained there living on the ground floor. Revealingly, the partisans were not there to arrest Agnelli or to stop him from escaping, they were there to protect him.[27] While fascist snipers were still shooting at people in the streets, Giorgio Amendola went to give a speech at FIAT's largest factory, *Mirafiori*. He remembers he spoke in a very large canteen:

I brought them the news that the 'collaborator' Valletta was on the list [of those] that the Piedmont CLN had sentenced to death. Partisan forces were charged with arresting him and ensuring that the sentence was carried out (huge applause). Today this factory, which is part of the nation's heritage, is entrusted to you, to be managed by yourselves and the factory CLN.

Valletta was now in hiding, but was soon discovered by partisans in a villa along with Colonel Stevens, who waved a document stating that Valletta was now under the protection of the British army, due to his 'meritorious commitment to the Allied cause'.[28]

Milan

Compared to the fraught moments in Turin and the extensive fighting in Genoa, Milan saw the smoothest move to liberation of the three cities forming the 'industrial triangle'. Events began to unfold on 23 April, with railway workers declaring an indefinite strike. The following day GAP groups began to launch insurrectionary actions, attacking fascist barracks in open daylight, with many other minor actions occurring throughout the city. At this stage, individual parties were sometimes issuing verbal orders, which did not have much overall impact. The key event was the unitary insurrectionary committee ordering the uprising to begin at 2 p.m. on 25 April.[29]

By early afternoon factories in the working-class strongholds of Sesto San Giovanni and Porta Romana were under armed occupation. Workers were forced to abandon the *Pirelli* factory in the former suburb following an attack by German tanks, whereas the OM factory in the latter area resisted four hours of attacks from an armoured train. As with Turin, the factories became the organising centres for the Resistance.

Late in the afternoon, Mussolini met with Resistance leaders at the archbishop's palace in an attempt to negotiate favourable terms for a surrender, but since he was only offered unconditional surrender he stormed out of the meeting. He descended a flight of stairs just as Sandro Pertini was coming up. Pertini recognised his old colleague from the Socialist Party, whose government since then had given him six jail sentences for anti-fascism. Their passing was highly symbolic – Mussolini was about to become history while Pertini was destined to continue a long and illustrious political career, culminating in his period as head of state from 1978 to 1985.

By the evening the main public buildings were being occupied, as were the main radio station, newspaper offices and military barracks. The printing presses were immediately commandeered to produce huge press runs of the PCI, PSI and Action Party dailies.[30] Perhaps the flight of Mussolini and other fascist leaders had quickly demoralised the remaining fascists. Fighting continued the following day throughout the city, but with no focal points or large losses. At 9 a.m. the main radio station began broadcasting under partisan control. By the evening of the 26th liberation was practically complete, becoming clear to all on the morning of 27 April. Losses in Milan were far smaller than in Turin, only around 30 dead and 100 wounded,[31] even though the insurrection in Milan had always been potentially more risky, being relatively distant from the mountain areas, from where large numbers of partisans were due to arrive.

Indeed it was only at 5 p.m. on 27 April that 600 partisans of the 'Gramsci' Garibaldi division arrived near Porta Ticinese from the Oltrepò Pavese area, more than 48 hours after the insurrection had begun. General Cadorna, the Liberty Volunteers Corps (CVL) commander, was there to meet them, along with Luigi Longo, CVL deputy commander and commander general of the Garibaldi brigades.

The day after, at 1 p.m., Cino Moscatelli's Garibaldi brigades finally arrived in Milan and were met in *viale Certosa* by Longo and Secchia. Their arrival was later than expected, due to stiff German resistance on their way down from the mountains. Above them flew a captured German fighter – with 'Valsesia' (the area where these brigades were based) written on the underside of its wings – dropping welcoming leaflets down on the people filling the streets. Moscatelli's column was preceded by seven captured tanks. People were thronging the streets to celebrate, curious to see the legendary Moscatelli. Mothers offered up their children to the partisans for a hug. Moscatelli smiled at the crowds, but mumbled to his men on the open-top car: 'keep your eyes on the windows', as there were still some active snipers about. The column took four hours to crawl the seven miles to *piazza del Duomo*, the city's main square.[32]

Pietro Secchia, riding on Moscatelli's car, had spent over a decade in fascist jails and had probably been the most efficient military organiser of the entire Resistance: 'There were no longer any distinctions – workers, students, clerks, professionals – they were united by a single emotion. There was not a face that did not express joy, not a voice that didn't shout out in enthusiasm. The people of Milan felt that this was their army.'[33]

It was only on the following day that the first Allied troops arrived.

Genoa

In the lead up to the insurrection in Genoa there were about 30,000 German troops in the area, about half in the city itself, with many pieces of heavy artillery on the overlooking hills. The partisans had about 4,000 to 5,000 fighters in the hills and mountains, and 3,000 in the city itself – but most of these were armed with just handguns.

As with the other cities, the Allies did not want a mass insurrection. Major Basil Davidson, deputy commander of the 'Clover' mission to the Ligurian CLN, had spelt things out during a meeting in February: urban partisans should engage only in acts of anti-sabotage to save industry and infrastructures; and large numbers of partisans should not come down from the mountains into the city.[34]

As happened elsewhere, the CLN listened politely and pretended to agree, at least half way. Events began to move very rapidly when on 23 April the local military high command of the Resistance called for an immediate general strike. On the same day General Gunther Meinhold offered to leave the port and local industry untouched, if his troops were allowed to withdraw peacefully. Meinhold's offer had nothing to do with ending the war; he was under orders to withdraw to the river Po as part of a planned new general defensive line; and indeed, what precipitated events was the departure of a significant number of German and fascist columns from the city.

When Meinhold put his conditions to Archbishop Siri he was sure that his offer, which included the local clergy guaranteeing a four-day truce while the Germans evacuated, would be accepted by the CLN. It was not. But to stop the German withdrawal the partisans had to react immediately, and that meant the 3,000 fighters in the city moving straight away on their own, and with only light weapons. What haunted their thoughts was the tragic resistance of the Warsaw ghetto, when the Russian army did not intervene to stop massive German reprisals. The same night an emissary of General Meinhold, a Lieutenant Uthec, came to meet the commanders of a Garibaldi division in the mountains near Genoa and asked them to allow German forces to withdraw peacefully to the north. One partisan commander answered: 'Do you really think we've gone through so many months of war, enduring so many sacrifices and deaths, to just let you escape unharmed?'[35]

That night in Genoa the Resistance launched several attacks, particularly in the port area, as well as freeing political prisoners from the main city jail. The police headquarters, the town hall and the city's main newspaper were all occupied.[36] In addition, five suburban train stations and some major factories were seized.[37] But the insurrection in Genoa would not be characterised by large concentrations of workers in factories. A PCI questionnaire from earlier in the year had reported: 'In our province [of Genoa] there are 100 large and medium factories, including the port. From the figure of 60,000 workers employed in 100 factories cited, today, due to decentralisation, round-ups, sackings and bombings, this number has fallen to about 25,000 workers.'[38]

After arguing all night, at dawn on 24 April the CLN agreed by a majority vote to proclaim an insurrection, and further fighting broke out early in the morning. As the Germans tried to form more columns and leave the city partisan groups repeatedly attacked, forcing them to withdraw back into their well-defended barracks. Fighting began in the docks, where partisans came under fire from SS squads as they tried to stop the destruction of ships and equipment. One advantage the Resistance had was that the general strike had begun on the morning of 24 April, hence all rail traffic was stopped, partly due to the strikes but also due to the electricity being cut off and the sabotage of steam trains.[39] If they could not destroy the Nazis the partisans could at least paralyse their forces and immobilise them. All telephone, water and electricity supplies were cut off to where the Germans were stationed.

The city's CLN issued a manifesto calling on people to arm themselves, and more arms were obtained after several fascist barracks had been stormed.[40] Crucially by now ordinary people were spontaneously joining organised partisan squads. Keen to get out of the city and back to Germany, a German colonel came to negotiate with Secondo Pessi and others members of the local CLN:

Colonel: I want to ask under what conditions I will be allowed to reach Giovi with my troops.
Pessi: You must surrender unconditionally – we'll give you a cast iron guarantee that you will be treated as prisoners of war.
Colonel: We're still able to destroy entire neighbourhoods and industrial plants.
Pessi: If the Germans were to commit further hostile acts against the city they will be considered war criminals, and as such executed immediately.
Colonel: (He complains that the local population has risen, and that he has no escape route.)
Pessi: The Germans have one escape route: surrender unconditionally.
Colonel: Are the partisans coming down from the mountains communists or supporters of Badoglio?
Pessi: They are freedom fighters.
Colonel: Do the partisans with the red neckscarves belong to the communist or socialist formations?
Pessi: The red neckscarf is the symbol of the Garibaldi brigades.

Colonel: I will try to contact my headquarters and explain to them the danger we're in.

Pessi: Given the operations currently under way, we cannot even promise you a phone link with your headquarters.

Colonel: I will speak to my men immediately. But as is natural, first I would like to talk to my commanding officer.

Pessi: It cannot be ruled out that tonight partisans will attack your position in *via Francesco Pozzo*.

Colonel: But I can't make a decision, I'm not a senior officer.

Pessi: There aren't any more senior officers. Berlin has fallen to the Soviet army.[41]

Through the archbishop, General Meinhold again threatened to bomb the city with their heavy artillery, but once more the CLN answered that if that happened then the thousand-plus Germans already in their custody, and those soon to be captured, would be executed. The Nazis' threats were starting to amount to bluster in any event, as from that afternoon and into the evening partisan brigades from the mountains were attacking artillery positions overlooking the city.[42] The CLN's steadfastness was not only a tactical decision: if the Germans withdrew quickly enough they could easily reach Turin or Milan and try to stop the uprisings there.

Back in the streets, after one night and one day's fighting, the docks were still controlled by the SS and fascists, the city centre was being fought over by fascists and anti-fascists, and heavy German weaponry controlled the outskirts of the city. The Allies were down the coast in La Spezia, nearly a hundred miles away, and between the two cities there were many mountains, and Germans. But by the morning of 25 April it was clear that insurrection had been successful. Fascists surrendered in the port, and partisan groups from the mountains, after marching for most of the night, had begun entering the city by the evening, forcing the surrender of outlying German positions, including artillery emplacements, along the way. All main roads out of the city were now controlled by partisans.

The Resistance had also conquered a radio station, which immediately started broadcasting to the people. The key to their strength was that the Resistance had the support of tens of thousands of Genoese – many of the actions that had taken place in the city were mass actions. The Germans in the city were trapped. After two nights and two days of fighting General Meinhold scuttled over to the Archbishop's palace, where at 7.30 p.m. on 25 April he signed a surrender document with an almost emaciated man in civilian clothes, a communist worker named Remo Scappini. An army of 10,000 Germans surrendered, and the city was saved.

Nevertheless, Hitler's own orders had been 'to die at your post', and to kill those who wanted to surrender. This ensured continued German resistance the following day, led by fanatical Nazis, with hundreds being killed in the last desperate attempt to break out of the city. But by the evening the city was essentially completely dominated by the Resistance. All told, 6,000 Germans and fascists were taken prisoner in the city, and 12,000 in nearby mountains, while the Resistance suffered between 187 and 400 dead and between 850 and 3,000 wounded.[44] Overall, partisans managed to defuse 219 bombs and mines planted in what was one of the Mediterranean's main ports.[43] The first Allied forces arrived in the city at 1 p.m. on 27 April and found all public services fully operational.

ALL THAT GLITTERS IS NOT GOLD

Many Resistance fighters were openly worried about the new Italy that was soon to be created. In May 1945 a Justice and Freedom partisan division wrote an article entitled 'Before we split up', full of pregnant warnings:

We're simply going to go back home, after twenty months of struggle and longing: we will find the warmth of a family's welcome, we'll see our blessed mothers have grown older. Read – study political problems in newspapers – these problems are our very interests, our well-being, our lives. Study in a serious fashion, not the form and the hot air but the thought behind things ... Mistrust politicians: those who want to earn a living from politics are above all layabouts, and they're always money-grubbing. Politics is what you do once the working day is over.[45]

Given the corruption that has characterised much postwar Italian politics, these views were remarkably accurate in their predictions. A month earlier, another Justice and Freedom bulletin had expressed similar views:

We can see from a thousand signals that reactionary forces are not dead; around us we can feel regret at the loss of big parades, rhetoric, big business and all that goes with it. If we could read the minds of many generals, police chiefs and industrialists we'd often come across the word fascism. It is up to us to eradicate these forces.[46]

Even Luigi Fiori, who came from a very traditional background and was a commander of a moderate partisan brigade, had his doubts:

About March I started to notice fascist soldiers coming up, unarmed, without uniforms – they wanted to join up. ... I sent them off to HQ, but I was amazed to learn they signed them up and gave them weapons. All of this may not have been a bad thing in some ways – but we had been a school of democracy for 20 months, talking and talking until gone midnight, changing our views radically – this lot had hardly changed at all. What are they going to do upon Liberation, with weapons, I wondered? Maybe I was being a bit too harsh, because I was the only one to act like this.[47]

Indeed such was Fiori's unease that he decided not to leave the mountains, but let his men go down and liberate Parma.

Figure 6.2   The liberation of Genoa. A partisan lorry drives down the city's main street.

The tension contained in all these statements was characteristic of all left-wing partisans to varying degrees, but particularly of the Justice and Freedom organisations, who were not affiliated to large left-wing parties and were therefore more likely to be cut out of any division of the spoils. What was about to happen on a deeper level was a fundamental settlement of Italian society and politics after the uncertainties, tragedies, expectations and hopes that had dominated the last two years. Claudio Pavone, a Justice and Freedom partisan himself, and decades later author of one of the most influential books on the Resistance, has said of April 1945: 'in fact what took place was not only the demobilisation of armed partisans, but of all "Resistance society", which entered into "political society" only in a minimal fashion'. And he continues: 'The burying of the machine gun becomes the symbol of the covering over of a road towards the future, a road which could still have been trod.'[48]

Indeed most history books reflect this shift. Nearly all end their story in April 1945. Those which do cover a longer time-span tend to mention the mass movements and hopes for a new society that emerged during the campaign for the first general election in spring 1948. It is as if the partisans went into hibernation for three years – though obviously they did not. The story that some people want to tell, far more familiar today, is that politics is just about elections. But the postwar history of the partisans is just like their wartime history: the story of a mass movement dedicated to effecting a generalised radical change in society, not merely to election campaigns aimed at securing a specific parliamentary majority.

7
Postwar Partisan Activity

Rosa Cantoni finally reached her home town of Udine late in the evening on 27 October 1945. The war had ended six months earlier, but Rosa had no idea what had happened to her family and friends because she had been in Germany. Like tens of thousands of other Italian women Rosa had taken an active part in the Resistance; she had been arrested in January and sent to Germany in a cattle truck. She had survived the horrors of Italian fascism, the height of Nazi barbarity in Buchenwald and Ravensbruck concentration camps, and was now finally home in liberated Italy:

> the last tram arrived. I recognised the driver, an oldish man, I knew he had been a fascist. I told him I didn't have any money to buy a ticket because I had just got back from Germany: he told me he didn't let people travel 'for free'. Then I said I wasn't getting off, and that he could try and chuck me off if he wanted. There was only one other passenger: he told the driver he should be ashamed of himself and threw him the money for my ticket. It wasn't the best of beginnings.[1]

This little vignette is quite emblematic. It shows the sense of confidence and defiance of a young woman, gained during the Resistance. But it also illustrates that in a democratic Italy active fascists did not have much to worry about. While the behaviour of the tram driver above may not have been epoch-making, the important thing to remember is that thousands of influential state officials remained in their jobs, working side by side with each other, often for the next 30 years.

WHY PARTISANS WERE ANGRY

Whatever their walk of life, partisans were generally confronted by quite a desolate scene once they arrived back home. For those who had been industrial workers, or became so after April 1945, they found that the factory bosses were still the same managers who had collaborated with the fascists and Germans, had informed on anti-fascists, and had often made a lot of money out of the war. The same was true in many a large office or agricultural enterprise. Very few managers were punished, hence there was a tendency to assassinate some of them. 'Purging' of the state apparatus was extremely limited in Italy. It was greater in France, where the number of politically-inspired killings after 1945 was almost double. Similarly, many other European countries inflicted comparatively much harsher prison sentences as well as death. Belgium probably experienced the highest proportion of postwar violence against fascists, with Italy experiencing the lowest. Here purging of fascists from public positions occurred at the same rate as in Luxemburg.[2]

Economic sanctions were also more severe outside of Italy: in France, the largest car producer, Renault, was nationalised, in part because of its collaboration with the Nazis; a similar reason lay behind the fate of Gnome-Rhone, the country's largest manufacturer of jet engines. In Germany, Volkswagen was taken out of private hands, as were the major chemical, electrical engineering and car manufacturers in Austria.[3]

The purging of certain notorious individuals from the Italian state apparatus was initiated by the Allies in the far south in late 1943 – with 360 out of 518 mayors in Calabria and Lucania being sacked – but the whole project ran out of steam once conservatives had time to regroup.[4] As we shall see, there was little change in northern areas, where violence organised by the fascist government had been far worse and lasted longer.

Clearly then, the majority of partisans did not get what they wanted after April 1945; the leaders of the PCI in particular did not intend to create the kind of society their followers wanted. Communist partisans, the largest section of the movement, did not see Italy move even close to becoming a communist society. For example, in late May the Action Party made the modest proposal for a national assembly of CLN delegates, which was rejected by the PCI.[5] But the disquiet and frustration were not necessarily only ideological. On a simplistic level, some 'men of action' missed the thrill and sense of power that comes with armed action. Yet most felt frustration that fascists were still walking the streets unpunished, and that surviving partisans and above all their fallen comrades had gone through hell almost for nothing. Furthermore, there was a sense of humiliation in having to endure the indignities of unemployment or of petty tyranny in workplaces – the society the partisans had fought to create was rapidly becoming a distant dream.

As the political coalition that had lasted throughout the Resistance inevitably fell apart, the growing political tension in Italian society meant that any organised action or revolt by ex-partisans – for better or for worse – carried great political importance. The conservative parties could point to partisan rebellions (on which more later) and argue that partisans had gone beyond the boundaries of acceptable behaviour, as they had frequently done during the Resistance. One of the pressure points for partisans in the new democratic Italy was the fact that many were facing a variety of economic and legal difficulties due to their wartime activities.

Economic Pressures

The whole country suffered hunger and rationing after liberation. Strikes quickly became very frequent, including that of the 140,000 workers in the province of Varese who took action on 2 October 1945 against the reduction in the daily bread ration from 325 to 200 grams.[6] Partisans had been promised positions in the army and the police if they wanted them, as well as help to find work back in civilian life. At a meeting of the Piedmont provisional regional government on 2 May, Colonel John Stevens said: 'after the battles they have fought in recent months, it's not just a question of taking weapons off partisans but of getting them back into civilian employment, obviously giving them precedence over others'.[7]

But none of these promises were kept: partisans who joined the police were soon put under pressure to resign, ordered to transfer to obscure parts of the country, or otherwise called upon to repress workers or peasants. The help promised for people to get a job in industry 'was turned into [political] monitoring within factories and the sacking of those who had saved factories'.[8] In the far north of Italy, partisan commander Pippo Coppo called for his men to demobilise in April–May 1945, but in his division of 1,200 men it was difficult for everyone to go back to a normal civilian life: 'We tried our best – some in the police, others with a bit of partisan booty (military lorries) set up some transportation cooperatives, others like me started work straight away.'[9] But many partisans could not find work. As a result, large numbers of those who had fought terribly hard for two years were often left unemployed, their demands for a public sector job from the new democratic government as a result of their sacrifices were in vain. Many faced poverty and unemployment, whilst ex-fascist bosses and bureaucrats carried on without any penalties.

Levels of unemployment and poverty grew throughout 1946. In July, shop stewards in Turin organised a general strike. In August there was a battle in Caccamo in Sicily over government requisition of wheat – 3,000 peasants fought against 600 police, leaving twelve killed and 100 wounded.[10] In October Roman building workers threatened with the sack invaded the prime minister's office; in subsequent clashes two people died and 150 were wounded.

Those partisans who did have jobs were not satisfied either; given the level of class consciousness that existed, they wanted big changes, as the prefect of Varese wrote to Rome on 5 October 1946: 'the mass of workers, who tend to escape the control of parties and trade unions, are showing signs of impatience due to the high cost of living, and the delay in beginning the public works programme announced to alleviate unemployment'.[11]

POLITICAL VIOLENCE AFTER LIBERATION

Rome was hot on the morning of 18 September 1944. It was even hotter in the crowded courthouse, where a man named Pietro Caruso was on trial. At the beginning of that year, one of Caruso's first acts upon becoming police chief was to order the arrest of all Jews in Rome.[12] In March, following a partisan attack, he had played a central role in providing the Germans with 335 prisoners selected indiscriminately from Roman jails, who were then killed by the Nazis in a mass reprisal at the Fosse Ardeatine, to the south of the city.

Many of the relatives of those executed wanted to follow the trial, in a city which had been liberated just three months earlier. Such was the prominence of this massacre, that the film director Luchino Visconti was given permission to film the proceedings. However, before the trial started the judge cancelled the hearing due to the number of people jamming the courtroom. The crowd became angry, and one of them suddenly recognised another man, Donato Carretta. Incredibly, Carretta had decided to come to the hearing, a totally foolhardy move given the fact he had been the governor of Rome's main jail, Regina Coeli, during the German occupation. The crowd quickly learnt of his presence and exploded with rage; overcoming police and court ushers they dragged him out of the building, punching and kicking him. He was then thrown in the nearby Tiber, where he drowned. His body was taken in an angry procession to his old jail, tied to a railing, and left bloody and dishevelled for an hour.[13]

Also in Rome, just before midday on 3 June 1946, Costanza Astrologo was walking through *piazza Sant'Ambrogio* when she suddenly recognised another woman, named D'Orazio, whom she immediately started to hit, drawing blood with her blows. Other people joined in the attack, making moves to lynch the woman, before the police arrived in time to arrest her. The attackers were Jewish, and had recognised D'Orazio as the fascist spy who reported them to the Germans, who had then transported them to concentration camps.[14] Of the 1,024 Jews deported from Rome, just 17 survived.

A few basic facts need stressing due to the growing influence of 'revisionist' historians: the fascist regime rounded up Italy's 40,000 Jews and transported between 6,000 and 8,000 to their death in Germany. A recent estimate has been made that between 1938 and 1945 the Italian government robbed Italian Jews of property worth $800 million at 2001 prices.[15] Even before the fall of Mussolini and the Nazi invasion, the fascist government had ordered the building of four internment camps for Jews.[16] These preparations were clearly central to the four internment camps built by the Germans later in 1943, as transit centres for the death camps. But Mussolini's government had already set up 50 internment camps in 1940, holding mainly anti-fascists, but also gypsies, foreign nationals, Slovenes and Croats. Up to 30,000 from the latter two groups were imprisoned, with several thousand dying of hunger and disease.[17] Furthermore, nearly 5,000 Jews, Slovenes, Croats, communists and Roma were also murdered in the gas chambers or by firing squads in the Italian concentration camp at Risiera di San Sabba, on the outskirts of Trieste. Another 25,000 people left the camp alive, only to be taken to Auschwitz, Buchenwald and Dachau.

For Jews, the relatives of those massacred by Nazis or fascists, and many other groups in society, 20 years of fascism and nearly two years of Nazi occupation had created an intense thirst for justice. The anger of these victims did not, however, derive from mass hysteria, but from a fully rational political calculation that justice was unlikely to be achieved in the courts. And as we shall see, in these early postwar years most arrests and convictions for violence during the Resistance period involved prosecuting anti-fascists and partisans, thereby adding insult to injury.

As a result, acts of political violence occurred in every walk of life. In factories summary justice was sometimes meted out, such as at *Magneti*

Marelli in Milan, where three managers were killed between liberation and the arrival of the Allies.[18] Generally though, there are only vague passing references to partisans carrying out executions in documents dating from the first days and weeks following liberation – the details are deliberately left hazy. Most of this anti-fascist political violence took place in northern and central Italy, particularly in Emilia, and there is a very simple explanation for this. If one superimposes three maps together – one showing fascist mass violence during its rise to power in 1920–22, another showing the areas of fascist and Nazi massacres and sustained violence in 1943–45, and a third illustrating anti-fascist violence in the immediate postwar years – the areas involved in the latter map will largely mirror the areas which suffered political violence in the first two.[19]

Nevertheless, the most well-known example of violence in late April 1945 was the execution of Benito Mussolini, his mistress Claretta Petacci and other fascist leaders. Mussolini had fled Milan on 25 April, and disguised as a German soldier had been captured by a partisan group on the morning of 27 April close to the Swiss border, with the news reaching Milan at 8.30 that evening. The following day two men representing the military high command of the Resistance arrived from Milan to confirm that two days before Mussolini's capture the CLNAI had passed the death sentence against fascist leaders who had not surrendered. Meanwhile in Milan, Allied HQ had cabled the CLNAI: 'Allied command immediately wants presumed location Mussolini ... it is ordered that he is held for immediate handover to Allied command'.[20] Anticipating such a reaction, as this telegram and others arrived, the squad from Milan decided to execute Mussolini and other members of his entourage.

One member of the group sent to the Swiss border was Aldo Lampredi, who had spent several years in fascist jails and had fought in the Spanish Civil War. Although he was acting for the whole high command, he could not stop himself from saying to Mussolini seconds before he shot him: 'Who would have said that Communists, who you persecuted for so long, would settle their accounts with you?'[21] On the road back to Milan, after loading up a truck with the bodies of Mussolini and 15 other fascist leaders who had been executed nearby, Lampredi suggested they all be taken to *piazzale Loreto*. The rest of the group agreed, and the bodies were dumped there at about 3 a.m. on 29 April.[22] At about the same time the CLNAI released a communiqué written by Sandro Pertini, signed by all parties including the Christian Democrats, which stated:

> the execution of Mussolini and his accomplices is the necessary conclusion of an historical period which leaves our country covered in rubble ... Only by making this clean break from a shameful and criminal past can the Italian people be sure that the CLNAI has decided to firmly embark upon the road of the country's democratic renewal.[23]

As the news spread and people came to see the bodies, a mood of rage and euphoria quickly developed. Such was the size and fury of the crowd, kicking and spitting at Mussolini and the others, that the corpses were hung up from a petrol station to avoid the situation totally getting out of control. Pertini was unhappy when he heard the news, but communist leader Luigi Longo approved: 'not out of sadism, but so it could be clear to everyone – in a very obvious fashion – that justice had been done. I think further bloodshed and vendettas were avoided by showing that the main people responsible for fascism had been executed.'[24] Charles Poletti, who had been nominated Allied governor of Lombardy, had just arrived in the city: 'We went for a walk round Milan. We saw order and discipline, and we also went to *piazzale Loreto*. We would like to express our satisfaction to the CLNAI and the partisans for the magnificent work they have done, we are glad to be here.'[25]

Figure 7.1   Mussolini, his mistress and other fascist leaders were executed near the Swiss border on 28 April 1945 and their bodies were taken to *piazzale Loreto* in Milan. Claretta Petacci can be identified by her skirt, Mussolini is to her left. Credit: Publifoto Milan.

By today's standards, the scenes in *piazzale Loreto* were highly undignified, but there were concrete reasons for the popular anger, and the choice of the location was far from arbitrary. The previous August partisans in Milan had attempted to bomb a German lorry, and although just one soldier was wounded, the SS ordered the Italian authorities to select 15 prisoners at random from jails, who were executed by the fascist militia, their bodies left lying in *piazzale Loreto* for 24 hours. The head of provincial government wrote to Mussolini on that very day: 'the pile of dead bodies was shocking beyond all description because the bodies were strewn about, full of blood and terrible wounds. Women were terrified and fainted, it was clear that everyone was filled with horror and disgust.'[26] Many workers on their way to factories saw the bodies, as did commuters coming into the city to what was a transport hub at the time. Many of their relatives came and saw their loved ones lying in a heap, but they could not remove them due to a fascist military guard which openly boasted about their actions, with one soldier saying to another: 'See? There's no need for the Germans to get rid of subversives, we can do it!' One woman, clearly a supporter of the fascists, cleaned her shoes on the dead bodies with a defiant air. Such was the brutality of the fascists that they even shot at the dead bodies again during the day. Six of the 15 worked in factories in the industrial suburb of Sesto San Giovanni, and such was the sense of outrage that many Milan factories went on strike the following day.[27] Mussolini commented prophetically when he heard the news: 'We will pay a very high price for the blood in *piazzale Loreto*.'[28]

Figure 7.2   Fifteen prisoners were killed and left in a main square of Milan, *piazzale Loreto*, for a whole day in August 1944. Credit: Bundesarchiv, Koblenz.

One other strong contributory factor that should not be overlooked in this period was the violence of democratic state institutions. Even before full liberation, government forces were committing what can only be described as massacres in the South. For example when council workers went on strike in Palermo in October 1944 against abuses in the rationing system, troops began firing and throwing hand grenades into the crowd, killing 30 and wounding 150.[29] The fact that there was considerable political violence after April 1945 should therefore surprise nobody. After a brutal dictatorship lasting 20 years, and a virtual civil war in the centre and the North, it is close to ludicrous to expect the violence to have suddenly stopped on a single day. Thousands of people had endured their loved ones spending long periods in prison and possibly dying there, or being beaten up and dying from their wounds, or simply being killed in massacres. Then there were the lesser but more common problems of suffering daily humiliation and abuse from fascists. With the fall of fascism, and the fact that it had been defeated by the Italian people, it is not surprising that the idea of 'do-it-yourself justice' was fairly widespread. However, it is also important not to exaggerate the scale of the killing: most reliable accounts suggest a maximum national figure of not more than 8–10,000 people killed, the vast majority between April and June 1945.

It is also essential to try to make a distinction between personal or popular justice, and partisan or political justice. As one historian has argued: 'The line between the emotional and political killing is a very difficult one to trace.'[30] Some people were killed, wounded or beaten up by ordinary people for 'emotional' or 'personal' reasons. Other people who were killed were attacked by organised groups of people, or alternatively individuals who in one way or another identified with a collective organisation. Yet because both acts risked being classified as illegal, many attacks, particularly assassinations involving a collective element, were largely carried out anonymously. Some historians in recent years, driven by a zeal to attack the Resistance, have failed to distinguish between these two categories. As another historian has written: 'It is strange that one could believe today that if somebody killed their neighbour because he had tortured their son or raped their wife, that Palmiro Togliatti or Pietro Secchia were responsible – or the partisans in general.'[31]

LEGAL ATTACKS AGAINST PARTISANS

Following on from an amnesty concerning partisan violence enacted in 1944 under the Allied government, in July 1946 Communist Party leader and now Minister of Justice Palmiro Togliatti passed another amnesty in which civil-war type actions, or in other words, acts of political violence, were depenalised up to 31 July 1945. Obviously this meant that anti-fascists who had killed fascists from 1 August onwards were liable to prosecution.[32]

One feature of the amnesty that enraged partisans was its effective decriminalising of those found guilty of 'ordinary torture', while only those convicted of 'tortures of a particularly atrocious nature' generally faced some kind of punishment. But due to the mentality of many members of the judiciary, shocking crimes frequently went unpunished. One notorious case involved the acquittal of seven fascists who had raped a female partisan, then knifed her to death before impaling her naked body in a vineyard. The judges found the first act to be rape not torture, the use of the knives was then defined as 'ordinary' killing rather than something 'particularly atrocious', and impalement was deemed merely an insult to the woman's body, given that she was already dead.[33] In a similar verdict, a fascist militia captain was held to fall under the amnesty because the repeated rape by his men of a bound and blindfolded female partisan 'did not constitute torture but only the highest possible offence to the woman's honour and decency'.[34]

As with any law, this amnesty was being applied by judges and magistrates. Leaving aside the intrinsic conservative traditions of the Italian judiciary of this period, the simple fact was that many judges were reactionaries, if not fascists, and had been allowed to stay at their posts. As one historian has argued: 'They had moved ahead in their careers during the twenty-year period of fascism and they had attained the highest posts in the judicial administration as a result of meritorious service during the dictatorship.'[35] There are many shameful examples, but to mention just two: Giuseppe Azzariti was president of the racist 'Tribunal of the Race' from 1938 to 1943, before becoming a member of the first postwar Constitutional Court and working closely with Togliatti during his period as Justice Minister. When Togliatti was asked about Azzariti's past he commented: 'I don't care, I need someone good at carrying out orders, not a politician.' During the years 1943–45, Luigi Oggioni was president of the fascist Appeal Court in Brescia, an area of high partisan activity, only to become in later years president of the national Court of Appeal; he remained in this most prestigious judicial position in the legal system until 1962, and was also a member of the Constitutional Court.[36]

What emerges is the essential lack of fundamental change within all institutions despite liberation – the continuity of state offices remained largely intact. Therefore judges felt free to express a kind of caste or class solidarity by refusing 'to enforce sanctions issued against civil servants and administrators who had served under the same regime. To enforce those sanctions would have meant bringing their own roles into question and punishing themselves.'[37] Furthermore, these judges were operating at the height of the Cold War, with intense political accusations being thrown from one extreme of the political spectrum to the other. Many judges began to use legal loopholes to launch a campaign against partisan actions, strengthened by the fact that amnesties did not necessarily invalidate previous laws, and in the early postwar years judges had mainly fascist criminal codes and public security laws to apply. So those hostile to the Resistance made use of these laws, often those relating to lesser crimes. For example, magistrates would sometimes order the exhuming of fascists executed by partisan firing squads, and if personal jewellery was not found on the body, try to mount a case for theft. Another common accusation was that partisans had stolen or looted goods from the local population. In some cases, partisan execution of spies was treated as premeditated murder, and imprisonment by partisan groups was viewed as kidnapping.[38] Although most of the early cases brought against partisans led to acquittals, it is easy to imagine the mood this created among them. As one recalls: 'when Scelba [the Minister of the Interior] started to free fascists and put partisans in jail, all the partisans from Veneto had a demonstration in which we burnt the Alexander award, which had been given to all partisans.'[39]

To look at some cases: in May 1947 a Turin court brought partisans to trial for robberies committed between July 1944 and March 1945, using evidence from SS police of the time, which stated that the partisans involved were in fact simply a criminal gang.[40] In October 1946 a Roman court convicted three GAP members for the killing of a police officer in March 1944, claiming it had not been carried out for political reasons.[41] As Pietro Secchia pointed out to a speech in the senate, during 1948–49 police questioned 3,500 partisans in the province of Modena, out of a total of 18,411 – so 20 per cent of former freedom fighters. Although the majority were released and never went to court, many spent several months in preventative custody awaiting a decision over whether they would be brought to trial.[42]

While under the Italian legal system it is magistrates who lead investigations, the supervisory work and material aspects such as arrests are dealt with by the police. Even as late as 1960, all of the 135 local police chiefs had begun their careers under fascism,[43] any attempt to democratise the police by appointing ex-partisans having been quickly reversed. Although not a fascist, the man responsible for the police in this period was the hard-line Christian Democrat Mario Scelba. Forty years later, he recounted what he did when he became Minister of the Interior early in 1947:

> Throughout 1947 I got rid of the 8,000 Communists who had *infiltrated* the police, either through offering packages or transferring them to islands, and hired 18,000 *extremely reliable* officers. ... I didn't limit myself to setting up trustworthy police forces. I also created a power structure for emergencies: a network that was parallel to the official one, and also superior to it.[44]

The key man Scelba selected to carry out this purge of partisans from the police was *Carabinieri* general Giuseppe Piéche. Before the Second World War Piéche had been a fascist prefect, and was later a senior officer in the fascist secret police during the Spanish Civil War. In addition, he was one of Mussolini's personal informers, and during the war was apparently sent to organise the fascist 'Ustaci' police force in Croatia.[45]

Another very telling move was the 1946 appointment of Guido Leto to supervise all police academies, despite the fact that under fascism he had been national chief of the secret police – hence someone who possessed vital secrets.[46] Early the same year it emerged that partisan leader Cino Moscatelli was being systematically followed by police agents.[47] It is not surprising in this atmosphere to find anti-democratic opinions being widely expressed; for example in the March/April 1949 edition of *Rivista di polizia* (Police Review), a police chief complained about the lack of a law which 'finally spells out the insurrectionary nature of political strikes'[48] – a clear example of a fascist mentality.

As with the judiciary, the lack of purging of the state apparatus produced some horrendous scenes. One ex-partisan recounts how he was obliged to 'help with enquiries':

> We were taken to the place where the four fascist soldiers were buried [the partisans involved openly admitted they had shot them in wartime], and were presented with something we didn't expect. There was a big crowd,

with the relatives of the dead at the front, and on one side a lot of parked cars. There were also journalists from the *Giornale dell'Emilia, Avvenire d'Italia* and the *Gazzetta di Modena*, the police, Lieutenant Rizzo and the investigating magistrate. Sergeant Cau told me: 'pick up the shovel, murderer.' The photographers moved closer and I tried to turn away. The sergeant pushed my face upwards, saying: 'Come on you criminal, hold your head up and get to work.' ... The dead men's relatives were just inches away from me and were shouting like lunatics – 'murderer, criminal.' 'Once you've finished digging', an old fascist said to me, 'you'll end up in that grave.'[49]

This partisan, whose two brothers had been killed in the Resistance, was then forced to pick up the bones of the dead. Eventually, after 14 months in jail, he and his fellow partisans were released from preventative custody and the case was dropped. A case such as this involved a public act of humiliation, but in addition many partisans reported what amounted to virtual torture taking place in police stations during this period.

Hundreds of ex-partisans were being brought to trial, particularly in Piedmont, Emilia-Romagna and Veneto. Between July 1948 and August 1950, 1,955 ex-partisans were arrested, with the 60 who were convicted serving a total of 214 years in jail. This led senator Umberto Terracini to set up a support organisation named 'Solidarietà democratica', which between 1948 and 1953 had to deal with an incredible 20,000 trials involving tens of thousands of ex-partisans, according to Terracini's estimate.[50]

The lowest point in this judicial campaign was probably reached in 1954, and carries echoes of the legalistic conveniences employed more recently by the White House in defining certain individuals as 'illegal combatants' in order to deny them ordinary legal protection. In one case the Supreme Military Tribunal ruled that fascist military forces acting as part of Mussolini's puppet government be given ordinary 'belligerent' status, whereas the same rights were not accorded to partisan units, defined as 'irregulars'.[51] One of the most notorious convictions was that of Franco 'Gemisto' Moranino, sentenced to life imprisonment in 1956 – a man whose anti-fascism was plain to see. Moranino was first arrested by fascists in 1941, given a twelve-year sentence, but was freed in August 1943. He then went on to lead a partisan division in Piedmont, was wounded by eight bullets in his legs, and went on to become one of the youngest ever MPs and an under-secretary in 1946. He was also the first MP to have his parliamentary immunity lifted, in 1951, and was convicted for the execution of presumed fascist spies, although the sentence was reduced to twelve years in 1957. He was later pardoned by the President of the Republic and was elected as a senator in 1968, for the very area in which he had been active as a partisan commander.[52]

The judicial harassment of partisans continued for many years. Indeed there were even communities of exiles abroad, the most famous case being in Czechoslovakia, where 466 Italian communists went to live in exile – facing serious charges related to partisan activity, the PCI had a secret network that smuggled them out of the country. Giulio Paggio, the leader of the *Volante*

Rossa (Red Flying Squad) in Milan, was one of them, as well as the former MP Franco Moranino.[53] These people lived in Prague for many years, some for the rest of their lives, and one of their most remarkable activities was to broadcast an Italian language radio news programme into Italy for much of the 1950s and 1960s.[54]

Simultaneous with the harassment of former partisans, senior fascists were being released from jail or acquitted. Perhaps the most controversial decision occurred in 1949 with the release on an appeal verdict, due to 'extenuating circumstances', of Junio Valerio Borghese. Two years earlier the Vatican had already intervened in an attempt to save him. The future Pope Paul VI, Giovanni Battista Montini, at the time Vatican secretary of state, had written positively about him to the Allies, on behalf of his wife.[55] Borghese had been commander of the infamous X MAS regiment, deployed specifically to combat partisan actions. This regiment had 800 documented murders to its name, as well as the looting and burning of entire villages, and the torture of hundreds of partisans. The appeal court that released Borghese was presided over by a family friend and ex-fascist, and many jurors were known to be former fascists too.[56] When the decision to release him was announced, it was greeted in the courthouse by fascist salutes. Pietro Secchia prophetically warned at the time that his release 'represents a serious threat to the freedom of the Italian people'.[57] The prefect of Milan had written three weeks after liberation: 'Partisan formations are openly reluctant to obey the order to disband and disarm. ... It is beyond doubt that these people, enthusiastic about the victory obtained, galvanised by a flattering and subtle propaganda, are moving towards transforming themselves from patriotic squads to the armed forces of political parties.'[58]

While the motivation for holding onto weapons in the summer of 1945 could have been 'positive' or offensive, the broader political context of the following years – in which a government increasingly dominated by the Christian Democrats accused the partisans of having behaved in an excessively bloodthirsty way during the war, of having killed people unnecessarily, and often for personal reasons – meant that partisan and therefore working-class resentment remained high. Not surprisingly, deeds often followed from feelings of frustration at the lack of justice.

PARTISAN REBELLIONS

Mass partisan actions were fairly common after 25 April 1945, even though most historians have concentrated on activities carried out by very small groups of people involving political killings. An example of the type of action that was far more common was the attack by 300 armed partisans against the police station in Binago, near Varese, in December 1945, when they managed to free other partisans who had been arrested on the charge of illegally possessing weapons.[59]

The first major partisan revolt took place in the town of Asti in Piedmont during 1946, where tension had been simmering for months. In April anonymous leaflets had been thrown from a cinema balcony: one side had a death symbol imposed over a fascist symbol with the slogan 'This is what awaits you.' On the other side the difficult living conditions of partisans were condemned, as well as the release of notorious fascists and their return to a comfortable life.[60] Over the summer a group of frustrated partisans had been meeting to talk about 'doing something'. One participant recalled their thinking: 'they intended to create an armed protest movement to criticise the fact that over the last 16–17 months nothing had been done'.[61] On 9 July a nebulous 'Asti 1st GAP command' distributed a leaflet which was far from conciliatory: 'If the sacrosanct rights of the people are not recognised, of those who have always suffered and who only ask to be able to work and live in a world made up of *justice, equality* and *freedom*, then *we will take up arms in a second war of liberation.*'[62] Connections with other nearby towns had also been made,[63] but their planning was interrupted by an unexpected event towards the end of August: the sacking on a pretext of Carlo Lavagnino, a captain in the auxiliary police force. Although Lavagnino had only had contacts with the Resistance as a police officer, for many local people – partisans or otherwise – it was the straw that broke the camel's back. Outraged, a group of partisans and auxiliary police officers met, and on 20 August decided to go up into the mountains with two lorries in protest, the very place where some of them had been active as partisans. Many had deserted their police posts, essentially an act of sedition – so in effect this was an armed revolt against the government, a crime for which the death penalty was still in place. One of the reasons for their desertion was that with Lavagnino's sacking the auxiliaries were now under the command of an unreconstructed officer from the fascist police.

Left-wing parties were embarrassed and confused. This emerges most clearly in the Socialist Party daily *Avanti!* On 22 August the headline article was: 'Asti like Chicago. Armed gang of 30 ... policemen'. Yet the following day's headline expressed a completely different perspective: 'Partisans take up their guns and disappear in protest against continuing injustice'.[64] Somehow, telegrams got through to the partisans up in the Santa Libera mountains from other partisans in Foggia, Savona, Biella and Treviso – clearly showing the impact the protest had made. Partisans in Macerata expressed their 'full, enthusiastic vigilant solidarity', while those in San Remo wanted to develop further contacts. Partisans improvised meetings in the nearby towns of Pinerolo, Casale, Biella and Voghera to discuss the events. And in Turin FIAT workers kept lorries ready for several days in order to join the partisans up in the mountains.[65]

The rebels immediately published their demands: no arrests for their actions; jobs for all partisans and unemployed people in Asti; application of government decrees on the employment of partisans and war veterans; recognition of and compensation for damage caused by Nazi or fascist revenge attacks; and immediate payment of debts incurred by partisans during the Resistance. The communist mayor of Asti met with Lavagnino and visited the partisan groups. Such was the sensitivity of the issue that a delegation took the demands to Rome where they met with acting prime minister Pietro Nenni, who promised to resolve them.[66] The PCI deputy leader, Pietro Secchia, secretly visited the rebels, applying pressure on them to drop their protest. At its highest point, about 400 armed men were involved,[67] spread out over seven campsites. Food was obtained either by raiding local barracks, or paying peasants for their goods. Large donations had quickly been given to the rebels.

At the same time, a poster was produced by the 'First Group Revolutionary Partisans' which demanded in particular employment for ex-partisans and the cancelling of Togliatti's amnesty law.[68] The diary entry of deputy prime minister and Socialist Party leader Pietro Nenni on 26 August gives an excellent account of the scale of the revolt:

> Partisan actions are spreading. Incidents have been reported today at Dozza Imolese due to the arrest of three partisans, on charges relating to the civil war period and therefore pardoned. Events in Mantova are more serious, where two hundred partisans have taken their weapons and disappeared, and in Piacenza, where one partisan has been killed and another wounded in a clash, with a subsequent general strike. Also in Genoa a squad of railway police have armed themselves. Yesterday lorry loads of armed partisans were seen in Milan, at the demonstration against the fascist attack on the Lambrate *Casa del popolo*.[69]

Two days later the cabinet discussed the crisis and the partisans' demands, and agreed to their requests: employment of up to 15,000 ex-partisans within various police forces, payment for war damage and war pensions for both partisans and civilian victims of Nazi and fascist outrages, as well as their families.[70] So after six days the protests around Asti ended, the government had met most of their demands and promised no arrests. One of the partisan activists wrote in *l'Unità*: 'We are going back home in a disciplined fashion, in the certainty that the government will keep its promises.'[71]

Meanwhile, partisans took to the hills south of Pavia with the weapons they had held onto following liberation: 'we felt that the struggle for Liberation hadn't ended. We only gave the Allies weapons that didn't work, we kept the rest because we didn't trust the bureaucrats in the CLN'.[72] By the end of August 1946 the police were estimating that 1,300 armed partisans were up in the hills. These numbers were probably even higher, although each local revolt lasted only a week or less.[73] In late August a group of partisans met in Milan to set up the Partisan Resistance Movement (MRP). Most had been left-wing partisans, and came from anarchist, socialist and Action Party backgrounds; in fact they inherited the Milan headquarters of the Action Party. Their best-known activist was Carlo Andreoni, a doctor with a long and troubled political career behind him. Originally a PCI member, he had spent many years in jail under fascism, and had then been active in socialist organisations, becoming deputy national secretary of the party in 1943. Very active in the Roman resistance, he had managed to coordinate a significant group of partisans in open opposition to the CLN.[74] Another well-known member was Giuseppe 'Vero' Marozin, a controversial partisan who had led a division in Veneto.[75]

The MRP's manifesto placed them outside the growing dominance of parliamentary politics and 'reasons of state': 'It is the fault of a Communist Minister of Justice and a Christian Democrat Minister of the Interior that fascist criminals are freed and that freedom fighters are imprisoned. ... Our big mistake is to sincerely and selflessly demand a republic, freedom, socialism and the rebuilding of our country.'[76] The PCI was worried by such a development, and in typically Stalinist style presented a false picture of it. Giancarlo Pajetta wrote in *l'Unità* in early September: 'Fascist elements have intensified their activity, false partisans have tried to "recruit" volunteers to be sent into the mountains.'[77] In a communiqué of mid-September, the MRP made a number of harsh criticisms of the largest partisan association, ANPI. They said that its leaders 'have approved or at least taken no action to stop an amnesty that has freed the worst fascist criminals while *leaving partisans in jail*'.[78] In further points the lack of a purging of fascists is stressed repeatedly, but it is perhaps in the following section that the existential crisis of some partisans emerges most clearly:

> The Communist leaders of ANPI do not want partisans to take part in public life apart from as members of political parties, and they would like to reduce it [ANPI] to a purely administrative body.
>
> On the contrary, the MRP believes that in the current serious situation partisans have to unite and take part in political struggle as partisans, and defend the same ideals of justice and freedom which they fought for during the war of liberation.[79]

The rebellions continued. In October another revolt occurred in Curino, near Biella in Piedmont. This took place under the direct influence of the MRP, and was led by Enzo 'Selva' Plazzotta, who had been a political commissar of the 'Cesare Battisti' brigade in the Verbania mountains. As early as May 1945 he was publishing dissident partisan newspapers in his local area.[80] The action began on 20 October when 'Selva' brought at least 100 men, and perhaps many more, into Curino – one of their ideas was to rebuild local roads as a sign of what they could do as employed workers. A few days later they were joined by 40 partisans from Emilia: total numbers amounted to about 200. They put up a poster which explained: 'The ideals of the MRP are justice and freedom ... the movement does not believe that the parties in power offer any guarantees that will allow for the solution of the problems that afflict the country'.[81]

As with previous revolts, the PCI sent a leader to talk to the rebels, in this case local MP Franco Moranino. Despite the peaceful conclusion of all the recent protests, after a few days 300 heavily armed policemen reached the town of Curino, along with two tanks. The explanation for this was party political: by now the PCI feared being outflanked on its left, and so reverted to Stalinist accusations. On 27 October the party daily accused Carlo Andreoni of being a 'fascist, Trotskyite, a well-paid servant of reactionary industrialists'. The following day Moranino accused the movement of 'creating difficulties for Italian democracy, the working class, behind a radical and revolutionary Trotskyist mask. We believe that its positions are curiously linked to those of today's right-wing, who want to create disorder.'[82] Two days later Giancarlo Pajetta wrote an editorial in *l'Unità* asking 'do the police know there are light weapons at Curino?'[83] This was quickly followed by Pietro Secchia suggesting Andreoni was a secret agent during fascism.

A big argument erupted among the left: the Action Party and the Republican Party defended all the MRP members arrested, while PSI leaders such as Sandro Pertini attacked the nature of the criticisms made against Andreoni.[84] The police then made a potentially inflammatory move, something they had not done in any of the previous rebellions: they raided the MRP offices in Milan, arresting several people, as well as taking Andreoni and other leaders into custody near Curino.[85] The local PCI MP Moranino was now egging the police on, making the following statement to the press:

> They've only got 20; there are another 150 hiding up there. They need to be found and encouraged to go back home. Otherwise someone else will turn up in their midst and the farce will be repeated. Let's not forget that there are still a lot of weapons in that area, and that too many people have an interest in sending help and supplies to feed the disorder.[86]

On 3 November the partisans arrested at Curino were released without charge. That same evening anonymous posters were put up in Verbania defending the leader of the Curino protest: '"Selva" wants nothing. He is only demanding jobs and a living for a country which has been destroyed and bled dry by people representing other interests.' Accusation and counter-accusation continued to fly.

Three weeks later several hundred partisans, closely linked to the PCI, drove from Verbania to Novara, where they demanded immediate jobs in public administration and the military (the government had promised these jobs three months earlier, during the crisis in Asti). They also smashed up the offices of a right-wing paper,[87] throwing furniture into the street and burning the premises. This protest had nothing to do with the MRP; in all likelihood the PCI allowed the attack on the newspaper to happen in order for partisans to let off steam, even though they later accused the MRP of being behind the vandalism.

The witch-hunt continued. On 21 November the Ministry of the Interior released a communiqué in which it was announced that 'left-wing subversives' from Florence and Grosseto were preparing to move on Rome, occupy public buildings and attack right-wing newspapers.[88] Facing both police repression and the strong hostility of the PCI, the MRP quickly folded. Overall though these small-scale rebellions – which continued on a sporadic basis in Piedmont during 1947 – were political dynamite. The stark truth is that they appealed to the guilty conscience of the left: the rebellious partisans were attacking the very basis of what the Resistance had created. They were not calling the Resistance as such into question but the fact that political parties – principally those of the left – had not fought nearly hard enough to realise partisan ideals.

THE NON-MONOLITHIC COMMUNIST PARTY

While generally supporting their demands, the PCI leadership frequently criticised or lied about the rebellions, even though considerable numbers of party members were at the heart of them. This gap between rank and file and leadership runs throughout the PCI during the Resistance and afterwards, contradicting one of the major stereotypes of this kind of party – that it was a monolith. While it is true that all of the leadership were fanatically pro-Stalin and blind to the many imperfections and outrages committed in the Soviet Union, the PCI was nevertheless a mass working-class party, based on class solidarity – something the leadership felt obliged in theory to uphold. National membership mushroomed from 90,000 in February 1945, to 1,676,013 in 1946 and over 2 million by 1948. As regards its social composition, in 1946 59 per cent of the membership were manual workers.[89] As a document of the time put it: 'apart from a few exceptions, our party is a party of the poor'.[90]

While most of this book concentrates on the experience of ordinary people, this section deals primarily with the perceptions and arguments within the party leadership. The tensions between the leadership and the rank and file first emerged in the liberated South, where veteran communist leader Velio Spano recalled how he was generally greeted by experienced party members: 'by some with scepticism, by others with indignation. Many old comrades judged the party line to be an out-and-out betrayal of communism.' Speaking of the January 1944 Bari congress of the CLN, he states that 'the vast majority of communist delegates felt the need for a policy of class opposition within the CLN, and were strongly against any notion of working with the government'.[91]

This is not to say that the southern masses were consciously revolutionary; they had not reached that stage of development. But they often lined up against the PCI's moderate line, which in the South still explicitly stressed the fight against the Germans only, or the question of the king. Initially the party paid very little attention to burning questions concerning food supply and the economy. Soon after the liberation of Naples there was a very serious but short-lived split in the PCI within the city, with the oppositionists declaring themselves against the king and for a working-class revolution.

In November 1943 Enrico Russo refounded the old CGL union federation, the largest organisation of its kind before it was banned under fascism. It quickly grew to 150,000 members, and in February 1944 over 2,000 delegates met for its refoundation congress in Salerno.[92] In an editorial in the first issue of the CGL's newspaper, Russo called for 'the creation of the proletariat's emancipation', basing his opinions on his own formative experiences. Russo had been Neapolitan secretary of the FIOM engineering union, and regional secretary of the PCI during the early 1920s.[93]

Across the country, disagreements broke out among experienced leaders over a whole range of issues. For example a row developed at the September 1946 central committee meeting over Togliatti's wish to bring the purging of civil servants to an end. It was Velio Spano again who complained:

> very often we find ourselves facing reactionary state officials who even manage not to enact measures approved earlier by Cabinet, and we have not raised this problem in a precise fashion within government ... Lenin has taught us that if you want to create new things you need to try and break up the machinery of state and create another one.[94]

One of the main problems had to do with the leaders themselves, in the sense of their own personal history – in some cases they physically and mentally represented the evolution of a small revolutionary party, formed over 20 years earlier, into a mass working-class party committed to parliamentary change. Spano himself had joined the PCI youth wing in 1923 aged 18, spent five years in fascist jails, and then fought in the Spanish Civil War.

An interesting vignette of this difficulty is provided by Ada Gobetti, an Action Party activist in Turin who coordinated the activities of female partisans in the city. During the insurrection she was travelling to the town hall, under sniper fire, to take up her position as deputy mayor. On the way she met the man about to become mayor, Giovanni Roveda, a PCI leader who had been a founder member of the party back in 1921. He had also set up *Ordine Nuovo* (New Order) with Gramsci and Togliatti, and had been secretary of the last democratic trades council in Turin during the early 1920s. Later, together with Gramsci, he was sentenced to 20 years' imprisonment in 1928. Gobetti was travelling to the town hall in the same car as Roveda, which had to stop because of a march by workers:

> A man, who looked like an industrial worker, gazed inside and recognized my companion. 'Roveda!' he said in a voice I will never forget. He was probably an old worker, who had fought and hoped alongside him, believed in him, and who after 8 September had cried believing him to be dead. But now he saw Roveda in front of him, ready to take on board the destiny of his city. I saw tears run down his face as he took his hat off with a deferential gesture and bowed. It was at that moment I understood what real authority was![95]

The party of Gramsci – an organisation committed to creating a classless society through revolution, led by workers' councils – was long gone. But the echoes were still strong, and the rank and file had never had time to absorb the changes, or rather the change in party policy had never been clearly explained to them. Coordinating this volatile organisation with hundreds of thousands of armed working-class people, who believed in traditional communism, was not an easy task. In the early postwar years the bridge built within the organisation was that of the *doppio binario*, or twin track. It was an unstated strategy, in which the party openly and loyally participated in conventional democratic and parliamentary activities, while at the same time the rank and file believed – and large sections of the leadership allowed them to believe – that there was another track upon which the party was travelling. When the moment was right, the word would come to launch a working-class insurrection – taking part in elections was just a Trojan Horse, to be discarded at the right time.

Although the existence of a twin track policy was vehemently denied at the time, many years later some PCI leaders admitted the truth. For example a leader very much associated with the moderate wing, Giorgio Amendola, wrote in 1977 of the *doppio binario*:

> this viewpoint was very widespread among the rank and file and cadre members of the party. Yes, we needed to use all legal openings, win seats on councils and in parliament, but winning these seats would have been useful when D-Day finally arrived. ... The keeping of arms dumps ... a widespread attitude of intimidation ('Your time will come!' 'We'll make you pay for this'), these were not all invented by Christian Democrat propaganda.[96]

A semi-official history of the PCI is quite honest about the scale of the problem: 'after Liberation above all the PCI's leadership set out with determined and concrete activities to win the entire party to democratic behaviour; repressing without hesitation the fringes, which were tempted by an insurrectionary perspective. In effect, it can be said that the leadership's first political battle is against the "twin track".'[97] But this was far from being a simple operation. The same historian is equally clear that the leadership could not wave a magic wand: 'Reigning in extremist surges, which have very obvious political reasons to exist, only occurs gradually: through clashes and repression, but also through compromises and verbal concessions towards the rank and file's "revolutionary" tendencies.'[98]

Deputy leader Luigi Longo largely had the role of turning the PCI in the North into a parliamentary party. At a leadership meeting at the end of June 1945 he was blunt about the problems, stating that 'the party is still a crowd'.[99] While at another meeting a month later he reported the presence within the party of a 'machine gun disease'. Tormented by the evolution of their own party, members of the central committee were fully aware of clear political opposition within their ranks. As Armando Fedeli outlined at a central committee meeting in September 1946: 'the majority of those who today make the weight of sectarianism felt within the party believe that we have an opportunist practice, that we are on the wrong road, that we are collaborators, and that the party is therefore sliding down the slope towards a kind of 1914–18 social democracy'.[100] Togliatti also defined these insurrectionary views as 'sectarian'. But even more seriously, at the same meeting he was at pains to point out that these temptations existed not only within the rank and file: 'even in our central committee we can feel the repercussions of the political weaknesses that exist at the base of our party. There are comrades who, when facing these political weaknesses, are not able to overcome them once they understand them but let themselves be dragged along by them.'[101]

OCCUPATION AND INSURRECTION, 1947–48

These 'sectarian weaknesses' were given a new lease of life in May 1947, when Christian Democrat prime minister Alcide De Gasperi removed the PCI and the PSI from government. The Cold War was now gathering pace, battle lines were being drawn up, and the coalition of the Resistance was now long past.

With the beginning of Cold War tension, and the openly hostile attitude towards communism shown by the Allies, many partisans were strongly convinced that they might still need their weapons in the future. Throughout the late 1940s it was strongly believed at all levels of the Communist Party that the government could suddenly declare the party illegal. Many years after the war, large quantities of partisan arms were still being discovered. In Emilia-Romagna 413 kilos of medium and heavy calibre ammunition were found between 1970 and 1995, as well as a hundred anti-tank mines.[102] In large factories one or two workers were delegated to keep weapons, which were often hidden in cellars, in working order. In subsequent decades, as these factories were knocked down, these arms dumps would emerge: at a steel factory in Milan in 1996 two hand grenades, a machine gun and ammunition were found in underground passages.[103] Police seizures of weapons also give another indication; in Rome alone 402 military rifles, 78 pistols and 3,209 hand grenades were confiscated in 1947.[104]

The PCI's ejection from government had in some senses confirmed these fears and allowed the rank and file to breath a sigh of relief: now they could really be themselves, setting themselves up in opposition to the DC and other moderate parties. But the relief was short-lived: economic pressures and political attacks continued unabated, and their hopes were also dashed by the PCI leadership. The following statement, made by Togliatti at a central committee meeting on 3 July, illustrates both his overriding concern of maintaining an alliance with the middle classes but, equally, his fear of the radicalism within his party:

> the most favourable element for us has been the fact that we left government without launching the slogan of an insurrection, something which has led to a growth in our party's prestige amongst specific social strata, and especially amongst the middle classes, which would not have occurred had we declared a general strike as soon as we left the government.[105]

The rank and file found a focus for their anger in Milan in November, with the sacking of the last 'partisan prefect'. In what was seen as a deliberate strategy, the 'partisan' composition of these local representatives of national government up and down the country was being changed. Following the fall of fascism, many of these positions had been taken up by individuals who had played a significant role in partisan struggles. And the prefect in Milan,

Ettore Troilo, was the last still holding his position. Troilo was a Roman lawyer and member of the PSI who had led a partisan formation in Abruzzo, before passing through the front line in December 1943. From January 1944, starting with 100 men, Troilo's group was almost unique in that it saw front-line service along with the Allies until May 1945.[106]

But Troilo's firing was far from being a symbolic act against the Resistance. There was a sharp economic downturn in the second half of 1947, and workers were resisting widespread sackings. Troilo had irritated the hard-line Minister of the Interior Mario Scelba because he had refused to take a strongly repressive line against a general strike called in response to these lay-offs. The news of his sacking was announced just before midnight on a Thursday evening, and by 7 a.m. the next morning thousands of people were outside Troilo's office, demonstrating in solidarity with him.[107] At roughly the same time, the Milan city council met and the mayor resigned in protest, soon followed by 160 mayors in the province of Milan. A worker involved in the movement describes the speed of the working-class response:

> The comrades who had been in the various (partisan) brigades, through a phone call, or on their bikes ... went round to inform people that they should meet up because they wanted to sack Troilo, and that they should occupy the prefecture. Once the prefecture was occupied, the roads were blocked in towns as well, to stop the passage of military columns which might have wanted to enter Milan. And once you've occupied the prefecture, you've got control of the city![108]

PCI sources confirmed the 'partisan' nature of the event: 'lorry loads of workers and patriots from all over the province arrived singing *Fischia il vento* [*The wind whistles*, perhaps the most famous partisan song]'. Indeed the PCI was not averse to stressing the continuity with the Resistance period: 'the songs of the Resistance were sung. There was the same spirit, enthusiasm and firm commitment to fight; yesterday to win freedom and independence, today not to allow an abuse of the democracy and the Republic which partisans and workers have won.'[109]

What quickly emerges from this account is that at a crucial moment the Resistance model of action was resurrected. Two and a half years after liberation the structure still existed in organisational terms, and crucially also in terms of weapons. Yet the decision to launch the occupation among the working class of Milan was both spontaneous and unitary: the response to Troilo's sacking was decided upon immediately in workplaces, without the guidance of political leaders, and perhaps for this reason it was particularly radical. But it is also true that it was a measured and disciplined response, and that no shots were fired or violence inflicted on individuals; in other words, the response illustrated a high level of political maturity amongst workers.

A government representative arrived from Rome near midnight and negotiations went on all night. It was finally agreed that Troilo could keep his position temporarily, and would then be replaced by someone presumably acceptable to the occupiers. The organiser of the occupation, PCI leader Giancarlo Pajetta, announced the end of the occupation to hundreds of people assembled in the courtyard: 'on this occasion, once again, partisans put their weapons back under their jackets and coats and returned home, cursing'.[110]

These developments also had an international echo; the departure of the last Allied troops from Italy was delayed due to the events. An Italian Foreign Office report written soon afterwards stated: 'General Gaither, the new American head of Civilian Affairs, asked for news on the evening of 28 November, stating that he was very concerned about a potential seizure of power by an extremist movement.'[111] In the Cold War climate, the US had strong suspicions that many of these activities happened because of encouragement from Moscow. But Soviet leaders had made their peace with the Allies in 1945 and were not interested in the Italian working class launching unpredictable movements with which Stalin would be associated. As an infuential PCI leader of the time recalled: 'Scelba had been able to weigh up what the party was – faithful to the line from Moscow – which didn't want an insurrection even if there were the conditions to launch one.'[112]

The insurrection which did eventually explode, on 14 July 1948, was to an extent conditioned by what had happened three months earlier, in the first democratic elections in Italy for nearly 30 years, held on 18 April. Against the expectations of the Communist and Socialist Parties, the Christian Democrats won a crushing victory, to a significant extent thanks to support from the Catholic church. A new activist group, Catholic Action, had created an organisation of 300,000 people who conducted election campaigning within Italy's 20,000 parishes. For all members of the PCI it was a rude awakening: the leadership had even produced posters celebrating their victory just a few days before the election. They responded quite aggressively in public to their defeat. In his parliamentary speech after the swearing in of De Gasperi's new government, Togliatti mentioned the question of hidden arms which had been talked about since April 1945:

> People talked about it, they whispered left right and centre ... that there were a lot of hidden weapons, and that they would have been brought out the day in which there was an attempt at fascist revival. Blessed be the hidden weapons, therefore, if they have saved us from another disaster of that kind, from an adventure that could have taken us even lower! Blessed be the hidden weapons![113]

Clearly Togliatti came close to admitting that his party had a hidden arsenal of weapons, and this was not just for internal consumption within the PCI. As mentioned above, the entire party, in the Cold War climate, was seriously worried that it would be declared illegal and forced to go underground. (There was paranoia within the party too: many PCI leaders believed that the young female MP Togliatti had taken up with, Nilde Jotti, was a spy, and for a period she was put under surveillance.) There was further aggression when serious fighting broke out in the parliamentary chamber between PCI and Christian Democrat MPs on 9 June.

It was in this climate that Togliatti, as he left parliament on 14 July, was shot three times by a 25-year-old student. Although he appears to have acted alone, Antonio Pallante was closely linked to right-wing circles. He was found to have a Liberal Party card in his pocket, as well as an entry pass to parliament given out by a Christian Democrat MP from his home town of Catania. A copy of *Mein Kampf* was found in his hotel room, together with 'a diary full of notes on nationalism'; furthermore the hotel was regularly used by known neo-fascists. At the time of his arrest he stated that he wanted to eliminate 'the most dangerous element in Italian political life, who through his activity as an agent of a foreign power, is impeding the rebirth of the Fatherland'.[114]

The Times described what happened next: 'The attempt upon Signor Togliatti caused a deep sensation here when it was made known by the Italian radio on the midday news bulletin. In the early afternoon work stopped in all factories and offices, shops were closed, and tramways and other essential services interrupted.'[115] No time limit was given to this strike, and decisions varied as to whether to remain inside the factory or to send delegations outside. In either case, if weapons were hidden within a factory they were often brought out and prepared for use.

Such a strong and immediate reaction is clear proof of both the esteem in which Palmiro Togliatti was held by the working class, as well as the political tension latent in Italian society at that time. It is interesting to read an editorial published in *The Times*, a newspaper hardly known for its communist sympathies, because its analysis was probably shared by nearly all protesters. It began by saying that the attempted assassination recalled:

the barbaric violence of the murderers whom Mussolini paid to silence his opponents. This irruption of a past which all had hoped that Italy had set firmly behind her is lamentable. ... but it is hard not to believe that he [Pallante] and others who have yet to be apprehended were not influenced by the continuous incitement to violence indulged in by right wing extremists and neo-fascists. The most shocking of these outrages was committed on May 1 last year, when 41 workmen and their families were machine-gunned to death by unknown persons during a political meeting in Sicily. ... Signor De Gasperi has so far refused to disband neo-fascist organizations, believing that this would only drive them underground.[116]

What is particularly important to understand when analysing the following three days of insurrection – during which it was initially uncertain whether Togliatti would recover – is the nature of the movement's leadership. As described by one historian: 'With the disappearance of Socialist leaders and the indecision of Communist leaders, the movement, which had arisen spontaneously, ended up being characterised by the most determined and radical elements of the PCI, that is, those who had joined the party because they believed in something which to Togliatti seemed very odd.'[117] In other words, the established national leaderships did not direct the popular response, particularly during the first day.

Small towns and cities all experienced revolts. In Venice workers invaded the RAI radio studios; in Naples two people were killed in clashes, and one in Taranto; in Arezzo the jail was attacked and prisoners freed; in Livorno a policeman was killed; and at Abbadia San Salvatore in southern Tuscany there was a full-scale uprising in which two policemen were shot dead; and so on.[118] Nearby in Siena a march of 400 people was stopped by three police armoured cars; a man appeared from a turret and shouted: 'Comrades, I'm with you. I'm a partisan from Lombardy, tell us what to do.' The reply from the crowd was 'go back', which the patrol did immediately.[119]

Genoa: The Eye of the Storm

The maritime city of Italy's industrial triangle saw the strongest reaction to Togliatti's shooting. Here is a contemporary account of the initial spontaneous response by industrial workers:

> 50,000 workers, who had mainly come from Sestri, had occupied the city centre by early afternoon. Police headquarters ordered a patrol of five armoured cars to go out, which the crowd rapidly took possession of; by late afternoon the city – as was the case in most of Liguria – was practically under the control of the masses, led by Communists.[120]

The prefect of the city – instinctively hostile to the protesters' behaviour – described events rather differently:

> numerous ex-partisans and large groups of armed hooligans were busy with acts of violence in various points of the city; immobilising trams and other vehicles, imposing the closure of shops, setting up road blocks, and attacking and disarming all isolated soldiers and policemen. A lieutenant has been wounded, and 10 *Carabinieri* were captured, disarmed, mistreated, and taken to the headquarters of the PCI and the ANPI.[121]

Such a rapid and mass unitary response clearly had to have a common point of reference, and that was the Resistance, both in terms of its military actions and its political practice of direct democracy exercised by rank-and-file workers. Yet although the Resistance model was reproduced on a military level in Genoa, the movement did not last long enough to create a stable political effect. This is how a communist trade union leader described the military connection with the Resistance:

> everything was stopped, the entire city had been divided into sections and was in our hands even more so than in the period of the partisan war. There was only one public authority in Genoa; it was a huge emotional factor which had unleashed the most revolutionary elements who were saying:

the time has come to settle accounts. Sectarian comrades dominated over the others.

There was the training of the partisan war, there were all those young people who had fought in the mountains in a complete military environment, they were an army excellently prepared for this kind of war. They passed the word amongst each other – 'let's get the armoured cars', and it took them a second because they were used to it. They had taken armoured cars and tanks off the Germans for so many years in the same way.[122]

The question then needs to be asked, who was leading these people? It would appear to have been rank-and-file workers, although local communist leaders were also equally outraged by the attack on Togliatti and enthused by the strength shown in such a impressive wave of anger. This is how the secretary of the PCI's Genoa Federation recalls events:

I went into the federation, where there was a lot of confusion. ... Nobody knew what was happening; we were unable to contact the leadership as the phones weren't working; ... At a branch level everyone had got carried away, even the leading members, until we arrived with our instructions. These were people who had gone through the struggle for liberation, there were some excellent comrades who had dived into it all, but nobody from the federal committee had done that. ... as I was regional secretary I received an invitation to take part in a meeting to be held outside Genoa on that very day to discuss with other leaders, even though the [national] leadership did not agree, how to coordinate action in the North. I didn't go because I didn't believe a revolution was possible.[123]

Not only does this quote illustrate the extent of support for an insurrection, it also shows that even important local leaders, as was the case in Milan, were also tempted to support the movement and see where it led. The communist trade union leader again takes up the story:

the crowd had taken over from the police and had captured the armoured cars, we were practically in a state of civil war. That evening Genoa was already in the hands of the people, so much so that at eight o'clock, if I remember right, the chief of police phoned the ANPI offices and said: 'Send me a group of partisans to defend the police headquarters, because I'm completely isolated here.' All the police had fled, the whole lot, it was a terrifying situation.[124]

Public order was now in the hands of members of the Communist Party and the rest of the left, the phone lines to the prefecture had been cut. Barricades were everywhere, and there was frequent sniping between the two sides as a result of which several people were killed. The reality quickly dawned on PCI leaders in major cities: they either had to launch an insurrection or stop one.

One of the first key setbacks suffered by the potential insurrectionary wave was the arrival of the PCI mayor of Genoa, Gelasio Adamoli, who made a speech where the armoured cars had been seized stressing the symbolic nature of the action and the need to remain within the law.[125] Yet it was fitting that the major role appears to have been played by the Federation secretary, who after refusing to attend a meeting which would have discussed the prospects for a revolution, went to see the city's prefect:

The prefect wanted me to speak to the people from the balcony of the Prefecture, something I refused to do. I had told the prefect: 'you must withdraw the police because if you let them run around there could be some clashes. We have given out instructions, and we're continuing to give out instructions, we are keeping the situation under control. You withdraw everything, and we'll tell people to go back to their party branches.'

He had been in contact with Rome, where Scelba was in control; it was hard for him, much harder than for us. It is not surprising that he lost his authority, he had to accept; he saw that we had told people to go away. There would have been hell to pay if we hadn't made that decision, we did a really good job.[126]

The First Day in Milan

Although Milan may not have experienced such an immediately strong insurrectionary upsurge as Genoa, the protest movement here ended on perhaps a higher or more militant note. Another factor which helped to push events along was a kind of united front formed between the PCI, the Socialist Party, and the CGIL, the main trade union federation, dominated by communists. Furthermore, in Milan there was the even more recent precedent of the occupation of the prefecture for two days, eight months earlier.

At Sesto San Giovanni, the area with the greatest concentration of large factories, a mass meeting of 40,000 workers was held in the early afternoon, and in accordance with initial instructions, workers returned and occupied their factories. On a broader level, the Milan edition of the PCI's daily newspaper *l'Unità*, distributed that afternoon, struck a strident tone demanding: 'Down with this murderers' government!'

The situation began to change significantly in the course of a mass rally held in the city's main square, *piazza del Duomo*, during the early evening. These mass rallies, compared to those which occur today, were far more important at that time due to the lack of television and the perceived untrustworthiness of radio bulletins. They were occasions when workers could glean the precise nature of an organisation's suggestions and respond in a unified manner. Here is an eyewitness account:

at 5 p.m. tens of thousands of workers filled *piazza del Duomo*, the Social Democrat mayor Greppi tried in vain to speak, whilst the PSI secretary of the trades council Mariani, and the PCI federation secretary Alberganti, invited the crowd to 'occupy the factories, fortresses of the working class'; Alberganti added: 'this is not a strike that will end up like others'.[127]

Another account confirms this last phrase, and also adds a reference made by Alberganti concerning the left's electoral defeat three months earlier, not reproduced by his newspaper *l'Unità* the following day: 'In Italy on 18 April we were all counted, today we are being weighed. This strike will not end either today or tomorrow.'[128] Such extreme language could only encourage radical elements, and as regards Alberganti personally, he was consistent with the militant stance he took during the occupation of the prefecture at the end of the previous year.

In individual factories the response was similar to that of Genoa, although the same kind of spontaneous movement towards outright insurrection was largely lacking. Here is an example from a light-engineering factory, in which a communist worker outlines the immediate response to the shooting and also admits to the existence of two tendencies within the party: those who wanted to wait for 'the line' and those who wanted 'to go further':

straight away there was a ferment in the factory, everybody stopped work. It was a kind of uprising; everyone downed tools, an immediate strike and so on. ... There was some resistance within the party: there were those who wanted to go beyond a strike and a demonstration, which they agreed with in any case; they wanted to go further.[129]

Another worker illustrates a quite well thought-out approach to the question of insurrection. Whilst light weapons held within a factory were probably sufficient for defensive purposes, a successful insurrection would involve the seizure of important positions within a major city, and so it was essential to at least get hold of heavy weapons: 'we wanted to go to the *Carabinieri* barracks in *via Lamarmora* and get their armoured cars and tanks. But our leaders were there, who advised us not to take that course of action. ... otherwise our intention was to get into the barracks, take their armoured vehicles, and then drive them around the city.'[130]

The Second Day in Genoa and Milan

Overall there was an uneasy stand-off between demonstrators and government forces during the second day, with neither side trying to gain supremacy. Although the protest movement may have lacked leadership, the second day nevertheless gave the protesters time to organise some kind of structure to their activities, and to begin to feel the weight of their collective power.

In Genoa electricity had been cut overnight, and there were sporadic attacks on police barracks and Christian Democrat party branches in city suburbs, together with further disarming of policemen and soldiers. A mobile police battalion was halted by barricades on the city outskirts during the morning and the prefect declared a state of siege at 1 p.m.[131] The city was criss-crossed by road blocks and barricades, and when a patrol of riot police – perhaps significantly made up mainly of ex-partisans – met a group of 'rebels' in the city's main square, they handed over their weapons. A police colonel, captured elsewhere, was unceremoniously thrown in the square's fountains. The police and army were confined to barracks.[132]

However at a joint meeting of communist, socialist, trades council and ANPI leaders it was decided to call on their members to abandon the road blocks. The mayor then went to visit the major barricades to invite people to go home. In this fashion the initiative which demonstrators had held the day before was dissipated. The police and the armed forces began to circulate again, though not because they had managed to impose their will, but because protesters had been persuaded to stop their most militant activities and let them pass.

In Milan the trajectory of protest was if anything moving in the opposite direction. A member of the *Volante Rossa*, or Red Flying Squad, recalled his impressions of the second day in an interview conducted many years later:

> Driving around the city we checked on where police and army vehicles were stationed. I remember that we had contacts with army detachments who were ready to support us if the need arose … Furthermore a meeting had been planned with the rank and file of the police, and one presumed that not all of them would have gone over to the other side … Just imagine that even without needing to fight the major public buildings had been occupied: the city council, the regional council, the prefecture, the radio station.[133]

What is interesting to note at this point is that according to the prefect, at a series of workers' rallies held at 11 a.m., 'Speakers stressed the theme of the government's responsibility and the necessity of continuing the strike until its resignation.'[134] At Gallarate just to the north of Milan the PCI MP Giovanni Grilli stated in a rally: 'either this black [fascist] government goes or we continue this strike till the end'. At nearby Busto Arsizio there was a shoot-out with a police patrol, which was disarmed. The same group, which by then had grown to 2,000 people, went on to free from custody two PCI prisoners who had been arrested with weapons.[135] Further confrontations seemed to be looming. The prefect reported that at 5 p.m. 'passenger transport began with the use of 14 vehicles set aside by the Civil Transportation Inspectorate and escorted by policemen. But this was terminated after a few hours due both to the lack of passengers and the fact that following several incidents drivers did not want to continue providing the service.'[136] There were even more worrying signs for the prefect by the evening:

> At 6 p.m. three under-age women were arrested in the vicinity of the S. Ambrogio barracks whilst they were trying to give guards type-written strips of paper which called on police not to fire on workers. In the evening persons unknown positioned posters in *via Torino*, which were immediately taken down, inviting policemen to join with the workers.[137]

The printing of written material and the use of under-age women to distribute them clearly indicates a high degree of organisation, and the intention to carry on.

As in Genoa, in Milan workers were still solidly in control of many factories. Indeed, as is the case with the *Vanzetti* factory, participation seems to have even increased by the second night: 'The number of comrades occupying the factory *increased* significantly, and organisation is more disciplined.'[138] The situation was stark. A young worker at the *Innocenti* factory in Milan recalls a mass meeting of 3,000 in the canteen, in which two arguments were put: 'Muneghina put the argument that in essence the response to the provocation – the attack on Togliatti – had shown the great strength of the working class, and that at that point we should go back to work. Other arguments ... put two alternatives to workers: we either launch a revolution or we're defeated.'[139]

The Final Day

In Genoa and along the Ligurian coastline on the third day 'Everything had stopped ... from Sarzana to Ventimiglia not even a bicycle was moving.'[140] The reality of an insurrection, and the difficulties involved, had been posed more starkly in Genoa than elsewhere, and perhaps this was why even on the second day a sense of disorientation had set in. Yet the number of factory occupations and the fact that the city had in effect experienced an indefinite general strike is clear evidence of workers' commitment to continue the struggle. But the 'insurgents' found themselves without any alternative leadership, and were therefore forced to accept that of PCI leaders who argued for a return to work. Some dockers bitterly complained: 'we're one step away from taking power, why stop now?'[141]

In Milan, the trades council's intransigent stance of the day before was suddenly turned into farce by the use of a ridiculous justification for ending the protest: 'to get more precise information on the situation, and to be able to judge things in greater detail'.[142] Union leaders in Milan must have suddenly realised that they were seriously out of step with other cities and hurriedly tried to fall in line. But it is hardly surprising that in Milan the decision to end the strike encountered widespread disbelief and resistance. *L'Unità*, whilst calling on people to end their protest, also acknowledged that 'throughout the morning the combativity of the working class has grown, such that they arrived at the time established for the end of the strike with the movement even better organised than it had been on the first day'.[143]

Many workers believed that the call for a return to work was the result of government misinformation, whilst others smelt a rat within their own ranks. Thousands marched on the trades council building to demand an explanation. Yet somehow the police had got to the building before them, making workers very angry: 'You've called the police to protect yourselves against us', shouted some *Pirelli* workers.[144] Others shouted: 'We've started and we want to finish it.'[145] The trades council denied they had called the police; yet local PCI leaders refused to speak to the demonstrators, as did

Colombi, the PCI leader sent up from Rome. For several hours the building was virtually under siege.

It was with a very heavy sense of irony that Minister of the Interior Mario Scelba could tell cabinet on the morning of the 17th: 'Last night in Milan the police "protected" Alberganti.'[146] Giuseppe Alberganti was the secretary of the PCI federation, who just two days earlier had thundered to tens of thousands of workers in *piazza del Duomo*: 'this is not a strike that will end up like others', and indeed for him it ended with police protecting him from angry workers who had taken him at his word.

This was also how the movement generally ended throughout the country; with workers resentfully ceasing their occupations and protests, and with the country taking two or three days to get back to normal.

THE END OF THE RESISTANCE?

The following day the country's most influential newspaper, the *Corriere della Sera*, had a headline eight columns wide: 'The country is moving towards normality'. Naturally the sense at the time referred to people going back to work, but in terms of the history related in this book such a headline represents the end of the final throw of the dice for 'Resistance politics'. The movement had not forced any concessions from the government, and with the Cold War climate that now dominated, over the coming years hundreds of participants would receive prison sentences. Indeed, at least seven protesters had died during the three days, with 84 being wounded.[147]

And the killing would continue; one study has revealed that 64 demonstrators were shot dead by police forces between 1948 and 1952, with one of the worst massacres taking place at Modena on 9 January 1950, when six workers were killed and 50 wounded.[148] Figures based on PCI sources state that during between 1948 and 1950 a total of 92,169 party members were arrested, with 19,306 being convicted and receiving a total of 8,841 years in custodial sentences.[149]

Police seizures of weaponry in 1948 were far higher than those of the preceding two years, and in some cases higher than in 1945: 28 cannons, 202 mortars and grenade launchers, 995 machine guns, 6,200 automatic rifles, 27,123 rifles and muskets, 9,445 pistols and revolvers, 49,640 grenades, 564 tons of explosives, 81 radio transmitters and 5.5 million rounds of ammunition.[150] Some of this weaponry was confiscated when it was brought out during the 'July days', but the vast majority was thrown away, abandoned after ex-partisans realised that the leaderships of their parties would not support an insurrection.

Indeed, that is the stark fact that emerges. Shortly before midnight on 14 July the PCI leadership decided to send their most experienced members to the major trouble spots. Togliatti's secretary recalls the following advice which Luigi Longo gave Ilio Barontini, and which characterised the leadership's role throughout the crisis: 'If the movement increases let it grow, if it decreases suffocate it completely.'[151] Whilst the leadership may have felt unable to disown the protest movement, they were even less enthusiastic about encouraging it and giving it a sense of purpose and direction.

In its crucial explosive phase national leaders went to ground, but as disorientation increased, they intervened decisively to bring things to an end. Ordinary members held the fort for two long days, hoping and waiting for 'D-Day' to be proclaimed. One PCI worker in Genoa later commented: 'At that moment people believed that the real party line was emerging, yet the central leadership of the party immediately fought against this line, circumscribing the protest.'[152] Many leading members in cities had actively supported moves towards an insurrection, such was the belief in the 'twin-track' strategy. But events had shown it to be a fantasy, PCI leaders were not prepared to launch an insurrection.

This was a political defeat for the Resistance generation. They now understood that the parties and organisations they had felt were theirs actually had different policies to what they had believed. The militaristic emphasis that many had was found wanting, a spontaneous explosion was just that – an unplanned and uncoordinated upsurge, a movement with no internal agreement on its objectives or on how to proceed. Any real insurrectionary movement has to build political support for a seizure of power – something the PCI and others had certainly done in order to create a parliamentary system in April 1945. What people were cruelly disabused of in July 1948 was the idea that the PCI wanted to create a communist society.

For those who still believed in creating a classless society the prospects were bleak. It meant leaving an organisation of over two million members, a movement in which, in solidarity with close friends, they had probably risked their lives on a day-to-day basis during the Resistance. It meant starting again from scratch, trying to explain patiently to those who would listen that neither the PCI nor the PSI were intending to create communism or socialism. In a Cold War climate, with industrialists and Christian Democrat politicians constantly attacking the left, only very few wanted to swim against the tide. Many perhaps remained bitter inside, maintaining their disagreement silently. Indeed one of the habits learnt very well by activists during the years of clandestine political activity under fascism was how to keep their views to themselves.

Yet some of these ideas remained alive, or rather resurfaced later. Twenty years after the events of 1948, Giuseppe Alberganti, although now 70, threw in his lot with the mass student movement that exploded in Milan in 1968. Indeed throughout the 1970s the number of ex-partisans who would join or relate to a large radical left was not insignificant. But this is a subject for another book.

8
The Long Liberation

As we have seen, the leadership and rank and file of fascism emerged largely unscathed from their military and political defeat in 1945. For this reason, it is important not to exaggerate the impact of the Resistance movement on the anti-democratic traditions of the state. During the war the movement was immensely powerful – liberating many cities in northern and central Italy before the arrival of the Allies and forcing many German divisions to be stationed throughout the country to ward off their guerrilla attacks. But after liberation the movement's key failure was its inability in many cases to prevent certain notorious and powerful fascists from maintaining their positions of power and influence. If this is not borne in mind then one runs the risk of 'imposing on Italy the perception of a "fateful break" in the continuity of events, leading one to celebrate the armed uprising as the "Year Zero" of the democratic and republican era'.[1] Sadly, 1945 was not a 'Year Zero'. And echoes of Mussolini's regime have frequently been heard down the decades since 1945, ringing particularly strongly since the implosion of the 'First Republic' in 1992–94.

Most fascist leaders retired from politics, while most of the rank and file gave up any active involvement in fascism. But a hard core of both leaders and led were more than prepared to continue the battle in different forms. Their key ally in this was democracy itself: although the Fascist Party was banned, fascist activity in anything but name was allowed to gain a foothold.

On the ground, it was clear that militarist groupings existed and were active – even before the end of the war. In April 1944 a bomb was placed by fascists outside a Communist Party branch in Nicastro, in Calabria. Over the following two months the police chief in Catanzaro arrested 60 people for belonging to fascist organisations and illegal possession of arms.[2] In 1945 a cinema showing that year's most popular film – Rossellini's homage to the Roman resistance, *Rome Open City*, was bombed but only the building was damaged. On 28 October, the anniversary of Mussolini's 1922 March on Rome, a black flag was rung up a flagpole in a major building in Rome.[3] And in June 1946 the PCI headquarters in Naples was attacked for three hours, with seven dead and 51 wounded.[4]

Fascist leaders, meanwhile, spent the early months after the Resistance's victory either in custody or avoiding arrest or execution. At the end of the war Junio Valerio Borghese, commander of the infamous X MAS regiment which had taken direct orders from the German army, was in hiding in Milan with a death sentence over his head. Admiral Ellery Stone, US Proconsul in occupied Italy, was a close friend of the Borghese family, and ordered James Jesus Angleton to rescue him.[5] Angleton already knew Italy well, having as a young man worked in the country for his father's banking firm. He quickly became the leading figure in the Rome office of the counter-espionage agency known as the Office of Strategic Services, the forerunner of the CIA, and obviously took the view that men such as Borghese could prove useful. In one early move, for example, Angleton was to send 20 former X MAS officers to the US to train as saboteurs.

The first record of an organised political regrouping of fascists dates from January 1946, when a number of fugitives from justice created a secret organisation named FAR, the Armed Revolutionary Front. Only those who had fought for Mussolini were allowed to join, and Jews were banned.[6] Among the individuals involved were Giorgio Almirante, Julius Evola, Rodolfo Graziani and Pino Rauti, who will be briefly examined in turn, since they reappear later in this chapter.

Almirante had been a junior minister in the fading months of Mussolini's regime, but from 1938 until June 1943 had been editor in chief of the viciously anti-Semitic journal *In Defence of the Race*. In the 5 May 1942 issue, for example, he wrote: 'If we really want an awareness of race to exist and to be alive within all of us, then racism has to be food for everyone and for everything. Otherwise we will be playing the game of half-breeds and Jews – Jews who have too often been able to change their names and hide themselves among us.' As an officer in the fascist militia, in May 1944 he signed an order for the execution of 83 partisans and civilians in the town of Niccioleta in Tuscany. Although convicted by five different courts, he never spent a day in jail for this mass murder, thanks both to the postwar amnesty concerning fascist crimes, and to his remaining in hiding for 18 months.

Julius Evola was a Nazi rather than an Italian-fascist philosopher, who as far back as 1934 had been arguing for 'a return to tradition as a way to counteract the degeneration of a modern civilisation that was materialist in its philosophy and subversive of the natural, hierarchical order in its politics'.[7] Evola was closely involved with the fascist regime but never joined the party, partly because of his esotericism and mystical beliefs. He also frequently visited Nazi Germany, his trips being paid for by one of his admirers, Heinrich Himmler. Evola criticised Italian fascism in particular for its populism, since he believed the state had to be both truly elitist and based upon tradition rather than modernism.[8] In his postwar writings he attempted to distance himself from the interwar dictatorships by outlining a form of 'spiritual' racism rather than a biological one. He also had a strategic political mind, and in future decades his ideas came dangerously close to fruition; as one historian of the Italian far right has written: 'Evola envisioned the possibility of rallying all the forces of the Right (the MSI, the "healthy" corps of the state, the police, paratroopers, veteran groups, and the like) in order to take over Italian society.'[9]

Rodolfo Graziani, after a bloody colonial career in North Africa, was no less than head of the armed forces under Mussolini's puppet regime of 1943–45.

He had been sentenced to death by a partisan court in 1945, but luckily for him surrendered to the Allies, otherwise he would have ended up in *piazzale Loreto* with Mussolini, although he did spend a brief period in jail.

Pino Rauti was the youngest of the four, having been born in 1926. As a 17-year-old he had volunteered to join Mussolini's militia, and fought to the bitter end against anti-fascists. In this early period he was very much under the influence of Evola, and later came close to plagiarising his writings.

These unsavoury individuals were vastly helped by the 1946 amnesty, which allowed most of them to circulate freely again. Neo-fascism was publicly born in December, with the foundation of the MSI, the Italian Social Movement, which was to dominate extreme right politics for the next 50 years. The founding document was drawn up in the house of the ex-deputy leader of the Fascist Party in Rome, and Almirante became leader.[10] But in a mechanism that was to constantly resurface, nearly all new members of the public MSI kept their membership of the FAR a secret, until its disintegration in a series of arrests in 1951. Thirty-three terrorist attacks were attributed to its members and Julius Evola, Clemente Graziani (the son of Rodolfo), and Pino Rauti were put on trial for organising a bombing in Taranto.[11] However the FAR–MSI duality also reflected a deeper division within neo-fascism which lasted for decades, between those who were more 'revolutionary', nostalgic and militaristic, and those who were prepared to work within the democratic system.

Another constant of the fascist right has been its symbiotic relationship with elements of the Italian state. One of the first examples of this was the 'Anti-Bolshevik Front', a secret army set up by General Giuseppe Piéche in 1948. Making use of his secret service experience under Mussolini, Piéche reconstituted secret state files on individuals. He hired ex-fascist fighters, secured funding from US intelligence sources, and had false membership cards for the PCI and PSI – just the beginning of the many 'black ops' the far right engaged in.[12]

The rules of democracy allowed what was in essence an unrepentant neo-fascist party such as the MSI to exist legally, immediately after a fascist dictatorship had been overthrown. Naturally fascism had some support, and in the 1948 elections the MSI obtained 500,000 votes, two-thirds of them from the South, and six MPs and one senator were elected. In its early years the MSI enjoyed very close relations with the Roman bourgeoisie and the Vatican. It was made up largely of ex-fascist bureaucrats and activists, and middle-class people frightened of losing the privileges they had enjoyed under fascism. Furthermore, the growing climate of the Cold War helped the consolidation of the MSI as a fully legal party.

Despite the party's open association with fascism, Graziani and Rauti were not satisfied with the MSI and became influenced by Evola's critique of Western decadence and spiritual degradation. But they were also drawn to his Nazism – Evola's 1953 *Gli uomini e le rovine* (*Men Among the Ruins*) called for a select band of warriors to mould themselves in the tradition of the Waffen SS.[13] Yet these intellectual discussions always went hand in hand with practical action such as classic fascist street-fighting squads, who were frequently seen acting alongside the police in repressing various protests and demonstrations.

Street violence was neo-fascism's minor threat, however. Despite being numerically small and electorally weak, fascism enjoyed widespread support at the highest level of the state machinery. For example during the 1950s, all 241 prefects had begun their public service under fascism; and out of the 135 police chiefs and 139 deputy police chiefs who had started their service under fascism, only five had been involved in the anti-fascist Resistance movement.[14] Senior police and military figures who had been educated and had begun their careers during the fascist period were therefore by and large in control of the repressive arms of state power well into the late 1960s and 1970s.

This emerged in a more systematic form in the 'Gladio/Stay Behind' scandal. While the word 'Gladio' was consciously taken from the symbol of Juan Valerio Borghese's anti-partisan unit X MAS, 'Stay Behind' referred to secret military units which would go underground to resist the communists if they took power. The earliest official reference to 'Gladio' dates from a US National Security Council document dated 15 March 1954, which speaks of 'stay behind assets'. In the scenario outlined, the task would be 'to develop underground resistance and facilitate covert and guerrilla operations'.[15] A formal agreement became operative two years later; it was signed by General Giovanni De Lorenzo but kept secret from parliament.[16] It was the first of many clandestine joint operations between elements of the Italian state and small groups of neo-fascists. Funded by the CIA, many operatives – generally ex-fascists – received training from the British Intelligence Service. Prime minister Giulio Andreotti finally admitted to the existence of the operation in 1990, adding that there were 139 Gladio arms caches in the country.[17] As with many of the scandals and massacres recounted in this chapter, subsequent investigations have never managed to shed full light on the background.

THE TAMBRONI AFFAIR

Sometimes the ruling Christian Democrat party showed open political toleration of the parliamentary wing of the MSI. In the mid-1950s the DC had lost an absolute majority in parliament, and was therefore forced to rely on support from other forces. Periodically, the DC threatened to bring the MSI back in from the cold when it needed to unsettle other coalition partners, and in broader ideological terms the MSI could always be relied upon to act as a bulwark against communism. Little by little, such as with the election of state presidents or prime ministers, neo-fascism became tolerated if not openly acceptable.[18]

This sympathy came to a head in 1960, when Fernando Tambroni, who had been an officer in the fascist militia, only became Christian Democrat prime minister thanks to the parliamentary votes of the MSI.[19] Soon after forming his administration Tambroni called for a vote of confidence, which his government only narrowly survived – by 300 votes against 293 – again thanks to MSI votes. Naturally, widespread opposition began to develop, and in anticipation Tambroni ordered all prefects and local police chiefs to vigorously repress any demonstrations against his government.[20]

It is worth examining this period in some detail, as it represented probably the country's most serious political crisis since 1945–48. Disquiet and outrage continued to spread throughout the country, and it was not hard to understand why: unrepentant fascists were being integrated into the heart of democracy, just as they had been in 1920–22. It is likely that in return for their parliamentary support the MSI was allowed to hold its party conference in Genoa, which had witnessed intense fascist violence just 15 years earlier. The MSI predictably upped the stakes, by announcing that the chair of the conference would be Carlo Emanuele Basile, head of government in Genoa during the German occupation, with direct responsibility for the deportation of workers and torture of partisans. On the eve of the March 1944 strikes he warned those intending to take action: 'Whether you strike for a few hours or walk out of your workplace, in both cases some of you, selected at random, will after a few hours be sent ... to concentration camps.'[21] Such was the ferocity of repression in Genoa that when Basile was initially sentenced to twelve years imprisonment in 1945, a crowd estimated at over 200,000 demonstrated outside the courthouse.[22]

Potentially the proposed MSI conference could be a turning point: if allowed to pass then neo-fascism would have gained full legitimacy within a democratic system that had had to fight fascism to create itself. The first ex-partisan meeting to contest the MSI conference was held on 2 June, and further meetings mushroomed throughout the month. On 19 June the MSI tried to open a branch in a suburb of Genoa, but thousands of people blocked the road. Police infiltrated the meetings of anti-fascists, and sent worried reports down to Rome, but similar protest movements were building up in Bologna, Reggio Emilia and Rome.[23] Four days before the conference was due to start, on 28 June, in a city and country awaiting a serious confrontation, a massive demonstration was held. Local socialist Resistance leader Sandro Pertini began his speech by saying:

People, partisans and workers, Genoese of all classes. The Roman authorities are particularly hard at work looking for those they consider the instigators, the inciters, the leaders of these anti-Fascist demonstrations. But they don't need to struggle so hard: I can tell you, sirs, who our instigators are: here they are, next to our flags: the dead of Turchino, Benedicta, Olivella and Cravasco, the tortured of the Student Residence [all sites of fascist and Nazi atrocities], where the terrifying screams of the victims and the cries and slaughter of their sadistic torturers still ring out today.[24]

On 30 June general strikes were held in Milan, Livorno, Ferrara and other cities. And on the same day – two days before the planned conference – tens of thousands marched through Genoa; many were also taking part in the general strike that had been proclaimed. As demonstrators were making their way home through the main city square the police attacked them. It was the spark that lit a fire, as a contemporary account describes:

> Policemen were ferociously hitting people with short truncheons. It lasted a second – a terrible cry of anger rose up from the crowd. The red cars of the police were surrounded, overwhelmed by an angry tide and pushed up against the walls. Next to me I saw a boy wielding a steel chair taken from a bar, who then attacked the front of the car. Another young man, almost an adolescent, with a little striped cotton t-shirt and drainpipe jeans, was whirling a big stick in front of two policemen. They were forced to stand with their backs to the wall, crossing their hands across their face. Another thin young man, his eyes burning behind his student glasses, threw himself on a policeman, snatching his truncheon away.
>
> Then, as the police moved back, in the blue haze left by the tear gas, long-range action began with stones. Every rock and projectile that went flying (cobblestones, bricks, small tables from bars, planks from god knows where) was accompanied either by a shout, an insult in dialect or a cry of anger. Above all it was young people who were throwing things.[25]

Perhaps the most important fact is that many of those fighting had been barely born during the Resistance. These events were the coming together of a new generation with the Resistance generation – and to a significant extent outside the control of the PCI. The rioting continued for several hours, with police reinforcements arriving the next morning; but meanwhile local partisans had set up a 'liberation committee' which ominously threatened 'to take over the government of the city'. A new general strike was announced, with strikers asked to take to the streets. Overnight dozens of barricades were built, hundreds of Molotov cocktails prepared, presumably to be used the following morning.[26] Meanwhile, the local prefect spoke with prime minister Tambroni, and decided to cancel the MSI conference. That evening the whole city celebrated, and the Resistance monument was covered in flowers.[27]

Despite the anti-fascist victory in Genoa political outrage over MSI involvement in government continued unabated, as did police repression of protesters. The most notorious incident occurred in Reggio Emilia on 7 July, when five people were shot dead by the police, and in Sicily it was almost open season, with four demonstrators being killed in Palermo and one in Catania.[28] Bomb attacks against left-wing and trade union offices were now common, and many people drew the conclusion that Tambroni wanted to rehabilitate fascism in its traditional form.

Following the killings in Reggio Emilia, on the following day there was a general strike throughout the country, but by this stage many senior Christian Democrats had become alarmed, and on 19 July Tambroni was forced to resign. Three very significant developments emerged from these weeks of crisis: first, anti-fascism had proved to be a unifying force throughout the country, but particularly among the working class – where a new generation had driven forward the uncompromising movement against Tambroni; second, three years later there would be an 'opening to the left' in Italian coalition government – the Socialist Party joined a government with the Christian Democrats; third, on the far right the most extreme and militaristic elements were now in the driving seat – because not only was the parliamentary road to fascism in tatters after Genoa, the hated Socialists were now in government.

ATTEMPTED COUPS

Bearing all this in mind it is not surprising to discover ex-fascists at the head of two aborted military coups in this period: 1964 and 1970. *Carabinieri* General Giovanni De Lorenzo had been a fascist career officer under Mussolini, one of the many who had not been purged after 1945. As a senior military officer during the 1950s he was head of SIFAR, the Italian secret services.[29] He was also paid by the CIA to organise the 'Gladio' secret army, made up of the nation's 'vital forces', prepared to take action if the PCI ever gained a parliamentary majority.

In 1964 De Lorenzo took the first steps in launching a military coup but mysteriously aborted his plans. It was called the 'Piano solo' because it mainly involved just the *Carabinieri* (in this case the Italian word 'solo' means 'only'), albeit three whole divisions, yet the broad plan included all the classic actions of a full-blooded coup. Up to 2,000 left-wing leaders, journalists, trade unionists and intellectuals would be arrested and detained at Gladio's training camp in Sardinia; public offices, television and radio stations would all be seized, as well as the offices of certain political parties, and left-wing newspapers would be shut down.[30]

What had outraged De Lorenzo in particular was the creation of a centre-left government coalition in December 1963, which included the Socialist Party. He had a series of meetings with senior politicians in the early summer of 1964, and although the whole story is still shrouded in mystery, it seems very likely that the coup was called off because De Lorenzo was able to frighten the Socialists and force Christian Democrats to take a more conservative line in government. What remains chilling are the powerful forces involved in the preparation of these plans:

> a number of very senior officers of law enforcement, the intelligence service, and the armed forces, working in close contact with their international counterparts (especially the CIA), with some reactionary political leaders and with a segment of the financial and business world. In the event it had been necessary, irregular civilian groups (obviously of the Right), illegally recruited, would have joined the fray.[31]

As ever, the only punishment De Lorenzo received was being relieved of his command several years later. Following a familiar path, he became an MSI MP shortly before his death in 1973.[32]

In the late 1960s Junio Valerio Borghese began plotting another coup with elements of the armed forces and members of the business community in

Genoa. The plan was to seize key government ministries and television stations in Rome, as well as government buildings throughout the country. Support this time was even wider: neo-fascists were mobilised to take over cities in Calabria, the Sicilian Mafia was on board, as was the P2, the secret Masonic lodge. So in December 1970 Borghese finally began operations to occupy the Ministry of the Interior; a group of about 50 former parachute regiment members led by Stefano Delle Chiaie probably penetrated the Ministry's armoury, but withdrew without a shot being fired. As with De Lorenzo, Borghese had been a member of the 'Gladio' secret army, and perhaps these connections made this aborted coup all the more serious, as it appears to have had the approval of US intelligence services.[33]

In both planned coups, manoeuvres were called off at the last minute. In all probability this was because the plotters received less support than expected from within the state machinery. Yet in both cases it was clear that a high number of senior military figures were either aware of the plots beforehand and kept quiet, or refused to move against the conspirators or to reveal their knowledge afterwards. In any event Borghese, an experienced plotter, infiltrator and double-agent, would not have taken things so far had he not been certain of substantial support within the state.

Finally, in August 1974 preparations for the 'Sogno coup' were also suddenly aborted. Edgardo Sogno was another murky figure, who had been financed first by FIAT and then by the US in the 1950s, and as with Borghese had experience from the Second World War – but interestingly enough as a conservative partisan commander. Plans were already at an advanced stage, and preliminary paramilitary action had already taken place when arrest warrants were issued for Sogno and others in May. In a familiar pattern, the original magistrate was taken off the case and the investigation transferred from Turin to Rome, where the defendants were quickly acquitted. Years later Sogno made it clear in an interview what his plans were: 'The country was slowly slipping into [leader of the PCI] Berlinguer's hands. Together with [former Christian Democrat defence minister] Pacciardi I had devised a plan. ... Had the PCI entered government, even as part of a coalition, military action would have taken place. Everything was ready, including the *Carabinieri*.'[34]

The common political motivation, and the overwhelming evidence of repeated involvement of high state figures in these attempted coups, make it hard not to agree with the verdict given by the magistrate who investigated Borghese's 1970 coup: 'the involvement of state organizations in the development of right-wing terrorism should not be considered a deviation, but instead normal activity, part of their institutional function'.[35]

THE STRATEGY OF TENSION

While the perhaps more sophisticated neo-fascist activists plotted within the Italian state, the traditional fascist street-fighting strategy was stopped in its tracks by a growing mood of left-wing radicalism among students. For example, after many successful 'punitive expeditions', on 15 March 1968

Giorgio Almirante led an attack of 200 neo-fascists at Rome University, along with another MSI MP Giulio Caradonna, but this time it was repulsed. Faced with a rapidly growing mass movement of left-wing students, a change of tactics was needed.

The first step was a trip by Stefano Delle Chiaie, Pino Rauti and others to Greece in spring 1968, as guests of honour of the military regime of the time. It was here that they heard first-hand experience from a neighbouring country of how to provoke violence at left-wing demonstrations and infiltrate far-left groups. At the same time the wave of student radicalism was spreading rapidly, indeed it was followed by the 'hot Autumn' of working-class unrest in 1969. Demands of all kinds were voiced by the newly radicalised workers – from wage increases to free evening classes and greater trade union rights. The government went some way to meeting workers' demands in 1969, but to do so they had to increase taxes and rents, thus hitting traditional DC supporters. Some industrialists conceded an eight-hour reduction in the working week to 40 hours, and equal wage increases for both white-collar and blue-collar workers, at every level. In 1970 the 'Workers Statute' became law: this provided for greater trade union negotiating rights, and introduced the crime of 'anti-trade union behaviour' to the statute book. Union meetings could now be held in the workplace, albeit outside working hours, although ten hours a year of *paid* union meetings were allowed.

But it was the militancy of young workers – best summed up by the slogan 'we want the lot' – that worried the 'captains of industry'. Factory owners were at a loss in 1969 as to how to respond. Socially and politically there were some similarities with the 1919–20 period in Italy – the so-called *biennio rosso* or 'two red years', in which the working class came close to seizing power, but which ended in 1922 with Mussolini being invited to form his first administration. Both the threat of working-class militancy and fears about it were very real, and neo-fascists were not slow to draw historical comparisons. It was from these considerations that the 'strategy of tension' emerged.

Neo-fascist thinking was in essence this: working-class insurgency needed to be stopped, but also 'spun' to their advantage to create an authoritarian outcome. This strategy involved government and secret services spinning the story that the left, and particularly anarchists, were behind terrorist attacks – that is, it was the left that was creating 'tension'. The police would give credibility to this illusion by promptly arresting anarchists or other activists after every attack, while the general public, faced with such an apparent abuse of democracy by anarchists and other leftists, and with general working-class rebellion, would, it was hoped, call for some kind of 'strong state' – essentially fascism – to resolve the situation. In April 1969 a secret neo-fascist meeting adopted the 'strategy of tension'. Perhaps not uncoincidentally, Almirante once again became MSI leader almost simultaneously, and called for an end to 'political appeasement', given that all institutions were declared to be corrupt. The MSI stressed that as a party it was outside the system, unwilling to make concessions to a communist-inclined working class.

The mad dogs of fascism were then let loose. On 25 April – the date was hardly coincidental – two bombs exploded in Milan wounding 20, and in August eight bombs exploded on trains within 24 hours. The scale of the ensuing attacks was bewildering: one source has estimated that there were 145 terrorist attacks throughout 1969, one every three days. Of these, 96 could be immediately classified as neo-fascist because of the nature of the arrests that were made, or because of targets such as PCI branches, synagogues or partisan monuments.[36] This bloodletting continued for a decade, with hundreds of people being killed in public places, particularly on the railways.

The most notorious attack took place at the start of this cycle: in December 1969 a bombing at a Milan bank in *piazza Fontana* killed 17 people. Two days before the bombing, the ever-present Almirante had stated in an interview: 'Fascist youth organisations are preparing for civil war ... to fight Communists all means are justified.'[37] Without any evidence, two hours after the bombing, police were rushing around the campus of Milan University looking for anarchists to arrest, and that evening local police chief Marcello Guida explained that police investigations were focused on anarchist groups. What many people were unaware of at the time was that as early as 1943 Guida was a senior officer at Ventotene jail, which included anti-fascists such as Sandro Pertini and Pietro Secchia among its inmates, and like thousands of fascist officials, he had been allowed to continue his career in 1945 undisturbed.[38]

Such a complex strategy could never have got off the ground, particularly on a logistical basis, had it relied only on existing right-wing terror groups such as *Ordine Nuovo* and *Avanguardia Nazionale*, which probably had no more than 1,500 active members. Given the history, and indeed the future history, of the Italian state, it is important to remember that, as one author has said: 'There was clearly collusion between some *Carabinieri* units (especially the secret police, SID) and the neo-fascists, and indeed the whole "strategy of tension" depended on such collusion.'[39] For example, Delfo Zorzi – one of the people strongly suspected both of planting the bomb in Milan and of organising the bombing of a trade union demonstration in Brescia in 1974 killing nine people – was subsequently given a lifelong diplomatic passport by the Foreign Ministry. Repeatedly tried *in absentia*, he currently lives comfortably in Japan, a country which does not have an extradition treaty with Italy. However, both Pino Rauti and a *Carabinieri* general have recently been indicted for the Milan bombing.[40]

Initially, the combination of encouraging terrorism and blaming the left worked well for Almirante electorally. In the May 1972 general election the MSI achieved its best vote since 1945 (it was not to get a higher vote until 1994), with its national average reaching 8.7 per cent, including peaks of 26 per cent in Naples and 36 per cent in Reggio Calabria. On 4 June, just a few weeks later, Almirante said in a speech in Florence that the MSI was ready to 'substitute' for the state if the government was not up to the task, and invited young neo-fascists to engage in physical clashes with the far left.

Despite Almirante's denials, over the next few years most people began to associate the MSI with terrorism. This was because the 'new left' movement, which had consolidated itself to the left of the PCI, exposed the links between the fascists and elements in government. Furthermore, in 1978 Almirante was charged with aiding and abetting one of the key perpetrators of a car bomb attack at Peteano that had killed three *Carabinieri* six years earlier.[41] This is a truly chilling story: years later two *Carabinieri* generals were convicted of destroying evidence and perverting the course of justice, in regard to the murder of three of their officers. Guido Abbatangelo, an MSI MP, was subsequently given an eight-year sentence for possession of explosives.[42] The key figure in the tale was a man named Carlo Cicuttin, secretary of his local MSI branch, whose voice had been recorded luring the three policemen into the trap at Peteano, which was why he and his accomplice fled to Spain. Almirante had a brilliant idea to get Cicuttin off the hook, sending him what was at the time a very large sum – $34,650 – to be used for a throat operation to change the sound of his voice. Nevertheless, both men were later convicted of the bombing, whereas Almirante avoided any serious legal sanctions due to his own personal amnesty law passed by parliament before the trial began.[43]

In a broader context, as these links between neo-fascist terror groups (who shared a history with the MSI) and terrorist attacks became clearer, support for the MSI declined. Another part of the equation was that the militancy of the working class decreased, so many conservatives no longer felt the need for such an extreme solution.

As a consequence, the MSI's electoral gains of 1972 were quickly cancelled out: from a high of 8.7 per cent the MSI's vote fell to 6.1 per cent in 1976, 5.3 per cent in 1979 and 5.4 per cent in 1992 – vital fluctuations in a proportional electoral system. Both Almirante and his protégé Gianfranco Fini understood that they had to return to the mainstream, and that this meant breaking with the more hard-line and nostalgic elements of their party.

THE POLITICAL DEFROSTING OF THE MSI

When the Christian Democrat government had tried to form an alliance with the MSI in 1960 they almost faced an insurrection in the North of the country. Not only did this contribute to the 'strategy of tension' developing from within neo-fascism, it also proved that any rehabilitation of the MSI, or indeed of fascism itself, would take a considerable period of time to achieve. Centre and right-wing politicians understood that a party viewed by most Italians as being made up of unreconstructed fascists could not be brought in from the cold at a stroke, so a slow creeping legitimisation of the MSI ensued. Much of this had to do with electoral calculation rather than establishment politicians embracing the ideology of fascism. The relative decline of the Christian Democrats and other centre parties meant that eventually they had to countenance some form of electoral alliance with the MSI in the future. Yet it was a party of the centre-left, led by the ambitious and ruthless Bettino Craxi, that led the way in beginning a very limited 'defrosting' of the MSI, given the unexpectedly high vote it had achieved at the June 1983 election.

What accelerated this process was the explosion of *Tangentopoli* ('Bribesville') from early 1992 onwards. Together with the subsequent 'Clean Hands' investigation, by early 1994 the political centre, in the shape of the DC and the PSI, had collapsed after its rampant corruption had emerged into the light of day. The party system that had emerged in 1945 was now seriously discredited, as conservative and right-wing politics came to be represented by two new forces – Silvio Berlusconi, who first entered the political fray and became prime minister in spring 1994; and the racist Northern League, which began to gain large votes in northern regions and stabilise itself organisationally and electorally. From now on both forces were to give a tremendous boost to revisionism.

Up until the explosion of *Tangentopoli* the MSI's vote had largely been a protest vote: but now the widespread popular revulsion against establishment parties was something the MSI could tap into because it had always been an anti-system party, railing against corruption year in year out. Given the inexperience of Berlusconi and the volatility of the Northern League, the MSI's new leader Gianfranco Fini sensed that great opportunities were ahead. In January 1994 he announced that the MSI would be transformed into National Alliance (AN) the following January. One of the main justifications for this move was the need to reach out to ex-DC voters and members, and to 'block the left's road' to what seemed like an inevitable victory in the upcoming general election.

Due to the chaos and uncertainty in conservative politics, legitimisation of the MSI and Fini by democratic politicians now became overt. During the mayoral campaign in Rome in 1993, when asked who he would vote for if he were registered in Rome, Berlusconi coolly replied: 'If I were in Rome, I would certainly vote for Fini.'[44] Fini had decided to stand as mayor of Rome and came very close to winning, gaining 46.9 per cent in the second ballot, as opposed to Francesco Rutelli's 53.1 per cent. Another significant electoral shift in the MSI's favour happened at the same time in Naples, where Alessandra Mussolini, granddaughter of Benito, received over 40 per cent of the vote but lost to the centre-left candidate for mayor.[45]

Although Berlusconi made a triumphant entry into politics at the 1994 elections, the MSI became the third largest party with 13.4 per cent of the vote, 105 MPs and 43 senators. Very soon after his election victory Fini made it clear that he wanted to put some distance between historical fascism and AN, telling a journalist on a major news weekly: 'the one thing the secretary of National Alliance has to avoid is comparisons with Mussolini'.[46] In the meantime, conventional politicians rushed to embrace him. The British ambassador in Rome, Sir Patrick Fairweather, had lunch with Fini just days after his victory. Similarly Bill Clinton, interestingly enough in Europe to commemorate the 50th anniversary of D-Day, had dinner with him.[47]

The MSI definitively came out of the cold when Berlusconi brought them into his first government in spring 1994. In a *Washington Post* interview in May 1994 he justified his decision by defending Mussolini's early period in government and denying the MSI's fascist heritage:

Later of course [Mussolini] would take away liberties and lead the country into war, so obviously the total outcome was to be condemned. But for a while, Mussolini did some good things here and that's something that history says is correct. ... Fascists do not exist in my government. They do not exist. There is nobody in my government who is against liberty and democracy.

In other words, fascism, or at least the MSI/AN, was being legitimised. Fini and his party were being pulled in two directions at once: there was the pull of the past on a very ideologised party, and the pull towards wielding power within democratic institutions.

Despite their absorption into conventional politics in the second half of the 1990s, former MSI leaders have nevertheless remained compulsively obsessed about justifying Mussolini's dictatorship. During the 1994 election campaign MP Alessandra Mussolini declared: 'If my grandfather had won the war we wouldn't be sitting around chatting', while in June she criticised American cinema on the grounds that it was 'dominated by the left, which is Jewish'. In May Piero Buscaroli, AN candidate for the European Parliament stated: 'Poofs disgust me ... if it were up to me, I'd send them all to concentration camps.' Sometimes Fini was no better. Soon after their spring election victory he described Mussolini as 'the greatest statesman of the century'.[48] The following month, a journalist visited Fini's local branch of the MSI, at Nomentano in Rome, and reported: 'Mussolini reigns like a monarch in every room. His portrait, either in profile or full-face, with or without helmet, is to be found on every wall and behind the desks of the branch's officers.'[49]

Fini was going to take his party on a long journey, though the road would be difficult since the party he had inherited was thoroughly fascist. In a survey carried out by the MSI and its youth wing in 1991, 88 per cent of those interviewed said their main historical point of reference was fascism; only 13 per cent were happy to define themselves as 'democrats'.[50] The first real step away from fascism was taken at the Fiuggi conference in January 1995, where the MSI was wound up and AN created, with the party increasingly defining itself as 'post-fascist'.[51] Despite the ongoing tensions within his party, what Fini had going for him once he gained definitive control of AN was both electoral success and, increasingly, strong representation within the highest levels of national government. As the party strived to become more respectable, its electoral appeal increased – in early 1996 AN received the largest approval rating of any political party, 15.7 per cent.

Fini has deliberately tried to avoid being a controversial figure such as Almirante, Berlusconi or Jean-Marie Le Pen in France. Until 1994 the MSI had been beyond the pale for almost 50 years. Fini's strategy was all about making the newly born AN a party of government, both theoretically and practically. So as a leader, Fini quickly distinguished himself by making many conciliatory gestures. He first visited the Fosse Ardeatine in Rome in December 1993, the site of a massacre of over 300 people by the Nazis, who had acted with the collusion of Italian fascists. He went on to visit Auschwitz in 1999, the Italian concentration camp Risiera di San Sabba in 2001, and in 2004 he took part in the 80th anniversary celebrations to commemorate the murder of Socialist Party MP Giacomo Matteotti.

The 'post-fascist' label that AN applied to itself in the mid 1990s was a serious move, and by the new millennium no significant examples of classical and overt fascism could be seen within the AN leadership. But the uneasy cohabitation of moderates and hard-liners finally blew up in November 2003, when Fini made an official visit to Israel for the first time. Although he was speaking in Jerusalem and not Damascus, his speech had all the trappings of a full conversion as he defined fascism's 1938 racial laws as 'absolute evil', and for the first time condemned fascism for passing them.[52] Since then, more nostalgic fascists such as Alessandra Mussolini and open Nazis such as Pino Rauti have left AN for other shores.

History can never repeat itself in an identical fashion. The far right have understood perfectly well for decades that, in order to gain a foothold in the political mainstream, they have to distance themselves from the interwar dictatorships. Overall they have done this successfully. Although it is wise to be cautious about AN's apparent conversion to democracy, with its dozens of ministers, MPs, senators – and thousands of local councillors – a professional political class has inserted itself fully into mainstream capitalist democracy. To all appearances AN seems to have transformed itself into a right-wing democratic party. The series of small split-offs to the right of the party over the years has slowly strengthened Fini's position internally, and obviously given him more freedom to make the party less and less fascist. Indeed Fini could easily lead the right-wing coalition after Berlusconi – and given the perennial controversy surrounding the latter, Fini is now incontestably better poised, more reasonable, even verging on the charming. In fact, at the time of writing, AN and *Forza Italia* are finalising arrangements for their fusion into the 'Party of Freedoms'.

THE UNDERMINING OF THE RESISTANCE

One of the factors allowing the Resistance to be undermined and fascism to be exonerated of its crimes has been the weakness of the historic memory created in Italy. Apart from the specific arguments over the Resistance, Italy did not have its own 'Nuremberg trials'. Furthermore, the widely documented war crimes of fascist forces outside of Italy have been a taboo subject.

In 1945 the Yugoslav government asked for the extradition of 302 presumed Italian war criminals, but none of the demands were ever granted.[53] Yet when looking at statistics for illegal incarceration alone, a recent Yugoslav report estimated that 149,639 people had been interned by the Italians, and 92,902 imprisoned[54] – while deaths through massacres could run into hundreds of thousands. The following year the Greek government published a white paper detailing horrific war crimes, torture, famine and destruction. It was later estimated that 100,000 Greeks died from malnutrition alone as a result of the country being invaded by Italian forces.[55] Yet the Italian government has never even apologised for war crimes in the Balkans.

The governments of Greece and Yugoslavia – and of Ethiopia – all applied to the UN for international trials concerning Italian war crimes, but their requests fell into a void. Initially, in the Cold War climate, it was the British Foreign Office who contrived to bury such matters. As one author has argued: 'In Anglo-American political attitudes towards Italy, the prevailing point of view favoured avoiding international trials that might have weakened the hold of the moderate governments that were leading the country.'[56] And once Rome was given jurisdiction similar concerns prevailed. As a consequence, individuals who in all likelihood would have been convicted as war criminals in an international court initially hung around in the shadows, with some then emerging into public life, writing their own memoirs and claiming they had been suspected unjustly. The end result was that while for many people the Resistance of 1943–45 had redeemed Italy, the behaviour of fascists during 1940–43, and even before, were issues that registered with relatively few people.

But some of the reasons for the weakening of the Resistance came from within, or more precisely from the very political parties and historians who celebrated and defended its values and achievements. While generally not downgrading the Resistance, the left felt the need to show it in a particular light. Therefore it was presented as a war of national liberation – which of course it was. But German violence was stressed, and the role of Italian fascists tended to be put into the background. To put fascists into the limelight would have brought into play the fact that Italians had fought Italians, that to some degree Italy had experienced a civil war, and as in every war of this kind there were two distinct sides. This was a formulation that the left tried hard to undermine, as one of the major historians of the movement argued in 1991: 'Anti-fascist unity as embodied in the CLN system, and which is today still a source of legitimisation of the Italian Republic and what has been called its "constitutional arch", is reinterpreted as mere anti-German unity, almost as if the Republic was founded on opposition to Germany and not instead to fascism.'[57] Or in other words, what was stressed was the wartime unity of the forces within the CLN, who then went on to create the 'constitutional arch' of postwar Italian politics. As the same author goes on to argue elsewhere, dealing specifically with the largest political force within the Resistance:

In order to legitimise itself as a national party during the postwar period, the Communist Party has put into quarantine, erased the memory, of the civil war in which it was involved. This has been one of the elements that has stopped the definition of civil war being used to study what really happened, and to understand the emotions created by such a definition.[58]

This deliberately restrictive interpretation of reality was unable to withstand a growing campaign from the right, which increasingly stressed the civil war fought during 1943–45, an experience lived directly by many Italians and handed down to their children. This gave neo-fascists and their fellow travellers a tactical advantage when they argued for reconciliation because they were talking about a traumatic experience the left denied, a tactic used as part of reaching the greater goal of gaining full political respectability.

But there was another underlying reason for the PCI's caution. It was, after all, a Communist Party in name at least, and was perceived as such by many. Yet it had not been allowed to enter a government coalition since 1947. So, as part of its drive to earn greater respectability and therefore votes, the left engaged in its own form of 'revisionism' of the Resistance.

Left-wing Revisionism

It is difficult to pinpoint a specific moment when this revisionism began, since it was a process that played out over many years. One of the first occasions was undoubtedly in 1988, when Giorgio Almirante died. The cult of death in Italian society is such that it is normal for funerals of national political leaders to be attended by leaders of other parties. But Almirante was different – as a leader of a party outside the 'constitutional arch' and an unrepentant fascist. Nevertheless, of all people, it was Giancarlo Pajetta who went to 'pay his respects' of behalf of the PCI.[59] Pajetta had spent ten years in fascist jails, had lost two brothers as partisans, and played a leading role in the Resistance. In the 1950s he was one of the most rebellious MPs in parliament, often coming to blows with fascists in the chamber. Even today people remember his total refusal to converse with fascists during a television debate in the 1960s – 'we settled accounts with you in *piazzale Loreto*'.

This process was accelerated in 1991, when the PCI decided to dissolve itself. For many years the party had had a very limited ideological link to a Marxist understanding of society, and was slowly evolving into a social democratic formation. The collapse of the Soviet Union and the Eastern bloc states accelerated this trend; it became increasingly ludicrous to defend Stalinist states whose demise was celebrated and indeed precipitated by their own people. Furthermore, constant references to the PCI's 'communism' during election campaigns were seen to constitute a drawback.

The name of the new party created from the ashes of the PCI was the Democratic Party of the Left (PDS), and the goal was to become a party of government, though success eluded them with Berlusconi's victory in 1994. Closely linked to this ditching of 'communism' was a growing distancing from the defence of the Resistance. In the summer of 1995 the then Green Party Mayor of Rome, Francesco Rutelli, attempted to rename a square in front of the Museum of Modern Art 'in honour' of Giuseppe Bottai, a Minister in Mussolini's fascist government. Bottai was Minister of Education in the late 1930s, when 'teaching staff of Jewish race' were sacked from universities and schools. Rutelli's initial justification was that Bottai had a particularly good environmental policy as regards safeguarding Roman monuments. He then claimed that his proposal 'would only be understood over time', whilst at the same time rushing the decision through council committees.

This move was even more incredible because Rutelli had been elected in a wave of united anti-fascism in autumn 1993 – his opponent in the close-fought campaign being Gianfranco Fini. His narrow victory was helped by the fact that for the first time ever, Jewish leaders had called for a vote for a specific candidate: Rutelli. Doubly significant was that Rutelli was helped throughout by ex-communist councillors of the PDS: as members of the ruling group they refused to vote against his decision, and also declined to lead any campaign on the ground. This attitude was consistent with the fact that in the very same period the PDS had invited Fini to speak at its annual festival for the first time. What united both Rutelli's proposal and the PDS's attitude was an open move towards 'national reconciliation' between fascists and anti-fascists.

Anti-fascists and ordinary people more generally were incensed by Rutelli's decision: demonstrations were held in the square, and signatures were collected to rename it in memory of murdered anti-fascists; 3,500 signatures in particular were collected in support of a proposal to rename the square after Jerry Mazlo, a South African migrant worker murdered by Italian racists in 1989. As the organisers said, he was the 'the first victim of Italian neo-racism', and if Rutelli's proposal had succeeded it would have done nothing but encourage further attacks. Indeed even Fini himself had said of this latter proposal: 'it's a good and correct initiative, which I share'.[60] Although Rutelli backed down, it was a highly emblematic episode.[61]

After 50 years in opposition, the ex-communist PDS finally became a major part of Romano Prodi's coalition government in May 1996, and they lost no time in making controversial statements about the Resistance. The opening speech of the new parliamentary session made by Luciano Violante, the newly elected leader of the lower house, caused uproar. He put forward the notion that the reasons young people fought for Mussolini's puppet regime between 1943 and 1945 should be understood and, by implication, accepted. He also said that 'shared values' needed to be created. While the actual words used were measured, it was another step towards the rehabilitation of fascism, albeit to an unknown degree.

A few months later, the ex-Christian Democrat head of state, Oscar Luigi Scalfaro, took up the ball that Violante had set rolling. On the rough equivalent of Remembrance Day, Scalfaro made it clear in his speech that for him: 'the first devout thought goes to the memory and a prayer in remembrance of those who fought, albeit on opposing sides but with an honesty of intentions, until the ultimate sacrifice'. Things were now becoming explicit: the fascist cause should be accepted, their deaths should be officially honoured. The uproar continued: an ex-partisan leader and one of Italy's most famous journalists, Giorgio Bocca, wrote an editorial in the country's best-selling newspaper arguing that 'official mourning for the dead who were alive during the Republic of Salò and were on that side, means recognition of that side. It means putting the liberation movement and collaborationists on the same level. It means, albeit in a creeping fashion given that considerable time has passed, that the two things were almost the same.'[62]

Violante, meanwhile, continued to legitimise Fini and, crucially, to put fascist ideas on the same level as anti-fascist ideas. They held a public meeting together with students in Trieste in March 1998, during which Violante spoke of 'the serious responsibilities of the fascist and communist movements. It's not a question of counter-posing one memory to another, but of understanding and measuring yourself up to the other one, on the basis of your own memory.' Naturally Fini was more than happy to reciprocate, speaking of the need to 'define a shared historic memory'. The scale of the revisionism was enough to move around 100 Italian historians and intellectuals to publish a joint public letter in which they attacked 'the historic groundlessness of the argument and the inconsistency of the demands put forward' by both politicians. It went on to state: 'Initiatives such as that of Trieste are incompatible with historical truth and the fundamental values of the constitution.'[63]

But the leadership of the PDS, now renamed simply Left Democrats (DS), were undeterred. At the funeral in 2000 of Carla Capponi, a leader of the Roman resistance, party leader Walter Veltroni directed a calculated insult against his audience. Repeating Violante's notion of four years earlier, he called on respect for those 'who fought and died in good faith at a very young age for the Republic of Salò'.[64] Although later out of government, it was their very conviction that led Violante and DS leader Piero Fassino to support a proposal put forward by AN in February 2004, to make 10 February a 'day of memory' for the forced exodus of Istrians, Dalmatians and *Fiumani* from Italy's eastern frontier. Once more, the racist policy of Italian fascism towards Slavs, the invasion of Yugoslavia in 1941, and the killing of around a million Yugoslavs, were deemed unworthy of recognition. In a climate of 'national unity' and 'reconciliation', what mattered far more was the loss of a small piece of territory and the exodus of a few thousand Italians.

Despite its steady move to the centre ground of politics, and a further renaming from Left Democrats (DS) to Democratic Party (PD), this still did not mean a total abandoning of the Resistance – when somebody says or does something outrageous against it PD leaders will generally issue a condemnation. But as with most major political parties around the world today there is very little activity among the membership, discouraged as it is by a leadership often made up of 'control freaks'. For example, to celebrate 25 April in 2008 in Turin, 200 PD activists made up special flags with their party's symbol but with a red background. Such was the nervousness created that the regional secretary of the party described this is a 'serious mistake', and called on the national leadership to 'criticise the event'.[65]

Right-wing Revisionism

In recent years the right, in its own terms, has begun to proclaim the Resistance as its own, accepting the values of 'anti-fascism'. But it also insists the period was one of civil war, and that therefore fascist deaths and sacrifices should be given equal value to anti-fascist ones. Coupled with this shift there has been an obsessive media campaign concerned with the excesses of the Resistance, in a context in which the average Italian remained unaware of the scale of fascist repression and violence. Newspaper articles, television documentaries and debates, and the cinema, all stressed the violence of the partisans.

Having won significant ground in the ideological battle, the right then went on the offensive. As early as 1994 the Berlusconi government – deliberately communicating its decision on 28 October, the anniversary of the March on Rome – announced an anniversary stamp commemorating the fascist philosopher Giovanni Gentile, killed by partisans 50 years earlier. This tendency towards revisionism accelerated under the Berlusconi government of 2001–06. For example in April 2003 the *Forza Italia* mayor of the Sicilian town of Agrigento decided to rename a major square in honour of Giorgio Almirante. The fact that two other councillors, both in AN, supported the initiative shows that it was not just a provocation by one individual. And to announce the decision on 25 April, the national holiday to celebrate the liberation of northern cities by anti-fascists, was no coincidence.[66] The following month AN organised dozens of meetings throughout Italy to commemorate the fifteenth anniversary of Almirante's death. In a meeting held in Milan, Fini called him an 'unforgettable master of democracy'.[67]

Such revisionist statements now generally provoke no reaction, such as Fini's recent claim that Almirante 'has honoured Italian democracy'.[68] However revisionism can never consolidate its position without receiving support from centre ground or left-wing forces. In May 2008 the inevitable Luciano Violante spoke at a meeting called to 'celebrate' a five-volume publication of Almirante's parliamentary speeches, praising him for having brought 'those who did not identify with the 1948 Republic into the bosom of democracy'.[69]

Politicians nowadays merely pay lip service to the Resistance, particularly when they attend official commemorations. In April 2008 a documentary about the battle of Licciana Nardi, when a major German column surrendered to partisans in northern Tuscany, had its premiere in a local cinema. Renato Occhipinti, one of the partisan commanders now well into his eighties, released himself from hospital against doctors orders to come to speak to the audience. When he gave his brief speech the local MP was sitting in the front row, just a yard away, but rather than listening to Occhipinti he continued to speak on his mobile phone.

The way Italian institutions now celebrate their own emergence from fascism has become both offensive and bizarre. For example on 8 September 2008 the President of the Republic went to Porta San Paolo in Rome to commemorate the improvised defence put up by soldiers and ordinary people against fascism and the invading Germans in 1943. Another speaker was the Minister of Defence (and ex-MSI hard-liner) Ignazio La Russa, who commemorated just the opposite:

> I could not live with my conscience if I did not remember other soldiers in uniform, such as those from the Nembo of the RSI army who subjectively, from their own point of view, fought believing in the defence of the Fatherland, who over the following months opposed the Anglo-American

landings therefore deserving the respect – albeit in the diversity of positions – of all those who look at the history of Italy with objectivity.[70]

La Russa certainly does raise a crucial issue for young generations: the growing impossibility of an accurate and full picture of the Resistance and fascism being communicated by government institutions and leaders. The fact that there was relatively little debate after La Russa's remarks illustrated the frequency nowadays of such statements. To appreciate their seriousness, however, one need only imagine ministers from the German government praising the SS.

As can be seen, in Italy revisionism has not been restricted to the field of historical or to some degree journalistic debate, it has been a prominent aspect of the profile of major politicians. Berlusconi in particular has built a successful political career on generically attacking 'communism', and has deliberately avoided ever taking part in the 25 April celebrations, including during his three stints as prime minister. He explained why on the eve of the 2007 anniversary: 'Historical reality is overturned at these commemorations. I won't take part in celebrations used by one side against the other. I've never taken part in 25 April events.'

This wave of institutional 'anti anti-fascism' has also created a climate in which there are widespread neo-fascist terror attacks. Between 2005 and 2008, activists have monitored attacks clearly having a fascist element to them, as regards either the attackers or the targets, and the results are chilling. There have been 350 attacks overall, including three murders. Ninety-eight of the attacks were described as 'Nazi-fascist vandalism', whereas 88 were attacks against the meeting places of the centre-left, 98 were physical attacks against left-wingers, and a further 88 were attacks against immigrants, homosexuals, journalists, and so on.[71]

However, since there is clearly a limit to the extent to which today's fascists can relive the past, the targets for racial intolerance and political violence have changed. Particularly since the election of Berlusconi's third government in April 2008, there has been an alarming rise in xenophobia and official racial harassment. The racist Northern League, having organised vigilante patrols in immigrant areas for many years, has increased the stridency of its anti-Islamic campaign. Gypsies quickly became a target, either through mobs burning down their camps, or the government announcing the racially profiled fingerprinting of all gypsies, including children. Many politicians and institutions outside of Italy have expressed their concern, and after just four months in power even the Pope was moved to issue what was seen as a veiled attack on the racism of the Berlusconi government.[72]

Yet all this political traffic has not been passing down a one-way street. The Resistance has been defended and fascism has continued to be criticised. One of the first mass examples was the national demonstration to commemorate 25 April in Milan in 1994. Berlusconi had just been elected, and for the first time Gianfranco Fini's 'post-fascist' AN was set to join government. A left-wing newspaper, Il Manifesto, called for a special anti-fascist mobilisation on that day, and people responded in large numbers. Up to 300,000 people marched through the rain-sodden streets, coming out in such numbers because of the threat they saw from the AN. But more revealing was the perception that this would not be one of the ossified cotton-wool commemorations that had come to characterise 25 April celebrations. Even the country's biggest selling daily, *La Repubblica*, although in the process of becoming a conservative paper, reported the protest positively, its banner headline referring to the proposal to allow AN into government: 'Don't you dare'.

But the attitude of the party leaders directly descended from the majority radical wing of the Resistance, who increasingly distanced themselves from their heritage, became a growing problem. Despite the popularity of the Resistance and the validity it holds for many people, this growing gap was simply one facet of a broader 'democratic deficit' that has rapidly increased in Western democracies over the last decade, in which many people find that their opinions about a whole range of important issues are not represented in parliament. Two examples of how these needs then emerge elsewhere come from the young anti-capitalist movement which developed in the early years of this century. First, perhaps the most popular song on the movement's marches throughout Europe was the partisan song *Bella ciao*. Second, as part of the European Social Forum held in Florence in November 2002, a million-strong demonstration was held against the impending war in Iraq, and the organisers felt it natural to place ANPI, the ex-partisans' association, as the lead contingent of the march. In the interviews the few remaining partisans gave, their common message was that while war in Iraq would be wrong, their war of resistance against fascism and foreign domination had been right. The dwindling numbers of surviving partisans, who would always speak with such authority and humanity, also necessitated a generational change. Nowadays active defence of the Resistance and its ideals often occurs outside of the bubble of institutions.

The arguments will continue, but they now occur in a very different political environment. While anti-fascism formed a large part of the political glue that held the 'First Republic' together from 1945 to 1994, its institutional appeal has withered both on the inside and the outside. The Resistance, presented so positively for much of the 1960s and 1970s, is now depicted in the opposite light by most of the mass media. As occurred with the Resistance itself during the 1943–45 period, its values and relevance today will be won on the streets and in workplaces.

PART II

9
Female Fighters

Women's involvement in the Resistance was highly significant, and the fact that it occurred at all is very clear proof of the general impact the Resistance had on Italian society. For the first time in Italian history women came out of their homes in large numbers, voluntarily, and got involved in politics. Their role was absolutely central, as the (male) partisan commander Arrigo Boldrini acknowledged: 'If in an ordinary army the ratio between fighters and support services is one to seven, in partisan warfare it is one to fifteen. Behind every fighting partisan there were fifteen people, the great majority of whom were women.'[1]

While Italian society had rapidly industrialised under fascism, culturally women were still second-class citizens. Under fascist law a man could be sentenced to three years' imprisonment for killing his wife in a 'crime of honour', whereas the penalty for abortion was normally five years. But fascism was contradictory in how it treated women: on one hand it wanted to impose traditional values, but on the other it sought to modernise society. Women's lives were therefore changing, despite fascist policies which made migration from the countryside virtually impossible, gave substantial tax subsidies to births, and imposed higher tax rates for unmarried men. Despite all this, in 1939 Italy's overall marriage rate was lower than that of both Britain and Germany, a sign that traditional gender roles were changing.[2] Because women were strongly discouraged from working from the early 1930s onwards, particularly in the North they looked to alternatives, one of which was going to university. So while in 1921 only 10.5 per cent of university students were women, by 1941 this had doubled to 22 per cent, albeit from a low numerical base.[3]

Along with their changing role in society in general, many women had also been involved in anti-fascist activities before the Resistance. During the 20 years of the regime, a total of 300 women had been sentenced to prison for anti-fascism. With the outbreak of war in 1940 men left for the front and these trends increased, with significant numbers of women starting work in industry, the civil service and the public transport system. Indeed women's participation in the Resistance as workers has largely been buried over time, although traces emerge occasionally, such as a court's verdict in Asti following the March 1943 strikes – in total ten workers were convicted, but eight of them were women.[4] Although women left the home and began working in large numbers together, in terms of breadwinning, a female wage was much lower than a male wage, so those women with children were hardly able to solve their own economic problems independently. Furthermore, from October

1940 butter and olive oil started to be rationed, followed in December by pasta and rice.[5]

In the hills and mountains of the countryside it was often women who first spontaneously became involved in resistance. It has been estimated that at least 50,000 Allied POWs walked out of their prison camps on 8 September 1943, soon followed by even larger numbers of Italian soldiers.[6] As both groups tried to either cross enemy lines or reach home, it was generally women who fed them, gave them clothes, let them sleep in decent conditions, thus exposing themselves to fascist and German reprisals. As we saw in general in Chapter 4, 'without the silent but continuous help of these women, the military-political movement would not have been born, gained so many recruits or reached the goals it had set'.[7] And as one author has argued, when Italian society went into crisis in 1943, 'as is usually the case in wartime, women crossed the lines between private and public worlds as social necessity demanded that they act in unusual ways'.[8] Finding food, and then later clothing and heating, became key objectives in people's lives. This not only led women into conflict with the authorities, but also increased their sense of confidence. As the same author continues: 'Women who struggled to feed their children, lived through bombings, watched neighbours and loved ones being deported to Germany, and bore the brunt of Nazi and Fascist abuse and brutality were keenly aware of immediate threats to survival and fearful of future perils.'[9]

One of the earliest examples of mass female protest took place in Parma in October 1941. The bread ration had just been reduced to 150 grammes per person per day, but Olga Bianchi, who took part in a 'bread riot', recalls: 'people came to steal, to take bread away, because they had already rationed it – but in any event there wasn't any'.[10] The chance that presented itself was a lorry making bread deliveries, which took the same route every day. So early in the morning about 40 kilos of bread were stolen by dozens of women; news of the successful action spread and a few hours later another lorry was relieved of its load. The next move, like the two earlier events, was not fully spontaneous, but neither was it organised beforehand. Women working in the many shoe factories of Parma realised that the authorities were likely to take a repressive line, and so a counter-measure was needed. Grolli Bici witnessed what happened next: 'What did they think when they went back to work in the afternoon? To organise a strike, a demonstration, so all the women in the *Balzarini* shoe factory came out and went to [lists names of local streets] to get women out of [other] factories, to go into a central square to demand that they did nothing.'[11]

In February 1942 70 women demonstrated in a suburb of Genoa in front of the headquarters of the Fascist Party. They carried empty shopping bags, and demanded an increase in the milk ration and distribution of potatoes.[12] As conditions worsened so too did anger, but the more the Resistance became a stable structure, the greater the number of activists who were able to organise protests. But protests were also a risky gamble. On 7 April 1944 a group of women launched an attack on a bakery in Rome; the Germans reacted violently, immediately lining up ten of the women against a wall and shooting them.[13]

For many women who became active in the Resistance in Parma, action against food shortages was their first step. Looking back, most women found it hard to pinpoint exactly when and how they joined the Resistance, but many said they had no other choice. And if women didn't actually get involved in armed actions, the reason, as one author has argued, was quite simple: 'It would be ridiculous to view civilian resistance as separate and opposed to armed resistance because, in some cases, it had nothing to do with a refusal to fire weapons but with the impossibility of finding them.'[14] Yet as the same author has argued, women used their private and public spheres to great effect: producing leaflets or newspapers in family homes, quietly involving other relatives in activities, shopping and carrying out anti-fascist propaganda at the same time, and passing off partisans or activists as refugees, sons, husbands or even lovers.[15]

An American academic has carried out invaluable statistical work on women's involvement in the Resistance, analysing data on 936 women activists to produce general profiles. The first thing to note is that there was nothing unusual about these women: in 1943 a total of 27.4 per cent were aged 19 or younger; 42.4 per cent were 20–29 and 15.4 per cent aged 30–39. Occupational categories also represented the population and the Resistance at large: 21.7 per cent were housewives (although classifying teenagers as such is not fully accurate), 19.4 per cent were agricultural workers of some sort, 15 per cent worked in industry and 12.8 per cent in commercial activities, mainly retail or clerical work.[16] In terms of party affiliation, only 8 per cent of women were members of any party in 1943, although another 16.6 per cent had joined a party by 1945. So roughly three-quarters of women never joined a party during the Resistance, but interestingly enough 18 per cent had been involved in anti-fascist activities before 1943.[17]

Furthermore women were real volunteers, as opposed to men who were often forced to choose between conscription or the mountains – women could have waited at home and sat it all out.[18]

NON-MILITARY ACTIVITIES

As with men, there was also a form of passive resistance, that of simply turning a blind eye. Then there were activities which were almost exclusively the domain of women such as knitting socks – an absolutely vital task. Such mundane occupations also created vital opportunities. Many of these women were also seamstresses or laundresses, common occupations at the time. It was normal for clients to visit houses for fittings, or for bundles of clean washing to be delivered by bicycle – easy 'cover' to transmit messages or take ammunition or bombs. It wasn't uncommon for women to take young children along with them to provide greater protection.

The most common activity of women partisans though was that of a *staffetta*, roughly translated as courier. Carrying information or orders was obviously vital in a society where the vast majority of people did not even have a telephone. In the beginning, older and more experienced women took on this delicate and demanding role, but as the movement grew and younger women gained experience, the ranks were widened. To then move from carrying information to carrying money, ammunition, medical supplies or bombs was not a big organisational leap, although it obviously involved a far greater risk and commitment. But any activity could be notably complex, such as providing financial help to the families of partisans who had been killed or arrested, or to families who were simply very poor. In Genoa this network began helping 165 families in July 1944 with 125,000 lire, rising to 1,000 families in March 1945 and an expenditure of 1,175,000 lire.[19]

Women could be called upon at almost any moment. For example, although Benissone Costa had joined the PCI in 1938 in Turin, her first actions in 1943 were rather low-level:

We were discontented with the war, the cold, the hardships. Propaganda work could be done best in the lines in front of the shops. There we talked, discussed and began to understand that it was fascism that wanted war and now we should end it. It was time the women organized because on us there was, perhaps, the greatest burden.[20]

As with so much of the Resistance, the growth of the movement was the coming together of two strands: a spontaneous drive towards action caused by extreme circumstances, and a political organisation offering answers and logistics – broadly speaking women's involvement followed the same trajectory as men's. So given that in big cities many women worked in factories, on 8 March 1943, International Women's Day, 3,000 women workers at the *Venchi Unica* factory in Turin went on strike, with several hundred then demonstrating against the war in Turin's main square.[21]

One of the highest points of mass activity occurred in July 1944 in the town of Carrara which then had a population of around 65,000. By this point, the German 'Gothic Line' (the front line) was very near. Not only that, there were very close links between activists in Carrara and partisans in the mountains above the town. Due to the proximity of the front line the Germans suddenly ordered the evacuation of the town by 9 July, giving just 48 hours notice. The Nazi commander, a Lieutenant Tobbens, also ordered that people gather in a local square: 'to be sent to a new destination', which many local people presumed meant being called up to join Nazi labour brigades.[22] For the local resistance, an empty city meant the end of activities, and in economic terms the creation of a ghost town would spell disaster. (Tourist facilities on the local beaches, an important focus for the town, had already been destroyed in 1943 out of fear of an amphibious landing). The local resistance had been growing throughout the year, and tension had been rising as the front line grew closer. On 16 June the local Women's Defence Group (see below) had put out a leaflet demanding that rations be immediately increased, as well as warning of the possibility of the Germans stealing all local food: 'Show your anger in the streets, in the market place and at the rationing office. We invite you to support the Women's Defence Committee en masse, that is supported by the National Liberation Committee, which in turn relies on your strength to help to drive out German invaders and fascist traitors.'[23] Long queues for food and low rations had tried the patience of all local people.

With news of the German plan, speakers were now sent out into the town: 'flying speeches' were made in local workplaces, along with leafleting both at night and during the day. Women went from door to door, or to local markets, arguing for a protest against the German orders. Furthermore, 'In the meantime SAP military commands had organised to protect the population from any possible revenge attack.'[24] The day of the proposed evacuation came and went, as did the following day. On 11 July several dozen women assembled, bolstered by the fact that male and female armed partisans were mixing with the crowd: they moved through the market, turning over stalls if people hesitated in showing support.[25] As the march started to move through the main streets it grew to several hundred. One partisan leader remembers: 'other women, some of them very young, came in from side streets; shops lowered their shutters'.[26] Some people were carrying placards reading: 'We're not moving'. German soldiers tried to stop the march with rifle butts but without success. Arriving outside the German HQ they found both German soldiers and fascist militia ready for them with machine guns, but they refused to be intimidated. A squad of Germans came out of the building and arrested four women, but that just enraged the crowd further.[27]

As the protests continued the Germans felt they could not commit a massacre, and the demonstration ended peacefully. Meanwhile, no local people had gone to the collection point for deportation, and the evacuation order was effectively dropped, signifying a total victory. Afterwards there was daily leafleting by the local Resistance. Activists in Carrara were quickly galvanised: on 14 July partisans attacked a fascist barracks in the centre of town which housed 350 people, killing two militia members and wounding one.[28]

The Women's Defence Groups

The *Gruppi di Difesa della Donna* (GDD, or Women's Defence Groups), were set up in Milan at the end of November 1943. Agreement was reached at a meeting of two PCI women, one from the PSI, two from the Action Party and one from the Catholic Left, a group that eventually joined the PCI[29] – the GDD groups were to be 'open to women of any social class, of any religious or political belief, who want to take part in the task of liberating the nation and fighting for their own emancipation'. They were all about providing a structure for women who had started to become involved in struggle spontaneously. Experienced female activists would be sent out and travel round whole regions, having been informed about who to contact. They would generally meet up with new women on Sundays. Not only in houses – often in gardens behind hedges, in attics and even in cemeteries.[30]

The basic unit of the GDD was the nucleus, or cell: five or six women who generally had already worked together. The cells were created in neighbourhoods, schools, workplaces and hospitals, and were then grouped into broader geographical networks. In agricultural areas of the Po valley it wasn't uncommon for rice workers to go on strike soon after being contacted – and then form their own GDD.[31] But above all the groups were an urban phenomenon; in the countryside many women supported the Resistance, but not as a result of accepting a new ideological and organisational framework. Although recruitment to local groups often occurred thanks to a pre-existing relationship with the Resistance, which was generally rather vague, this was far from being a uniform explanation for involvement. In early 1944 a heavily pregnant Vittorina Rifredi, an agricultural worker, had to go to Modena to get ration coupons. After several unsuccessful trips, in which the coupons were not ready, she went there with a rolling pin and threatened the clerks – who promptly produced the coupons. Other people involved in the Resistance witnessed this behaviour, and soon after she was approached about joining the Women's Defence Group.[32]

Statistics show that the GDDs fulfilled a need. Milan had 2,274 full GDD members and 6,719 associate members by November 1944, divided into 47 workplace groups and 32 neighbourhood groups. Just four months later, in March 1945, this had risen to 3,398 and 9,823 respectively, divided into 126 workplace and 58 neighbourhood groups. On the eve of liberation in northern regions (Piedmont, Lombardy, Liguria, Veneto and Emilia-Romagna), there were 24,028 full members and 15,823 associate members.[33] One of the groups' key actions was organising demonstrations, another was printing local leaflets. Elda Morelli was just 16 when she started producing leaflets in Parma:

> With these leaflets or small posters, once I had learned how to prepare the plate and duplicate we needed a typewriter for the plate and reams of paper … I wrote, typed, prepared the plate and printed. I represented the Women's Defence Groups and I had a contact and … when this stuff was ready I either had a rendezvous with someone to whom I gave a certain amount, or I had addresses where I used to leave them in packages. … Generally we used to meet up at the *Annunciata* church, inside it, and I came along with a shopping bag and we shared them out. Everyone had a different sector of the city to throw them off [off bridges, in the streets, off trams, into cinemas, etc.] … apart from throwing them off we had to paste them up and we went to get the glue. A women prepared some jam jars for us containing a brush and some glue.[34]

As is clear from this quotation, something which is relatively easy to do today – the production and distribution of a leaflet – involved a high degree of personal commitment and very detailed organisation.

In a bigger city such as Genoa leaflets were produced on a much larger scale. The following details illustrate how all activities were carefully focused: In October 1944 GDD groups distributed 1,000 copies of a leaflet entitled 'It's what we would have expected (deportations)'; 2,000 entitled 'People of Genoa – women and mothers'; 300 entitled 'Genoese women, the Germans are leaving the Ligurian coastline'; 1,000 copies of '1 and 2 November'; 100 copies of 'Agenda of Ligurian schools' CLN'; 2,000 copies entitled 'Teachers'; 100 copies entitled 'The CLN informs all committees'; 50 copies of 'CLN decree for occupied Italy' and finally 50 copies of a leaflet entitled 'To CLN railway workers'.[35] Whenever a situation arose in which people potentially wanted to discuss events, a leaflet quickly appeared.

Women also gathered food, medicine and clothing for the Resistance. A key mobilising factor was the possibility of stopping food falling into the hands of the fascist authorities or the Germans; this sometimes meant attacks on grain warehouses, from where grain would then be distributed to needy families. Butter and cheese dairies were another target. Carolina Generali recalls that her GDD group in a village west of Bologna emerged in late 1943 from a struggle to stop wheat being taken away: 'I organised some women to stop the convoy, and despite the drivers' protests we forced them to travel round the town giving a bit of wheat to every family.'[36] Sometimes agricultural workers would destroy their produce rather than let it fall into the wrong hands, or would simply not deliver it to public authorities. Other more immediate clashes occurred when fascists or Germans tried to requisition livestock. However, the main urban public action as regards food was against rationing and the lack of supplies.

In April 1944 in Imola, fascists called out firemen to hose down protesting women, but the women managed to turn the hoses on the fascists. Shots were then fired by reinforcements, and two protesters were killed. The women stood their ground, and officials ended up seeking refuge in the town hall.[37]

Women made an equally important contribution to the production of local newspapers. The main publication however was undoubtedly the national newspaper, *Noi Donne* (*Us Women*), which first appeared in May 1944. Although its first print run was just 500, in a few months it rose to 6,000, and varied between that figure and 10,000 for the rest of the Resistance period.[38] To the extent that discrimination and sexism were discussed, they were generally seen as the product of fascism rather than part of more fundamental social structures; tradition would apparently be discarded in a 'new' and progressive Italy.[39]

GDD members were by and large non-party political, although the left tended to dominate. For example at the end of 1944 three GDD groups in Emilia-Romagna detailed the political breakdown of their membership: in the first, out of 55 members 19 were in the PCI; the second group was again made up of 55 members, with 11 in the PCI; whereas the smaller group, consisting of 20 members, had 8 PCI members. Another report from Ravenna in 1945 mentioned a breakdown of 60 republicans, 43 communists and 8 independents.[40] In the summer of 1944 the 7 GDD groups in La Spezia had 95 PCI members and 145 members of other parties.[41] This detailed breakdown demonstrates an important fact, given the accusation made by Christian Democrats and others (an accusation used to stop the GDD from becoming unitary women's organisations) that these groups were dominated by communists.

In big cities there were also factory-based groups in workplaces with high numbers of women workers: statistics show there were GDD groups in 25 Milan factories, and the same number in Turin. In June 1944 a GDD group at the *Mira Lanza* soap factory in Genoa organised a protest against the deportation of women in Germany, and the following month at the *Rolik* knitwear factory there was a strike against the sacking of 150 women workers.[42] There were also limited attempts at education and discussion groups. Maria Bocchi, then aged just 15, remembers them as follows:

> They explained what the partisan struggle was and why they did what they did, and all the damage caused by fascism – in short they preached at us a bit. ... we talked about the role of women, above all the role of mothers. The argument was that our men were away, and we needed peace so our sons could come back home ... The thing I remember in general was a more just world being talked about, and in this better world there was some talk about women's rights, that women were equal and had the right to vote, understand? In other words the first time I heard arguments about equality was back then, even if I probably understood only about 5 per cent of what was being said ... the family was the family, and equality meant voting, employment, this wasn't a period in which there were discussions about relationships between men and women.[43]

The growth and politics of the organisation caused a clash within the CLNAI. On 18 June 1944 a GDD letter sent to the CLNAI requested recognition and financial support – something that was only finally agreed on 16 October. The proposal had been supported by the PCI, PSIUP and Action Party and opposed by the DC and the Liberal Party.[44] Despite the October agreement, on the ground many Christian Democrat organisations, such as those in Liguria, continued to snub what were in effect unitary organisations.[45] And on 11 February 1945 the national DC instructed its female numbers not to join the GDD, out of dissatisfaction at the left's apparent numerical dominance.[46]

So not all women involved in the Resistance in an organised fashion came under the GDD. Catholic women often became involved through their local parish church, generally by priests allowing them to be approached by women who were already active. In Turin Catholic women often visited partisans held in jails to take them food and clothing, pretending to be a relative. In preparation for the insurrection, a whole network of Catholic women were prepared to act as nurses.[47]

The underlying political tension surrounding the GDD was ultimately a reflection of its mass working-class nature. Although open to women from all classes, inevitably working-class demands tended to keep the middle class and the rich at a distance. When it was announced that the bread ration in Genoa would be halved from 200 to 100 grammes, 'For a day and a half at Cornigliano market women demonstrated; yelling and launching themselves against fascist policemen. To calm them down, a fake discovery of a few tons of flour was announced so [more] bread could be baked.'[48] These were hardly the kind of activities that genteel ladies were inclined to get involved in.

The GDD also continually demanded that more accurate and professional categories be used for their activity, rather than the vague word *staffetta*. Their demands were that women attached to partisan units be classified as 'nurses', 'facilitators', 'information officers', and so on.[49] While participating in the Resistance technically as equals, women were obviously facing a male mindset that frequently did not view them as such – a tension that will be examined further below.

MILITARY ACTIVITIES

As we have seen in earlier chapters, a distinction needs to be made between urban Resistance activity and action up in the mountains within larger formations. In both instances the most likely cause for activity was previous arrests or the impending probability of arrest. Some urban squads were even led by women, such as the 7th 'Gianni' GAP group in Emilia-Romagna, commanded by Novella 'Vanda' Albertazzi, who had joined as a courier in December 1943 after one of her brothers had been shot and another imprisoned. Out of 200 members, 80 were women. As Albertazzi once said: 'it seemed absurd and impossible to stay bent over a table ten hours a day, to gossip with friends, while the Germans walked in the streets, while the Fascists arrested young men'.[50] In November 1944 she led her unit in a major battle among the ruins of the Maggiore hospital in Bologna against German tanks, armoured cars and cannons.[51]

Many women did not want to take on just a supporting role, and had to 'fight' within partisan brigades to be given the right to fight. Elsa Oliva was from an anti-fascist family, and luckily managed to escape from a transit camp in September 1943 before being sent to Germany. She went up into the hills, looking for her brother who was already a partisan, and joined the 2nd Brigade of the Beltrami division in May 1944.[52] After several days she told the commander and the rest of the men: 'I didn't come here to find a lover. I'm here to fight and I'm only going to stay if you give me a gun and put me in the group for guard duty and military action. ... In my first firefight I showed I wasn't handling a gun just for show.'[53] Because she showed herself to be a good fighter she was given the command of a group, and when moves were made to relieve her of command she managed to hold on to the position only because her men defended her. She was also a severe disciplinarian, tying up men to posts as punishment from time to time.

Another remarkable story concerns Laura Seghettini, who went up into the hills as a 22-year-old and asked to join her local group as a fighter, a request that was agreed to after initial hesitation. A few months later she was asked to form and lead her own squad of 40 men.[54] Her group operated around the Cisa pass, a vital link over the Apennines because it was the main supply route to German forces fighting the Allies further south. Seghettini remembers: 'I always went into battle, perhaps more than others, precisely

Figure 9.1   Female partisan.

because being a woman I didn't want people talking behind my back.'[55] In the beginning she was as inexperienced as her men – in one of her first actions she ran out onto the Cisa pass brandishing a rifle, and forced the first truck in a 30-vehicle column to come to a halt. This was very bad tactics because it allowed the rest of the column to open fire – the norm was to stop the last few trucks. Nevertheless, the action was a success, the sheer unexpectedness of Seghettini's actions having wrong-footed the fascist soldiers, who were presented with the curious sight of a small woman brandishing a rifle almost taller than she was. As did Oliva, Seghettini would sometimes tie a man to a post for disciplinary reasons, in one case concerning the sexual pestering of local women by a male partisan.[56]

Gabriella degli Esposti formed a Women's Defence Group in the countryside outside Modena. Even though she had two young daughters she also took part in partisan actions, as well as organising mass demonstrations in her hometown. She was picked up in December 1944, and tortured for several days during which her breasts were cut and her eyes gauged out. Her dead body was found with its stomach ripped open – it transpired she was pregnant. A women-only detachment was formed in her honour in Modena the following month – 55 women divided into five squads, part of the Modena 1st M division that ended up fighting in the Montefiorino area.[57]

There were other all-female units. For example 38 women in Piedmont were attached to the 19th 'Eusebio Giambone' Assault Brigade, formally recognised from August 1944. The group quickly received praise for their military actions from a nearby Socialist Brigade commander, who also suggested they: 'React against the social democratic tendency of some comrades who are still unable to understand that an Italian woman can be worth as much as one from the Soviet Union or the Balkans.'[58]

Once the individual stories are assembled together an interesting picture emerges of tens of thousands of women shaking off the stereotype of being passive home-carers. Most accounts estimate that 35,000 women took part in military actions, out of a total resistance force of 300,000; indeed recent research from Emilia-Romagna also indicates that 10 per cent of the partisans who fought in battles were female.[59] A total of 623 women lost their lives in battle or in revenge attacks; 4,600 were arrested, tried and tortured, while 2,750 were deported to concentration camps. Women's activities were not just military but also involved political leadership – after the war 512 women were recognised as having been political commissars at various levels.[60] Just as it is difficult to be accurate about the precise numbers of people involved in military resistance as a whole, after the war women were less likely to demand recognition since for cultural reasons they were still expected to be 'seen and not heard'.

Developing a mass movement meant developing mass female involvement. Perhaps it was this need for women's participation that led to a remarkably low level of open sexism. One local command wrote in reply to some questionable (male) comments: 'A number of prejudices need to be removed – that women are the weak sex, unable to use weapons. Such prejudices are the fruit of our backwardness and habits.'[61] It is impossible to be precise about what drove such appeals to treat women as equals, but with hindsight the desperate circumstances rather than a profound belief in women's equality seem to have been the most influential factor.

MILITARY VERSUS WOMEN'S LIBERATION

The issue of women's liberation ran through the Resistance, just as issues of economic and political liberation criss-crossed all military activities during the period. One of the key problems for female emancipation was that the 'unwillingness to consider gender oppression was tied to another, more general concern in the Resistance – a desire to maintain unity at all costs. The success of the struggle was linked to an insistence on the homogeneity of goals and interests of all Italian citizens.'[62] In other words, tensions over broad political and gender issues were generally put to one side in favour of short-term unity.

Within the most powerful organisation of the Resistance, the PCI, there was a lot of contradictory behaviour. The leadership criticised male comrades for their 'indifferent or suspicious' attitudes towards working with women, but also avoided coming out strongly in favour of women's rights. In autumn

1944 the party took the position that women should meet in separate groups in order to develop more freely. Many women opposed this, such as Marcella Ferrara, party member since 1943 and active in the Rome GAP, who later said: 'Men and women comrades should work together ... Enclosing oneself in a ghetto, as I always define the women's committees, was something that cut one off from the outside.'[63] While this was proposed for perfectly understandable reasons, a major article published in the party's theoretical journal in November was quite conservative in how it argued for women's rights in a free and democratic Italy. It was clearly stated that more women should be in leadership positions, but the overall vision was that 'Italian women will have the task of solving people's serious problems in terms of looking after children and families, the supply of food, collective canteens; they will have to participate in the appropriate resolution of demands for housing and education, etc.'[64] In practice women tended to be brought into policy discussions only over issues such as maternity and infant care, health care, food and housing. The PCI thus essentially supported traditional gender roles; though it publicly called for equality, it ignored the tensions intrinsic to such traditional roles and values, particularly religious values.

Yet the common purpose of partisan activity was such that it tended towards unity and equality, and as the Resistance neared its end demands for women's rights increasingly emerged from the rank and file. Three weeks before the insurrection a mass meeting of partisans in southern Lombardy heard a woman speaker express the hope 'that women are able to obtain social emancipation, which up till now has been held back by bourgeois prejudices, which wanted to make woman either a beast of burden or a luxury item'.[65] It is interesting to note that what repeatedly emerges from such discussions are accusations not against men, but against capitalist society as being chiefly responsible for holding women back. This attitude emerged even more clearly in a speech by a male PCI member at a meeting of communist factory workers in Padua in March 1945:

Women make up 50 per cent of humanity and it is pointless to talk about democracy without taking into account the strength they represent. The fascist state in particular, and the bourgeois state in general, has always wanted them to be slaves, to exploit them in order to divide the workforce. The party is for woman's emancipation and for her economic independence, without which she cannot be called free. What do women represent in the liberation struggle? A vitally important factor. 90 per cent of our couriers are women and the same can be said for the partisan army: we see them in the streets during the big demonstrations where they surge forward and win all manner of things – from demands over foodstuffs to the freeing of patriots whom fascist courts have condemned to death. We have women workers in some factories: I believe that if [male] comrades from a factory get involved with them they'd obtain far more than what they have done so far. Women are a goldmine of energy and know how to do marvellous things. It is necessary for us to start forgetting old fascist and bourgeois concepts about them.[66]

Although GDD groups were now frequently talking about women's rights in a new Italy, all the language was non-threatening as regards traditional values and the domination of Catholic values. While women's rights were to be fought for at work – to the extent that women worked outside the home – behind closed doors everything was to be left as it was. As the magazine *Noi Donne* headlined on 15 May 1945: 'Leaving our rifles, we will rebuild our families'. In other words PCI women were operating in a party that avoided any discussion of issues such as abortion or divorce. In a speech to the first conference of communist women in June 1945 Togliatti argued: 'We need a renovated family ... that is a center of simple human solidarity. It is because of this that we are opposed to setting up any problem which tends to disrupt or weaken family unity ... In the end, to resolve the problems of children we need to defend the family.'[67]

Nevertheless, in terms of membership much of this paid off for the PCI. By late 1945 the party had between 250,000 and 280,000 female members, 14–15 per cent of the total membership. By 1946, women made up 401,202 out of a total party membership of 1,676,013 – 24 per cent – with 134,306 of these classified as housewives.[68] Given the ideological positioning of the Resistance as a whole, overall women did not end up thinking that equality and an end to oppression could only be achieved by revolutionary means. The fight against fascism

provoked violent and radical reactions and resistance, but focus on the struggle itself allowed little time to discuss and unmask basic causes for gender equality. ... The radical potential that had characterized certain factions of the Resistance was dissipated as parties of the Left modified revolutionary goals in favor of moderate and pragmatic political agendas and a focus on electoral victory.[69]

But it has to be said that most women did not want emancipation and the kind of equality experienced today. Indeed for those who joined partisan groups in the mountains there is considerable evidence that their rebellion consisted in wanting to behave like men.[70]

Giving his opinion on the place of women in 1932, Mussolini had said: 'she must not count in our state'.[71] The Resistance represented an enormous victory over such prejudices, and the women who had participated in it had a lot to celebrate. Vitalina Lassandro was an 18-year-old woman who had already worked in a number of Turin factories, and recalls her own celebration upon liberation:

Who knows how, but there was a record player with music, and in every house, hovel and courtyard people were dancing. I was dancing with these boys – over the last five years we had lost track of each other – but here we were again young men and women. And I remember they had big pistols in their belts, we were dancing along with a pistol ... Everything exploded: happiness and the beauty of freedom, or the illusion of freedom.[72]

The bitter final note mentioned by Lassandro derives from the fact that the interview was recorded many years later. But the limitations of women's liberation were visible even before the whole country was freed. In October 1944, 2,000 partisans marched through the town of Alba in Piedmont, which they had just liberated:

> Women marched with the men, in male clothing, and some of the crowd began to mutter – *What have we done to our country?* – because these young women had a way of moving and an appearance that made people start winking at each other. There were no illusions about this among commanders, and the evening before the parade they had ordered women to stay up in the hills, but they told them to get screwed and surged down into the city.[73]

The same backward mentality emerged during the final parades to mark the partisans' victory. One woman in Milan remembers people insisting that they wear armbands indicating they were nurses rather than partisans. In Turin women were not allowed to march at all with the Garibaldi brigades out of fear people might think they were prostitutes, whereas in the more moderate formations women were allowed to march.[74] But given the unevenness of the Resistance, and the ambiguity and uncertainty with which women's roles had been treated, in Genoa apparently women marched with no restriction.[75]

10
The Partisan Republics

A previous invader of Italy, Napoleon, ordered the building of a road over the Alps in September 1800. It took French engineers five years to complete the 2,000-metre high Simplon pass, and when it was finished they told him: 'the Alps no longer exist'. Nearly 150 years later German invaders were to discover that the Alps still existed, but so too did the Apennines and other remote areas – these were the places where 'partisan republics' briefly came into existence. Although some were small and lasted just a few days or weeks, in others a new political system started to take its first steps.

Overall, as one author says, once these republics were created 'a whole series of social, political and economic problems explode. In dealing with them, the divergent ideologies of anti-fascist parties, as well as the expectations of partisan organisations and the civilian population emerge and are tested.'[1] The key barometer of success was political participation. As one PCI leader wrote at the time: 'Where partisans have passed by an indestructible political lesson needs to remain: partisan villages and liberated zones must all be models of a democratic Italian state. Their men, women and youth must be able to tell everybody that it is possible to live in freedom.'[2] After 20 years of dictatorship, people suddenly and briefly had a chance to experiment with building their own collective future.

Concepts of democracy could vary widely, however, as we shall see with the Ossola republic. So the existence of these republics was double-edged: on one hand their very creation was a sign of the movement's strength. But on the other hand they also revealed some of the political tensions and limitations the Resistance was putting to one side for as long as the war needed to be fought – for example no republic ever stated that women should have the right to vote. In essence, what immediately emerged for all republics was the question: *what are we fighting for?*

As regards economic policy, most republics were established in rural areas, dominated by agricultural production. Therefore, food prices were raised to ensure the support of those who produced agricultural commodities, while the authorities had a strong welfare policy to compensate people who did not work on farms (in effect prices were subsidised through direct assistance). In rural areas any new republic had to have the support of peasants, but what is interesting about the Ossola republic is that there were large numbers of factory workers – so mass support could theoretically have been guaranteed immediately by the elimination of factory owners, something that never happened.

Another key issue of principle was whether local goods could be transported and sold to the enemy. Given that these were small mountain and hillside areas, they were not self-sufficient in food and essential goods. There were widely varying tax and price policies too. The most radical policy was implemented in Carnia, where all direct and indirect taxation was abolished, and there was a simple tax on property – although collection was not particularly efficient. However in the longer-lasting republics the new national state taxes which were collected went to the partisan movement, more than any other body the representative of a new national state – whereas council taxes went to the newly elected municipality.[3]

The problem that came before all others was military: these republics existed just a few dozen miles away from enemy forces that were far more powerful. Each of them had to plan for an eventual attack, but militarising the territory and the population would mean denying political debate about what choices a free people now wanted to make. Given this irremovable difficulty, striking a correct balance between military preparation and creating new democratic structures was never going to be perfect.

We shall look at three of the most important republics, which overall numbered about 15.

THE MONTEFIORINO REPUBLIC

This republic existed for around 40 days (from 18 June 1944 to early August) in the Apennines between Modena and La Spezia. Strategically, it controlled two vital mountain passes from the Western side of Italy over to the Po valley. It had begun with an element of luck, when on 8 September the previous year many Italian soldiers had left large numbers of weapons in an area where the first organised resistance groups were based, around the four ceramic factories in the town of Sassuolo.[4] Another stroke of luck was the presence of local priests who were active in persuading local people not to obey the call-up to the fascist army in spring 1944; they refused to announce the call-up at Sunday mass and advised parents to hide their male children. This was mirrored by the local CLN, which produced leaflets calling on people to join 'the patriotic formations active in our mountains' rather than obey the fascist call-up.

The other key factor – a purely tragic one – was the policy of massacres and reprisals, which inevitably pushed the local population towards the partisans. On 8 March fascist militia killed two people in the town of Palagano; ten days later Germans burnt down whole villages and killed 130 people, with many more being taken away. The fascist prefect of Montefiorino visited the area and described what he saw to his head office: 'Destroyed houses have largely been reduced to a pile of rubble under which all furniture has been burnt, along with food, bedding, cash savings, agricultural tools, cows ... Bodies will be buried in mass graves due to the lack of space in cemeteries.'[5]

Naturally many young male peasants felt they had nothing left to lose, and so joined partisan groups. One of the most successful groups was led by Mario Ricci, a veteran of the Spanish Civil War, who in early April attacked a local airfield destroying all the planes. By late spring partisans had been so successful in launching attacks on small enemy positions that on 15 June all members of the fascist National Guard were ordered to leave the area.[6] Three days later the republic was created, and in the lowland area around Modena a clear safe zone now existed for anti-fascists. Given that in 14 months of bombing 1,300 people had been killed in the Modena area alone, many now decided to leave the lowlands around the city and head up into the hills simply for safety. Two years after the events, the 'peasant general' Mario Ricci explained how it was the very appeal of the Resistance that had led to this republic's spontaneous formation: 'Given the continuous arrival of young men from the lowlands and from the entire region, and the need to organise, train and arm all these new forces, it was no longer possible to follow the classic partisan tactic of moving camp daily, which had allowed us to surprise the enemy and hit them hard.'[7]

The level of democracy was direct, almost rudimentary. Partisan commanders asked heads of families in villages to meet and designate their own representative. Mass meetings were held in squares and people raised their hands to make decisions – to an extent the local population delegated power to partisan commanders, who in turn appointed a local provisional council.[8] A contemporary report describes one of the fundamental reasons why the local population tended to support the partisans: 'Apart from work on fortifications, partisans still without arms are mainly employed working in the fields beside peasants; given the scarcity of labour and transportation difficulties in the mountains this represents a great help for the peasants, and resolves food problems for these partisans.'[9] Nevertheless, the local peasants, used to a life of near subsistence through scrimping and saving, viewed the frequent partisan celebrations as a waste. The presence of many unaccompanied women from outside the area also jarred with traditional values; so too did wall slogans such as 'Viva Russia' and 'Viva Stalin'.[10]

Democratic decisions were made concerning a new tax system, financial help for the needy, the prices of essential goods – particularly wheat, while partisan doctors set up a rudimentary health service. Two other specific policies were that the richest grain producers would provide the wheat needed to feed partisans, as well as giving a free amount of wheat to those people made homeless in the raids that had occurred in March. But as the report cited in the previous paragraph comments, the adherence of local people to this new system was far from total:

A certain reluctance still exists in relation to the fact that they are not sure about the safety of the liberated areas and fear the fascist and German reprisals which would follow upon their return. Such fears vanish happily to the extent that the brigades' strength, seriousness, order and discipline increase.[11]

A feature specific to this republic was direct Allied involvement. Major Johnston, who had been parachuted into the area, was in daily radio contact with Allied HQ, and, unusually, air drops would take place almost every night. Such was the coordination that when the Allies were preparing to launch a major offensive against the Gothic Line, the Germans feared that a parachute battalion was going to be dropped in the Montefiorino area, that is, behind German lines.

Given that there were spies even in liberated areas, the Germans were aware of developments, and in July launched an attack on Piandelagotti, which was quickly repulsed due to a rapid partisan counter-attack. A few weeks later, on 30 July, the Germans attacked again, but this time with between 5,000 and 8,000 men, artillery, armoured cars and flamethrowers. Italian fascists gave support by controlling the main roads. The scale of the attack created divisions among the local population: some helped the partisans by loading munitions onto lorries, digging trenches or erecting barbed wire. Others just thought about fleeing. As the Germans advanced from the north, there was hand-to-hand fighting in the town of Roteglia, and their advance was halted by a group of Russian ex-POWs. The following evening, after five days of fighting, partisans decided to retreat and move higher up into the mountains. The Nazis had suffered 2,080 deaths: it had been their biggest ever battle with partisans.[12]

But the Germans quickly realised that they had failed to seriously damage partisan forces, even though partisans had suffered around 200 casualties, killed or wounded. They therefore took their frustration out by bombarding the towns of Montefiorino and Piandelagotti, and burning Villa Minozzo to the ground.[13] Partisan forces meanwhile regrouped further up in the mountains, and a few weeks later began operations again. Indeed what is remarkable is that a second Montefiorino republic was established in January 1945, and lasted, despite enemy attacks, until liberation in April.[14]

THE REPUBLIC OF CARNIA

High up in the mountains north of Venice, Carnia is next to the Austrian and Slovenian borders. Here a republic was created gradually, through a series of small battles between August and October 1944. In the far north partisans had already turned the Resistance international, when they attacked a military barracks in Austria at the end of July.[15] The precise boundaries of such a huge territory naturally varied, but it involved a local population of between 80,000 and 100,000, spread out over 37–45 local councils and 2,500 square kilometres.[16]

Partisan activity began comparatively early in this area, thanks to a local PCI organiser, Mario Lizzero, who managed to win over his local party federation to supporting armed struggle as early as March 1943.[17] With the general influx of soldiers following the collapse of the armed forces on 8 September, by spring 1944 the confidence of local groups was already high: on 2 April in Ampezzo partisans arrested a local police captain in a bar, forcing him to release one of their comrades.[18] By the end of the month, local towns openly challenged the authorities – thousands of women attended the funeral of a partisan killed during a raid on a barracks in Tolmezzo; while a few days later hundreds marched through the Pesarina valley celebrating Mayday, singing songs that had not been heard for 20 years.[19]

Such a remote mountain area clearly favoured partisan activity, but another key factor in the development of the local movement were the fascist and German acts of violence, such as the complete destruction of Forni di Sotto in May, which overnight made 1,500 people homeless, followed in July by the murder of 52 people by the SS in the But valley.[20] A further turn of the screw was the decision by the Germans in July to ban the movement of foodstuffs from the lowlands, in a deliberate move to punish local people by starvation.[21]

Compared to the difficulties of the Ossola republic, in Carnia partisans were far more disciplined and respectful of democracy, indeed in August democratic elections were held for local councils. Partisan commanders limited themselves to taking part in council meetings; the main reason for them keeping a distance was that local National Liberation Committees had been functioning in the territory since June, so a strong political as opposed to merely military tradition existed.[22] However partisan accounts reveal real changes and tensions at political meetings: 'Various interests have come into collision: the mountains against the lowlands, the poor peasant against the average and rich peasant, the worker against the bourgeois, office workers against management, etc., etc., however they all agree that they don't want yesterday's leaders – the fascists.'[23]

As larger areas were liberated, a CLN for the whole Carnia area was announced on 11 August, made up of a representative of each local CLN and two military advisers. The local Garibaldi division had a clear analysis of the central importance of elections: 'to really arrive at a total liberation of the area, in order that activity of a military nature be truly efficient, and finally to call the broad popular masses to actively struggle for national liberation, it is necessary to proceed towards the creation of new popular organs of power'.[24] Following these elections, a provisional council for the whole of Carnia was declared at Ampezzo on 26 September. Although military commanders did not interfere in local political affairs, democratic life was not very lively – perhaps due to the mountainous territory – and there were no free newspapers.[25] On the other hand, many Garibaldi brigades published fortnightly wall newspapers.[26]

As part of the shift from a pure militarisation of the area, the Garibaldi brigades called for the immediate setting up of a 'People's Guard' in the liberated zones, made up not of partisans but able-bodied men aged between 16 and 55. To achieve this, the brigades argued, 'The best weapon is propaganda: only in this fashion will support for this village protection service become total.'[27] But on a broader level, as was the case in other partisan republics, military commanders were divided politically, so there was no unified command structure.

The second meeting of the provincial council, held on 30 September, dealt mainly with new democratic education. Local CLNs were invited to examine the situation of each teacher carefully and to sack those 'who cannot guarantee the teaching of democratic lessons'. Communist-inspired youth organisations also persuaded the council to agree that schools would put on classes in basic education for manual workers.[28] Text-books were also assessed for the extent of their fascist propaganda.

Factories were reopened, and some were specifically asked to produce munitions. For example the *Solari* watch factory in Pesariis repaired and adapted partisan weapons, such as converting rifles to be able to fire 120 mini-mortar bombs, an invention that was used successfully in subsequent battles.[29] Elsewhere, a manager of a coal mine gave partisans explosives. The reopening of these workplaces was not the only measure to reduce unemployment: the building of military roads also helped to lower the number of those without jobs. However the greatest problem was food, and many women would walk down from the mountains into the occupied lowlands to get basic foodstuffs from partisan bases.[30] A local hospital was set-up in Ampezzo in mid-August, in a building that the authorities requisitioned, and had on average 20 overnight patients.[31]

In this republic the problem of finance was dealt with in a fairly original way. The area had no industry and very little large-scale agricultural production, so capital reserves were small. When peasants began withdrawing their bank deposits, to avoid widespread economic uncertainty the council abolished all direct and indirect taxation, and created an 'asset tax', which began at 2 per cent for 200,000 lire and above, rising to 8 per cent for assets above a million.[32] The situation was greatly helped by a loan from the Bonomi government in Rome. The administration of justice, meanwhile, saw interesting developments: trials would be decided upon by juries, the death penalty was abolished and the entire process was cost-free for those involved.[33]

Meanwhile, an international army of 40,000 had finally been assembled in an attempt to extinguish the republic, including Germans, Italians, Austrians, Vichy French, Croatian Ustascia, Georgians and Don Cossacks. That the Resistance controlled such a redoubt was unacceptable to the Nazis: when they had to retreat to their home country their route would inevitably take them through this area. Reoccupation of the entire territory took 80 days of fighting, with partisans losing many men. The republic ended in the first few days of December, having lasted roughly three months. As was the case with nearly all other partisan republics, the territory was not totally conquered: over 12,000 men remained high up on Prescola mountain, which by then was covered by two metres of snow.[34]

THE OSSOLA REPUBLIC

This republic, with a population of 60,000 to 80,000, lasted just over a month, from 10 September to 14 October 1944. It took its name from the main town, Domodossola, which is in a valley north-west of Milan that borders Switzerland. At just 250–300 metres above sea level, most of the lower Ossola valley cuts through much higher strategic Alpine valleys. Compared to many other partisan republics, the Ossola area was highly industrialised. It included Italy's only gold mine, as well as marble and granite quarries – indeed much of the marble for Milan's cathedral came from this area. Overall, by the Second World War heavy industry characterised the area, including steel and engineering factories, as well as hydro-electricity plants: Ossola power stations produced about two billion kilowatts a year. With its industries, and the Simplon pass into Switzerland, it was hardly surprising the Germans took a strong interest in the area once they had invaded Italy.

The communists, after suffering long years of arrests and prison sentences, had by 1942 managed to create a stable local structure and distribute newspapers. Pippo Coppo, who had joined the PCI in 1932, was able to enrol 50 people into the Omegna branch by August 1943, many of them fellow workers at the *Cobianchi* factory.[35]

The following month, not long after 8 September, the German forces arrived. A member of the future provisional council of government recalled the arrival of the SS:

tough, threatening and contemptuous. They lined up in large numbers at factory gates. Managers and shop steward committees were ordered to guarantee and maximise production, otherwise they would be killed. ... There was a total ban on helping refugees or allied prisoners, the punishment for doing so was a death sentence. Threats and terrible experiences were not enough: every single refugee continued to be fraternally helped, or protected in safe hiding places.[36]

The collapse of Italian fascism had produced a huge movement of people throughout Italy: anti-fascist prisoners were released, Allied prisoners-of-war walked out of unguarded camps, Italian soldiers left army units which were now lacking any command structures – and most, along with assorted refugees, were heading for the Swiss border. It was a mixture of these transient individuals, politicised local people, and peasants simply drawn into events, who made up the first elements of organised resistance in the valleys of the Ossola.

One specific contribution to the Resistance in this area first emerged just to the south in the town of Novara, where on 9 September two young career army officers, Alfredo and Antonio Di Dio, refused to hand their weapons over to the Germans, preferring to form a partisan group above Lake Orta. Another man in Novara named Eraldo Gastone responded in the same way, but headed for the Sesia valley with about 30 men, in this case many of them workers. This was to be the initial group that grew into one of the most legendary partisan formations, led by Cino Moscatelli.[37]

Workers in the town of Villadossola got hold of weapons from Milan quite soon after 8 September. Quickly basing themselves in nearby hills, in early November they decided to head back down to their home town, relying on a positive reaction from their fellow workmates. This move led to one of the first acts of insurrection of the entire Italian Resistance. On the morning of 8

November road blocks were set up, police stations were occupied, workers walked out of their factories, and the German garrison surrendered. However, being somewhat inexperienced and naive, the group had not planned for a major counter-attack. Additionally, they did not think of blowing up bridges or barricading the main roads, nor of how or where to retreat to. Consequently an attack the following day by an SS armoured column supported by three Stukas was successful.[38]

Despite its bad ending, the brief occupation of Villadossola created a huge sense of confidence in the valleys, and at the end of the month the nearby town of Omegna was briefly liberated. This was led by two commanders – Filippo Beltrami and Cino Moscatelli – at the head of brigades which were now well organised. A poster announcing liberation was stuck up in the town, and in the space of just two hours both men gave a speech to an enthusiastic crowd, the fascist headquarters were burnt down, and several tons of weaponry and ammunition taken from a local factory and police barracks. But having learnt the lesson of Villadossola, the brigades never thought about holding onto the town.[39]

Over the following winter, partisan forces were severely diminished in the Ossola area. Being in general badly armed, and not ready for the winter, demoralisation and disorganisation set in. Things picked up again in spring 1944, and as partisan attacks grew, the enemy began withdrawing in early summer, leaving 2,000 armed men operating in the valley. By August it was impossible for the fascists and Germans to use the railway lines that passed through the valleys,[40] and meanwhile the high valleys were freed one by one. The 400 Germans and fascists stationed in Domodossola understood they were surrounded and began negotiations through a local priest, though not with the Garibaldi brigades because they never negotiated special surrender terms. They had discussions with Dionigi Superti and the Di Dio brothers – commanders of moderate partisan forces. The strange outcome was that the city was liberated at dawn on 9 September with partisans marching in and Germans marching out without a shot being fired. Negotiations had allowed them to leave the city, deprived only of their heavy weaponry – indeed the partisans accompanied them to the outskirts.[41]

Not surprisingly, the Germans immediately attacked the Beltrami and Garibaldi divisions in the first town they came to, Gravellona Toce, with the latter group suffering 39 dead. It was scandalous that the 'Valtoce' and 'Valdossola' divisions did not come to their help – because after all it had been their commanders, Di Dio and Superti, who had agreed to let the Germans go the day before. Even more controversial was the fact that the Garibaldi and Beltrami divisions had been excluded from these negotiations, but nevertheless then had to suffer the consequences.[42]

It was politics rather than military stupidity that lay behind this, and it was the first of many such clashes that plagued the Ossola republic. The Garibaldi division was communist and the Beltrami socialist, while the other groups claimed they were 'non-political'. But, as is still the case today, being 'non-political' is in itself a political stance. In the case of the moderate brigades, there was a refusal to discuss political issues in general which led to serious problems: not only could leaders of these formations act more or less without any argument from the rank and file, it was also easy for them to manipulate their men, who were unaccustomed to and suspicious of 'political' partisan brigades. At the end of June a political commissar visited one of the moderate brigades led by Superti and noted: 'to me it seemed I wasn't in a partisan formation but among the defunct army prior to 8 September [1943], and naturally they greeted me courteously but rather coldly. ... there is no political organisation'.[43] This commissar was also banned from giving a speech to the brigade he was inspecting.

Crucially, therefore, the Ossola republic came into being with its military commanders profoundly divided. Indeed on the very eve of the liberation of Domodossola Superti issued an order 'according to which whoever moves from his formation to ours [Garibaldi] is be treated as a *deserter*'.[44] This was literally unheard of: migrations between partisan groups, while not particularly numerous, had always taken place for a wide variety of reasons. Given these attitudes it is not surprising that the more conservative partisan commanders were determined to interfere with the democratic process of a liberated area. Indeed such were the tensions that in the government's early days there were seven officially recognised police forces – some belonging to the provisional government, others to the partisan groups.[45] Crucially, the new ruling civilian body, the provisional council of government, also suffered from a democratic deficit – in essence deriving from a virtually non-existent CLN. In other words there had been no broad democratic tradition pre-existing the republic, on the basis of which to create a united organisation with widespread credibility.

After the Germans' withdrawal, the following morning the new council announced in a wall poster both the town's liberation and its own constitution. Office holders were listed, but the power they had given themselves came from the 'designation of military command' rather than by popular acclaim or democratic election. It was not set up 'in the name of the people' through mass meetings. Although formally democratic, it came very much 'from above', or to be more precise, from conservative partisan commanders. A further crucial weakness was that before the creation of the republic all experienced political leaders had been forced to leave for Switzerland as they were known to the fascist police. Following the creation of the republic there was a tendency for the more careerist among them to hop back across the border and demand they be given public office.

Nevertheless, things changed immediately. There were no crimes during the whole 35-day period, not even street fights. In the republic's 220 primary schools, all fascist norms were cancelled. Any books of a clearly fascist nature were dropped, and to some extent text-books from Italian cantons in Switzerland were brought in. Foreign languages, banned under the nationalist fascist regime, were put back on the curriculum. On 25 September 1,500 people crowded into a local cinema to hear a speech by the famous Latin scholar, Concetto Marchesi, and other political leaders.[46]

A 'Popular University' was quickly announced by Mario Bonfantini, a socialist member of the provisional government. His three (free) lectures a week on the history of modern Europe were always well attended, by students, manual workers, peasants, white-collar workers, partisans, priests and nuns. And they continued right up to the eve of the fascist and Nazi invasion. Here a historian recounts the last lesson:

> Bonfantini almost forgot about his lesson, but out of a sense of duty he goes to the venue, a cinema, where he finds at least 150 people. They're not unaware of what is happening, but they are relaxed, they want to learn calmly, and ask questions. 'The situation is serious', Bonfantini says, 'the enemy is approaching Finero and could even arrive [here] in Domodossola overnight. Superti and Di Dio are preparing a counter-attack. Maybe it's better to go home.' But then he smiles: 'If you want, I'll take the lesson.' They agree.[47]

Italy's first ever female Minister – for Welfare – was the communist Gisella Floreanini, who immediately organised the putting up of posters asking local people to donate any surplus food at collection points, so that more needy people could make use of it. The response was significant, a sign of a fundamentally new attitude.[48] By mid-September timetabled train services were already running on the tracks that led into Switzerland. Roads were opened, as was the postal service – by 22 September new stamps had been produced. There was even a football match between the 'Valtoce' division and Domodossola's local football team, which the partisans lost 5–1.[49]

Two days after liberation workers were in their factories again. At power stations the lines to occupied Italy were cut, causing cities such as Novara to be plunged into darkness. In steel and engineering factories hand grenades, mortar bombs, anti-tank devices and smoke bombs were all produced very quickly. If the liberation had lasted slightly longer, mortars and automatic weapons would have been produced. Other factories started producing goods that could be traded with Switzerland.[50] Another measure was that all workers sacked for anti-fascism were to be re-employed. Political meetings were held inside factories, but there was no talk about workers running the factories themselves: class positions were to stay as they were; this was not a revolution.

Trade unions were set up again, and the local trades council soon began operating from what had been the fascist union offices. On 3 October unions sent employers a demand for an immediate 4 lire per hour pay increase for all industrial workers, and specified that the working week be limited to 48 hours.[51] A newly formed teaching trade union supported these demands, something unheard of at the time, when white-collar and blue-collar workers lived almost separate lives and teachers were viewed as highly privileged.[52] Industrialists such as Severino Cristofoli naturally resisted the demands, but most private employers did grant pay rises very quickly. And where employers had announced sackings, these were withdrawn in favour of drastically reducing everybody's working week.[53] Another interesting detail is that large local factories made major donations to the provisional government – the electrical energy company Edison gave half a million lire, and Montecatini 750,000.[54]

Railway workers demanded an increase of 30 lire a day, but in their case the employers were the provisional government. The council had a real debate about this and two motions were presented – the one that was passed provisionally agreed to the increase, but specifed that it could only be ratified once pay rates in liberated southern and central Italy were known.[55] In its second meeting on 14 September the government authorised the publication of two new daily papers. One was its own official information sheet, whereas the second – *Liberazione* – was more the paper of the partisan formations and the CLN of Domodossola. Two editions of *l'Unità* and one each of *Avanti!* and *La nostra lotta* (*Our Struggle*) were produced, as well as an edition of *Fronte della gioventù* (*Youth Front*). Furthermore, the 2nd Garibaldi division published two editions of their *Unità e Libertà*, the same number of *Il Patriota* was published by the Matteotti brigade, and eight editions of *Valtoce* by the division of the same name. The creation of the republic was rightly treated as a significant news event: even in the US the *Chicago Daily News* carried a lengthy and positive article about the republic during its lifetime.[56]

However, the underlying weakness of the Ossola experience was the desire of some partisan commanders to dominate civilian political affairs. These leaders tended to hark back to the *Risorgimento* period of Italian unification, when society was more deferential and hierarchical. The worst example of this were the Di Dio brothers, and their 'Valtoce' division, who were openly contemptuous of the provisional government's authority. Alfredo Di Dio was the son of a Sicilian police chief, and a puritanical Catholic.[57] Pippo Frassati was another ultra-moderate, a monarchist who walked around in shiny high boots, and who once arrested two communists who had crossed the Swiss border with a bundle of newspapers.

One highly emblematic crisis involved a stand-off in Villadossola, when communist *garibaldini* and moderate partisans were about to fight it out over the ownership of an arms dump found in a factory, until a mediator arrived from the provisional government.[58] Indeed after Domodossola was liberated, moderate partisan commanders quickly set up armed road blocks and stopped *garibaldini*, disarming them before they could come into town. The underlying issue was always the desire of moderate commanders to isolate their men from political discussions. Moscatelli understood this kind of behaviour needed to be contested, and organised a big march and speech in Domodossola. After Di Dio made all kinds of threats if Moscatelli spoke in the main square, he subsequently agreed to speak elsewhere in the town. On 23 September Di Dio even threatened to stop a public meeting of the provisional government because his permission for it had not been sought.[59] Incredibly, he even intervened very heavily over the fact that the provisional government was publishing its documents on red paper, and successfully had the colour changed to white.[60]

On occasion he would also 'see red' with *garibaldini* partisans if they ventured into his area, ripping off their red neckscarves.[61]

Many of the more conservative formations requisitioned vehicles and foodstuffs, and local people could not fail to notice their use of such precious resources. One communist report characterised the Di Dio formations thus: 'the old anti-democratic mentality of the Royal Army exists; officers who live luxuriously in hotels with their families or lovers, and rush around everywhere in cars'.[62] But crucially, the provisional government had not built up popular political support to a level strong enough to allow them to challenge the conservative partisan groups. Indeed the government decided to nominate local councils on the basis of equal representation of the parties represented in the national CLN, a bureaucratic imposition that often did not match local opinions on the ground. At times this became ludicrous, such as in the town of Premosello when Dr Raffaele Einaudi discovered one morning from reading a poster that he had become mayor 'due to the people's will'.[63] Although the time frame of the republic was short, there is no evidence that local elections were ever planned.

Some of the tensions amongst partisans were understandable, particularly with regard to what to do with the fascists who were now in custody. Alfredo Di Dio (whose brother had been killed by the Germans) once threatened the authorities: 'If you don't give us those two fascists we'll come and take them away from the jail ourselves.' The man in charge of the republic's justice commission answered him: 'Fine. But I'll give the order to not hand them over and I'll be at the prison door to stop anybody gaining entry through force.' On the opposing side of the partisan divide, when Cino Moscatelli visited the prison camp containing 300 fascists and saw that the radiators in huts were already switched on in early October, he complained: 'These people, who in all likelihood are just bastards, are given two blankets – my boys up at six thousand feet get one blanket if they're lucky.'[64]

Indeed, since most partisan units felt that justice was too meek – not one death sentence was passed – at least some units simply never handed over captured fascists to the courts and dealt with them on their own.[65] However new values were being forged: the best example of this was the clemency of legal sentences as defended by Justice Minister Ezio Vigorelli, who had suffered the death of his two sons in partisan actions just three months earlier, but despite this now resisted knee-jerk executions of fascists.

One other important issue was that of obtaining official recognition from the Swiss government, which would have allowed goods and military help to pass freely across the border. The Italian government in Rome had spent 30 million Swiss francs on buying arms, which could be transported once an export licence was granted.[66] In the Italian-speaking Ticino Canton there was a great deal of solidarity; in fact, the first Swiss Red Cross convoy had arrived on 22 September in Domodossola. The Red Cross were quickly sending in 20 tons of potatoes a day, but also flour, condensed milk, tinned meat and medicine.[67] A Swiss political leader had visited the Ossola republic on 28 September and wrote asking for solidarity in a local Swiss paper: 'The food situation is tragic ... There is no winter clothing ... There's nothing ... Children are starving.'[68]

The Allies, for their part, did not drop any arms or food to the new authorities in the Ossola for the whole 35 days.[69] Partisans had even rebuilt an old landing strip, and another runway existed elsewhere, but no Allied plane ever landed.[70] The Allies just made promises – almost every night Radio London announced air drops – and every night fires were lit on the airstrips to guide the planes in. The Allied secret services had originally talked about sending in US and Yugoslav soldiers currently interned in Switzerland over the border, but nothing came of it.[71] At a meeting of the CLN and Allied representatives held in Switzerland on 17 October a British colonel blamed bad weather, the 'scarce strategic importance of this area, the patriots' bad timing and difficulties in providing air drops'.[72] However the Allies did make at least two air drops to the forces led by the Di Dio brothers,[73] in one alone dropping 85 drums containing four machine guns, 30 Sten guns and even a typewriter.[74]

Hunger became severe, and although formally the civilian authorities had supreme powers, partisan commanders found it difficult to accept increasing food restrictions being applied to their units, thus ratcheting up the civilian–military tension. But some of this tension can also be explained by inexperience: three of the five partisan commanders were aged just 23.[75] Furthermore, the political and economic change achieved by the Ossola republic was not that of a revolution abolishing an old class system, but the creation of a new democratic system to replace a dictatorship, so the collective political leap forward was not as extensive as it could have been. Although people tried to pull together in such desperate circumstances, the initial divisions were never overcome.

A Garibaldi brigade newspaper published on 28 September was scathing about what was happening: 'popular, democratic and progressive participation of the whole population in the management of common affairs is totally lacking'.[76] This meant that the unity needed in preparing for either military offence or defence was lacking. A single military command structure was agreed only near the end of the republic, yet in essence it remained a dead letter. It was impossible to prepare a meaningful defence plan, for example, if organisations did not come clean about the number of partisans and weapons they had in the field. While partisan units had proved themselves able in rapid guerrilla attacks, defending an extensive territory against large enemy forces was a fundamentally different kind of warfare.

These political divisions led to military weaknesses, which then led to political and military defeats. As one communist inspector warned a week before the fatal attack: 'the military situation is pretty serious, and if there is not joint cooperation [and] Ossola is attacked from various fronts it will undoubtedly fall'.[77] One of the obstacles towards creating a single unitary military command was that every formation would then have to have a commander and a political commissar, of equal rank to a commander, both of whom had to jointly agree every decision taken. The stumbling block therefore was not just the moderate's desire to be 'non-political', it really illustrated resistance to the general drift towards a more collective command structure.

Although the Garibaldi divisions in particular asked for and obtained many new recruits from the local population, most had to be turned away because there were no weapons for them. And when in early October the enemy began assembling up to 20,000 well-armed men, mainly Italian fascists, with heavy artillery, on the edge of the republic, no moves were made against them. Partisan formations were still squabbling about how to create a unified military structure. Due to these kinds of problems, the republic could only muster a total of between 3,000 and 3,500 men, who were not very well trained and lacked munitions.

By now bread had run out, and people were living on chestnuts and milk. Despite these difficulties, in the southern areas of the valleys workers were called out of their factories by sirens, and paid to dig anti-tank trenches. Peasants, summoned from the fields by church bells, were eventually persuaded to spread barbed wire from the river bed to the mountain slopes, and to cut down their crops to create an open field of fire. Massive blocks of granite were also placed on the roads by mine workers.[78]

The enemy attack began on 10 October, with the main assault inevitably coming from the south. The partisans were outnumbered four to one, and facing artillery fire from an armoured train. They had limited ammunition, only light weapons, and very little food – despite all this they resisted for four days as they were driven back up the valley, until the fascists entered Domodossola on the evening of 14 October.[79] Overall the moderate partisan forces put up the greatest resistance, as the Garibaldi brigades had withdrawn to higher ground, mistrustful and mindful of the betrayal they had suffered at Gravellona Toce a month earlier.[80]

The provisional council of government evacuated the town, with the enemy in hot pursuit. About 2,000 partisans ended up crossing the Swiss border, where they were disarmed and put into internment camps. The same choice was made by around 35,000 civilians, about half the permanent population, who preferred to do this rather than undergo further occupation.[81] One reason so many people acted in this fashion was that since the region had been a democracy for over a month, fascist spies would have had a field day informing on those who had supported democracy.

The republic was defeated, but despite its internal weaknesses the main causes of its defeat were ultimately external. Obviously it was ended directly by the Nazis and fascists, but it probably could have lasted much longer had it been given help by the Allies, who clearly did not like the idea of Italians developing their own democracy independently. A German newspaper commented: 'General Alexander, commander of the British army in Italy, must bear the responsibility for the Italian blood spilt in Valdossola.'[82]

The PCI leader Giancarlo Pajetta and about 120 others decided to try to avoid internment in Switzerland and set out on a 'long march'. Gisella Floreanini, despite having a young daughter, was the only minister of the provisional government to join them. It took the group, which was eventually whittled down to just ten people, 20 days to cross over high mountains and six valleys and reach Val Sesia, where Moscatelli's forces were based.[83]

As was the case with the other partisan republics, by the following spring resistance in Ossola had been rebuilt, and on 24 April 1945 Domodossola was definitively liberated. Combined forces from the Ossola and other valleys then met up in the Po valley, at Varese, moving on to liberate Tradate and Como, arriving in Milan on 29 April.

11
Organising 'Terrorism'

The Prussian military strategist Carl von Clausewitz once famously remarked that 'War is merely a continuation of politics'. Equally so, guerrilla fighting is the prosecution of conventional war by other means. The legal and political legitimacy of such a response has been enshrined in many United Nations resolutions since 1945, such as resolution 3070 from 1973, which 'Reaffirms the inalienable right of all people under colonial and foreign domination and alien subjugation to self-determination, freedom and independence', and indeed restates 'the legitimacy of the peoples' struggle for liberation from colonial and foreign domination and alien subjugation by all available means, including armed struggle'. Yet over the last two decades in particular, this kind of struggle has been demonised by the word 'terrorism'.

Even so, many governments in the world have derived their legitimacy from waves of mass or clandestine 'terrorism' – indeed US democracy itself emerged from guerrilla warfare against British colonialism. Many highly respected political figures of the last few decades – such as Nelson Mandela, convicted in 1964 for leading the armed wing of the African National Congress – were for long periods pariahs in the eyes of powerful leaders around the world. During Ronald Reagan's presidency Mandela and the ANC were on the US government's terror watch list, and in 1987 Margaret Thatcher explicitly called the ANC a terrorist organisation. Yet by 2006, Tory leader David Cameron was applauding Mandela's 'leadership, his humanity and generosity of spirit' and defined him as 'one of the greatest men alive'.

Similarly, the current deputy leader of the Northern Ireland Assembly, Martin McGuinness, is widely believed to have been the IRA chief-of-staff for much of the 1970s and 1980s. Given the IRA's waging of a guerrilla campaign, it may be useful to consider briefly how Irish republicanism organised itself militarily. What was rarely explained during 'the Troubles' was how the IRA was in a position to carry out thousands of military actions. Most of all, it was hardly mentioned that people joined the IRA freely, hence the organisation calling its members 'volunteers'. Having a continuous stream of recruits, the IRA then needed weapons, which were generally bought, mainly through fund-raising in the United States, or various legal or illegal activities in the North and South of Ireland. Having obtained recruits and weapons, when they launched an attack against an individual policeman or soldier, or against a barracks, people in the street heard the noise, turned round and saw people running away. Equally, there could be dozens of people looking through the windows of their houses, shops or offices, but who then looked the other way. In short, to sustain a military campaign of this kind a significant degree of popular support was needed. Indeed Sinn Fein, the IRA's political wing, regularly scored percentage votes in double figures at election time.

These same conditions applied in the Italian Resistance, with some variations. Although a steady stream of new recruits was available, most weapons were not bought but obtained by disarming individual policemen or attacking their barracks en masse. And in launching any military attack in a city, or act of sabotage, it was inevitable that activists would be seen – so such actions were predicated on there being a high level of passive support, or in some cases on maintaining a fearsome reputation to convince people that despite their disagreement it was better to remain quiet. Moving weapons, explosives and publications was also highly problematic in streets that were patrolled so frequently, so a network of non-combatants to reduce the risks was needed – these were generally the *staffette* – who was going to stop a 70-year-old woman or a 12-year-old boy at a checkpoint?

As with guerrilla warfare in the mountains or countryside, urban resistance took the form it did because it was impossible militarily to organise large static numbers in cities. However one city more than others – Bologna – periodically launched significant military challenges to fascist and Nazi rule. When the Germans first organised an auxiliary police force in February 1944, local GAP groups were ordered not to attack them, as most policemen were very young and not particularly vicious. However when the police clearly became oppressive, GAP groups killed 17 officers in five days, which resulted in mass desertion: at least 150 out of 500 left the police force, many of them joining partisans in the mountains as it was impossible to stay at home.[1]

Indeed it was in Bologna that the only mass urban engagements of the Resistance took place. Within the space of a week in November two furious battles broke out; the bravery and desperation behind such an unusual decision stemmed from the fact that the city was straining at the leash, given that the Allied front line was just ten miles away (and was to remain there for the next six months). The first battle erupted in the Porta Lame area, and was perhaps the most important military engagement in an Italian city during the Resistance, outside of an insurrection. As a result of two partisans going to buy bread, 75 well-armed *Gappisti* (GAP members) stationed in an abandoned barracks were discovered by the enemy, who in the course of the day built up their forces to 1,500 men. The partisans resisted for eleven hours, coming first under mortar and then cannon fire. Finally, a Tiger tank was brought in from the nearby front line. Aware of all this, a partisan group of 250 based in the cellars of the bombed out Maggiore Hospital left the building to help in the battle, launching a surprise attack on the enemy from behind from four different points. After a total of 16 hours of ferocious fighting partisans suffered twelve dead, including a New Zealander named John Klemlem, while the enemy lost 216 men.[2]

The second battle occurred very close by a week later, but in this case the Germans and fascists knew of the partisans' hideout beforehand, and apart from assembling 900 men had brought in 18 Tiger tanks – it was almost as if Bologna now constituted the front line. Once again, fighting went on all day, with the partisans losing six men. One of these deaths was a successful suicide attempt, while one of the five wounded was an unsuccessful attempt – all partisans knew they would probably be either shot or tortured to death once captured.[3]

As discussed earlier, there were two types of partisan groups operating in the cities: GAP groups and SAP squads. Initially these abbreviations meant *Gruppi* or *Squadre di azione proletaria* – proletarian action groups or squads – but the communists, who were to create the first GAP groups in the autumn of 1943 and who made up the overwhelming majority, decided to define their activities as 'patriotic' action, so the 'p word' was changed from proletarian to patriotic.[4] The difference between GAP and SAP groups lay in the scale of military commitment: *Sapisti* were part-time 'terrorists', who kept their normal job and engaged in lower-level military activities. SAPs were created in the summer of 1944, once again by the PCI. The reason for their creation was the expectation by workers of a significant partisan armed intervention during the March 1944 strikes, hopes that were not fulfilled. The leadership's rhetoric was exposed by events, everybody could see it did not have masses of militarised personnel to call on, and so the PCI rapidly tried to create a situation in which large numbers of people had access to weaponry. SAP squads were therefore far more mass-based, and had a clearly defined territorial base.

Figure 11.1   Partisans being tortured by the infamous Muti squad in Milan.

Individual members of SAP squads knew only three or four other members, and then only by their *nome di battaglia*, or military nickname. If they were arrested they could not name many people, and those named could not be traced by the police because the nicknames were used only by SAP members. Their activities were extremely varied, particularly as regards propaganda. They would distribute leaflets in various ways – through letterboxes of individual flats, throwing them off bridges or from a moving tram – or alternatively would paint or chalk messages on walls or pavements. By early

1945, they were conducting 'flying rallies' in markets, factories and cinemas, in which armed *Sapisti* would secure the area before one of them would get up to make an anti-fascist speech to a surprised audience.

Militarily, SAPs first step was to disarm soldiers and policemen. Getting hold of their first weapons could often be very quick, if risky. One tactic was to simply walk up behind a policeman, stick a screwdriver in his back, and demand his gun, hoping he would not turn round. The tactic worked overwhelmingly well, and as one ex-partisan put it: 'When you got hold of a few guns it seemed like you'd conquered the world.'[5]

Leaflets were produced explaining to railway workers how to sabotage trains. They were told to put a specific amount of glass or sand, ground to a fine powder, in the oil or grease used to lubricate train wheels. After a few hundred kilometres the wheels would seize up, but the origin of the sabotage would be difficult to trace. Many such methods were summed up in one of the most fascinating documents of the entire Resistance, *Prontuario del Sapista* (*A Sapista's Manual*), a booklet written in 1944. The document was printed presumably because there was a need for many people to read it – after all this clandestine urban army could not be trained in the open. Many of the techniques already mentioned are explained in detail over its ten pages – for example that disarming should be done in groups of five: 'During the evening or the day a group can carry out at least four disarmings.' In order to paint slogans on walls it is recommended that a SAP group goes armed with two revolvers and two hand grenades. Instructions are also given for leafleting on foot, on bicycles, in cars and in public buildings. The manual notes that many such actions could be carried out by fewer people and with little or no weaponry, but it emphasises the political nature of these activities: 'Those who do not have an awareness about why they are fighting will not be good fighters, they will not face danger with courage if they do not believe in the need for that action in order to reach a political end.' And the final aim is spelt out in detail:

> These preparatory actions are aimed at the creation of a revolutionary area. Every *Sapista* must act, and at the end of every week he must be able to say: 'I've taken part in this disarming, leafleting, writing of wall slogans, etc., I've contributed to the preparation of the national insurrection and the liberation struggle, I've trained for the final phase of mass attack against the enemy.'[6]

Indeed the actions themselves could raise the general population's morale, as a Florentine *Sapista* points out, outlining yet another form of action: 'A comrade used to bring three-pointed nails to my house, that we then spread across roads to sabotage vehicles and German lorries. Not only to make them waste time, but also to show people that there was partisan activity.'[7]

Gappisti were the full-time 'terrorists', who from time to time would kill soldiers and policemen in the street, in their barracks, in bars, etc. They would also attack telephone lines, electricity sub-stations, railway lines, and more or less any kind of military or official target. While enthusiasm could carry people into direct involvement in 'terrorism', the constant tension of such a life meant that not everybody could stand the pace. The planning before an assassination or a major act of sabotage was meticulous; as the Florentine *Sapista* quoted above recalls: 'When you carried out a five minute action it was preceded by three days of preparation, or sometimes by a week. To be able to strike you had to become familiar with how your target moved about and when he did so, and all other crucial factors.'[8] To blend in better with the crowds nearly all attacks took place in broad daylight rather than under the cover of darkness, given that a curfew was also in force. Rather than recruiting 'hot heads', *Gappisti* needed to be patient, cool and calculating.

Carla Capponi, a highly active *Gappista* in Rome, recalled how her commander once ordered her to meet a woman, already active in the Resistance, who wanted to join the organisation. Noting that the small blond woman was well dressed, with gloves that went up to her elbows, Capponi quickly explained what her own life was like:

Look, you sleep in cellars, you eat when you can and what you can. Forget about hot water. I haven't changed my jumper for two weeks and I've been wearing these old tights for two months now. You're always on the move, you never go anywhere regularly, you mustn't meet any of your relatives, not even your mother – it's as if she's dead. You're hunted 24 hours a day. You need to know how to shoot, and go out under curfew to attack fascists and Germans.[9]

Activists in GAP groups also needed to be ruthless. The legendary *Gappista* Giovanni Pesce, soon after moving from Turin to take command of a GAP group in Milan, complained in a report in July 1944:

a group that had to carry out a specific act of sabotage arrives on the scene to plant some bombs without creating suspicion, in the meantime a woman starts shouting 'Don't do it – they'll execute my husband' [Who was presumably in jail] and the GAP withdraw without carrying out the action. This must not happen again. We cannot consider the interests of one single person, one must always consider the general interest. There are thousands of men today who give their lives for freedom, therefore we must act in solidarity with them: we cannot be sentimental.[10]

As such, one of the most delicate jobs was choosing the individuals who would join GAP groups. Pesce explains:

This was a really difficult job; they were chosen by political parties and unions and sent on to me. I used to see one or two at a time. Some of them would say: 'I'm not going to start shooting in the streets, I'll get arrested straight away.' So you'd have to explain at length why it needed to be done, that everybody's lives were at stake. Loads of people were being killed, strung up, or deported. What were we meant to do – nothing? If you do nothing you're accepting all of this. By doing something you gave people hope.

And then you could tell that many of them weren't brave enough. I remember that one week I saw a hundred volunteers, and out of them I only chose three.[11]

The classic selection process tended to initially favour people with a proven political record, such as Irene Castagneris. Castagneris had joined the PSI in Turin just after the First World War, and then the Communist Party when it was founded in 1921, with which she stayed in contact throughout the 1920s and 1930s. When the regime began to collapse in 1943, she took anti-fascist leaflets into her factory, until, after 8 September, 'the party was forming some squads ... They decided that the only woman who could do that kind of work – given that they had been watching – was me.'[12] In other words, people were often selected beforehand and then approached. Castagneris ended up doing all kinds of work, such as carrying bombs, ammunition, or guns through the streets of Turin.

When fellow fighters were arrested the fear immediately arose that they would talk, revealing where other partisans lived. Prisoners could also be taken round the streets and asked to identify fellow partisans. So sometimes fighters such as Castagneris were forced to spend a few weeks in a safe house without ever going outside. Once the immediate danger had passed, it was prudent to change your appearance, hair colour, etc. Activists needed nerves of steel. Castagneris remembers coming back to Turin on a bus carrying some weapons:

I got off and saw a dead partisan right in front of me, stretched out on the ground. They'd hung a sign on him: 'Whoever is found carrying weapons will suffer the same fate.' I thought about what I had in my bag, and then I had an anti-aircraft shell as long as this – we used to take the explosives out of them to make bombs – and I was carrying it in my arms, like a big bottle.[13]

Following an assassination, the average *Gappista* tended to just collapse:

Look, every time it was over, when you went back home or to the house they gave you or another one that you used – because sometimes there was a curfew and you couldn't get home in time – so you went there ... As soon as you got in you collapsed onto the bed. Then you grabbed the bottle of gin and downed a couple of mouthfuls, threw yourself on the bed because you couldn't stand it any more, your nerves were on such an edge. Afterwards, about an hour later, you felt better. And you started to talk: 'Did you see that guy? What an idiot! Could you ever imagine someone behaving like that! They didn't even know what was happening.' Well, that gave you the strength to do it all over again. ...

Your courage came from knowing why you were doing it, why it was necessary. ... people did it because they wanted it all to end quickly.[14]

Getting caught was a terrible prospect, and women prisoners were treated no better than men. When Irma Bandiera of the 7th GAP group in Bologna was captured by the SS she was repeatedly tortured. This culminated in her being blinded and then executed in a main street.

The general military model of operations was brought in by Ilio Barontini and Ateo Garemi from France, who had already fought in the *Franc-tireurs partisans*. Garemi, however, was killed in Turin very soon after his return, with his place being taken by Giovanni Pesce. Many of the *Gappisti* in the North had seen action in Spain: not only Barontini and Pesce, but also Vittorio Bardini, Egisto Rubini and Bruno Roda.[15] Barontini had perhaps the greatest experience of all: he had fought not only in Spain and France, but also in Ethiopia and even in China. Since he had commanded a Garibaldi brigade in Spain, and had played a significant role in France, he was able to offer plenty of practical and organisational suggestions. He knew how to make bombs, how to handle explosives, make up slow and fast fuses and so on.[16]

Apart from the purely military aspects, much of what urban partisans did had a political impact, in the sense that they aimed at to keep the morale of the Resistance high, and to demoralise the enemy. The PCI initially had difficulty in politically convincing its most committed members to become *Gappisti*, as an internal report detailed: 'The concept they hold is that a Communist can't behave like a thief; in this case all they see is the form, and forget the substance.'[17] But their activities were also political in another sense, since other political forces argued that 'terrorist' attacks would simply encourage reprisals. In reply PCI members in particular argued that Nazis and fascists were terrorists anyway, and that terror needed to be answered by terror, otherwise demoralisation and passivity would increase. Indeed over time there is evidence that the Germans and fascists became conditioned by partisan actions, particularly those carried out as reprisals, and consequently thought twice about immediately launching indiscriminate attacks on the population.

In a broader sense, these actions were vital because the fascist regime wanted to present itself as a legitimate government, and constantly claimed there was no resistance in the cities. To remain silent and inactive would have led to an incalculable level of demoralisation. Although the regime rarely admitted to the Resistance having any support, certain measures revealed the effect the frequent attacks were having. One of the main tools in the arsenal of a 'terrorist' was a bicycle, which allowed fighters to leave the scene of an attack quickly. As a result, in a major city such as Bologna, from 1 March 1944 people aged over 16 were not allowed to use bicycles.[18] For similar reasons, in the town of Mirandola to the north of Modena, the mayor banned the wearing of cloaks in January 1945, at the height of winter.

There was also an element of psychological warfare being played out on the large chessboard of city streets. For example in October 1943 Roman communists put up a wall poster entitled 'Whoever collaborates with the Germans is a traitor'. Examples of resistance and sabotage were then listed, but much of the text made it clear that both the Germans and their Italian fascist allies were destined for defeat, and that any excuses made later would not be heeded. 'In any event', the poster concluded, 'whoever collaborates with the Germans is a traitor – from now on they are condemned to death!'[19] Pressure was also applied personally: in many cities the Resistance sent letters to fascist leaders and senior bureaucrats threatening to kill them.[20]

A TALE OF TWO CITIES

Rome

The Italian capital experienced German occupation for nine months, half the period of northern cities. But despite that Rome had many powerful GAP groups, which developed very quickly. What was politically different was the existence of the *Bandiera Rossa* (*Red Flag*) group, formally known as the Communist Movement of Italy, an organisation which placed class divisions rather than national unity at the top of its agenda, and therefore concentrated on developing support among the working class, refusing to be part of the CLN. The shanty towns of the periphery, the *borgate*, were their strongholds, and it was from here that many raids on barracks were launched in the week after 8 September 1943, when large quantities of weapons were seized.[21] Indeed on 9 September some Communist Movement members had fought at Porta San Paolo against the invading Germans, where somewhere between 240 and 400 died for the Resistance.[22] Their politics and organisational talent enabled them to pull together many different strands of opposition, and a significant movement that in essence argued for revolutionary change had developed as a sizeable force by late 1943. So much so that by the latter months of 1943 they probably had slightly more members in Rome than did the PCI. They were particularly strong in workplaces, though there were very few large factories in Rome, and had informers within the police and government ministries. In the *borgate* they even had a children's organisation for those aged 7–14, called 'Koba', a false name Stalin had used in his youth.[23]

Throughout the autumn and winter of 1943 the Communist Movement of Italy continued to grow, not least through its propaganda – *Red Flag* was the name of the party's newspaper and also the name most people used to describe the organisation itself. Activists repeatedly attacked the city's two main airports, frequently destroying aircraft and blowing up fuel dumps. Additionally, a week never went by without a major attack on rail traffic.[24] But the *Red Flag* activists were not as tightly organised as those in the PCI; indeed in a mass attack on Forte Tiburtino on 22 October, 22 *Red Flag* partisans were captured, ten of whom were executed the following day.

Crucially, a relative openness in recruitment policy led to a series of fatal round-ups in the coming months.[25] One man who was particularly sadistic in his torture of prisoners was SS Captain Erich Priebke, who had joined the

Nazi party back in 1933 and the SS in 1936. As one partisan recalls: 'they tied my hands to the door handle; Priebke carried on hitting me, he broke my nose ... When I fainted he stomped on my chest with his boot saying "Talk"'.[26] As ever, 'terrorist' actions were accelerated by Nazi atrocities, the first major one being a raid on the Jewish ghetto on 16 October 1943, when German soldiers arrested over 2,000 Jews from a list supplied by the Italian Ministry of the Interior.

The PCI grew rapidly too, but far more in the central areas of the city. Taken together these two groups quickly developed a phenomenal strike rate. Two days after the raid on the ghetto PCI *Gappisti* launched an attack with hand grenades against a fascist militia barracks. The two political strands then came together on 7 November, the anniversary of the Russian Revolution, when many posters were put up, and at least three 'flying rallies' were organised. Furthermore, a big slogan was painted on the side of the tomb of the unknown soldier: 'Death to fascists and Germans', and a huge hammer and sickle was painted on the Spanish Steps. A large flag with a hammer and sickle was also fixed on a tall tree in one of the city's main squares.[27]

On 16 December 1943, in just one day, the Roman resistance was able to kill the leader of the fascist militia, attack a fascist patrol wounding one soldier, damage a German vehicle, and bomb the fascist militia headquarters, causing severe damage and wounding several people. Two days later they bombed a restaurant used by Germans, killing ten; while Rosario Bentivegna threw a bomb at Germans on leave from the front line as they left a cinema, killing eight.[28] On 19 December four *Gappisti* attacked Hotel Flora, headquarters of the Germans' War Tribunal, with dynamite and hand grenades, probably killing several officers.[29]

Although the Germans' normal practice was never to reveal the number of casualties they had suffered, subsequent research shows that partisans' attacks were causing them serious problems. As the German commander-in-chief Kesselring admitted when he was put on trial just after the war: 'Rome had become an explosive city for us ... Security immediately behind the front line was a serious problem. The morale of front line troops was directly affected because they could no longer be sent to Rome for brief rest periods or for leave.'[30]

As with partisans in the mountains, the men and women of the Roman resistance came from all walks of life. The man in charge of the PCI explosives dump was a young university chemistry lecturer, Gianfranco Mattei, while Rosario Bentivegna was a medical student.[31] Franco Calamandrei, deputy commander of GAP groups, would translate French literature at home while waiting to launch his next attack. To a significant degree this typified the social composition of Roman PCI partisans – which was thus not fully representative of the city as a whole. Coupled with the lack of large factories, the Roman resistance was not characterised as having a high level of active support – although hostility towards it was no greater than in any other city. The dynamics of Resistance activity was certainly not uniformly upward, as it was difficult to quickly replenish groups whose members had been killed or arrested.

One constant political drawback was the influence of the Vatican over the moderate parties, which often argued for reducing or entirely eliminating 'terrorist' actions that could lead to reprisals. Overall, the Vatican feared communism and the Soviet Union far more than it did Nazism and the Third Reich. Cardinal Luigi Maglione, Vatican secretary of state, put it very clearly when writing of a meeting with German officials immediately after they had occupied Rome: 'I made it clear to the German ambassador the seriousness of the situation which could arise if the Germans had to abandon Rome a few days before the Allies arrived. ... the police that were left would find it impossible to prevent or repress a Communist insurrection'.[32]

Paradoxically, the enthusiasm of partisans was to be put to the test after 22 January 1944, when the Allies landed at Anzio, just under 30 miles south of Rome. From then until liberation, naval bombardments and artillery fire were periodically heard in the capital. The Action Party's paper quickly headlined with: 'This is the moment [we've] waited for. Men and women of Rome – to your posts!' L'Unità too called for an 'insurrectionary general strike' in the next few days, and widespread sabotage occurred across the city. Just two days after the landings, a German restaurant at the city's main station was bombed by a 19-year-old student who entered the bar on her own, causing at least four dead and 19 wounded. The reason for the attack was that many trains were leaving the station for the new front line at Anzio.[33] Another very effective action took place on 15 February, when a bomb planted on the Rome–Naples railway line caused the death of 310 German soldiers.[34] Faced with such difficulties the Germans imposed a curfew that started at 5 p.m., in the heart of winter.

As with the landings at Salerno, the Allies were unwilling to make use of the surprise factor, and built up their supplies and vehicles slowly. This gave the Germans time to bring in reinforcements and launch a counter-attack, so much so that after a couple of weeks long lines of captured American soldiers were made to march through Rome city centre in order to demoralise the local population. The PCI had made comprehensive preparations for a general insurrection, but the German counter-attack forced them to cancel their plans.[35] Having placed the Resistance on an insurrectionary footing, many activists had put themselves in danger, and indeed from February until liberation on 4 June many were arrested, suffering death and torture.

Because the Allies were so near, promising imminent liberation, the Germans regularly engaged in mass round-ups and were even more violent than usual towards the local population. By now, almost every house or flat in the city had a hiding place either in use or ready for use. On 2 March the Germans rounded up over a thousand men for transportation to Germany. A crowd of a similar number, mainly women, quickly assembled outside the jail to protest, and tension increased when Gappisti started throwing leaflets into the crowd. At one point Teresa Gullace, a mother of five who was six months' pregnant, was trying to throw a parcel of food to her husband through a window when she was shot by an SS soldier.[36] Such a cruel act of intimidation in front of a large crowd could not be allowed to pass without a response. Local PCI women first laid a bunch of flowers, which quickly became a focal point. A few hours later, as the crowd loitered outside the barracks, mainly women *Gappisti* launched an attack in the same spot, killing a fascist militia man and wounding another. In the chaos that ensued, many prisoners managed to escape.[37] In the meantime, one *Gappista* ran into a bar to take shelter from the fascists who were shooting randomly, when a member of the militia came in:

> he's young, exhausted, wearing a black leather jacket. He then says to the women who are looking at him in fear and with disgust – 'If only you knew how I feel! I can't stand it any more, I can't stand it any more! That Italians are doing this to each other!' – he then bursts into tears, throws his machine gun away and collapses into semi-consciousness. Upset, women crowd round and nudge him, they are crying as well. A man says 'Get the gun out of the way' – I take the machine gun and its cartridge and carry them out the back into the toilet.[38]

Another man who had taken part in the same attack ran into a nearby church and hid in a confessional booth. Hearing the shooting outside, the priest asked him whether he had anything compromising he wanted to hand over. After the *Gappista* passed over his gun the priest gave him a mini-sermon against violence.

The fascists and Germans clearly understood that the Resistance would reply to terror with terror, but the fascists in particular were becoming very demoralised, being only too aware that the Allies were very close to liberating the city. GAP attacks were now almost daily in the capital, and were to continue until liberation. On 9 March Carla Capponi, acting on her own, blew up a German lorry and trailer carrying petrol very close to the Colosseum. The following day fascists marching through the city were attacked by partisans with light weapons and hand grenades – nine were killed and many wounded.[39]

The most notorious act of the entire Italian Resistance took place in *via Rasella* on 23 March, the anniversary of the founding of the Fascist Party. Rosario Bentivegna lit the fuse that exploded ten kilos of dynamite placed in a street cleaner's cart as a column of SS soldiers marched by, something it did at the same time every day – completely ignoring the agreement to Rome being an 'open city'. Another partisan group immediately attacked the shell-shocked Germans with hand grenades and machine guns, and when the dust cleared 33 Germans were dead and around 100 wounded. Until that point partisan actions had been daring, but they generally involved attacking fixed targets in enclosed areas which allowed for a relatively easy escape. This was a serious escalation: the Resistance had decided to attack 156 fully armed soldiers marching through a street preceded by a motorbike with a machine gun mounted on a sidecar.

The German generals who came to inspect the scene were hysterical. The orders from Hitler's headquarters called for exemplary punishment. Despite their vindictiveness, the Nazis now understood how vulnerable they were. The attack, although shocking, was not yet controversial within the Resistance because there had been no act of reprisal. However the following day, with the fascist authorities adding dozens of prisoners of their own accord at the last minute, 335 prisoners – including 75 Jews along with Resistance leaders and ordinary criminals – were massacred in the *Fosse Ardeatine* quarries to the south of the city, with SS Captain Erich Priebke playing a leading administrative role, as well as later admitting to executing at least two prisoners. The biggest problem for GAP groups became not how to respond to this, but the fact that in mid-April they were betrayed by one of their own under torture. Rosario Bentivegna, Carla Capponi and many others had to leave the city. From now on most Resistance actions took place in the suburbs rather than the city centre.

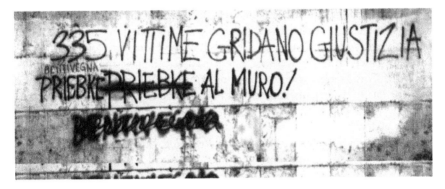

Figure 11.2 '335 victims cry out for justice. Bentivegna/Priebke up against the wall!' Contemporary graffiti (both men are still alive) arguing over the responsibilities of Rosario Bentivegna, leader of the attack on an SS column in Rome, and SS Captain Erich Priebke, one of the key officers in the massacre of 335 prisoners as reprisal.

Politically, the shock of the *Fosse Ardeatine* massacre allowed the Vatican to condemn not only the German reprisal, but particularly the partisan attack. The important thing for the Vatican was not to try to lengthen the period of German occupation, but to ensure that there was a smooth handover to the Allies without the involvement of the Roman masses. As Pope Pius XII had argued in his 1943 Christmas message to Romans: 'we recommend calm and moderation, and the avoidance of any rash act that would do nothing but provoke even more serious disasters'.[40] Although the Roman CLN did not criticise the attack in *via Rasella* (just as it had never criticised any other partisan action), the left was thrown on the defensive.

Throughout April and May *Red Flag* continued widespread resistance in the *borgate*,[41] but the central area of the capital was often very quiet compared to previous months. Despite this trend, in mid-April the city's CLN had agreed on an insurrectionary general strike, to be held initially on 24 April, but then delayed until 3 May. But the number of large workplaces listed in the plans revealed a key weakness: only tram drivers, women working at the main tobacco factory, and printers at the main newspapers were mentioned. Although 300,000 posters and leaflets were distributed in preparation for the event the strike failed, partly due to the German's repressive moves beforehand, and partly due to the political argument put forward by moderate forces about Rome being an 'open city' and that the capital and its monuments should not be destroyed by street fighting. Militarily, partisan attacks on electricity pylons just outside the city also failed, so trams could be run; and the night before German soldiers and tanks had occupied tram depots, forcing the morning shift to go to work on the morning of 3 May.[42]

In broader terms the city was tired and hungry, and not ready to launch an insurrection. Both the PCI and the Resistance at large had suffered too many arrests and losses to feel strongly enough about a full-blooded uprising. Crucially, their slightly tenuous relationship with large masses of workers meant they were not able to grow significantly in numbers. Furthermore, at a meeting with a British major in Villa Borghese at the end of May, it was made very clear that the Allies did not want an uprising.[43] This matched perfectly with a speech made by Churchill in the House of Commons on 24 May, in which he said: 'We have good reason to believe that Rome will be excluded from being a war zone for our armies.'[44] When the Vatican let it be known that the Germans had agreed to leave the city without defending it, the city's CLN had neither the willingness to object, nor an insurrectionary plan to enact.

As the Germans began to withdraw *Red Flag* partisans initiated several firefights in the far south of the city.[45] But by and large the Germans left Rome without a shot being fired at them, a unique withdrawal given their experience in other Italian cities.

Milan

What made Milan's experience different to Rome's was its greater number of factories. Although 'terrorism' took place on the same basis, with sudden attacks by anonymous individuals, the organisational backbone of much urban resistance came from the large industrial workplaces. The number and concentration of factory workers made this an almost natural development, and something that in some cases emerged very quickly. In summer 1943 some socialist workers and railwaymen in south-east Milan not only formed a military organisation, but used factories as collection points for clothes, food and medicine for soldiers deserting from the Italian army. Some escaped British POWs were even hidden in a small factory before being smuggled into Switzerland.[46]

The first series of 'terrorist' actions in Milan took place on 29 September, when an anti-aircraft battery was blown up, as well as a German ammunition dump. Three days later a munitions dump at Taliedo airport was destroyed. In the same period, and in a harbinger of the kind of 'dual power' that was to prevail in Milan factories by late 1944, fascist spies were also killed in two factories, *Breda* and *Caproni*.[47] But the partisans' most famous early action was the assassination of Aldo Resega on 18 December, an attack that already indicated a tight military organisation. Resega was the fascist leader in Milan, the birthplace of fascism. His daily movements were studied for a month beforehand by a group of *Gappisti*, and then two other *Gappisti* – kept unaware of his identity in order reduce their stress levels – were sent to kill him, walking either side as he crossed the road in front of his house.[48] As one of the two *Gappisti* recounts:

I had a pistol underneath the newspaper I was pretending to read, and from not more than 4 inches away from his side fired off four rounds. He falls forward without a sound, dead on the spot – 'Lupo' [nickname of the other partisan] wants to do his bit so he fires four bullets into him as he's lying on the ground. After that we cross the street in four paces and get on our bicycles.[49]

The fascist leadership decided to kill eight prisoners in reprisal the following day, and then held a huge funeral in the centre of Milan. Thousands of fascists from all over Italy were called upon to attend, but the funeral was attacked with a few shots and hand grenades from rooftops. The reaction by fascists illustrates the mass panic that 'terrorist' attacks could create, as the Minister of the Interior later estimated that over 5,000 rounds had been fired at shadows, and all the while Resega's coffin was left standing in the street.[50]

However, the rise of urban partisan activity also led to greater expectations, which were not realised, particularly before and after the March 1944 strikes. The PCI had emphasised that this was going to be a lot more than a conventional strike, but it simply did not have the military strength to impose a qualitative breakthrough. The party's Milan newspaper *La Fabbrica* (*The Factory*), headlined after the strikes: 'Towards the decisive struggle – Let's organise the insurrection!'[51] Although many GAP groups suffered arrests beforehand, the strikes had been built up as political, almost insurrectionary strikes, which were due to receive widespread military support. Yet as one author has argued as regards Milan:

Nobody knew that there were just fifty men available, of which the youngest was 17 and the oldest 30, with the majority being little more than boys of around 20. There was a kind of messianic expectation, but the partisans are never seen and this leads to a lot of demoralisation. Furthermore, the strike had been organised as a mainly political strike, and no relevant demands were even made to management. Compared to December, this time people don't bring home either an extra kilo of coal or an increase of five cents.[52]

What is only mentioned in passing here, 'partisans are never seen', exemplifies one of the weaknesses of 'terrorist' actions – the vast majority of people are meant to wait passively for a far smaller number of brave people who will achieve change on their behalf, only here the number of brave people was too small to make any substantial difference. This was why the PCI's military organiser in Milan, Italo Busetto, called for a large expansion of the SAP network after the March 1944 strikes. By the end of the month the PCI federation calculated that it had 220 to 250 SAP members; that is, people who were generally still active at work but who were also trained militarily. Yet the fact that at least 16 had no access to arms, and that many others had only taken part in actions such as leafleting, suggests that the figures were rather inflated.[53]

The initial lack of growth came down to political disagreements between SAP and GAP groups: SAP commanders did not want to hand over their best members to GAP groups, because it meant losing them forever. The PCI wanted to increase its military organisation, but found a high level of resistance amongst workers, who often stated that when they were called upon to take part in an armed insurrection they would take up arms, but not before. This problem, which was just one facet of what the PCI termed *attendismo*, was viewed quite severely. For example on 30 November 1944 Busetto told a PCI Federal Committee: 'Despite the F.C.'s efforts incomprehension as regards armed struggle still exists ... there is an indispensable need for close collaboration between military and political cadres, which doesn't yet exist ... the problem of military struggle is understood as a problem for partisans in the mountains and not one of SAP groups.'[54]

Furthermore, the life of a *Gappista* in particular was very difficult and demanding. People lived an incredibly isolated existence, as the most famous *Gappista* who operated in Milan, Giovanni Pesce, confirmed in an interview:

Sometimes when we needed revolvers we went and disarmed people, other times we got guns from the big brigades up in the mountains – that's where we got our explosives from as well. Then we needed to find a bomb-maker too.

But I never met these people. And it was women who used to bring revolvers and explosives to me. ...

Nobody knew where I lived, it was terribly lonely. I never went out, nobody was meant to see me, these were the instructions I got from the party.[55]

Although Pesce was a front-line fighter, the same experience held true for the commissar of all GAP and SAP groups, Amerigo Clocchiatti: 'Activity was frenetic, but nevertheless you had the impression you were organising nobody. An open and physical contact with groups was lacking.'[56] In other words, the life of an urban 'terrorist' was very lonely, and far from that of a courageous romantic hero.

Despite all these difficulties, Busetto's call for the creation of SAP squads was of profound importance in maintaining morale between March 1944 and the insurrectionary period – both as regards workers in factories and the population in general. Some 'terrorist' attacks also provided the spark for a qualitative leap of confidence among industrial workers, and a reciprocal demoralisation among fascists, as Pesce explains:

> More than anything else, our actions had both political importance and an impact on morale. You need to understand that the vast majority of Italians were passive, they were frightened. But deep down they hated the Germans. So the important thing was that every time there was an attack, it gave people hope and confidence.
>
> The second aspect was that these actions created links with the strikes which workers were leading in the factories. It also showed the partisans up in the mountains that people were fighting in the cities as well.
>
> The really important thing wasn't killing a spy, but the repercussions this had on public opinion. I'll give you an example: the *Caproni* factory in Milan. The boss, Cesarini, had got more than 150 workers deported to Germany, where about 70 died in concentration camps. So these workers were really frightened, absolutely terrified – they never went on strike – they did nothing.
>
> They had ordered some partisans from the mountains to kill him, but they weren't courageous enough. Then they ordered me to do it. So on my own – I was crazy – at 7.40 in the morning I went up and killed him and two other managers.
>
> At the same time, all the workers who were getting off the tram for the shift change and who had seen what happened started shouting 'Well done!' So the very same day, the entire factory went on strike. And that factory was 'strike happy' until liberation day. The important thing wasn't the killing, but the effect it had.[57]

A partisan response to the 15 people killed in *piazzale Loreto* on 10 August was vital in terms of keeping anti-fascist morale up. Pesce happened to pass by and saw the dead bodies piled up, but did not stay long in order to avoid being recognised. Many factories went on strike that very afternoon or the following day, and rallies were held in some workplaces. The following day Pesce went to his bomb-maker and asked him to make up eight bombs immediately. That evening four bombs were placed on the window sills of German headquarters, and the entrance was also mined with more timed bombs, so that soldiers trying to leave the building were continually hit. The German casualties, although numerous, were never released.[58] Three days later another partisan threw a hand grenade through a window into the main courthouse, killing three German officers.[59] Both Germans and fascists knew that every outrage they committed against the local population would be followed by a response from GAP or SAP squads.

By the winter of 1944–45 Busetto and Clocchiatti had managed to create a unified structure for all 'terrorist' groups operating in Milan, and, as Clocchiatti recounts, the results were remarkable:

Panic took hold of the enemy. Bravery increased among the *garibaldini*, they saw you could act and hit the enemy without too many losses. Our men learnt the technique of urban guerrilla warfare – strike and leave the area, strike and disappear. Create terror – insecurity within the enemy's ranks was the basic law of urban warfare.

We organised flying rallies in working-class markets. We stationed observation and protection squads at various points within the market: the speaker made a brief and incisive statement over current economic problems and called for peace. Then – away. ...

For New Year's Eve 1945 we organised speeches in three cinemas ... they were notorious for being used by fascists and Germans. Our men were due to speak in the interval, so with the house lights on. Squads were meant to keep Nazi and fascist groups in their sights from the stalls and the balcony (if there was one), and the speaker was to get up on the stage, and then everybody would have withdrawn. It worked well at two, but at the *Pace* cinema men from the X MAS shot at the comrade who was speaking; we replied by killing two of them.[60]

Workers were now using military threats to deal with pressing problems, such as the danger of deportation to Germany. A report from the *Motomeccanica* factory recounts: 'As regards the question of deportation, the issue was raised in no uncertain terms, that is management were told they will be held personally responsible if round-ups were to take place in the factory.'[61] The undoubted epicentre of these activities was the industrial suburb of Sesto San Giovanni, where around 40,000 workers were employed. One of the most militant factories in what became known as the 'Stalingrad of Italy' was called *Breda*, and as with the factory cited above, workers were trying to turn their workplace into an environment where they were free from harassment. A PCI report of events in October 1944 recounts:

comrades became aware of some policemen at the front security entrance and so they got all work to come to a halt throughout the factory, and put the workforce on alert. A delegation was sent to management to demand an explanation. Management initially stated that it was about a theft, but put under pressure and with the threat of keeping the factory idle they were forced to mention the name of the worker they wanted to arrest (one of our members), who then left. People subsequently went back to work.[62]

Obviously management did not want to accept that their control was being usurped, and would repeatedly try to regain lost ground, but workers' sense of self-confidence was simply too high. Two weeks later another strike broke out at the same factory demanding early payment of wages, but other demands were also made – common at the time – that management give their workforce foodstuffs, clothes and coal. One manager named Bovone 'Confronted the workforce using expressions which workers took as an insult, and he was slapped by a woman. Workers tend to aggressively invade management offices. ... Management leave the factory: the strike continues until the end of the shift.'[63]

By the autumn of 1944 even small factories had what clandestine documents referred to as 'sporting activity', or their own 'football team' – a codeword for SAP squads. Over the winter each squad slowly built up its numbers, weaponry and scale of activity. This growth was bound to effect the management, who were also aware that in a few months anti-fascists would be in power and factory owners would be called to account for their actions. Perhaps this strength explains why the insurrection was so smooth and successful in Milan. Liberation meant an end to violence. In describing the end of his 'terrorism' as he walked out onto the streets of Milan on 25 April, Giovanni Pesce illustrates how the partisans' violence had been a necessary evil rather than a way of life:

> there are people, there are armed workers, groups of young people running towards the barracks the fascists had left overnight. ...
>
> Finally I feel I'm living in a world that is complete, full, alive. For months I had been fighting with little groups of determined patriots, for months I moved around like a shadow, isolated, with just a few sporadic contacts with members of the brigade. Now, in the midst of all these people – workers, young people, women, I feel immersed in a huge sea of affection. Until yesterday I walked the streets of this city viewing passers-by as potential enemies, doubting everyone, trusting no one. Today, I'm confused in this friendly crowd. It's like waking up from a nightmare. Then I realise that the houses are lovely houses, that the streets are wide, and that above there's the sky.[64]

Here Pesce is hinting at the future of the 'Resistance generation' and the fallacy of pigeon-holing those forced to engage in political violence as 'terrorists'. After liberation, Pesce and tens of thousands of others went back to civilian life and led a completely normal existence – although many of them remained politically active in conventional terms for decades to come.

12
An Uneasy Alliance:
The Resistance and the Allies

It is important to remember that there were two levels to the Allied contribution to the liberation of Italy. The one that is often forgotten is the help given by ordinary soldiers and low-level officers. Some of the soldiers who battled their way up the peninsula fighting conventionally were genuinely touched by the humanity of ordinary Italians; but the most interesting contact was the direct involvement of Allied soldiers in the Resistance.

On 8 September 1943 approximately 85,000 POWs found themselves suddenly freed from Italian prison camps. (This number includes Americans, Russians, Yugoslavs and people from the British Empire such as Australians, Canadians, South Africans and New Zealanders.) Their military duty was to move south and try to cross the front line and rejoin their unit. However many of them preferred either to go to ground working on peasant farms or to join the Resistance. This was a mass phenomenon, and one that has been largely overlooked ever since: 'there may have been an understandable disinclination by military historians to look too closely into the virtual resignation from the war of the equivalent of two to three divisions of British and Imperial soldiers'. Equally, Italian historians have generally failed to recognise the scale of spontaneous help given to escaped POWs by Italian peasant families out of a sense of common humanity. To the extent that the Allies later became aware of this phenomenon, they revealed a complete misreading of what had happened, as evidenced at the beginning of the Cold War by General Eisenhower's request that the details of those Italians who had helped should be kept, because such people 'might be useful in covert intelligence operations'.[1]

Several of those soldiers who chose to join the Resistance movement later wrote memoirs of their experiences. Almost inevitably they were from the officer class rather than lower ranks, but what emerges from all tales is a sympathy for the common humanity shown to them by ordinary Italians, in a situation marked by a very strong language barrier. Most officers tended to preserve their class spirit however, and were suspicious and critical of communist partisans.

Gordon Lett was a 33-year-old British major who, after being freed on 8 September, rather than trying to cross the front line, quickly pulled together an international battalion made up of eight nationalities in the hills above La Spezia. Typically, the dedication at the start of his book reads: 'His International Battalion was limited in arms and equipment but not in courage, and behind them to a man, incredibly poor, heart-warmingly loyal, were the *Rossanesi*, the people of the valley.'[2]

Eric Newby, who later became a world famous travel writer, was a year older than Lett, and a lieutenant in the Special Boat Section. After his release from a camp west of Parma on 8 September he was hidden for three months in the Apennines by Italians, among them his future wife. Similarly to Lett's, the dedication to his book reads: 'To all those Italians who helped me, and thousands like me, at the risk of their lives.'[3]

Stuart Hood was a 27-year-old intelligence officer in the Eighth Army, freed from the same camp as Newby. After working on several peasant harvests, he joined two separate partisan groups in Tuscany and was later awarded an MBE.[4]

The affinity also worked the other way, with members of the Resistance coming to appreciate individual Allied soldiers. On 15 July 1944 Roberto Battaglia was parachuted into northern Italy to command a partisan unit and met 'Tony' Oldham, a British officer who had escaped from a prison camp after 8 September. Battaglia was struck by the fact that Oldham was a career officer who had decided not to attempt to rejoin British forces:

Through these regions and the families who have given him shelter he has come to love Italy in a completely new and unique way: not as a different nation but as a part of humanity that is rising up against the Germans ... I will never tell him explicitly why I have been sent here: yet it is this simple feeling, this faith in the war we're fighting, that unquestionably makes us brothers.[5]

AN ALLIANCE FOR MILITARY NEEDS

The second level of Allied contribution to the liberation of Italy was the top-level military planning. Even before the Second World War the Allies had been prepared to enter into an alliance with European anti-fascists, but this was only in pursuit of their own strategic aims. As early as April 1938 the British government had decided to set up networks in France, Czechoslovakia and Poland, aimed at gathering information and potentially engaging in future acts of sabotage. Yet the strategy was to encourage only small numbers of specialist saboteurs, not to create the basis for a mass movement.

The British Special Operations Executive (SOE), which united the three armed forces, was set up in 1940. The following year it started talking about overcoming 'factions' within European Resistance movements, and bringing them all under a single authority, that is, under British command. This meant Resistance movements providing military help through sabotage and supplying important information.

The Allies wanted a military network without politics. They certainly did not want the creation of guerrilla armies, but small organisations they could direct and control, such as the Dutch and Norwegian movements. This model, however, could not work well in Italy, where the movement developed later and where the left was much stronger – something which the Allies were not aware of initially. Contact with the Italian Resistance began in Switzerland in November 1943, and only at the beginning of June 1944 were important operative contacts made – most significantly during the liberation of Ancona. The Allies sent around 200 'missions' into Italy, made up of one to five officers, so up to a thousand Allied personnel therefore operated behind enemy lines.[6]

At times, however, the Allies' racist attitudes towards Italians did not help their military cause. After just a few days in the liberated port of Brindisi, on 15 September 1943, General Frank Mason-MacFarlane wrote to Eisenhower in dismissive terms: 'virtually no advantage can be gained from the Italian army, apart from the fact that soldiers can be used as slave labour in the docks and along our lines of communication'.[7] However the Labour MP Ivor Thomas pointed out the truth of Italian fighting abilities: 'Italians have not really fought in this war because they were fighting a war which for them was hateful. Give them a good cause and they will show they can fight as well as any other soldier ... In Spain the Garibaldi division fought well in many battles, and made a significant contribution to the fascist defeat at Guadalajara.'[8] Indeed on the limited occasions when Italian formations fought side by side with Allied units they acquitted themselves very well.

Equally, once resistance grew behind German lines they were able to give a good account of themselves. For example the 28th Garibaldi brigade prepared the plan for, and took a central role in, the liberation of Ravenna on 4 December 1944. The brigade commander Arrigo 'Bulow' Boldrini wrote in a report at the time:

> there were two concepts of how the war had to be fought: the partisan/popular one which wanted to speed up the country's liberation and bring the war to an end through incessant, continuous and decisive action. The Allied one started from the standpoint that, for obvious political reasons, liberation had to be as little as possible the achievement of the Italian people.[9]

At a conference years later Boldrini continued in a more sardonic vein:

> discussing and negotiating with the commander of the 8th Army, flanked by a large number of generals, was an interesting and I must say very positive experience – because I realised that at the end of the day the plan worked out by peasants, farmhands and intellectuals was also valid for the senior officers of 8th Army high command. Ultimately, we knew the area like the back of our hand, and above all we were determined to liberate our country.[10]

But once the Allies began to understand the strength of the Resistance in summer 1944, moves were made to reduce the power of the movement – the tension surrounding the attempted partisan disarmament in Florence in early August was probably the first concrete example of this. The examples began to multiply as the months wore on. In the Forlì area, the 700 men of the 8th Garibaldi brigade had been forced to cross to the Allied side due to German pressure. They wanted to carry on fighting alongside the Allies, but were ordered to disarm – they indignantly replied 'we'll hand over our weapons by the sharp end' – and only then were allowed to fight. Yet when Forlì was finally liberated on 12 November the brigade was formally banned from taking part. Interestingly enough, when the Allies moved into Forlì GAP groups had already liberated the city anyway.[11]

By the final quarter of 1944 the Allies were clearly aware of the strength of the left within the movement. The new heights reached by the Resistance throughout the country worried both the Germans and the Allies in different ways. This was the background to a notorious proclamation made by General Alexander on 13 November, in which he told partisans: 'The summer campaign which began on 11 May and has been conducted without interruption, including the breaching of the Gothic Line, is over. The winter campaign will now begin.' This meant: 'ceasing large-scale operations' and 'preparing yourself for a new phase of struggle to face a new enemy, the winter'.[12] Major battles between the opposing armies had ended in late September, and Alexander's proclamation made the Allies' intentions clear – the consequences for the partisans were terrible. On 1 October Kesselring ordered a 'week of struggle' against partisan bands from 8–14 October. He knew the Allies were not going to attack German forces until the spring, so he removed several divisions from the front line for a massive campaign against the Resistance. This week turned into a two-month campaign which concluded at the end of the year, and saw the extinguishing of major partisan republics such as Carnia, Monferrato and Ossola.

General Alexander's statement and the Allies' policy are therefore all the more inexplicable in the midst of such a sustained German assault – what was even stranger was that the statement was not broadcast in code, as was the norm. Even worse, Resistance leaders were not consulted or informed beforehand about such an important decision. The real reasons for this behaviour were in all likelihood political and not military. Having recognised the strength of the communists, it was in the Allies' interests to see them weakened, and they needed time to develop a political alternative to them. The fact that the announcement was made the day before an important meeting with a CLNAI delegation that had come from occupied Italy to Rome also gives rise to speculation that it was pitched to demoralise the more active sectors of the Resistance. And within the political alliance of the latter, it gave a boost to the arguments of those parties who wanted to stop all activities whatsoever, accusing the PCI of being irresponsible in wanting to continue fighting over the winter.

The other worry the Allies had besides the strength of the left in the Resistance, was the possibility of a too rapid German collapse and withdrawal. This was the period in which the Allies drew up 'Operation Cinders' – a plan to use 240 aircraft to drop on the outskirts of Turin the same parachutists who had recently suppressed Greek partisans, in order to ward off insurrections or revolutions. But this was not just a Turin affair; all Allied missions received detailed instructions on this matter.[13]

Just in case this seems far-fetched, in the same period two examples illustrate how serious the Allies were about keeping the left out of power. In early September the exiled Belgian government was installed in Brussels. It included two communists, who quickly resigned due to the rapid disarming of Resistance forces, leading to strikes and mass armed demonstrations, which in turn were put down by British troops at the behest of prime minister H. Pierlot.[14] Three months later in Greece the British encouraged a group of right-wing colonels to seize power, and sent tens of thousands of troops to support the conservatives. Indeed Churchill had first called for significant British involvement in Greece as early as 29 August. Tension built and culminated in a general strike in a liberated Athens on 3 December, during which police killed 28 demonstrators. At their funeral the next day, another hundred were massacred.[15] Not surprisingly an insurrection broke out in Athens on 5 December, just two days before the signing of the Rome protocols (see below), in which Greek partisans rose against the British-supported government. Fighting continued for six weeks between communists and the British expeditionary force, which suffered 868 dead and about 1,000 wounded.[16] At no point did the Russians complain about British behaviour.

BETWEEN A ROCK AND A HARD PLACE: THE RESISTANCE AND THE ROME PROTOCOLS

Soon after 8 September 1943, Ferruccio Parri, a senior member of the CLNAI and later Italy's first non-fascist prime minister after liberation, sent an emissary on behalf of the Milan military committee of the CLN, Alberto G. Damiani, to Switzerland to talk with Allied officers. The meeting with the British representative John McCaffery and the American Allen W. Dulles (who was also responsible for the OSS in general, as well as secret services in Germany) proved easy to arrange – but the two sides knew very little about each other.

The Allies had only a vague awareness of the political forces emerging to lead Italy out of 20 years of fascism, although the Resistance probably had more accurate ideas about the Allies. What particularly worried the left of the CLN in this period was the open British support for the king and Badoglio, as it was a sign of clear conservative preferences, in opposition to the majority mood for radical change. Two major historians say that Parri was urgently looking for help from the Allies, and not just for military reasons: 'what created this was not only the desperate needs of the first partisan groups, but also the big issue of the "wait and see attitude" (*attendismo*) that had arisen within the CLN'.[17] Unless the Resistance built up its forces quickly, conservative parties were likely to dominate and dampen down further growth. Parri was prepared to make some compromises with the Allies to get weapons to fight 'a big war', but this was the very opposite of what the Allies wanted.

Parri decided to cross the Swiss border himself, with Leo Valiani, and met with Dulles and McCaffery near Lugano on 3 November. The two Allied officers said they could not make binding decisions, but accepted that the Resistance could be a political movement. Yet when they started talking about military strategy the Allied officers repeated that all they really wanted was small groups engaged in sabotage actions, which would be controlled by Allied missions. Valiani later wrote that the Allies agreed to four big immediate air drops, and that Allied liaison officers would be sent to the biggest partisan groups.[18]

Neither side ever really abided by their tentative agreement. The active part of the Resistance continued to build a swiftly growing movement with a strong political edge, while the last three promised air drops never took place (the first one did occur on 23 December). But what the Resistance could do was limited. Nearly a month after the meeting a CLNAI document outlined both what was intended by 'a big war', and the limitations of the situation:

> the situation is serious; if help doesn't come we will collapse. We're still awaiting an outcome on the first drops agreed at the beginning of the month! The lack of immediate financial help will force us to cancel any assistance to those born in 1924 and 1925 [those facing the call-up], and will also strongly limit any help for [escaped] prisoners. Giving us a cast-iron assurance of 50 million lire in 4–5 months we can conduct a big war.[19]

Down in liberated Italy relations were in many ways worse. When the CLN announced they were to hold their first conference in Naples in December 1943 the Allies banned it. They later softened their stance, insisting it be moved out of a big city to Bari, and not involve more than 120 delegates, with the conference finally being held in January 1944. They also insisted delegates could not organise any kind of demonstration, and the public was restricted to attending just the inaugural session. Furthermore, the opening speech by philosopher Benedetto Croce was not allowed to be broadcast on the radio, there were Allied military road blocks around the theatre, and delegates had to show their invites to pass through, with Italian police checking passes a second time at the theatre entrance.[20] General Mason-MacFarlane also recommended censorship of 'criticism likely to bring the [Badoglio] Government into disrepute'.[21]

Part of this intolerance stemmed from tensions in Italy's largest liberated city at the time, Naples. There had been clashes in the closing months of 1943 between students and political groups who wanted to hold meetings, but who were stopped by Allied forces. The party demanding greater freedom was actually the Action Party, rather than the PCI. However, the Allies' attitude was also influenced by Badoglio, who, resenting any platform being given to politicians hostile to entering his government, pressurised the Allies to limit the nature and broadcasting of the debates.[22]

In the liberated South, people who wanted to publish newspapers had to appeal to, of all people, the Psychological Warfare Branch (PWB) of Allied government. Initially the only newspaper the Allies allowed in Naples was called *Il Risorgimento*, and was run directly by the PWB until March

Figure 12.1   Partisans tending a fire guiding in an Allied supply drop.

1944.[23] *L'Unità* and other left-wing papers were only able to publish legally by the end of March 1944. In early March three CLN parties in Naples called a strike, but it was banned by British commander General Maitland Wilson. Given the tense climate, Roosevelt was moved for the first time to tell Churchill that force should not be used.[24] Indeed the first political rally in Naples was only allowed on 12 March, six months after liberation,[25] and no public meetings were allowed without the express permission of Allied military government, AMGOT.

Despite the fact that throughout 1944 the Allies continued to work with politicians and organisations in both occupied and liberated Italy, their mistrust if anything increased as the Resistance grew in size and stature. In August 1944, McCaffery, head of British secret services in Switzerland, wrote an accusatory letter to Resistance leader Ferruccio Parri:

> A long time ago I said that the greatest military contribution that you could make to the Allied cause was continuous and widespread sabotage on a vast scale. You wanted [armed] bands. ... The bands have operated well, we are aware of this. But you have wanted to create armies. Who asked you to do that? Not us. You did it for political reasons.[26]

Underlying these accusations was probably recognition that the majority of the Resistance was prepared to carry on regardless of what the Allies wanted, or indeed of the formal agreements made between them and Resistance leaders.

The extent to which this was happening is difficult to establish, but one crucial element was the PCI, which was unwilling to submit to Allied pressure and blackmail in terms of the actual activity of its men and organisations. But there were significant objective limits to the movement. In mid 1944 the Resistance started to realise that it desperately needed money to continue, and that finance from the Allies would come with conditions.

On 14 November a team was sent by the CLNAI to negotiate with the Allies, made up of Ferruccio Parri, Alfredo Pizzoni, Giancarlo Pajetta and Edgardo Sogno, the latter very much the Allies' man – indeed the Allies insisted he came.[27] Although relations were good enough between the leadership of the movement in occupied Italy (the CLNAI) and the Italian government led now by Ivanoe Bonomi in Rome, the meetings with the Allies were largely left to the CLNAI alone. Indeed part of the Allied thinking in these December meetings was to try to pitch the CLNAI against the Rome government in a kind of divide and rule policy. The two main objectives for the Allies were clarifying that the CLNAI was subservient to Rome, and consequently that it was Rome's local representative in northern Italy.[28]

The final agreement – 'the Rome Protocols' – was signed on 7 December 1944 at Rome's Grand Hotel. The key clause was no. 4:

When the enemy withdraws from territory occupied by them the CLNAI will exercise its best endeavours to maintain law and order and to continue the safeguarding of the economic resources of the country until such time as Allied Military Government is established. Immediately upon the establishment of Allied Military Government, CLNAI will recognise Allied Military Government and will hand over to that Government all authority and powers of local government and administration previously assumed. As the enemy withdraw, all components of the General Command of the Volunteers of Liberty in liberated territory will come under direct command of the Commander-in-Chief, AAI, acting under the authority of the Supreme Allied Commander, and will obey any order issued by him or by Allied Military Government on his behalf, including such orders to disband and surrender their arms, when required to do so.

This point in particular established that the Resistance was fighting for the Allies, not for itself, and that it had no room for manoeuvre or scope for action when the North was liberated. Furthermore, the left agreed that upon liberation the new armed forces would be a reconstructed conventional force, and would not be based on the partisan brigades; all arms would be handed in immediately, and partisan units disbanded – they could not even be part of a new Italian army.

In return for signing the protocols the Resistance received from the Allies a commitment to more finance – 160 million lire a month – and a supply of arms, food and clothing.

One historian has defined this agreement as marking 'the substantial political defeat of the Resistance',[29] while socialist leader Sandro Pertini immediately denounced it as 'the subjection of the Resistance to British policy'.[30] Alternatively, he called it 'the enslavement of the CLNAI to British policy', and polemically threatened that the socialists would not abide by the agreement.[31]

On the other hand, it seemed that if the Resistance was to continue in its present form, it needed finance from the Allies. Politically, all parties accepted that some kind of agreement needed to be signed – but was it a defeat? The question can be answered with both a 'yes' and a 'no'. The 'yes' answer is already encapsulated in clause 4 of the agreement cited above; the 'no' answer relates to the growth of the Resistance the next spring, when it became bigger and better equipped, and had a decisive role to play in April 1945. But overall perhaps the defeat was clear, as following liberation the Resistance as a live force would no longer have any role to play: formally it was meant to disappear without leaving any direct imprint on Italian society.

THE ALLIES' POLITICAL STRATEGY

Although the Allies concentrated on a military struggle against the German army, from the very beginning it was clear they could not simply impose their political wishes on pre-existing political traditions which enjoyed sizeable popular support. Or rather, they needed to develop some alternative form of political support within the country. Throughout 1942 and 1943 the US had been agnostic about the king remaining as head of a new democratic state that the Allies would recognise in the midst of war. But as the Badoglio government continued to be unpopular and unrepresentative – also because the large left-wing parties were not initially part of it – the Americans became more concerned about the issue. Their fear was of the left gaining even more ground outside of the institutions, in the country at large, with potentially uncontrollable consequences. As such, in many ways the king himself was not the issue; the problem was finding an institution with some popular support they could work with, rather than being an invading force with no significant local support.

So in November 1943 the State Department developed a policy of supporting the Badoglio government with the king at its head, but only until the liberation of Rome, after which a new government could be set up.[32] As it transpired the timing was wrong: Rome was only liberated on 4 June the following year, and in the preceding months the left continued to grow rapidly. A worrying chasm was opening up: Italians were flocking to join the Resistance and the Communist Party, with many thinking that the institutional ballet around the king's future was essentially irrelevant in terms of the new society they were going to create.

The Americans' alarm grew in the early months of 1944, whereas the British were doggedly sticking by Badoglio and the king. In early March 1944 Roosevelt told Churchill that the time had come to ditch the king, and if necessary, Badoglio as well. But luckily for Churchill, he was able to hold his position thanks to some unlikely new allies – Russia and the

PCI.[33] One of the most remarkable aspects of this whole sequence of events is that – totally independently, and from a position of being sworn ideological enemies – the PCI developed a policy that was identical to that of Britain. Or rather Stalin, in order to undercut British influence in Italy, announced on 14 March that Russia would be the first Allied government to fully recognise the Badoglio government.[34] Togliatti, en route from Moscow to Italy, made a similar announcement on 29 March – that his party would join Badoglio's government under the king's banner – provoking uproar within his own party and the rest of the left. (See page 51)

Moscow and the PCI

One of the instinctive concerns of the Allies was that the Second World War could end like the First – in revolution. The role of national Communist Parties therefore became vital in their calculations throughout Europe. These parties had switched from opposing war with Germany when it was allied with Russia, to urging resistance alongside the Allies at all costs against the Nazis once they invaded Russia in 1941. Given that the Americans and British were now in alliance with Russia, the role of the Communist Parties became one of warding off any revolutionary developments emerging within the left. In other words, the scale of social and political change in liberated countries promoted by Communist Parties would always be subordinated to what Stalin had agreed with American and British leaders. And there is clear evidence that Stalin put his own strategic interests above the wishes of Communist Parties outside the Soviet Union by making secret deals with Allied leaders. The source for this is Winston Churchill, ideologically a sworn enemy of Stalin. Their agreement was made during talks in Moscow concerning which major power would wield influence in specific European countries. This is how Churchill recalled the key moment, in which he acted without informing the US or his own government, at a meeting held on 9 October 1944:

The moment was apt for business, ... I wrote on half a sheet of paper:

Romania: Russia 90% – the others 10%.
Greece: Great Britain 90% – Russia 10%.
Yugoslavia: 50% – 50%.
Hungary: 50% – 50%
Bulgaria: Russia 75% – the others 25%

I pushed this across to Stalin, who had by then heard the translation. There was a slight pause. Then he took his pencil and made a large tick upon it, and passed it back to us. It was all settled in no more time than it takes to set down. ... After this there was a long silence. The pencilled paper lay on the centre of the table. At length I said, 'Might it not be thought rather cynical if it seemed we had disposed of these issues, so fateful to millions of people, in such an off-hand manner? Let us burn the paper.' 'No, you keep it', said Stalin.[35]

Perhaps it was factors such as 'the percentages agreement' above that made the Allies work with Resistance movements they did not trust. One historian, when assessing Alexander's controversial proclamation in November 1944, views it as 'a direct and immediate consequence of the agreement reached between Churchill and Stalin in Moscow on the division of spheres of influence'.[36] At the end of the day, Stalin's strategic policy meant that independent Resistance movements were expendable.

Despite the faith that millions of communists had in Stalin, in his sphere of influence in Eastern Europe he had no interest in revolution, working-class power or independent action. And as he explained to Churchill at the same meeting, when it came to Italy he had the same attitude:

When the Red Army entered Bulgaria, Bulgarian Communists proceeded to form Soviets. The Red Army stopped it. The Communists arrested the Bulgarian police and the Red Army freed the police. However, Ercoli [Togliatti] was a wise man, not an extremist, and would not start an adventure in Italy.[37]

When the Warsaw resistance rose against the Nazis on 1 August, Stalin refused to move the nearby Red Army forward, and denied Allied aircraft landing rights during their air drops into the war-torn city. In a message to Churchill and Roosevelt on 22 August, he said: 'sooner or later everybody will know the truth about the group of criminals who have launched their adventure in Warsaw, in the hope of seizing power'. After two months of heavy fighting the Polish resistance had lost 20,000 partisans, half of its overall number, while an incredible one in five of Warsaw's population of one million was dead.[38]

There was enormous tension within many European Communist Parties, precisely because they were unaware of Stalin's cynical agreement with the Allies, affecting the fate of tens of millions of people. As the logic of this strategic division began to filter through to the leadership of individual parties, it was far from easy for communist leaders to disown their heritage, which was dead set against the capitalism and imperialism represented by Churchill and Roosevelt. Furthermore, in domestic terms they had a score to settle with those who had financed and supported fascism and Nazism. In Italy there were many examples of this latent tension, but in other countries such as Greece there was a fully fledged civil war after liberation, with the British fighting on the conservative side.

The public arguments put forward by the Russians and the PCI for joining the government were that Badoglio and his supporters were anti-fascists, and that the war effort was being delayed and derailed by squabbling and a lack of unity. Togliatti's sudden change of policy, announced when he arrived back in Italy after 18 years in exile, was the result of a meeting in the Kremlin with Stalin and other Russian leaders just before his departure from Moscow.[39] Furthermore, in another sign of his goodwill, in May Stalin made a key move that allayed many Allied fears by disbanding the international communist organisation known as the Comintern. Stalin was at pains to show he had no interest in or designs on Western Europe – hoping that he would then be given a free hand in the Eastern half.

In a speech in Rome on 9 July Togliatti was explicit about what kind of party the Allies were now dealing with: 'When we ask things from the Allies we know we're not talking in the language of a party or a class. We're speaking a popular and national language, we're speaking in the name of all of Italy, and we know we are speaking of the same interests of the great democratic nations.'[40] With remarks such as this, Togliatti was quickly able to gain the trust of senior Allied leaders. Robert Murphy, Roosevelt's personal representative in Italy, later described him as 'an agreeable dinner guest', who added 'a piquant touch to gatherings'.[41] The Socialists and the Action Party, however, were consistently to the left of the PCI, as were most rank-and-file communists. Although Togliatti repeatedly tried to reassure the Allies, once telling them he was 'the head of the only Communist Party in Italy with nationalistic and patriotic tendencies',[42] the situation on the ground was far from being solved.

The Unconsummated Marriage

The Allies needed the Resistance for military purposes – *but to what extent did they really need that help?* Inevitably, their military considerations became increasingly political, and short of outright revolution the Allies were prepared to tolerate potential dangers from the Resistance. In the final analysis, as two major historians of the movement point out, a complete break with the Resistance was not in the Allies' interest:

> Above all division would have made it impossible to closely and directly follow the changes in the CLN's organisational and political line. But this was not all: it would have meant the loss of the great help Allied agents received from contacts in the [Resistance] military committee, the information regularly received in Milan via Damiani, whether it be on the Italian [political] situation or a vast array of military matters – troop movements, defensive and building works, the intensity of traffic on main military supply routes, statistics on industrial production and much other useful information.[43]

But by the same token, an identical calculation was made by the left of the Resistance, which was less enthusiastic about an alliance with the Allies – what would the consequences of complete separation be? One potentially very worrying question for the PCI leadership was what would happen if the Resistance no longer received significant finance from the Allies? There is evidence from Piedmont that when the Resistance leadership could not get funds, partisans would force money out of capitalists. Written evidence for this is rarely available, due to the danger of prosecution after the war, although some references are sometimes made in code. A report from the Biella area in January 1944 states that 'The industrialists have been taught a lesson. You already know the details of these actions.'[44] The reference was to the owner of a textile factory being kidnapped following a strike, and who while in the mountains was 'persuaded' after a few days to meet the workers' wage demands in full.[45] Another industrialist was briefly kidnapped in Novara in September, and again made a contribution to the cause.[46]

A major military leader once put the question quite bluntly to the Piedmont CLN in December 1944: 'you either take strong action to find the means necessary to fight the war, or the armed formations themselves will impose a war tax'.[47] Albeit with differing degrees of emphasis, and for quite different reasons, both the Allies and the left of the Resistance did not want to take moves that undermined existing property relations, therefore there was an interest on both sides in the Allies financing the Resistance to a significant degree.

Although Britain and the US differed over the details, what united them was the desire to see Italy transformed from a hostile country which wanted to create a self-sufficient economy into a politically compliant free-market nation, highly dependent on foreign investment, imports and technology. They were willing to enlist any kind of help to ensure that this transformation took place, including the Mafia.

Breaking the spirit of their formal agreement with Britain, the US started to become the dominant Allied force in Italy in the second half of 1944, fully recognising the Italian government diplomatically, while the British did not. Behind all of this was economics: the US financed 80 per cent of civilian relief supplies being sent to Italy and clearly the Italian government recognised these resources and would feel beholden to its major donor. Furthermore, the Americans were immediately more accommodating than the British: in July 1944 the US invited Italy to attend the Bretton Woods summit on postwar economic policy, but British opposition prevented their participation.[48]

But there was very little real generosity behind the US expenditure, rather a cool-headed understanding that unless the Italians were guaranteed basic survival they would tend to look to more extreme solutions. So in September 1944 the US unilaterally arranged for Italy to receive help from the United Nations Relief and Rehabilitation Administration. The US government quickly made Italian economic recovery dependent on America: by 1946 the US was supplying Italy with 40 per cent of its fuel imports, 70 per cent of its food imports and 100 per cent of its imported medical supplies.

A week after the big northern cities were liberated on 25 April, General Alexander ordered that all radio transmitters, carrier pigeons, cameras, telescopes, and binoculars be reported to military authorities. All newspapers were subject to censorship by Allied military authorities. Partisans were also meant to hand in their weapons by 19 May – though many did not follow the order, viewing the Allies as potential enemies. Charles Poletti, heavily implicated with the Mafia,[49] became the Allied Military Government commissioner for Lombardy. All public meetings had to be authorised by the Allies, and indeed when on 18 May, just a few weeks after liberation, PCI leader Togliatti came to speak at the Milan Federation of the party, Allied police prevented him from speaking. In Turin they threatened him with arrest, as they did the Socialist Party leader Pietro Nenni. Why did this matter? Because both these men were ministers in the new democratic (*sic*) government!

Figure 12.2 Liberation of a town in central Italy. The first armoured car has a sticker reading 'Long live the Communist Party'; all the other vehicles are from the US army.

Pietro Secchia was one of the prime architects of the Resistance, but had begun his left-wing activism just after the First World War. He lived through many years of clandestine activity and imprisonment. Just two months after liberation he realised his hopes had been dashed:

The 'Allies' were the real bosses, the Italian government counted for very little. Nevertheless there was a lot of government/parliamentary bustle,

222 THE ITALIAN RESISTANCE

and over the last year even our lot were now inserted into this ministerial/ parliamentary work, the horse trading, intrigues, ministerial entourages and their underhand dealings – all concerned with very different issues from those which made up day-to-day experience in the North ... This situation made me really bitter. I understood that we had been beaten for a second time.[50]

Figure 12.3   A look-out.

Conclusion

The last fighting in Italy during the Second World War took place on 2 May 1945, very close to the Austrian border. After the surrender of a German tank crew in the main square of a town, partisans realised that their nightmare was over:

> We looked at each other in silence, none of us felt like speaking. Some people puffed up with tricolours and rosettes passed in front of us, the truckload of *Tommies* and girls went away. Sergio's deep, broken and staccato voice came out from beneath his weapons:
> 'Now the shambles is going to start, just you wait and see what kind of shambles they'll create.' ...
> We walked away from the square down the alleyways, foreigners, swallowing the bitter pill and with a flash of thought that we will try to make sense of tomorrow, in 'the shambles'; to continue to do what our dead wanted.[1]

The book from which this quotation is taken, published 18 years after the events but based on diaries written at the time, has a bittersweet tone, and stresses the worries and frustrations of ex-partisans. Official society resurfaced very quickly, people who had done little or nothing to defeat fascism and Nazism suddenly wanted to take credit for it. The shambles of postwar Italian politics was indeed about to begin.

The hopes of much of the Resistance movement were dashed. Unbeknown to nearly all partisans, on an international level Stalin had made a deal with the Allies that kept Italy within the Western camp, so PCI leaders obediently followed the Moscow line and actively discouraged their members from moving towards something more radical than parliamentary democracy.

On a more positive note, four days later, General Cadorna, commander of the Liberty Volunteers Corps, spoke at the final rally of partisans in Milan before their demobilisation. He concluded his speech by saying: 'if the organisations disband, the spirit of the partisans doesn't die. It will guide the country towards its new destiny.'[2]

For better or worse he was right, at least at an institutional level. For many years the political alliance of the Resistance formed the 'constitutional arch' of postwar politics. But for the Socialist and Communist Parties in particular, 'Narration of the Resistance is monumentalised, its concrete form is a mythical discourse, its public manifestation puts male partisans at the centre, forgetting the civilian population, the major victims of the war in Italy.'[3]

Similarly, for decades official Italy ignored the fact that Italian fascism had spawned its own racial laws. And the devastating effect of Allied bombings or rapes by Allied soldiers were also taboo subjects, given that they were carried out by Cold War allies. Most disturbing of all, the official institutions pretended there had been no Italian civil war: 'All these denials create resentment and disgruntlement, which deeply clashes with official discourse.'[4] In effect a mythology was created: of a united anti-fascist population in the North, and a backward elemental population in the South. This distortion became embedded in Italian politics, and although it contained some elements of truth, it was and still is a significant distortion.

The Resistance was a movement against fascism in all its forms, but primarily against Italian fascism. It was therefore a civil war in political terms, even though the war was also fought against German invaders. The fact that many people fought in or were victims of a civil war made the PCI's later claim that it was only a 'war of national liberation' a particularly damaging distortion. It was a combination of the Resistance being elevated into a unifying national myth, and a failure to accept that there had been both a civil war and a class war in Italy between 1943 and 1945, that stored up problems for the Resistance in the future.

For ordinary ex-partisans life could be very difficult – there was an intense sense of frustration and bitterness, which was often experienced in silence due to their loyalty towards the left-wing parties they did not want to embarrass. For ex-fascists there was a simmering resentment that was to gain significant rehabilitation decades later.

Much still remains of the Resistance. Dozens of books are published every year, and there are today's deadly boring official commemorations – one example among many of how democracy has become increasingly hollowed out and irrelevant to most people. A sign of just how far commemoration has become literally ritualised, and corralled within one of the most conservative institutions of Italian society, is the fact that from the late 1980s onwards many local councils have organised official commemorations that begin with a mass in the local church.

There is then a danger that the Resistance could become an ossified myth of national unity, seen by many people as being irrelevant today. One recent example occurred in Turin on 25 April 2008: in the city's main square 2,000 people assembled for the official Resistance celebrations. Yet a few hundred yards away 50,000 people came to watch the iconoclastic comedian Beppe Grillo perform his second 'Fuck off day' – the insult being hurled indiscriminately at professional politicians.

An old partisan had hinted at these dangers – the watering down of the Resistance and the general transformation of politics into bland soporific variations of spin – a couple of years earlier in a speech to the ANPI conference. Reflecting on the fact that 600 to 800 school students came to a meeting to hear him speak, he said:

These kids listened to me from 8.15 to 13.20 and asked me 17 questions, a sure sign of keen involvement. Well do you know what got the greatest consensus and applause? It was when I said that although I might take part in all the anti-fascist demonstrations I knew that attitudes needed to be updated. I know and understand how difficult unity can be. But I also know that unity is not unanimity – if so it has become a caricature or even a con.[5]

What remains of the Resistance – and this is a sign of a healthy democracy – is argument. Every time somebody wants to rename a public space after a fascist leader an argument breaks out over the historical record. Then there are the constant attacks of revisionists, who argue that all deaths – of fascists and anti-fascists alike – should be commemorated equally. Also in a broader context, the old and generally discredited accusations concerning partisan violence periodically resurface. One of the perennial responses was once given by the philosopher Norberto Bobbio: 'Instead of the partisans, what would have happened if those who fought with the Germans, even in good faith, had won?'[6]

Despite the difficulties the Resistance faces in preserving an accurate memory of itself, it is hard to see in the immediate future how a positive celebration of the Resistance could disappear from Italian society. After all, it was the greatest politicisation of Italian society there has ever been. From women to peasants, from industrial workers to students – hundreds of thousands put their lives on the line in the hope of creating a better world. Given the scale of commitment, the echo has remained for decades ever since.

Apart from public celebrations and discussion, the Resistance has been handed down from generation to generation, and nearly three generations later the whole period continues to inspire young people. For example in the mid 1990s a student born in 1978 criticised those who had not opposed fascism in a school essay: 'There were those who stayed at home and just worried about their own patch. These were the same people who, willingly, allowed a regime to develop. They just looked on quietly.' His father, a trade union official far too young to have taken part in the Resistance himself, got his son involved in a small television documentary on the Resistance in 1995. The son's job was to read out the last letters of partisans condemned to death, one of which read: 'Dear mum, this is my last letter, I will be executed very shortly. I fought for the liberation of my country and to create the right for Communists to be respected and recognised by all Italians. I will die calmly because I don't fear death.'

The boy's name was Carlo Giuliani; he was shot dead by a policeman in 2001 during riots in Genoa against a G8 summit. The following summer his mother Haidi went to speak at a meeting up in the mountains of northern Italy. At one stage an old man in his eighties came shuffling towards her. He had been a partisan leader: 'last July in Genoa your son Carlo was performing an act of Resistance. He was a partisan.' The links in the chain continue; to the crowd of over a thousand who commemorated Giuliani's death in July 2008, the broadcasting of him reading out partisan letters back in 1995 seemed a most appropriate thing to do.

Ordinary people's continued interest is shown by internet access to ANPI's website. In its first year of operation, 2000–01, weekly average hits varied between 10,000 and 20,000, rising to 30,000 to 45,000 the following year, and an average of 75,000 per week in the first quarter of 2003. In its first two and a half years of operation, the website totalled 6,643,000 hits.[7] ANPI held its first national festival in June 2008. This is surprising, given that it was founded way back in 1944. One of the reasons for it was the move to the right by Italy's equivalent of the UK Labour Party, the PD, and the end in 2007 of its popular *Feste dell'Unità* – despite or perhaps because of the fact that the final national *Festa* saw two million visitors and made a profit of €7 million.[8] Another reason for the success of the ANPI festival – attended by about 30,000 people over three days – was that ANPI opened up its membership to non-partisans in 2005. Therefore the vast majority of people attending were the children and grandchildren of ex-Resistance fighters.

The festival was not just a series of history lessons. Rita Borsellino, sister of a magistrate killed by the Mafia, called for a new form of resistance against the Mafia. Men and women well into their eighties also spoke passionately about what was happening today. Eighty-eight-year-old Luigi Fiori was worried about the recent election of the 'post-fascist' Gianni Alemanno as mayor of Rome: 'These people have learnt from the past and don't come across as fascists. That's what makes them even more dangerous.'

Wars against a powerful occupying force are not straightforward affairs. The overwhelming political and economic strength of the invader is such that local collaborators can be installed, financed and armed, dividing the population and thus creating the grounds for a civil war. People fight back against both forces – the invaders and the collaborators – at different times and in different ways.

Most wars against oppressive regimes or dictatorships take a long time to develop. Often there is a low-level permanent resistance, unable to operate openly – but it is there, despite everything the regime and its backers might say and do. There are different strands within each movement. People are not just fighting *against* a foreign invader or ideology, they are fighting *for* something, and while classical fascism is today largely discredited, what risks being forgotten are the positive aspects and demands of the Resistance.

The fact that in Italy today officialdom tends to either ignore or ossify any celebration of the Resistance should not be surprising. There is no space in neo-liberal capitalism for something as open-ended and self-creating as what the partisans did in 1943–45. Such sense of participation is not the kind of thing that the people who run today's democracies want to see. In its 15-year history, and through three election victories, Berlusconi's *Forza Italia* party has never really had a party congress or any real internal debate.

Spontaneous struggles moulded by underground political organisations do not readily combine with spin doctors and focus groups. The Resistance, with its intense participation in democracy, sits very awkwardly with the worrying possibility that the real meaning of democracy – 'rule by the people'

– will become hollowed out, leaving just neo-liberal consumption. Just as worrying is a tendency in left-wing circles to concentrate on remembering the victims of the Resistance and Nazi atrocities, rather than celebrating the Resistance as a struggle from below. Yet for the Resistance to continue to have a positive and contemporary hue it needs to be seen as a subversive and inspiring example that even the most powerful enemy can be defeated. The aspect of the Resistance legacy that is most important today is that workers and activists have a model to look back to, one of self-activity, generosity, improvisation and comradeship – a model which enabled big changes, but which could have made even bigger changes.

The historical record shows that the Italian Resistance was an inspiring story, in which a largely inexperienced movement took on vastly superior military and economic forces, often making their ability to rule over large swathes of the country impossible. The intensity of what was only a two-year period is in itself fascinating. As Laura Seghettini, who lived through a particularly indelible personal tragedy, once said: 'Back then living a month was a life.' It is the intensity and commitment of those lives – many cut tragically short – that put today's cynicism towards political change to shame. What the Resistance has left us with is the knowledge that everybody, in some way, can help to resist an oppressive government. And if a movement that develops holds out the hope of radical political change, even the most brutal and unpopular governments can fall.

Notes

ACS: Central State Archives, Rome
APC: Archivio del Partito Comunista Italiano, held at the Istituto Gramsci, Rome
ISRMO: Istituto milanese per la Storia della Resistenza del Movimento Operaio
ISRP: Istituto Storico della Resistenza di Parma

Introduction

1. A. Hitler, *Mein Kampf*, Boston: Houghton Mifflin, 1971, p. 681.
2. *The Times*, 23 May 1944.
3. J. Slaughter, *Women and the Italian Resistance*, Denver, Colorado: Arden, 1997, p. 51.
4. G. Kolko, *The Politics of War*, New York: Pantheon, 1990, p. 48.
5. P. Ginsborg, *A History of Contemporary Italy*, Harmondsworth: Penguin, 1990, p. 70.
6. A. Kesselring, *A Soldier's Record*, New York: William Morrow and Co., 1954, pp. 270–1.
7. S. Galli, 'Identikit resistenti. Anagrafe dei partigiani in Emilia-Romagna', *Zapruder*, No. 13 (magg-ago 2007), p. 106.
8. A. Gracci, *Brigata Sinigaglia*, Naples: La città del sole, 2006 [1945], p. 169.
9. M. Franzinelli, 'Chiesa e clero cattolico', in E. Collotti, R. Sandri and F. Sessi (eds), *Dizionario della Resistenza, Vol. 1: Storia e geografia della Liberazione*, Turin: Einaudi, 2000, p. 313.
10. P. Secchia and F. Frassati, *Storia della Resistenza*, Rome: Editori Riuniti, 1965, p. 732.
11. Ibid., pp. 817–8.
12. Kesselring, *A Soldier's Record*, p. 271.
13. Ibid., p. 272.
14. Ibid., p. 277.
15. Secchia and Frassati, *Storia della Resistenza*, p. 883.
16. G. Bocca, *Storia dell'Italia partigiana*, Rome-Bari: Laterza, 1977, p. 387.
17. A. Bravo, 'Resistenza civile', in Collotti, Sandri and Sessi, *Dizionario della Resistenza, Vol. 1*, pp. 272–3.
18. T. Carlyle, *The French Revolution, A History. Vol. 3: The Guillotine*, London: Routledge, n.d., pp. 82–3.
19. Interview with Mario Vezzoni, 24 June 1988.
20. M. Dondi, *La Resistenza italiana*, Milan: Fenice, 2000, 1995, p. 14.

1 Midnight in the Century

1. R. De Felice, *Mussolini il fascista: La conquista del potere*, Turin: Einaudi, 1966, pp. 766–7.
2. D. Guérin, *Fascismo e gran capitale*, Rome: Erre Emme, 1994 [1945], p. 176.
3. T. Behan, *The Resistible Rise of Benito Mussolini*, London: Bookmarks, 2003, p. 25.
4. Ibid., p. 31.
5. Ibid., p. 50; and A. Lyttelton, *The Seizure of Power. Fascism in Italy 1919–1929*, London: Weidenfeld and Nicolson, 1987, p. 70.
6. A. De Grand, *Italian Fascism. Its Origins and Development*, Lincoln: University of Nebraska Press, 1989, p. 35.
7. Lyttelton, *Seizure of Power*, p. 96.
8. Behan, *Resistible Rise of Benito Mussolini*, p. 70.
9. P. Secchia, *La Resistenza accusa 1945–1973*, Milan: Mazzotta, 1973, p. 158. In turn citing *Il Messaggero*, 14 April 1923.

10. R. Zangrandi, *Il lungo viaggio attraverso il fascismo*, Milan: Mursia, 1998 [1947], p. 326.
11. Lyttelton, *Seizure of Power*, p. 243.
12. *Liberazione*, 10 April 2005, reviewing Arrigo Petacco, *L'uomo della Provvidenza*.
13. De Grand, *Italian Fascism*, p. 66.
14. Interview with Mario Vezzoni, 24 June 1988.
15. G. De Antonellis, *Napoli sotto il regime*, Milan: Cooperativa Editrice Donati, 1972, p. 231.
16. A. De Bernardi, *Operai e Nazione. Sindacati, operai e stato nell'Italia fascista*, Milan: Franco Angeli, 1993, pp. 108–9.
17. Ibid., p. 112.
18. Gianni Alasia, speech at the 14th National Congress of ANPI, 25 February 2006.
19. Zangrandi, *Il lungo viaggio attraverso il fascismo*, p. 331 and 342; the latter citing an interview in *Giornale d'Italia*, 9 July 1924.
20. See F. Locatelli, 'Ordine coloniale e disordine sociale', *Zapruder*, No. 8 (sett–dic. 2005).
21. *Il Manifesto*, 21 September 2004, reviewing Angelo Del Boca, *La disfatta di Gasr Bu Hàdi*.
22. Historian Angelo Del Boca, writing in *Il Manifesto*, 1 November 2002.
23. *Il Sole-24 Ore*, 16 March 2008, reviewing Eric Salerno, *Uccideteli tutti*.
24. D. Mack Smith, *Mussolini's Roman Empire*, London: Longman, 1976, p. 79.
25. Ibid., p. 75.
26. N. Poidimani, '"Facetta nera": i crimini sessuali del colonialismo fascista nel Corno d'Africa', in L. Borgomaneri (ed.), *Crimini di guerra. Il mito del bravo italiano tra repressione del ribellismo e guerra ai civili nei territori occupati*, Milan: Edizioni Angelo Guerini, 2006, p. 49.
27. Ibid., p. 57.
28. *Il Manifesto*, 1 October 2008.
29. *Il Manifesto*, 3 April 2007, reviewing Jon Irazabal, *Durango, 31 marzo 1937*.
30. Interview with Giovanni Pesce, 6 April 2002.
31. P. Spriano, *Storia del Partito comunista italiano. III: I fronti popolari, Stalin, la guerra*, Turin: Einaudi, 1970, p. 85.
32. G. Pesce, *Un garibaldino in Spagna*, Rome: Editori Riuniti, 1955, pp. 32–4 and 57–9.
33. See Behan, *Resistible Rise of Benito Mussolini*, pp. 78–97 and 114–15.
34. Interview with Pesce.
35. Mack Smith, *Mussolini's Roman Empire*, p. 101.
36. Pesce, *Un garibaldino in Spagna*, p. 115.
37. Spriano, *Storia del Partito comunista italiano*, pp. 93–4.
38. C. Pillon, *I comunisti nella storia d'Italia*, Rome: Il calendario del popolo, n.d., p. 599.
39. Interview with Pesce.
40. E. Francescangeli, *L'incudine e il Martello. Aspetti pubblici e privati del trockismo italiano tra antifascismo e antistalinismo (1929–1939)*, Perugia: Morlacchi Editore, 2005, p. 241.
41. B. Gombac, 'La patria cercata', *Zapruder*, No. 15 (genn–aprile 2008), p. 34.
42. P. Secchia and F. Frassati, *Storia della Resistenza*, Rome: Editori Riuniti, 1965, p. 551.
43. E. Gobetti, *L'occupazione allegra. Gli italiani in Jugoslavia (1941–43)*, Rome: Carocci, 2007, p. 177.
44. *Il Manifesto*, 23 April 2000.
45. H. Burgwyn, 'General Roatta's war against the partisans in Yugoslavia: 1942', *Journal of Modern Italian Studies*, Vol. 9, No. 3 (2004), p. 321.
46. Gobetti, *L'occupazione allegra*, p. 236.
47. L. Santarelli, 'Muted violence: Italian war crimes in occupied Greece', *Journal of Modern Italian Studies*, Vol. 9, No. 3 (2004), p. 285.
48. Ibid., p. 289.
49. Gobetti, *L'occupazione allegra*, p. 179.
50. De Antonellis, *Napoli sotto il regime*, p. 211.

51. A. Ballerini and A. Benna, *Il muro invisibile. Immigrazione e Legge Bossi-Fini*, Genoa: Fratelli Frilli, 2002, pp. 164–5.
52. P. Gallo, *For Love and Country. The Italian Resistance*, Lanham: University Press of America, 2003, p. 18; and S. Zuccotti, *The Italians and the Holocaust*, London: Peter Halban, 1987, p. 36.
53. C. Baldoli, *Exporting Fascism*, Oxford: Berg, 2003, p. 138.
54. *Il Manifesto*, 1 December 2006.
55. G. Bezzecchi and M. Pagani, 'Porrajmos. Storia di uno sterminio dimenticato', operano-madimilano.org/viaggio/viaggioterza/porrajmos.htm
56. De Bernardi, *Operai e Nazione*, p. 215.
57. Secchia and Frassati, *Storia della Resistenza*, p. 34.
58. P. Coppo, *Conversazioni sulla guerra partigiana*, Omegna: Fogli sensibili, 1995, p. 43.
59. E. Artom, *Diari gennaio 1940–febbraio 1944*, Milan: Centro di Documentazione Ebraica Contemporanea, 1966, p. 49.

2   The Mafia and Street Kids: How Fascism Fell in the South

1. N. Gallerano, 'La disgregazione delle basi di massa del fascismo nel Mezzogiorno e il ruolo delle masse contadine', in AA.VV, *Operai e contadini nella crisi italiana del 1943/1944*, Milan: Feltrinelli, 1974, p. 453.
2. Report dated 17 December 1942; cited in ibid., p. 457.
3. M. Pantaleone, *The Mafia and Politics*, London: Chatto and Windus, 1966, pp. 60–1.
4. L. Cortesi, *Nascita di una democrazia. Guerra, Fascismo, Resistenza e oltre*, Rome: Manifesto libri, 2004, p. 68; and G. Rochat, 'La campagna d'Italia 1943–45', in E. Collotti, R. Sandri and F. Sessi (eds), *Dizionario della Resistenza*, Vol. 1: *Storia e geografia della Liberazione*, Turin: Einaudi, 2000, p. 194.
5. G. Di Capua, *Il biennio cruciale. L'Italia di Charles Poletti*, Soveria Mannelli: Rubbettino, 2005, p. 79.
6. J. Follain, *A Dishonoured Society*, London: Little, Brown and Co., 1995, p. 220.
7. Ibid., p. 225.
8. U. Santino, *Storia del movimento antimafia*, Rome: Editori Riuniti, 2000, p. 135.
9. P. Ginsborg, *A History of Contemporary Italy*, Harmondsworth: Penguin, 1990, p. 462, note.
10. Ibid., p. 60.
11. M. Occhipinti, *Una donna di Ragusa*, Palermo: Sellerio, 1993, pp. 86–97.
12. R. Battaglia, *Storia della Resistenza italiana*, Turin: Einaudi, 1964, p. 60; and L. Ganapini, 'Crisi del regime fascista', in Collotti, Sandri and Sessi, *Dizionario della Resistenza, Vol. 1*, pp. 23–4.
13. Battaglia, *Storia della Resistenza italiana*, p. 60.
14. P. Secchia and F. Frassati, *Storia della Resistenza*, Rome: Editori Riuniti, 1965, p. 79.
15. A. Clocchiatti, *Cammina frut*, Milan: Vangelista, 1972, p. 201.
16. Secchia and Frassati, *Storia della Resistenza*, p. 12.
17. Ibid., p. 14.
18. M. Dondi, *La Resistenza italiana*, Milan: Fenice, 2000, 1995, p. 20.
19. E. Artom, *Diari gennaio 1940–febbraio 1944*, Milan: Centro di Documentazione Ebraica Contemporanea, 1966, pp. 55 and 57.
20. Secchia and Frassati, *Storia della Resistenza*, p. 6.
21. Ibid., p. 15.
22. A. Agosti and G. Sapelli, *Dalla clandestinità alla lotta armata. Diario di Luigi Capriolo, dirigente comunista (26 luglio–16 ottobre 1943)*, Turin: Musolini, 1976, p. 2.
23. Secchia and Frassati, *Storia della Resistenza*, p. 40.
24. Agosti, and Sapelli, *Dalla clandestinità alla lotta armata*, p. 3.
25. F. Amati, 'Il Movimento di unità proletaria (1943–1945)', in G. Monina (ed.), *Il Movimento di unità proletaria (1943–1945)*, Rome: Carocci, 2005, p. 45.

26. G. Rochat, 'L'armistizio dell'8 settembre 1943', in Collotti, Sandri and Sessi, *Dizionario della Resistenza*, Vol. 1, p. 33.
27. Ibid., p. 34.
28. Secchia and Frassati, *Storia della Resistenza*, p. 32.
29. Rochat, 'L'armistizio dell'8 settembre 1943', p. 35.
30. Dondi, *La Resistenza italiana*, p. 22.
31. E. Collotti, 'L'occupazione tedesca in Italia', in Collotti, Sandri and Sessi, *Dizionario della Resistenza*, Vol. 1, p. 43.
32. Secchia and Frassati, *Storia della Resistenza*, p. 106.
33. Rochat, 'L'armistizio dell'8 settembre 1943', p. 36.
34. Artom, *Diari gennaio 1940–febbraio 1944*, p. 75.
35. N. Lewis, *Naples '44*, London: Eland, 2002 [1978], p. 15.
36. Secchia and Frassati, *Storia della Resistenza*, pp. 178–80.
37. L. Borgomaneri, 'La resistenza armata in Milano', in AA.VV, *Conoscere la Resistenza*, Milan: Edizioni Unicopli, 1994, p. 22.
38. L. Leris, *Dal carcere fascista alla lotta armata*, Parma, 1964, p. 25.
39. G. Ricci, *Storia della Brigata Garibaldina 'Ugo Muccini'*, La Spezia: Istituto Storico della Resistenza, 1978, p. 26.
40. G. Vaccarino, C. Gobetti and R. Gobbi, *L'insurrezione di Torino. Saggio introduttivo, testimonianze, documenti*, Parma: Guanda Editore, 1968, p. 38.
41. Amati, 'Il Movimento di unità proletaria (1943–1945)', p. 105.
42. Secchia and Frassati, *Storia della Resistenza*, pp. 108–9.
43. Ibid., p. 113.
44. Interview with Luigi Fiori, 10 August 2007.
45. Secchia and Frassati, *Storia della Resistenza*, pp. 212–14.
46. Battaglia, *Storia della Resistenza italiana*, p. 105.
47. Gallerano, 'La disgregazione delle basi di massa del fascismo nel Mezzogiorno e il ruolo delle masse contadine', p. 455.
48. G. Gribaudi, *Guerra totale. Tra bombe alleate e violenze naziste. Napoli e il fronte meridionale 1940–44*, Turin: Bollati Boringhieri, 2005, p. 49.
49. G. De Antonellis, *Napoli sotto il regime*, Milan: Cooperativa Editrice Donati, 1972, p. 223.
50. Ibid., p. 234.
51. I. de Feo, *Diario Politico 1943–1948*, Milan: Rusconi Editore, 1973, p. 18.
52. De Antonellis, *Napoli sotto il regime*, p. 237.
53. Gribaudi, *Guerra totale*, pp. 415–17.
54. Ibid., pp. 160–2; and Secchia and Frassati, *Storia della Resistenza*, p. 188.
55. de Feo, *Diario Politico*, p. 30.
56. De Antonellis, *Napoli sotto il regime*, p. 214.
57. Ibid., p. 229.
58. C. Barbagallo, *Napoli contro il terrore nazista 28 settembre–1 ottobre 1943*, Naples: Città del sole, 2004 [1944], p. 10.
59. Ibid., p. 11.
60. Gribaudi, *Guerra totale*, p. 230.
61. de Feo, *Diario Politico*, p. 39.
62. Barbagallo, *Napoli contro il terrore nazista*, p. xvii.
63. Ibid., p. 43.
64. Ibid., p. 41.
65. G. Chianese, 'Napoli', in Collotti, Sandri and Sessi, *Dizionario della Resistenza*, Vol. 1, p. 383; and Gribaudi, *Guerra totale*, p. 194.
66. Barbagallo, *Napoli contro il terrore nazista*, p. 51.
67. G. Bocca, *Storia dell'Italia partigiana*, Rome-Bari: Laterza, 1977, p. 61.
68. Gribaudi, *Guerra totale*, p. 194.
69. De Antonellis, *Napoli sotto il regime*, pp. 251–2.
70. Barbagallo, *Napoli contro il terrore nazista*, p. 54.

71. Gribaudi, *Guerra totale*, p. 195.
72. Barbagallo, *Napoli contro il terrore nazista*, p. 61.
73. Ibid., p. 72.
74. Ibid., p. 68.
75. Gribaudi, *Guerra totale*, p. 198.
76. Bocca, *Storia dell'Italia partigiana*, p. 65.
77. Gribaudi, *Guerra totale*, p. 233.
78. De Antonellis, *Napoli sotto il regime*, p. 261.
79. L. Longo, *Un popolo alla macchia*, Milan: Mondadori, 1947, p. 102.
80. De Antonellis, *Napoli sotto il regime*, p. 275.

3   People, Parties and Partisans

1. V. Castronovo, *Giovanni Agnelli*, Turin: UTET, 1971, p. 617.
2. R. Gobbi, *Il mito della Resistenza*, Milan: Rizzoli, 1992, p. 33.
3. R. Battaglia, *Storia della Resistenza italiana*, Turin: Einaudi, 1964, p. 49.
4. Ibid., p. 47.
5. Ibid.
6. C. Dellavalle, *Operai, industriali e partito comunista nel Biellese 1940/1945*, Milan: Feltrinelli, 1978, p. 42.
7. Ibid., pp. 46–9.
8. P. Spriano, *Storia del Partito comunista italiano. IV: La fine del fascismo. Dalla riscossa operaia alla lotta armata*, Turin: Einaudi, 1973, p. 178.
9. Battaglia, *Storia della Resistenza italiana*, p. 49.
10. G. Bottai, *Diario 1935–1944*, Milan: Rizzoli, 1989, p. 369.
11. A. De Bernardi, *Operai e Nazione. Sindacati, operai e stato nell'Italia fascista*, Milan: Franco Angeli, 1993, p. 224.
12. N. Bobbio, *Ideological Profile of Twentieth-Century Italy*, Princeton: Princeton University Press, 1995, p. 128.
13. Spriano, *Storia del Partito comunista italiano*, p. 190.
14. Ibid., pp. 193–4.
15. Castronovo, *Giovanni Agnelli*, p. 609.
16. Spriano, *Storia del Partito comunista italiano*, p. 142.
17. Ibid., p. 181.
18. Battaglia, *Storia della Resistenza italiana*, p. 50.
19. G. Amendola, *Lettere a Milano*, Rome: Editori Riuniti, 1973, p. 74.
20. See T. Behan, 'Gillo Pontecorvo: Partisan Film-maker', *Film International*, Vol. 6, No. 1 (2008). Pontecorvo would later go on to become a film director, and made one of the best-known films about a national liberation struggle, *The Battle of Algiers*.
21. F. Amati, 'Il Movimento di unità proletaria (1943–1945)', in G. Monina (ed.), *Il Movimento di unità proletaria (1943–1945)*, Rome: Carocci, 2005, p. 16.
22. Ibid., p. 79.
23. Spriano, *Storia del Partito comunista italiano*, p. 234, note.
24. Amati, 'Il Movimento di unità proletaria (1943–1945)', p. 106.
25. A. Boldrini, *Enciclopedia della Resistenza*, Milan: Teti, 1980, p. 291.
26. G. Kolko, *The Politics of War*, New York: Pantheon, 1990, p. 59.
27. Bobbio, *Ideological Profile of Twentieth-Century Italy*, p. 147.
28. G. De Luna, *Storia del Partito d'Azione*, Rome: Editori Riuniti, 1997 [1982], p. 39.
29. Boldrini, *Enciclopedia della Resistenza*, p. 43.
30. Guido Calogero, one of the main supporters of 'liberal socialism', cited in Bobbio, *Ideological Profile of Twentieth-Century Italy*, p. 152.
31. E. Artom, *Diari gennaio 1940–febbraio 1944*, Milan: Centro di Documentazione Ebraica Contemporanea, 1966, p. 172.
32. Ibid., p. 93.
33. Boldrini, *Enciclopedia della Resistenza*, p. 211.

34. Spriano, *Storia del Partito comunista italiano*, p. 335.
35. Ibid., p. 340.
36. Ibid., p. 342.
37. L. Borgomaneri, *Due inverni un'estate e la rossa primavera. Le Brigate Garibaldi a Milano e provincia 1943–45*, Milan: Franco Angeli, 1995, p. 380.
38. J.B. Urban, *Moscow and the Italian Communist Party. From Togliatti to Berlinguer*, London: I.B. Tauris, 1986, p. 175.
39. Amendola, *Lettere a Milano*, pp. 214–5.
40. Urban, *Moscow and the Italian Communist Party*, p. 173.
41. *L'Unità*, 15 March 1943.
42. Battaglia, *Storia della Resistenza italiana*, pp. 53–4; and Urban, *Moscow and the Italian Communist Party*, p. 163.
43. Urban, *Moscow and the Italian Communist Party*, p. 163.
44. T. Abse, 'Palmiro Togliatti: Loyal Servant of Stalin', *Revolutionary History*, Vol. 9, No. 2 (2006), pp. 86–7.
45. Amendola, *Lettere a Milano*, p. 300.
46. L. Cortesi, *Nascita di una democrazia. Guerra, Fascismo, Resistenza e oltre*, Rome: Manifesto libri, 2004, p. 303.
47. Ibid., p. 299.
48. P. Secchia and F. Frassati, *Storia della Resistenza*, Rome: Editori Riuniti, 1965, pp. 116–17.
49. Ibid., pp. 200–1.
50. F. Catalano, *Storia del CLNAI*, Bari: Laterza, 1956, p. 118.
51. E. Bonatti, *Il Revisionismo allo specchio della storia*, Rovigo: Istituto Polesano per la storia della Resistenza e dell'età contemporanea, 2006, pp. 68–9.
52. R. Battaglia, *Un uomo, un partigiano*, Bologna: Il Mulino, 2004 [1945], p. 19.
53. Ibid., p. 26.
54. Artom, *Diari*, p. 85.
55. M. Dondi, *La Resistenza italiana*, Milan: Fenice, 2000, 1995, p. 52.
56. Ibid., p. 29.
57. P. Coppo, *Conversazioni sulla guerra partigiana*, Omegna: Fogli sensibili, 1995, p. 17.
58. Ibid., p. 16.
59. See Artom, *Diari*, p. 88.
60. F. Colombara, 'Memorie di una guerra infinita', *Ieri Novara Oggi*, No. 4–5 (April 1996), p. 44.
61. Coppo, *Conversazioni sulla guerra partigiana*, p. 66.
62. D. Gorreri, *Parma '43. Un popolo in armi per conquistarsi la libertà*, Parma, 1975, p. 218.
63. D. Fo, *Compagni senza censura*, Vol. 2, Milan: Mazzotta, 1977, p. 298.
64. Artom, *Diari*, p. 76.
65. C. Pavone, *Una guerra civile. Saggio storico sulla moralità nella Resistenza*, Turin: Bollati Boringhieri, 1991, p. 180.
66. C. Pavone, 'Il movimento di liberazione e le tre guerre', in AA.VV, *Conoscere la Resistenza*, Milan: Edizioni Unicopli, 1994, p. 14.
67. Pavone, *Una guerra civile*, p. 256.
68. Ibid., p. 249.
69. *La Nostra Lotta*, No. 1 (October 1943), p. 19.
70. Pavone, 'Il movimento di liberazione e le tre guerre', p. 15.
71. *L'Unità*, 9 April 1945.
72. *La Repubblica*, 25 April 2008, reviewing Giuseppe Mayda, *Mauthausen*.
73. See *La Nostra Lotta*, No. 6 (December 1943), pp. 11–3.
74. Spriano, *Storia del Partito comunista italiano*, p. 142.
75. Pavone, *Una guerra civile*, p. 352 and p. 345.
76. Pavone, 'Il movimento di liberazione e le tre guerre', p. 15.

4   Resistance in the Mountains

1. P. Secchia and F. Frassati, *Storia della Resistenza*, Rome: Editori Riuniti, 1965, pp. 202–3.

2. Ibid., p. 204. Four or five of these squads then came together in a brigade, but what in turn constituted a brigade often varied between 100 and 200–250 partisans, or sometimes up to 300. A division was then made up of two or three brigades, so a total of 600–1,000 men. But all these figures are only approximate, there was a lot of variation. See also A. Boldrini, *Enciclopedia della Resistenza*, Milan: Teti, 1980, pp. 46, 58–9, 158–9.

3. C.S. Capogreco, *Il piombo e l'argento. La vera storia del partigiano Facio*, Rome: Donzelli, 2007, p. 206.

4. F. Colombara, *La terra delle tre lune. Classi popolari nella prima metà del Novecento in un paese dell'alto Piemonte: Prato Sesia*, Milan: Vangelista, 1989, p. 253.

5. Interview with Luigi Fiori, 10 August 2007.

6. M. Avagliano (ed.), *Generazione ribelle. Diari e lettere dal 1943 al 1945*, Turin: Einaudi, 2006, p. 109.

7. L. Seghettini, *Al vento del Nord. Una donna nella lotta di Liberazione*, Rome: Carocci, 2006, p. 88.

8. G. Fellicani, *Il Battaglione Partigiano 'Dino Gotti'. La Resistenza nella bassa bolognese di Aroldo Tolomelli*, Bologna: Futura Press, 2002, p. 12.

9. M. Casalini, and F. Verdelli, 'Gip e Falce. Ricordi resistenti', in *Pippo Coppo: partigiano e sindaco della Liberazione*, Omegna: Comune di Omegna, 2005, p. 32.

10. M. Nardi, *Otto mesi di guerriglia*, La squilla, 1976, p. 42.

11. P. Coppo, *Conversazioni sulla guerra partigiana*, Omegna: Fogli sensibili, 1995, p. 39.

12. Seghettini, *Al vento del Nord*, p. 24.

13. E. Artom, *Diari gennaio 1940–febbraio 1944*, Milan: Centro di Documentazione Ebraica Contemporanea, 1966, pp. 104–5. Further examples of punishment are given in C. Bermani, *Pagine di guerriglia. L'esperienza dei garibaldini della Valsesia*, Vol. 2, Vercelli: Istituto per la storia della Resistenza e della società contemporanea nelle province di Biella e Vercelli, 1995, pp. 153–4.

14. R. Battaglia, *Un uomo, un partigiano*, Bologna: Il Mulino, 2004 [1945], p. 101.

15. Interview with Fiori.

16. C. Pavone (ed.), *Le Brigate Garibaldi nella Resistenza*, Vol. 3, Milan: Feltrinelli, 1979, p. 331.

17. G. Ricci, *Storia della Brigata Garibaldina 'Ugo Muccini'*, La Spezia: Istituto Storico della Resistenza, 1978, p. 296. For further details see L. Galletto, *La lunga estate*, Carrara: Acrobat Media Edizioni, 2006, pp. 327–39.

18. Ricci, *Storia della Brigata Garibaldina 'Ugo Muccini'*, pp. 297–8.

19. Artom, *Diari*, p. 119.

20. Battaglia, *Un uomo, un partigiano*, p. 122.

21. Ibid., p. 123.

22. *La Stella Alpina*, 1 November 1944; cited in F. Colombara, 'Vesti la giubba di battaglia', *l'impegno*, a. xxvi, No. 2 (December 2006), p. 39–40.

23. C. Pillon, *I comunisti nella storia d'Italia*, Rome: Il calendario del popolo, n.d., pp. 816–7.

24. *La Nostra Lotta*, November 1943, p. 20.

25. Interview with Fiori.

26. A. Gracci, *Brigata Sinigaglia*, Naples: La città del sole, 2006 [1945], p. 90.

27. M. Dondi, *La Resistenza italiana*, Milan: Fenice, 2000, 1995, p. 72.

28. Ibid.

29. G. Carocci and G. Grassi (eds), *Le Brigate Garibaldi nella Resistenza*, Vol. 1, Milan: Feltrinelli, 1979, p. 311.

30. Boldrini, *Enciclopedia della Resistenza*, p. 104.

31. DVD, *La collina rossa, Voci della Resistenza*, Merizzo: Archivi della Resistenza Circolo Edoardo Bassignani, 2006.

32. A. Aniasi, 'Un uomo autorevole', in *Pippo Coppo: partigiano e sindaco della Liberazione*, Omegna: Comune di Omegna, 2005, p. 25.
33. Dondi, *La Resistenza italiana*, pp. 72–3.
34. Gracci, *Brigata Sinigaglia*, p. 210.
35. Carocci and Grassi, *Le Brigate Garibaldi nella Resistenza*, p. 171.
36. Seghettini, *Al vento del Nord*, p. 26.
37. Avagliano, *Generazione ribelle*, p. 105.
38. Ibid., p. 106.
39. Ricci, *Storia della Brigata Garibaldina 'Ugo Muccini'*, pp. 133–4.
40. Coppo, *Conversazioni sulla guerra partigiana*, pp. 87, 88, 89.
41. Colombara, 'Vesti la giubba di battaglia', p. 37. Originally in P. Secchia, *Il Pci e la guerra di Liberazione. Ricordi, documenti inediti e testimonianze*, Milan: Feltrinelli, 1973, pp. 882–3.
42. Colombara, 'Vesti la giubba di battaglia', p. 37.
43. Ibid., p. 34.
44. See F. Colombara, 'Il fascino del leggendario. Moscatelli e Beltrami: miti resistenti', *l'impegno*, a. XXVI, No. 1 (June 2006).
45. Colombara, *La terra delle tre lune*, p. 287, note.
46. E. Collotti, R. Sandri and F. Sessi (eds), *Dizionario della Resistenza*, Vol. 2: *Luoghi, formazioni, protagonisti*, Turin: Einaudi, 2001, p. 177.
47. Battaglia, *Un uomo, un partigiano*, p. 108.
48. *La Nostra Lotta*, 5 August 1944, p. 12.

5   Resistance in the Cities

1. P. Secchia and F. Frassati, *Storia della Resistenza*, Rome: Editori Riuniti, 1965, p. 344.
2. *L'Unità*, 1 August 1942.
3. G. Carocci and G. Grassi (eds), *Le Brigate Garibaldi nella Resistenza*, Vol. 1, Milan: Feltrinelli, 1979, p. 165.
4. P. Spriano, *Storia del Partito comunista italiano. IV: La fine del fascismo. Dalla riscossa operaia alla lotta armata*, Turin: Einaudi, 1973, p. 142.
5. C. Dellavalle, 'Lotte operaie, Torino', in AA.VV, *Operai e contadini nella crisi italiana del 1943/1944*, Milan: Feltrinelli, 1974, pp. 198–9.
6. Ibid., pp. 211–12.
7. J. Slaughter, *Women and the Italian Resistance*, Denver Colorado: Arden, 1997, p. 28.
8. D. Sassoon, *Contemporary Italy*, London: Longmans, 1986, p. 25.
9. Secchia and Frassati, *Storia della Resistenza*, p. 275.
10. V. Castronovo, *Giovanni Agnelli*, Turin: UTET, 1971, p. 611.
11. E. Collotti, R. Sandri and F. Sessi (eds), *Dizionario della Resistenza*, Vol. 2: *Luoghi, formazioni, protagonisti*, Turin: Einaudi, 2001, p. 260.
12. M. Calegari, *Comunisti e partigiani. Genova 1942–1945*, Milan: Selene, 2001, p. 88.
13. R. Battaglia, *Storia della Resistenza italiana*, Turin: Einaudi, 1964, pp. 146–7.
14. Ibid., p. 148.
15. Ibid., p. 150. Emphasis in the original.
16. *La Nostra Lotta*, No. 2 (January 1944), pp. 16–18.
17. Remo Scappini, writing on 14 December; cited in Calegari, *Comunisti e partigiani*, p. 155.
18. *L'Unità*, 10 December 1944. Even Catholic newspapers such as *Voce Operaia* could be moved to write of Valletta thus: 'This individual enslaved to the Germans [who] scornfully sends workers away, threatening them with a Nazi firing squad.' Cited in C. Pavone, *Una guerra civile. Saggio storico sulla moralità nella Resistenza*, Turin: Bollati Boringhieri, 1991, p. 353.
19. Battaglia, *Storia della Resistenza italiana*, pp. 187, 189.
20. Ibid., p. 188.
21. Ibid., pp. 188–9.

22. Ibid., p. 190.
23. Ibid., p. 191.
24. Ibid., p. 192.
25. *La Nostra Lotta*, Nos. 5–6 (March 1944), pp. 25–33.
26. R. Anfossi, *La Resistenza spezzata*, Rome: Prospettiva Edizioni, 1995, p. 37.
27. Battaglia, *Storia della Resistenza italiana*, p. 460.
28. Ibid., p. 461.
29. N. Labanca, 'Firenze', in E. Collotti, R. Sandri and F. Sessi (eds), *Dizionario della Resistenza*, Vol. 1: *Storia e geografia della Liberazione*, Turin: Einaudi, 2000, p. 466.
30. Ibid., p. 467.
31. *La Nazione*, 5 December 1943. Cited in P. Spriano, *Storia del Partito comunista italiano. V: La Resistenza, Togliatti e il partito nuovo*, Turin: Einaudi, 1975, p. 187.
32. Pavone, *Una guerra civile*, p. 288.
33. Battaglia, *Storia della Resistenza italiana*, pp. 332–3.
34. *La Nostra Lotta*, 5 August 1944, pp. 8–9.
35. Secchia and Frassati, *Storia della Resistenza*, p. 683.
36. Ibid., pp. 685–6.
37. Ibid., p. 683.
38. Battaglia, *Storia della Resistenza italiana*, p. 334.
39. See A. Gracci, *Brigata Sinigaglia*, Naples: La città del sole, 2006 [1945], pp. 66–7.
40. *La Nostra Lotta*, 5 August 1944, p. 9.
41. Collotti, Sandri and Sessi, *Dizionario della Resistenza*, Vol. 2, p. 288.
42. G. Occupati, *Campo di marte da sempre*, Florence: Morgana Edizioni, 2006, p. 102. There is a plaque at the end of platform 6 of Florence's main railway station that commemorates this event.
43. Ibid., p. 53.
44. Ibid., p. 94.
45. Secchia and Frassati, *Storia della Resistenza*, p. 690.
46. C. Francovich, *La Resistenza a Firenze*, Florence: La Nuova Italia, 1975 [1961], p. 270.
47. Secchia and Frassati, *Storia della Resistenza*, p. 697.
48. Collotti, Sandri and Sessi, *Dizionario della Resistenza*, Vol. 2, p. 178; and Gracci, *Brigata Sinigaglia*, p. 180.
49. Gracci, *Brigata Sinigaglia*, pp. 177–81; and Secchia and Frassati, *Storia della Resistenza*, p. 700.
50. M. Avagliano (ed.), *Generazione ribelle. Diari e lettere dal 1943 al 1945*, Turin: Einaudi, 2006, p. 128.
51. Secchia and Frassati, *Storia della Resistenza*, p. 702.
52. *L'Azione comunista*, 7 August 1944.
53. P. Secchia, *Aldo dice 26 x 1. Cronistoria del 25 aprile 1945*, Milan: Feltrinelli, 1963, p. 33.
54. Avagliano, *Generazione ribelle*, p. 130.
55. Francovich, *La Resistenza a Firenze*, pp. 279–80.
56. Battaglia, *Storia della Resistenza italiana*, p. 336.
57. Gracci, *Brigata Sinigaglia*, p. 131.
58. Battaglia, *Storia della Resistenza italiana*, p. 338.
59. Secchia and Frassati, *Storia della Resistenza*, p. 704.
60. S. Pertini, *Quei giorni della liberazione di Firenze*, Florence: Lucio Pugliese editore, 2006, p. 26.
61. Gracci, *Brigata Sinigaglia*, p. 137.

6 'Aldo says 26 for one'

1. See the statements quoted in C. Pavone, *Una guerra civile. Saggio storico sulla moralità nella Resistenza*, Turin: Bollati Boringhieri, 1991, pp. 360–2, for example.
2. R. Battaglia, *Storia della Resistenza italiana*, Turin: Einaudi, 1964, p. 438; E. Collotti, R. Sandri and F. Sessi (eds) *Dizionario della Resistenza*, Vol. 2: *Luoghi, formazioni,*

protagonisti, Turin: Einaudi, 2001, pp. 299–300; and Pavone, *Una guerra civile*, p. 322.

3. V. Castronovo, *Giovanni Agnelli*, Turin: UTET, 1971, pp. 638–43.
4. Ibid., p. 645.
5. Ibid., pp. 661–2.
6. Pavone, *Una guerra civile*, p. 324.
7. Castronovo, *Giovanni Agnelli*, pp. 668–9. Much of the money was channelled by a communist doctor named Coggiola, who later became PCI mayor of Turin. See also M. Rendina, 'Il falso ordine di Stevens. La liberazione di Torino', in A. Cassarà (ed.), *La scelta. Dalla Resistenza alla Liberazione*, Rome: Nuova Iniziativa Editoriale/*l'Unità*, 2005, p. 151.
8. *Europeo*, 30 March 1981, p. 48.
9. Castronovo, *Giovanni Agnelli*, pp. 649–50, 665–6.
10. P. Secchia, *Aldo dice 26 x 1. Cronistoria del 25 aprile 1945*, Milan: Feltrinelli, 1963, p. 62; *Patria indipendente*, March 2005, p. 27.
11. M. Avagliano (ed.), *Generazione ribelle. Diari e lettere dal 1943 al 1945*, Turin: Einaudi, 2006, pp. 292–3. Although the code word for the insurrection specified 1 a.m. on 26 April, in most cases events were brought forward.
12. Ibid., p. 296.
13. G. Amendola, *Lettere a Milano*, Rome: Editori Riuniti, 1973, pp. 554–6. See also Secchia, *Aldo dice 26 x 1*, pp. 60–1.
14. Amendola, *Lettere a Milano*, p. 556.
15. G. Vaccarino, C. Gobetti and R. Gobbi, *L'insurrezione di Torino. Saggio introduttivo, testimonianze, documenti*, Parma: Guanda Editore, 1968, p. 209.
16. B. Guidetti Serra (ed.), *Compagne. Testimonianze di partecipazione politica femminile*, Turin: Einaudi, 1977, p. 145.
17. Amendola, *Lettere a Milano*, p. 567.
18. Secchia, *Aldo dice 26 x 1*, p. 96.
19. Vaccarino, Gobetti and Gobbi, *L'insurrezione di Torino*, p. 35.
20. Amendola, *Lettere a Milano*, p. 566.
21. Secchia, *Aldo dice 26 x 1*, pp. 96–8.
22. Ibid., p. 99; and Vaccarino, Gobetti and Gobbi, *L'insurrezione di Torino*, pp. 381–3.
23. Secchia, *Aldo dice 26 x 1*, p. 103.
24. Ibid., p. 105.
25. Vaccarino, Gobetti and Gobbi, *L'insurrezione di Torino*, p. 265.
26. *Europeo*, 30 March 1981, p. 49.
27. G. Bocca, 'Con le segretarie Fiat non si scherza', in Cassarà, *La scelta*; and Castronovo, *Giovanni Agnelli*, p. 670.
28. Amendola, *Lettere a Milano*, p. 577.
29. Secchia, *Aldo dice 26 x 1*, pp. 78–9.
30. L. Borgomaneri, 'Milano', in E. Collotti, R. Sandri and F. Sessi (eds), *Dizionario della Resistenza, Vol. 1: Storia e geografia della Liberazione*, Turin: Einaudi, 2000, p. 542.
31. Secchia, *Aldo dice 26 x 1*, p. 89.
32. T. Behan, *The Long Awaited Moment. The Working Class and the Italian Communist Party in Milan, 1943–1948*, New York: Peter Lang, 1997, p. 135; and Secchia, *Aldo dice 26 x 1*, p. 91.
33. Secchia, *Aldo dice 26 x 1*, p. 91.
34. M.E. Tonizzi, 'A wonderful job'. *Genova aprile 1945: insurrezione e liberazione*, Rome: Carocci, 2006, p. 49.
35. G.B. Lazagna, *Ponte rotto*, Milan: Sapere Edizioni, 1972 [1945], p. 291.
36. Secchia, *Aldo dice 26 x 1*, p. 71.
37. A. Gibelli, 'Liguria, Genova', in Collotti, Sandri and Sessi, *Dizionario della Resistenza, Vol. 1*, pp. 498–9.
38. P. Spriano, *Storia del Partito comunista italiano. V: La Resistenza, Togliatti e il partito nuovo*, Turin: Einaudi, 1975, p. 536.

39. P.E. Taviani, *Breve storia dell'insurrezione di Genova*, Florence: Le Monnier, n.d. [1945], p. 15.
40. Tonizzi, 'A wonderful job', p. 86.
41. Secchia, *Aldo dice 26 x 1*, p. 73.
42. L. Balestreri, *La Brigata Balilla*, Genova: Sezione ANPI 'Monte Sella', 1982 [1947], pp. 161–7.
43. R. Battaglia and G. Garritano, *Breve storia della Resistenza italiana*, Rome: Editori Riuniti, 1964, pp. 224–6; and G. Bocca, *Storia dell'Italia partigiana*, Rome-Bari: Laterza, 1977, pp. 481–3.
44. Secchia, *Aldo dice 26 x 1*, p. 76; and Tonizzi, 'A wonderful job', p. 95.
45. Pavone, *Una guerra civile*, p. 583.
46. Ibid., p. 586.
47. Interview with Luigi Fiori, 10 August 2007.
48. Pavone, *Una guerra civile*, p. 590.

7 Postwar Partisan Activity

1. L. Tessitori, *I ricordi di Giulia. La storia di Rosa Cantoni*, Udine: Università della LiberEtà, 1995, p. 127.
2. C. Bermani, 'Dopo la Guerra di Liberazione (appunti per una storia ancora non scritta)', in AA.VV, *Conoscere la Resistenza*, Milan: Edizioni Unicopli, 1994, p. 108. See also M. Rossi, 'Il conto aperto', *Materiali di storia*, No. 13 (1999).
3. M. Kidron, *Western Capitalism Since the War*, Harmondsworth: Penguin, 1970, p. 25.
4. N. Gallerano, 'La disgregazione delle basi di massa del fascismo nel Mezzogiorno e il ruolo delle masse contadine', in AA.VV, *Operai e contadini nella crisi italiana del 1943/1944*, Milan: Feltrinelli, 1974, p. 469.
5. J.B. Urban, *Moscow and the Italian Communist Party. From Togliatti to Berlinguer*, London: I.B. Tauris, 1986, p. 199.
6. A. Pellegatta, *Cronache rivoluzionarie in provincia di Varese (1945–1948)*, Milan: Quaderni di pagine marxiste, 2004, p. 24.
7. G. Vaccarino, C. Gobetti and R. Gobbi, *L'insurrezione di Torino. Saggio introduttivo, testimonianze, documenti*, Parma: Guanda Editore, 1968, p. 349.
8. L. Borgomaneri, *Due inverni un'estate e la rossa primavera. Le Brigate Garibaldi a Milano e provincia 1943–45*, Milan: Franco Angeli, 1995, p. 391.
9. P. Coppo, *Conversazioni sulla guerra partigiana*, Omegna: Fogli sensibili, 1995, p. 31.
8. A. Peregalli and M. Mingardo, *Togliatti guardasigilli 1945–1946*, Milan: Colibrì, 1998, p. 84.
9. Pellegatta, *Cronache rivoluzionarie in provincia di Varese*, p. 51.
12. F. Wildvang, 'The enemy next door: Italian collaboration in deporting Jews during the German occupation of Rome', *Modern Italy*, Vol. 12, No. 2 (2007), p. 193.
13. G. Ranzato, *Il linciaggio di Carretta*, Milan: Il Saggiatore, 1997, pp. 35–51.
14. *L'Unità*, 4 June 1946.
15. P. Gallo, *For Love and Country. The Italian Resistance*, Lanham: University Press of America, 2003, p. 302, note. Interestingly enough, the number of industrial workers deported was far higher, around 12,000. In Genoa alone, following successful strikes, over 1,600 workes were deported to Germany. See Fondazione Giuseppe Di Vittorio, *Salvare le fabbriche*, Rome: Ediesse, 2005, pp.18–19.
16. *La Stampa*, 24 September 1994.
17. *Il Manifesto*, 25 April 2000.
18. P. Willson, *The Clockwork Factory. Women and Work in Fascist Italy*, Oxford: Clarendon Press, 1993, pp. 226–7.
19. See G. Crainz, 'Il dolore e la collera: quella lontana Italia del 1945', *Meridiana*, Nos. 22–3 (1995).
20. P. Secchia, *Aldo dice 26 x 1. Cronistoria del 25 aprile 1945*, Milan: Feltrinelli, 1963, p. 87.

21. A. Lampredi, 'Così fucilammo Mussolini e la Petacci', *Patria indipendente*, 20 April 2008. Originally published in *l'Unità*, 1972.

22. L. Borgomaneri, 'Milano', in E. Collotti, R. Sandri and F. Sessi (eds), *Dizionario della Resistenza, Vol. 1: Storia e geografia della Liberazione*, Turin: Einaudi, 2000, p. 543; and Lampredi, 'Così fucilammo Mussolini e la Petacci'.

23. C. Pillon, *I comunisti nella storia d'Italia*, Rome: Il calendario del popolo, n.d., p. 906.

24. *Panorama*, 3 December 1979.

25. Borgomaneri, 'Milano', p. 544.

26. Borgomaneri, *Due inverni un'estate e la rossa primavera*, p. 194.

27. E. Collotti, R. Sandri and F. Sessi (eds), *Dizionario della Resistenza, Vol. 2: Luoghi, formazioni, protagonisti*, Turin: Einaudi, 2001, pp. 72–3; C. Pavone, *Una guerra civile. Saggio storico sulla moralità nella Resistenza*, Turin: Bollati Boringhieri, 1991, p. 241; and Father Camillo De Piaz, in *25 aprile. Milano, la liberazione*, RAI Educational documentary by Aldo Zappalà, 2008.

28. Borgomaneri, *Due inverni un'estate e la rossa primavera*, p. 197.

29. P. Spriano, *Storia del Partito comunista italiano. V: La Resistenza, Togliatti e il partito nuovo*, Turin: Einaudi, 1975, p. 488.

30. L. Alessandrini, 'The Option of Violence – Partisan Activity in the Bologna Area 1945–48', in J. Dunnage (ed.), *After the War: Violence, Continuity and Renewal in Italian Society*, Market Harborough: Troubador, 1999, p. 62.

31. Bermani, 'Dopo la Guerra di Liberazione (appunti per una storia ancora non scritta)', p. 94.

32. C. Bermani, *Le storie della Resistenza. Cinquant'anni di dibattito storiografico in Italia*, Verbania: Fogli Sensibili, 1995, p. 50; M. Ponzani, 'La repressione antipartigiana negli anni del centrismo (1948–1953)', in AA.VV, *Senza memoria non c'è futuro. La democrazia italiana nasce dalla Resistenza*, Milan: Edizioni Punto Rosso, 2008, pp. 45–6; and P. Secchia, *La Resistenza accusa 1945–1973*, Milan: Mazzotta, 1973, p. 92.

33. F. Ferraresi, *Threats to Democracy. The Radical Right in Italy after the War*, Princeton: Princeton University Press, 1996, p. 209, note; and P. Ginsborg, *A History of Contemporary Italy*, Harmondsworth: Penguin, 1990, p. 92.

34. Crainz, 'Il dolore e la collera: quella lontana Italia del 1945', p. 263.

35. G. Neppi Modona, 'Postwar Trials against Fascist Collaborationists and Partisans: the Piedmont Experience', in Dunnage, *After the War*, p. 51.

36. M. Franzinelli, *L'amnistia Togliatti*, Milan: Mondadori, 2006, p. 28 and pp. 41–2; N. Tranfaglia, 'Legiferare e guidicare', in G. Santomassino (ed.), *La notte della democrazia italiana. Dal regime fascista al governo Berlusconi*, Milan: Il Saggiatore, 2003, p. 78; and R. Zangrandi, *Il lungo viaggio attraverso il fascismo*, Milan: Mursia, 1998 [1947], p. 362.

37. Neppi Modona, 'Postwar Trials against Fascist Collaborationists and Partisans', p. 53.

38. Ponzani, 'La repressione antipartigiana negli anni del centrismo (1948–1953)', p. 43; Pietro Secchia, writing in *Vie Nuove*, 27 February 1949. Reproduced in Secchia, *La Resistenza accusa 1945–1973*, p. 64.

39. D. Fo, *Compagni senza censura*, Vol. 2, Milan: Mazzotta, 1977, p. 300.

40. M. Ponzani, 'I processi contro i partigiani nel dopoguerra', *Rivista dell'Istituto Storico della Resistenza e della Società Contemporanea in Provincia di Cuneo*, No. 71 (June 2007), p. 253.

41. Ibid., pp. 264–5. One of those convicted was already deceased, having been killed in the Fosse Ardeatine massacre.

42. Speech made on 28 October 1949. Reproduced in Secchia, *La Resistenza accusa 1945–1973*, p. 72.

43. Ferraresi, *Threats to Democracy*, p. 8.

44. C. Bermani, '"Forze dell'ordine" e continuità dello Stato', in AA.VV, *Guerra civile globale*, Rome: Odradek, 2001, p. 126. My emphasis.

45. Ferraresi, *Threats to Democracy*, p. 207, note; and C. Troilo, *La guerra di Troilo, novembre 1947. L'occupazione della Prefettura di Milano, ultima trincea della Resistenza*, Soveria Mannelli: Rubbettino, 2005, p. 223.

46. Bermani, '"Forze dell'ordine" e continuità dello Stato', p. 122; and Franzinelli, *L'amnistia Togliatti*, p. 188.

47. T. Behan, *The Long Awaited Moment. The Working Class and the Italian Communist Party in Milan, 1943–1948*, New York: Peter Lang, 1997, p. 184.

48. Secchia, *La Resistenza accusa 1945–1973*, p. 83.

49. Ibid., p. 73.

50. Ponzani, 'I processi contro i partigiani nel dopoguerra', p. 255; and Ponzani, 'La repressione antipartigiana negli anni del centrismo (1948–1953)', p. 49.

51. Ferraresi, *Threats to Democracy*, p. 20. Following repeated uproar over such cases, a law passed four years later finally gave partisans 'regular' military status.

52. Ponzani, 'La repressione antipartigiana negli anni del centrismo (1948–1953)', pp. 61–3; and Secchia, *La Resistenza accusa 1945–1973*, pp. 299–300.

53. See G. Fiori, *Uomini ex*, Turin: Einaudi, 1993.

54. See P. Cooke, 'From partisan to party cadre: The education of Italian political emigrants in Czechoslovakia', *Italian Studies*, Vol. 61 (Spring 2006).

55. J. Greene and A. Massignani, *The Black Prince and the Sea Devils*, Cambridge MA: Da Capo Press, 2004, p. 181. For further details on Borghese see Chapter 8.

56. Peregalli and Mingardo, *Togliatti guardasigilli 1945–1946*, p. 52.

57. *Vie Nuove*, 27 February 1949. Reproduced in Secchia, *La Resistenza accusa 1945–1973*, p. 63.

58. ACS, PS, 1944–46, b.21. 'Relazione dei Prefetti', Milan, 14 May 1945.

59. Pellegatta, *Cronache rivoluzionarie in provincia di Varese*, p. 107.

60. L. Lajolo, 'I fatti di Santa Barbara', in AA.VV, *Contadini e partigiani. Atti del convegno storico*, Alessandria: Edizioni dell'Orso, 1986, p. 329.

61. T. Tussi, *La memoria la storia*, Naples: Laboratorio Politico, 1996, p. 92.

62. Franzinelli, *L'amnistia Togliatti*, p. 103. Emphasis in the original.

63. Lajolo, 'I fatti di Santa Barbara', p. 329.

64. Tussi, *La memoria la storia*, pp. 92–3.

65. Lajolo, 'I fatti di Santa Barbara', p. 334.

66. Tussi, *La memoria la storia*, pp. 96–7.

67. Pellegatta, *Cronache rivoluzionarie in provincia di Varese*, p. 57.

68. R. Gremmo, *L'ultima Resistenza. Le ribellioni partigiane in Piemonte dopo la nascita della Repubblica (1946–1947)*, Biella: Edizioni ELF, 1995, p. 65.

69. Franzinelli, *L'amnistia Togliatti*, p. 103.

70. Ibid., p. 104.

71. Cited in Lajolo, 'I fatti di Santa Barbara', p. 340.

72. Tussi, *La memoria la storia*, p. 100.

73. M. Dondi, *La lunga liberazione. Giustizia e violenza nel dopoguerra italiano*, Rome: Editori Riuniti, 1999, p. 173.

74. F. Amati, 'Il Movimento di unità proletaria (1943–1945)', in G. Monina (ed.), *Il Movimento di unità proletaria (1943–1945)*, Rome: Carocci, 2005, pp. 116–17.

75. Collotti, Sandri and Sessi, *Dizionario della Resistenza*, Vol. 2, pp. 169–71; Gremmo, *L'ultima Resistenza*, p. 97; and Pavone, *Una guerra civile*, p. 452.

76. Pellegatta, *Cronache rivoluzionarie in provincia di Varese*, p. 111.

77. Cited in Gremmo, *L'ultima Resistenza*, p. 122.

78. Pellegatta, *Cronache rivoluzionarie in provincia di Varese*, p. 106. Emphasis in the original.

79. Ibid.

80. Ibid., p. 109.

81. Gremmo, *L'ultima Resistenza*, pp. 126–7.

82. Ibid., p. 136.

83. Ibid., p. 144.

84. Perhaps it was the scale of these attacks – which in this climate could easily end with execution in the middle of the night, that later pushed Andreoni onto other shores. In 1947 he joined the Social Democratic party and then authored a notorious article in July 1948 commonly thought to have been a contributory cause to an attempt on Togliatti's life the following day. During a speech in parliament criticising the government's acceptance of the Marshall Plan, Togliatti had said: 'Today we respond to imperialist war with revolt and insurrection in defence of peace.' Three days later Andreoni had written in response: 'the majority of Italians will find the courage, energy and decisiveness to nail Togliatti and his accomplices to the wall of betrayal. And not with metaphorical nails.' Both cited in ibid., p. 191.
85. Ibid., p. 139.
86. Ibid., p. 141.
87. Ibid., pp. 167–8; and Pellegatta, *Cronache rivoluzionarie in provincia di Varese*, pp. 112–13.
88. Gremmo, *L'ultima Resistenza*, p. 158.
89. R. Martinelli, *Storia del Partito comunista italiano VI. Il 'Partito nuovo' dalla Liberazione al 18 aprile*, Turin: Einaudi, 1995, p. 176.
90. Ibid., p. 146.
91. Gallerano, 'La disgregazione delle basi di massa del fascismo nel Mezzogiorno e il ruolo delle masse contadine', p. 491.
92. D. Horowitz, *The Italian Labor Movement*, Cambridge: Harvard University Press, 1963, pp. 189–90.
93. See F. Giliani, 'Il Pci di fronte alla Resistenza: Democrazia progressiva o rivoluzione socialista?', www.marxismo.net/idm/idm8/giliani.html
94. Martinelli, *Storia del Partito comunista italiano*, p. 127.
95. A. Gobetti, *Diario partigiano*, Turin: Einaudi, 1996 [1956], pp. 409–10.
96. G. Amendola, 'De Gasperi e la lotta politica nel trentennio repubblicano', *Rinascita*, 2 September 1977, pp. 8–9.
97. Martinelli, *Storia del Partito comunista italiano*, p. 20.
98. Ibid., p. 22, note.
99. Ibid., p. 19.
100. Ibid., p. 128.
101. Ibid., p. 129.
102. M. Caprara, *Lavoro riservato. I cassetti segreti del Pci*, Milan: Feltrinelli, 1997, p. 26.
103. *La Repubblica*, local Milan pages, 10 July 1996.
104. Ranzato, *Il linciaggio di Carretta*, p. 188. See also table in Dondi, *La lunga liberazione*, p. 138.
105. A. Agosti, 'Il partito comunista italiano e la svolta del 1947', *Studi Storici*, No. 1 (1990), p. 59.
106. P. Secchia and F. Frassati, *Storia della Resistenza*, Rome: Editori Riuniti, 1965, pp. 422–5.
107. Troilo, *La guerra di Troilo*, p. 129.
108. Interview with Luigi Moretti, 30 June 1988.
109. *Voce Comunista*, 29 November 1947.
110. M. Mafai, *L'uomo che sognava la lotta armata*, Milan: Rizzoli, 1984, p. 57.
111. Troilo, *La guerra di Troilo*, p. 145.
112. Giulio Seniga, cited in Caprara, *Lavoro riservato*, p. 38.
113. Martinelli, *Storia del Partito comunista italiano*, p. 373.
114. A. Grillo, *Livorno: una rivolta tra mito e memoria*, Pisa: Biblioteca Franco Serantini, 1994, p. 31. The use of the word 'Fatherland' was common to all political parties, and was not particularly associated with Nazism.
115. *The Times*, 15 July 1948.
116. Ibid. The final death toll in the Mayday massacre the previous year at Portella della Ginestra was in fact twelve.
117. G. Galli, *La sinistra italiana nel dopoguerra*, Milan: Il Saggiatore, 1978, p. 240.

118. Caprara, *Lavoro riservato*, pp. 46–7; and *The Times*, 15 July 1948.
119. C.M. Lomartire, *Insurrezione. 14 luglio 1948: L'attentato a Togliatti e la tentazione rivoluzionaria*, Milan: Mondadori, 2006, p. 121.
120. Galli, *La sinistra italiana nel dopoguerra*, p. 256.
121. W. Tobagi, *La rivoluzione impossibile. L'attentato a Togliatti: violenza politica e reazione popolare*, Milan: Il Saggiatore, 1978, p. 22.
122. M. and P. Pallante (eds), *Dalla ricostruzione alla crisi del centrismo*, Bologna: Zanichelli, 1975, p. 86.
123. Ibid., pp. 86–7.
124. Ibid., p. 85.
125. Galli, *La sinistra italiana nel dopoguerra*, p. 260.
126. Pallante, *Dalla ricostruzione alla crisi del centrismo*, p. 87.
127. Galli, *La sinistra italiana nel dopoguerra*, p. 257.
128. G. Bocca, *Palmiro Togliatti*, Rome-Bari: Laterza, 1973, p. 513.
129. Interview with Gianni Ottolini, 18 May 1988.
130. Interview with Moretti.
131. R. Del Carria, *Proletari senza rivoluzione*, Milan: Edizioni Oriente, 1970, p. 389.
132. Lomartire, *Insurrezione*, p. 119.
133. C. Bermani, 'La Volante Rossa', *Primo Maggio*, No. 9/10 (inverno 1977/78), p. 100.
134. Tobagi, *La rivoluzione impossibile*, p. 42.
135. Lomartire, *Insurrezione*, p. 99; *Battaglia Comunista*, 27 July 1948, cited in Pellegatta, *Cronache rivoluzionarie in provincia di Varese*, p. 86.
136. Tobagi, *La rivoluzione impossibile*, p. 43.
137. Ibid.
138. ISRMO, b. 56, f. 3. A factory report written by 'E.M.', emphasis added.
139. G. Garigali, *Memorie Operaie. Vita, politica e lavoro a Milano 1940–1960*, Milan: Franco Angeli, 1995, p. 90.
140. Pallante, *Dalla ricostruzione alla crisi del centrismo*, p. 87. The two towns mentioned are at the two extremities of the Ligurian coastline, about 150 miles apart.
141. Lomartire, *Insurrezione*, p. 187.
142. M. Caprara, *L'attentato a Togliatti. Il 14 luglio 1948: il PCI tra insurrezione e programma democratico*, Venice: Marsilio, 1978, p. 68.
143. *L'Unità*, 16 July 1948.
144. Caprara, *L'attentato a Togliatti*, p. 69.
145. *Battaglie del Lavoro*, 20 July 1948.
146. Cabinet minutes, cited in P. Di Loreto, *Togliatti e la 'doppiezza'. Il PCI tra democrazia e insurrezione, 1944–49*, Bologna: Il Mulino, 1991, p. 316.
147. Total figures, including police and army, were: 16 dead and 204 wounded, although all figures probably underestimate the real totals. Lomartire, *Insurrezione*, p. 183.
148. E. Santarelli, *Storia critica della Repubblica. L'Italia dal 1945 al 1994*, Milan: Feltrinelli, 1996, p. 59.
149. C. Bermani, *Il nemico interno. Guerra civile e lotte di classe in Italia (1943–76)*, Rome: Odradek, 1997, p. 122.
150. Di Loreto, *Togliatti e la 'doppiezza'*, p. 320.
151. Caprara, *L'attentato a Togliatti*, p. 29.
152. Pallante, *Dalla ricostruzione alla crisi del centrismo*, p. 84.

8   The Long Liberation

1. N. Zapponi, 'Fascism in Italian Historiography, 1986–93', *Journal of Contemporary History*, Vol. 29, No. 4 (October 1994), p. 555.
2. J. Dunnage, 'Policing and Politics in the Southern Italy Community 1943–48', in J. Dunnage (ed.), *After the War: Violence, Continuity and Renewal in Italian Society*, Market Harborough: Troubador, 1999, pp. 38–9.

3. G. Scaliati, *Trame nere. Movimenti di destra in Italia dal dopoguerra ad oggi*, Genoa: Fratelli Frilli, 2005, p. 13.
4. G. De Antonellis, *Napoli sotto il regime*, Milan: Cooperativa Editrice Donati, 1972, p. 285.
5. S. Christie, *Stefano Delle Chiaie: Portrait of a Black Terrorist*, London: Anarchy Magazine/Refract Publications, 1984, p. 6.
6. Scaliati, *Trame nere*, p. 15.
7. N. Bobbio, *Ideological Profile of Twentieth-Century Italy*, Princeton: Princeton University Press, 1995, p. 194.
8. F. Ferraresi, *Threats to Democracy. The Radical Right in Italy after the War*, Princeton: Princeton University Press, 1996, p. 46.
9. Ibid., p. 48.
10. Scaliati, *Trame nere*, p. 18.
11. P. Ignazi, *Postfascisti? Dal Movimento sociale italiano ad Alleanza nazionale*, Bologna: Il Mulino, 1994, p. 14.
12. C. Bermani, *Il nemico interno. Guerra civile e lotte di classe in Italia (1943–76)*, Rome: Odradek, 1997, p. 115; and Scaliati, *Trame nere*, p. 22.
13. A. Cento Bull, *Italian Neofascism: The Strategy of Tension and the Politics of Nonreconciliation*, Oxford: Berghahn, 2007, p. 12.
14. A. Grillo, *Livorno: una rivolta tra mito e memoria*, Pisa: Biblioteca Franco Serantini, 1994, p. 97.
15. Ferraresi, *Threats to Democracy*, p. 77.
16. Bermani, *Il nemico interno*, pp. 96–7.
17. J. Greene and A. Massignani, *The Black Prince and the Sea Devils*, Cambridge MA: Da Capo Press, 2004, p. 201.
18. Bermani, *Il nemico interno*, p. 153.
19. Scaliati, *Trame nere*, p. 41.
20. Bermani, *Il nemico interno*, pp. 163–5.
21. P. Secchia and F. Frassati, *Storia della Resistenza*, Rome: Editori Riuniti, 1965, p. 477.
22. M. Dondi, *La lunga liberazione. Giustizia e violenza nel dopoguerra italiano*, Rome: Editori Riuniti, 1999, p. 53.
23. Bermani, *Il nemico interno*, p. 170.
24. P. Cooke, 'The Italian State and the Resistance Legacy in the 1950s and 1960s', in G. Bonsaver and R. Gordon (eds), *Culture, Censorship and the State in Twentieth-century Italy*, Oxford: Legenda, 2005, p. 125.
25. Bermani, *Il nemico interno*, p. 173.
26. Ibid., p. 178.
27. P. Ginsborg, *A History of Contemporary Italy*, Harmondsworth: Penguin, 1990, p. 257.
28. Ibid.
29. A. Silj, *Malpaese. Criminalità, corruzione e politica nell'Italia della prima Repubblica 1943–1994*, Rome: Donzelli, 1994, p. 55.
30. Ibid., p. 57.
31. Ferraresi, *Threats to Democracy*, p. 82.
32. For further details see Bermani, *Il nemico interno*, pp. 296–7; C. Bermani, '"Forze dell'ordine" e continuità dello Stato', in AA.VV, *Guerra civile globale*, Rome: Odradek, 2001, pp. 143–4; Ferraresi, *Threats to Democracy*, pp. 80–1; and Ginsborg, *A History of Contemporary Italy*, pp. 276–8.
33. See Cento Bull, *Italian Neofascism*, pp. 51–2; S. Ferrari, *Le stragi di stato*, Rome: Nuova Iniziativa Editoriale/l'Unità, 2006, pp. 70–3; Ginsborg, *A History of Contemporary Italy*, p. 334; Greene and Massignani, *The Black Prince and the Sea Devils*, p. 224.
34. Ferraresi, *Threats to Democracy*, pp. 136–7; Silj, *Malpaese*, pp. 152–9. See also A. Cazzullo, *Testamento di un anticomunista*, Milan: Mondadori, 2000.
35. Cited in Greene and Massignani, *The Black Prince and the Sea Devils*, p. 237.
36. Ferrari, *Le stragi di stato*, p. 157.

37. Ibid., p. 30.
38. P. Spriano, *Storia del Partito comunista italiano. IV: La fine del fascismo. Dalla riscossa operaia alla lotta armata*, Turin: Einaudi, 1973, pp. 339–40. There is a grim irony to the fact that an anarchist who died in police custody during investigations over the *piazza Fontana* bombing, Giuseppe Pinelli, had been a courier in the Milan Resistance.
39. M. Clark, 'Italian squadrismo and contemporary vigilantism', *European History Quarterly*, Vol. 18 (1988), p. 46.
40. *L'Unità* online, 15 May 2008.
41. *Liberazione*, 26 May 2003.
42. *Avvenimenti*, 19 February 1997.
43. Ferrari, *Le stragi di stato*, p. 89.
44. *La Repubblica*, 24 November 1993.
45. P. Ginsborg, *Italy and its Discontents*, London: Allen Lane, 2001, p. 289.
46. *L'Espresso*, 15 April 1994.
47. *Guardian*, 3 June 1994.
48. *La Stampa*, 1 April 1994.
49. Cited in Ginsborg, *Italy and its Discontents*, p. 447.
50. V. Bufacchi and S. Burgess, *L'Italia contesa. Dieci anni di lotta politica da Mani Pulite a Berlusconi*, Rome: Carocci, 2002, p. 172, note.
51. M. Tarchi, 'The political culture of the Alleanza nazionale: an analysis of the party's programmatic documents (1995–2002)', *Journal of Modern Italian Studies*, Vol. 8, No. 2 (2003), p. 141.
52. *Il Manifesto*, 25 November 2003.
53. E. Gobetti, *L'occupazione allegra. Gli italiani in Jugoslavia (1941–43)*, Rome: Carocci, 2007, p. 175.
54. H. Burgwyn, 'General Roatta's war against the partisans in Yugoslavia: 1942', *Journal of Modern Italian Studies*, Vol. 9, No. 3 (2004), p. 328.
55. See L. Santarelli, 'Muted violence: Italian war crimes in occupied Greece', *Journal of Modern Italian Studies*, Vol. 9, No. 3 (2004), p. 285.
55. Ibid., p. 283.
57. C. Pavone, *Una guerra civile. Saggio storico sulla moralità nella Resistenza*, Turin: Bollati Boringhieri, 1991, p. 223.
58. C. Pavone, 'Il movimento di liberazione e le tre guerre', in AA.VV, *Conoscere la Resistenza*, Milan: Edizioni Unicopli, 1994, p. 17.
59. G. Galli, *Passato prossimo. Persone e incontri 1949–1999*, Milan: Kaos, 2000, p. 322.
60. *Panorama* magazine, 28 September 1995.
61. Rutelli had been nothing if not consistent. In 1982 he had opposed the awarding of a medal to the Roman partisan Rosario Bentivegna. See A. Portelli, *L'ordine è stato già eseguito. Roma, le Fosse Ardeatine, la memoria*, Rome: Donzelli, 2005, pp. 416–7.
62. Bermani, *Il nemico interno*, pp. 79–80.
63. *Liberazione*, 19 March 1998.
64. *Il Manifesto*, 26 November 2000.
65. *Il Manifesto*, 25 April 2008.
66. *L'Unità*, 26 April 2003.
67. *Liberazione*, 26 May 2003.
68. RAI 3 news, 9 September 2007.
69. *Il Manifesto*, 29 May 2008.
70. *L'Unità*, 9 September 2008. The Nembo parachute regiment was formed only at the same time as the RSI, Mussolini's puppet government, a few after weeks 8 September. And the Nembo was in fact an integral part of the German army.
71. *Il Manifesto*, 6 May 2008. The article is essentially a presentation of the www.ecn.org/ antifa website.
72. *Guardian*, 19 August 2008.

9 Female Fighters

1. M. Cicioni, '"In order to be considered we must first have fought": Women in the Italian Resistance', in A. Davidson. and S. Wright (eds), *'Never Give In': The Italian Resistance and Politics*, New York: Peter Lang, 1998, p. 101.
2. J. Slaughter, *Women and the Italian Resistance*, Denver Colorado: Arden, 1997, p. 24.
3. Ibid., p. 26.
4. A. Bravo and A.M. Bruzzone, *In guerra senza armi. Storie di donne, 1940–45*, Rome-Bari: Laterza, 1995, p. 186.
5. M. Giuffredi (ed.), *Nella rete del regime*, Rome: Carocci, 2004, p. 153.
6. G. Petti Balbi, 'La donna nelle campagne e in montagna', in G. Benelli, B. Montale, G. Petti Balbi, N. Simonelli and D. Veneruso (eds), *La donna nella Resistenza in Liguria*, Florence: La Nuova Italia, 1979, p. 170.
7. Ibid., p. 172.
8. Slaughter, *Women and the Italian Resistance*, p. 49.
9. Ibid., p. 50.
10. ISRP, Fondo Testimonianza, busta TE5.
11. Ibid.
12. G. Benelli, 'La Resistenza femminile in città', in Benelli, Montale, Petti Balbi, Simonelli and Veneruso, *La donna nella Resistenza in Liguria*, p. 88.
13. *Il Manifesto*, 26 April 2008.
14. A. Bravo, 'Resistenza civile', in E. Collotti, R. Sandri and F. Sessi (eds), *Dizionario della Resistenza, Vol. 1: Storia e geografia della Liberazione*, Turin: Einaudi, 2000, p. 269.
15. Ibid., p. 280.
16. Slaughter, *Women and the Italian Resistance*, p. 39.
17. Ibid., p. 40.
18. See P. Willson, *The Clockwork Factory. Women and Work in Fascist Italy*, Oxford: Clarendon Press, 1993, pp. 223–42.
19. Benelli, 'La Resistenza femminile in città', p. 101.
20. Slaughter, *Women and the Italian Resistance*, pp. 44–5.
21. A. Boldrini, *Enciclopedia della Resistenza*, Milan: Teti, 1980, p. 161; and *Patria indipendente*, 30 March 2003.
22. M. Brucellaria, 'Testimonianze sulle caratteristiche e sulla specificità della Resistenza a Carrara', in D. Canali (ed.), *La Resistenza Apuana. Scritti e Discorsi*, Carrara: Casa di Edizioni in Carrara, 1994, p. 49.
23. G. Mariani, 'I quattro giorni del luglio 1944 a Carrara', in ibid., p. 157.
24. R. Serra, *Le S.A.P. di Apuania. I 'Volontari della libertà' nei ricordi di un Comandante*, Carrara: Società Editrice Apuana, 2006, p. 21.
25. Brucellaria, 'Testimonianze sulle caratteristiche e sulla specificità della Resistenza a Carrara', p. 50.
26. G. Ricci (ed.), *Retrovie della Linea Gotica occidentale. Il crocevia della Lunigiana*, Lunigiana: Comuni di Aulla, Fivizzano e Pontremoli, 1987, p. 262.
27. Mariani, 'I quattro giorni del luglio 1944 a Carrara', p. 160.
28. Ibid., p. 163.
29. Slaughter, *Women and the Italian Resistance*, p. 66.
30. Ibid., p. 67.
31. Ibid.
32. Ibid., p. 44.
33. Ibid., p. 68 and 100.
34. ISRP, Fondo Testimonianza, busta TE5.
35. Benelli, 'La Resistenza femminile in città', p. 111.
36. C. Bianchi, *Il Reno brontola, molte voci, una memoria. Testimonianze di lotte partigiane*, Bologna: Re Enzo, 2002, p. 107.
37. Slaughter, *Women and the Italian Resistance*, p. 69.
38. Ibid., p. 104.
39. Ibid., p. 111.

40. Ibid., p. 89.
41. Benelli, 'La Resistenza femminile in città', p. 110.
42. Ibid., pp. 107–8.
43. ISRP, Fondo Tesimonianza, busta TE5.
44. F. Catalano, *Storia del CLNAI*, Bari: Laterza, 1956, p. 296.
45. D. Veneruso, 'La donna dall'antifascismo alla Resistenza', in Benelli, Montale, Petti Balbi, Simonelli and Veneruso, *La donna nella Resistenza in Liguria*, pp. 66–7.
46. M. Addis Saba, *Partigiane. Tutte le donne della Resistenza*, Milan: Mursia, 1998, p. 48; and Slaughter, *Women and the Italian Resistance*, p. 90.
47. G. Vaccarino, C. Gobetti and R. Gobbi, *L'insurrezione di Torino. Saggio introduttivo, testimonianze, documenti*, Parma: Guanda Editore, 1968, pp. 42–3.
48. Benelli, 'La Resistenza femminile in città', p. 115.
49. Bravo, 'Resistenza civile', p. 274.
50. Slaughter, *Women and the Italian Resistance*, p. 58.
51. G. Nisticò (ed.), *Le Brigate Garibaldi nella Resistenza*, Vol. 2, Milan: Feltrinelli, 1979, p. 635.
52. *Il Manifesto*, 26 October 2001.
53. C. Pavone, *Una guerra civile. Saggio storico sulla moralità nella Resistenza*, Turin: Bollati Boringhieri, 1991, p. 442.
54. L. Seghettini, *Al vento del Nord. Una donna nella lotta di Liberazione*, Rome: Carocci, 2006, p. 86.
55. C. S. Capogreco, *Il piombo e l'argento. La vera storia del partigiano Facio*, Rome: Donzelli, 2007, p. 168.
56. Interview with Laura Seghettini, 16 August 2007.
57. Addis Saba, *Partigiane*, p. 100; E. Collotti, R. Sandri and F. Sessi (ed.), *Dizionario della Resistenza*, Vol. 2: *Luoghi, formazioni, protagonisti*, Turin: Einaudi, 2001, p. 530.
58. Nisticò, *Le Brigate Garibaldi nella Resistenza*, pp. 279–80. See also C. Bermani, *Pagine di guerriglia. L'esperienza dei garibaldini della Valsesia*, Vol. 2, Vercelli: Istituto per la storia della Resistenza e della società contemporanea nelle province di Biella e Vercelli, 1995, pp. 172–3. Sporadic attempts to create women-only formations were made in Val Sesia by Cino Moscatelli, but women preferred to be in mixed groups; ibid., pp. 166–73.
59. S. Galli, 'Identikit resistenti. Anagrafe dei partigiani in Emilia-Romagna', *Zapruder*, No. 13 (magg–ago 2007), p. 105.
60. Boldrini, *Enciclopedia della Resistenza*, p. 164.
61. C. Pavone (ed.), *Le Brigate Garibaldi nella Resistenza*, Vol. 3, Milan: Feltrinelli, 1979, p. 294.
62. Slaughter, *Women and the Italian Resistance*, p. 6.
63. Ibid., p. 78.
64. *La Nostra Lotta*, 25 November 1944, p. 30.
65. Pavone, *Le Brigate Garibaldi nella Resistenza*, p. 563.
66. Ibid., p. 494.
67. Slaughter, *Women and the Italian Resistance*, p. 82.
68. Ibid., p. 75.
69. Ibid., pp. 128–9.
70. Bermani, *Pagine di guerriglia*, p. 149.
71. *Patria indipendente*, 30 March 2003.
72. Bravo and Bruzzone, *In guerra senza armi*, p. 198.
73. B. Fenoglio, *Una questione privata. I ventitre giorni della città di Alba*, Turin: Einaudi, 1990 [1952], p. 161.
74. Pavone, *Una guerra civile*, p. 444.
75. Veneruso, 'La donna dall'antifascismo alla Resistenza', p. 75.

10   The Partisan Republics

1. M. Beltrami, *Il governo dell'Ossola partigiana*, Rome: Sapere 2000, 1994, p. 17.
2. L. Longo, *Un popolo alla macchia*, Milan: Mondadori, 1947, p. 190.

3. R. Battaglia, *Storia della Resistenza italiana*, Turin: Einaudi, 1964, p. 384.
4. E. Gorrieri and G. Bondi, *Ritorno a Montefiorino*, Bologna: Il Mulino, 2004, p. 50.
5. Ibid., pp. 62–3.
6. E. Collotti, R. Sandri and F. Sessi (ed.), *Dizionario della Resistenza*, Vol. 2: *Luoghi, formazioni, protagonisti*, Turin: Einaudi, 2001, p. 250.
7. G. Bocca, *Storia dell'Italia partigiana*, Rome-Bari: Laterza, 1977, p. 370.
8. Ibid., p. 343.
9. G. Nisticò (ed.), *Le Brigate Garibaldi nella Resistenza*, Vol. 2, Milan: Feltrinelli, 1979, p. 127.
10. Gorrieri and Bondi, *Ritorno a Montefiorino*, pp. 90–2.
11. Nisticò, *Le Brigate Garibaldi nella Resistenza*, p. 126.
12. C. Pillon, *I comunisti nella storia d'Italia*, Rome: Il calendario del popolo, n.d., p. 865.
13. Bocca, *Storia dell'Italia partigiana*, pp. 370–4.
14. Gorrieri and Bondi, pp. 123–35.
15. Bocca, *Storia dell'Italia partigiana*, p. 419.
16. Ibid., p. 406; and P. Secchia and F. Frassati, *Storia della Resistenza*, Rome: Editori Riuniti, 1965, p. 780.
17. Collotti, Sandri and Sessi, *Dizionario della Resistenza*, Vol. 2, p. 570.
18. A. Buvoli and C. Nigris, *Percorsi della memoria civile. La Carnia. La Resistenza*, Istituto Friulano per la Storia del Movimento di Liberazione, 2004, p. 18.
19. Ibid., pp. 20–3.
20. Ibid., p. 44.
21. Collotti, Sandri and Sessi, *Dizionario della Resistenza*, Vol. 2, p. 242.
22. Battaglia, *Storia della Resistenza italiana*, p. 409.
23. Nisticò, *Le Brigate Garibaldi nella Resistenza*, p. 328.
24. Circular dated 29 August 1944, cited in Ibid., p. 289.
25. Bocca, *Storia dell'Italia partigiana*, p. 408.
26. Nisticò, *Le Brigate Garibaldi nella Resistenza*, p. 328.
27. Ibid., p. 310.
28. Bocca, *Storia dell'Italia partigiana*, p. 410.
29. Buvoli and Nigris, *Percorsi della memoria civile*, p. 54.
30. Secchia and Frassati, *Storia della Resistenza*, pp. 784–6.
31. Buvoli and Nigris, *Percorsi della memoria civile*, p. 66.
32. Bocca, *Storia dell'Italia partigiana*, p. 412.
33. Battaglia, *Storia della Resistenza italiana*, p. 412.
34. Bocca, *Storia dell'Italia partigiana*, pp. 426–8; and Collotti, Sandri and Sessi, *Dizionario della Resistenza*, Vol. 2, p. 243.
35. C. Bermani, 'Un lavoro politico oscuro, ma molto importante', in *Pippo Coppo: partigiano e sindaco della Liberazione*, Omegna: Comune di Omegna, 2005, p. 11.
36. Beltrami, *Il governo dell'Ossola partigiana*, pp. 29–30.
37. Secchia and Frassati, *Storia della Resistenza*, p. 171.
38. Ibid., p. 224.
39. Beltrami, *Il governo dell'Ossola partigiana*, pp. 35–6; C. Bermani, *Pagine di guerriglia. L'esperienza dei garibaldini della Valsesia*, Vol. 1, tomo 1, Vercelli: Istituto per la storia della Resistenza e della società contemporanea nelle province di Biella e Vercelli, 2000 [1971], p. 32; and P. Spriano, *Storia del Partito comunista italiano. V: La Resistenza, Togliatti e il partito nuovo*, Turin: Einaudi, 1975, p. 211.
40. G. Bocca, *Una repubblica partigiana. Ossola, 10 settembre–23 ottobre 1944*, Milan: Il Saggiatore, 2005 [1964], p. 35.
41. Bocca, *Storia dell'Italia partigiana*, p. 405; and Secchia and Frassati, *Storia della Resistenza*, p. 768.
42. Beltrami, *Il governo dell'Ossola partigiana*, p. 38.
43. Nisticò, *Le Brigate Garibaldi nella Resistenza*, p. 81.
44. Ibid., p. 313. Emphasis in the original.
45. Bocca, *Storia dell'Italia partigiana*, p. 414.
46. Bocca, *Una repubblica partigiana*, p. 63.

47. Ibid., p. 108.
48. *Il Manifesto*, 26 October 2001.
49. Bocca, *Una repubblica partigiana*, p. 87.
50. Beltrami, *Il governo dell'Ossola partigiana*, p. 79.
51. Ibid., p. 83.
52. Bocca, *Una repubblica partigiana*, p. 105.
53. Ibid., p. 82.
54. Bocca, *Storia dell'Italia partigiana*, p. 413.
55. Beltrami, *Il governo dell'Ossola partigiana*, p. 84.
56. Ibid., pp. 94–5.
57. Bocca, *Una repubblica partigiana*, p. 17.
58. Ibid., pp. 99–100.
59. Beltrami, *Il governo dell'Ossola partigiana*, p. 63.
60. Nisticò, *Le Brigate Garibaldi nella Resistenza*, p. 374.
61. Bocca, *Una repubblica partigiana*, p. 18.
62. Nitsticò, *Le Brigate Garibaldi nella Resistenza*, p. 397.
63. Beltrami, *Il governo dell'Ossola partigiana*, p. 61.
64. Bocca, *Una repubblica partigiana*, p. 73.
65. Secchia and Frassati, *Storia della Resistenza*, p. 797.
66. Beltrami, *Il governo dell'Ossola partigiana*, p. 57.
67. Ibid., p. 87.
68. Ibid., p. 55.
69. Ibid., p. 58.
70. Pillon, *I comunisti nella storia d'Italia*, p. 869.
71. Secchia and Frassati, *Storia della Resistenza*, p. 822.
72. Ibid., p. 844.
73. Battaglia, *Storia della Resistenza italiana*, p. 410.
74. Bocca, *Una repubblica partigiana*, p. 90.
75. Secchia and Frassati, *Storia della Resistenza*, pp. 799–800.
76. Beltrami, *Il governo dell'Ossola partigiana*, p. 61.
77. Nisticò, *Le Brigate Garibaldi nella Resistenza*, p. 398.
78. Bocca, *Storia dell'Italia partigiana*, pp. 424–5; and Bocca, *Una repubblica partigiana*, p. 113.
79. Beltrami, *Il governo dell'Ossola partigiana*, p. 97.
80. Nisticò, *Le Brigate Garibaldi nella Resistenza*, pp. 519–20.
81. Beltrami, *Il governo dell'Ossola partigiana*, p. 98.
82. *Das Reich*, 3 November 1944.
83. See F. Giannantoni, 'Gisella Floreanini: un simbolo di coraggio e di altruismo', in A. Del Boca (ed.), *La 'Repubblica' partigiana dell'Ossola*, Crodo: Centro Studi Piero Ginocchi, 2004.

11 Organising 'Terrorism'

1. C. Pavone, *Una guerra civile. Saggio storico sulla moralità nella Resistenza*, Turin: Bollati Boringhieri, 1991, p. 497; and R. Romagnoli, *Gappista. Dodici mesi nella Settima GAP 'Gianni'*, Milan: Vangelista, 1974, p. 87.
2. R. Battaglia, *Storia della Resistenza italiana*, Turin: Einaudi, 1964, p. 446; Romagnoli, *Gappista*, pp. 128–62; and P. Spriano, *Storia del Partito comunista italiano. V: La Resistenza, Togliatti e il partito nuovo*, Turin: Einaudi, 1975, p. 479.
3. Battaglia, *Storia della Resistenza italiana*, p. 446; and Romagnoli, *Gappista*, pp. 169–81.
4. P. Secchia and F. Frassati, *Storia della Resistenza*, Rome: Editori Riuniti, 1965, pp. 392–3. Indeed this was part of a more general attempt at terminological change, in which all parties tried to replace 'partisan' with the more nationalistic word 'patriot', with varying degrees of success. See also Pavone, *Una guerra civile*, pp. 147–9.
5. T. Behan, *The Long Awaited Moment. The Working Class and the Italian Communist Party in Milan, 1943–1948*, New York: Peter Lang, 1997, p. 63.

6. The Italian original is fully reproduced in P. Cooke (ed.), *The Italian Resistance. An Anthology*, Manchester: Manchester University Press, 1997, pp. 70–80.
7. Interview with Silvano Sarti, 17 April 2007.
8. Ibid.
9. R. Bentivegna, *Operazione via Rasella*, Rome: Editori Riuniti, 1996, pp. 55–6.
10. G. Nisticò (ed.), *Le Brigate Garibaldi nella Resistenza*, Vol. 2, Milan: Feltrinelli, 1979, p. 140.
11. Interview with Giovanni Pesce, 6 April 2002.
12. B. Guidetti Serra (ed.), *Compagne. Testimonianze di partecipazione politica femminile*, Turin: Einaudi, 1977, p. 287.
13. Ibid., p. 290.
14. Ibid., pp. 296–7.
15. C. Pillon, *I comunisti nella storia d'Italia*, Rome: Il calendario del popolo, n.d., pp. 815–6.
16. Secchia and Frassati, *Storia della Resistenza*, pp. 390, 393.
17. Spriano, *Storia del Partito comunista italiano*, pp. 183–4.
18. Secchia and Frassati, *Storia della Resistenza*, p. 466.
19. Ibid., p. 208.
20. Pavone, *Una guerra civile*, p. 497.
21. S. Corvisieri, *'Bandiera Rossa' nella Resistenza romana*, Rome: Samonà and Savelli, 1968, p. 69.
22. A. Peregalli, *L'altra Resistenza. Il PCI e le opposizioni di sinistra 1943–1945*, Genoa: Graphos, 1991, p. 207; and G. Ranzato, 'Roma', in E. Collotti, R. Sandri and F. Sessi (ed.), *Dizionario della Resistenza, Vol. 1: Storia e geografia della Liberazione*, Turin: Einaudi, 2000, p. 414.
23. E. Collotti, R. Sandri and F. Sessi (eds), *Dizionario della Resistenza, Vol. 2: Luoghi, formazioni, protagonisti*, Turin: Einaudi, 2001, p. 182; Peregalli, *L'altra Resistenza*, p. 209.
24. Corvisieri, *'Bandiera Rossa' nella Resistenza romana*, p. 71.
25. Ranzato, 'Roma', p. 417.
26. A. Portelli, *L'ordine è stato già eseguito. Roma, le Fosse Ardeatine, la memoria*, Rome: Donzelli, 2005, p. 179.
27. M. Musu and E. Polito, *Roma ribelle. La Resistenza nella capitale 1943–1944*, Milan: Teti, 1999, p. 303; and Portelli, *L'ordine è stato già eseguito*, p. 154.
28. G. Amendola, *Lettere a Milano*, Rome: Editori Riuniti, 1973, p. 227; and Portelli, *L'ordine è stato già eseguito*, p. 156.
29. C. Capponi, *Con cuore di donna*, Milan: Il Saggiatore, 2000, p. 149.
30. Bentivegna, *Operazione via Rasella*, p. 9.
31. Ibid., p. 57; and Secchia and Frassati, *Storia della Resistenza*, pp. 396–7.
32. Musu and Polito, *Roma ribelle*, p. 183.
33. Capponi, *Con cuore di donna*, p. 166; Musu and Polito *Roma ribelle*, p. 312; and the interview with Maria Teresa Regard published in *Il Manifesto*, 22 February 2000.
34. Bentivegna, *Operazione via Rasella*, p. 46.
35. Amendola, *Lettere a Milano*, p. 273.
36. Capponi, *Con cuore di donna*, pp. 200–1; E. Piscitelli, *Storia della Resistenza romana*, Bari: Laterza, 1965, pp. 285–6. The death of Gullace inspired the most famous scene in Rossellini's film *Rome Open City*.
37. Amendola, *Lettere a Milano*, pp. 277–8.
38. F. Calamandrei, *La vita indivisibile. Diario 1941–1947*, Rome: Editori Riuniti, 1984, pp. 170–1.
39. Musu and Polito, *Roma ribelle*, p. 314; Secchia and Frassati, *Storia della Resistenza*, p. 498.
40. Musu and Polito, *Roma ribelle*, p. 182.
41. See Corvisieri, *'Bandiera Rossa' nella Resistenza romana*, pp. 124–31.
42. Amendola, *Lettere a Milano*, p. 326; Ranzato, 'Roma', p. 422; Secchia and Frassati, *Storia della Resistenza*, pp. 602–5.

43. Corvisieri, 'Bandiera Rossa' nella Resistenza romana, p. 161.
44. Piscitelli, Storia della Resistenza romana, p. 361.
45. Corvisieri, 'Bandiera Rossa' nella Resistenza romana, p. 165.
46. L. Cavalli and C. Strada, Nel nome di Matteotti: materiali per una storia delle Brigate Matteotti in Lombardia 1943–45, Milan: Franco Angeli, 1982, pp. 64–5.
47. L. Borgomaneri, Due inverni un'estate e la rossa primavera. Le Brigate Garibaldi a Milano e provincia 1943–45, Milan: Franco Angeli, 1995, p. 44.
48. Ibid., pp. 44–5; and Spriano, Storia del Partito comunista italiano, p. 184.
49. Borgomaneri, Due inverni un'estate e la rossa primavera, p. 45.
50. Battaglia, Storia della Resistenza italiana, p. 184; L. Borgomaneri, 'La resistenza armata in Milano', in AA.VV, Conoscere la Resistenza, Milan: Edizioni Unicopli, 1994, p. 26; and Secchia and Frassati, Storia della Resistenza, p. 393.
51. La Fabbrica, 15 March 1944.
52. Borgomaneri, 'La resistenza armata in Milano', p. 27.
53. Behan, The Long Awaited Moment, pp. 103–4.
54. Ibid., p. 104.
55. Interview with Pesce.
56. A. Clocchiatti, Cammina frut, Milan: Vangelista, 1972, p. 392.
57. Interview with Pesce.
58. G. Pesce, Soldati senza uniforme, Rome: Edizioni di Cultura Sociale, 1951 [1950], pp. 144–6.
59. G. Pesce, Senza tregua. La guerra dei GAP, Milan: Feltrinelli, 1995 [1967], p. 206.
60. Clocchiatti, Cammina frut, p. 401.
61. APC, 30-7-4, 'Relazione, Milano 30 settembre 1944'.
62. ISRMO, Fondo Olona, busta 6, f. 2, 'Agitazioni del mese di ottobre'.
63. Ibid.
64. Pesce, Senza tregua, pp. 305–6.

12 An Uneasy Alliance: The Resistance and the Allies

1. R. Absalom, 'Hiding History. The Allies, the Resistance and the others in Occupied Italy 1943–45', The Historical Journal, Vol. I, No. 38 (1995), p. 128.
2. See G. Lett, Rossano, London: Hodder and Stoughton, 1955.
3. See E. Newby, Love and War in the Appennines, London: Picador, 1983 [1971].
4. See S. Hood, Pebbles from my Skull, London: Hutchinson, 1964. Later published as Carlino.
5. R. Battaglia, Un uomo, un partigiano, Bologna: Il Mulino, 2004 [1945], p. 65.
6. E. Collotti, R. Sandri and F. Sessi (eds), Dizionario della Resistenza, Vol. 2: Luoghi, formazioni, protagonisti, Turin: Einaudi, 2001, pp. 310–13.
7. P. Secchia and F. Frassati, Storia della Resistenza, Rome: Editori Riuniti, 1965, p. 225.
8. Ibid., p. 248.
9. Ibid., p. 896.
10. Ibid.
11. Ibid., pp. 894–5.
12. P. Spriano, Storia del Partito comunista italiano. V: La Resistenza, Togliatti e il partito nuovo, Turin: Einaudi, 1975, p. 440.
13. D. Ellwood, Italy 1943–1945, Leicester: Leicester University Press, 1985, p. 161; and D. Ellwood, 'Gli alleati e la Resistenza', in E. Collotti, R. Sandri and F. Sessi (eds), Dizionario della Resistenza, Vol. 1: Storia e geografia della Liberazione, Turin: Einaudi, 2000, pp. 249–50.
14. Spriano, Storia del Partito comunista italiano, p. 446.
15. Ibid., p. 447.
16. S. Peli, La Resistenza in Italia. Storia e critica, Turin: Einaudi, 2004, p. 126.
17. Secchia and Frassati, Storia della Resistenza, p. 367.
18. Ellwood, 'Gli alleati e la Resistenza', p. 246.
19. F. Catalano, Storia del CLNAI, Bari: Laterza, 1956, p. 87.
20. Secchia and Frassati, Storia della Resistenza, pp. 441–3.

21. Ellwood, *Italy 1943–1945*, p. 80.
22. Ibid.
23. G. De Antonellis, *Napoli sotto il regime*, Milan: Cooperativa Editrice Donati, 1972, pp. 280–1.
24. G. Kolko, *The Politics of War*, New York: Pantheon, 1990, p. 56.
25. De Antonellis, *Napoli sotto il regime*, p. 282.
26. Secchia and Frassati, *Storia della Resistenza*, p. 730.
27. G. Ricci, *Storia della Brigata Garibaldina 'Ugo Muccini'*, La Spezia: Istituto Storico della Resistenza, 1978, p. 409.
28. See Catalano, *Storia del CLNAI*, pp. 326–50, for further details.
29. P. Ginsborg, *A History of Contemporary Italy*, Harmondsworth: Penguin, 1990, p. 57.
30. Cited in ibid., p. 58.
31. Spriano, *Storia del Partito comunista italiano*, p. 446.
32. Kolko, *The Politics of War*, p. 47.
33. Ibid., p. 50.
34. See T. Behan, *The Long Awaited Moment. The Working Class and the Italian Communist Party in Milan, 1943–1948*, New York: Peter Lang, 1997, pp. 75–8.
35. W. Churchill, *Triumph and Tragedy. The Second World War*, Vol. VI, London: Cassell, 1954, p. 198.
36. Catalano, *Storia del CLNAI*, p. 286.
37. Ellwood, *Italy 1943–1945*, p. 117.
38. G. Vaccarino, C. Gobetti and R. Gobbi, *L'insurrezione di Torino. Saggio introduttivo, testimonianze, documenti*, Parma: Guanda Editore, 1968, pp. 17–18.
39. L. Cortesi, *Nascita di una democrazia. Guerra, Fascismo, Resistenza e oltre*, Rome: Manifesto libri, 2004, pp. 276–80.
40. *L'Unità*, 11 July 1944.
41. Kolko, *The Politics of War*, p. 54.
42. Ibid., p. 55.
43. Secchia and Frassati, *Storia della Resistenza*, p. 381.
44. G. Carocci and G. Grassi (eds), *Le Brigate Garibaldi nella Resistenza*, Vol. 1, Milan: Feltrinelli, 1979, p. 225.
45. C. Dellavalle, *Operai, industriali e partito comunista nel Biellese 1940/1945*, Milan: Feltrinelli, 1978, p. 103.
46. C. Bermani, *Pagine di guerriglia. L'esperienza dei garibaldini della Valsesia*, Vol. 2, Vercelli: Istituto per la storia della Resistenza e della società contemporanea nelle province di Biella e Vercelli, 1995, p. 13.
47. C. Pavone (ed.), *Le Brigate Garibaldi nella Resistenza*, Vol. 3, Milan: Feltrinelli, 1979, p. 70.
48. Kolko, *The Politics of War*, p. 60.
49. T. Behan, *See Naples and Die. The Camorra and Organised Crime*, London: I.B. Tauris, 2009, pp. 50–1, 54.
50. E. Collotti (ed.), *Archivio Pietro Secchia 1945–73*, Milan: Feltrinelli, 1979, p. 192.

Conclusion

1. G. Zangrandi, *I giorni veri*, Recco: Le Mani, 1998 [1963], pp. 221–2. The word 'Tommies' to indicate British soldiers is used in the original.
2. P. Secchia, *La Resistenza accusa 1945–1973*, Milan: Mazzotta, 1973, p. 93.
3. G. Gribaudi, *Guerra totale. Tra bombe alleate e violenze naziste. Napoli e il fronte meridionale 1940–44*, Turin: Bollati Boringhieri, 2005, p. 624.
4. Ibid., p. 625. Eric Morris, in his *La guerra inutile. La campagna di Italia, 1943–45*, has estimated that while Britain suffered 56,000 deaths from Luftwaffe bombing raids, Allied bombers killed 64,000 Italians.
5. Gianni Alasia, speech at the 14th National Congress of ANPI, 25 February 2006.
6. *La Stampa*, 19 November 2000.
7. *Patria indipendente* (March 2003), pp. 49–50.
8. *La Repubblica*, 29 August 2008.

Index

Printed and bound by CPI Group (UK) Ltd, Croydon, CR0 4YY

09/06/2025

14685867-0005